Windows 98 Book

Alan Simpson

Illustrations by John Grimes

Peachpit Press
Berkeley ▼ California

The Little Windows 98 Book
by Alan Simpson

Peachpit Press
1249 Eighth Street
Berkeley, CA 94710
510 524 2178
fax 510 524 2221
Find us on the Web at http://www.peachpit.com
To report errors, please send a note to errata@peachpit.com

Peachpit Press is a division of Pearson Education
Copyright © 1998 by Alan Simpson
Cartoon Illustrations copyright © 1998 by John Grimes

Development Editor: Jeanne Woodward
Production Coordinators: Amy Changar and Lisa Brazieal
Cartoon Illustrations: John Grimes
Copy Editor: Carol Henry
Indexer: Carol Burbo
Compositor: Owen Wolfson
Interior Design: Robin Williams
Cover Design: TMA Ted Mader + Associates

Notice of Rights
All rights reserved. No part of this book may be reproduced or transmitted in any form by any means, electronic, mechanical, photocopying, recording, or otherwise, without the prior written permission of the publisher. For information on getting permission for reprints and excerpts, contact permissions@peachpit.com.

Notice of Liability
The information in this book is distributed on an "As Is" basis, without warranty. While every precaution has been taken in the preparation of the book, neither the author nor Peachpit Press shall have any liability to any person or entity with respect to any loss or damage caused or alleged to be caused directly or indirectly by the instructions contained in this book or by the computer software and hardware products described in it.

Trademarks
Microsoft and Microsoft Windows are trademarks of Microsoft Corporation. Screen shots reprinted with permission from Microsoft Corporation. All other trademarks are used in an editorial fashion only and to the benefit of the trademark owner with no intention of infringement of the trademark.

ISBN 0-321-19308-3

0 9 8 7 6 5 4 3 2 1
Printed and bound in the United States of America

*To Susan, Ashley,
and Alec*

Acknowledgments

Even though only one person's name appears on the cover of most books, every book is really a team project. This book is certainly no exception. My sincere thanks go to the many people who worked hard to bring this book from the "idea stage" to the finished product you now hold in your hand.

At Peachpit, I'd like to thank Nancy Ruenzel for giving me this opportunity. And also many thanks to Jeanne Woodward for her tireless support and patience. I also want to thank Amy Changar, Owen Wolfson, and Lisa Brazieal for their fine work in keeping this book on track and ensuring quality throughout its layout process.

Many thanks to Carol Henry at C^2 Editorial Services. Her skill, talent, and eagle eye kept me honest and on track.

To the gang at Waterside Productions, my literary agency, many thanks for suggesting I write this book. It certainly was a fun project!

And of course to my family, for their patience through yet another long Daddy project.

Contents

Read Me First xxi

Part One — Essential Basic Skills

1 Beginner's Basics 3

PC Basics 4
Ks, Gigs, and All That 5
What You Need for Windows 98 6
Don't Skimp! 6
Processors and Megahertz 7
The Bottom Line 7

Software Basics 8
Bundled vs. New 8
Types of Programs 9

So What Is Windows 98? 9
An Operating System in Every PC 9
How to Start Windows 98 10
Dialog Box 10
Passwords 10
The Windows 98 Desktop 11

How To Work It 13
Mouse Anatomy 13
Holding the Mouse 14
Pounding the Keyboard 15
Combination Keystrokes 16
About the Numeric Keypad 16
Typing Numbers 17
Arrow Keys 17
Num Lock 17
Toggles 17

CONTENTS

Practice What You'll Be Doing 18
Try a Keyboard Shortcut 19

To Click or Double-Click? 20
Using Web View 21
The Hand Pointer 22

Taking the Guided Tour 22
Hands-On Review 24

Shutting Down Your PC 24
Standby Mode 26

Summary 27

2 Understanding Programs and Documents 29

What Is a Program? 30
Starting a Program 30
Using Menus in Programs 32
Closing a Program 33

What Is a Document? 34
Saving a Simple Letter 34
The Cursor 36
Printing a Document 36
Saving a Document 37
Closing a Document 38
Reopening a Document 39
Opening from Within a Program 39
Opening a Document from the Documents Menu 40

Notes on Printing 41
Sheet-Fed vs. Tractor-Fed Paper 41
The Print Dialog Box 42

Summary 45

3 Icons, Windows, and the Taskbar 47

Using Icons 48
Opening and Closing Icons 49
Tooltips and Shortcut Menus 51
Moving Icons 52
Arranging Desktop Icons 53
Using Auto Arrange 54
Arranging Icons in the Start Menus 54

vi

Things That All Windows Do ... 56
Sizing a Window ... 58
Bringing a Window to the Forefront ... 60
The Active Window ... 61
Hiding and Showing Open Windows ... 62
Moving and Sizing with the Keyboard ... 63
Disabled/Enabled Options ... 63
Arranging Open Windows ... 64

Using the Taskbar and Toolbars ... 65

Setting Taskbar Visibility Settings ... 65

Positioning and Sizing the Taskbar ... 67

Taskbar Toolbars ... 68

Managing Toolbars ... 69

Changing the Appearance of Toolbars ... 70

Reinforcing What You've Learned ... 72

Summary ... 74

4 Dialogs, Menus, and Help ... 77

What Is a Dialog Box? ... 78
Tabs ... 79
Buttons ... 79
Using the Keyboard ... 79
Dimmed (Disabled) Controls ... 80
The Little Help Button ... 80
Option (Radio) Buttons ... 81
Checkboxes ... 81
Sliders ... 82
Drop-Down Lists ... 82
List Boxes ... 83
Text Boxes ... 83
Text Box Controls ... 84
Changing Text ... 84
Insert vs. Overwrite ... 85
Selecting Text ... 86
Using the Keyboard in the Dialog Boxes ... 87

Using Menus ... 88
Using Menus and Toolbars ... 88
Toolbar Button Equivalents ... 89

CONTENTS

Menu Keyboard Shortcuts 89
Menu Symbols 89

Getting Instant Help 90

Finding Information Using Tabs 91
The Contents Tab 91
The Index Tab 91
The Search Tab 92
Navigating the Help Window 93
Uncovering Help 94
Other Ways to Get Help 94

Summary 96

Part Two — Have It Your Way

5 Personalizing Your PC 99

The Control Panel 100

Setting Date/Time 101
Time Zones 102
Taskbar Clock 102

Your Own Desktop 103
Your Own Wallpaper 103
Your Screen Saver 104
Screen Saver Options 104
Screen Saver Password 105
Want to See What It Looks Like? 106
Want to Turn Passwords Off? 106

Screen Colors 107
Your Own Desktop Design 108
Changing Appearance Items 109

Effects Tab 110
Changing Icons 110
Visual Effects 111

Web Tab 112

Settings Tab 112
Choosing the Screen Area 112
Screen Area Options 113
Choosing a Color Depth 113

Desktop Themes 114
Previewing Theme Settings 115

When You Like It, Apply It 116
Changing a Theme 116
Saving Your Theme 116
Removing a Theme 116
Deleting a Theme 117

Your Own Keyboard 117
Cursor Blink Rate 118

Your Own Mouse 118
Southpaws, Take Note! 119
Need Slower Double-Clicks? 119
Choosing a Mouse Pointer 120
Want More Mouse Pointers? 121
The Mouse Motion 121
Mouse Wheel 122

Managing Your Computer's Power 123
EPA Guidelines 123
Your Power Settings 124
Advanced Power Settings 125
Forcing Standby Mode 126

Protecting Your Privacy 126

Using the Password 128

Changing/Removing a Password 128

Controlling Sound 129
The Lowest Setting Wins 129
Easy Volume Control 130
Test It Out 131
The Volume Control Dialog Box 132
Which Volume Controls Do You Want? 133
Saving the Settings 134

Changing Sounds Effects 134
Sound Schemes 135
Sounds Events 135
Changing the Sounds Properties 135
Saving a New Sound Scheme 136

Your Locale Settings 136

CONTENTS

Multiple Monitors...137
   Multiple Display Support..137
   Two Monitors, One Desktop...138
   Arranging Multiple Monitors..139
   Multiple Monitors: Some Guidelines..140

Summary...142

6   Exploring Your PC   143

Disk Drives..144
   Your PC's Drives..144

Files and Folders...145
   The Root Folder...146
   Changing the Label on Your Hard Drive.......................................146
   Other Folders Under Root...147

Windows Explorer...147
   Your Guide to the Hard Disk..148

Explorer in a Nutshell...149

Paths..150
   Parts of a Path...150
   Parents and Children..151
   Why So Many Folders?...151

Explorer View Options...152
   Using the Details View..153

Exploring with My Computer...154
   Levels in My Computer..155
   Going Backward Up the Hierarchy..155

Saving Your Stuff..156
   The Save As Dialog Box...157
   Choosing a Path...157
   Navigating to a Folder..157

Saving to the Desktop...158
   Naming Your Files...158
   Filename Extensions...158
   File Types...159
   Steps to Save a File..159

Opening a Saved Document..160
   From the Documents Menu..160
   From Explorer or My Computer...160

From a File Menu..161
From the Open Dialog Box...161

What You've Learned..163

Finding Stuff...164
Where to Search...165
Searching for a Filename..165

Real Files vs. Shortcut Files...165
Searching for Content...166
Searching by Date...167
Specify the Calendar Date...167

A Range of Dates..168
Searching by Type or Size...169

Search Results Are Cumulative..170

Summary..171

7 Copy, Deleting, and All That..173

Folder Options..174
Custom Settings for Folders...175
Settings for Web Content..175
Settings for Mouse Clicking..176

View Tab..177
Settings for Files/Folders..177
Settings for Hidden Files...178
Visual Settings..178

Finding the Files You Need..179
With My Computer..179
With Explorer..180
With the Find Program..180

Selecting Files and Folders...181
Steps for Selecting...182
Lassoing Files and Folders...182
Selecting All Icons..183
Selecting with the Keyboard..183

Renaming a File or Folder..183

Deleting Files and Folders...184
Steps for Deleting...185
Other Ways to Delete..185

CONTENTS

Using the Recycle Bin 186
Recycling Your Disk Space 186
"Undeleting" Deleting Files 187
Nukin' the Trash 187

Moving and Copying Files/Folders 188
Moving vs. Copying 188
Source and Destination 189

Steps for Moving/Copying 189

Using Disks and Other Media 190
Copying to Removable Media 191
When You Need Multiple Disks 192
A Quick Summary 192

Copying within a Folder 193

Moving/Copying with the Clipboard 193
About the Clipboard 194
Steps for Using the Clipboard 194

Undoing a Recent Action 195
Uncutting 195

Creating a New Folder 195
Creating a New Document 196

File Attributes 197
Looking at Properties 197
Attribute Definitions 198
CD-ROM File Attributes 198

Changing Attributes 199

Major Backups 199
Planning Ahead 200
Using CDs for Backup 200
Backup for Documents Only 200

Guidelines for Backup 210

Summary 202

8 Installing New Programs and Such 203

Installing a New Program 204
A General Installation Procedure 204
Follow Screen Instructions 206

CONTENTS

Starting Your New Program ... 206
Finding the Icon ... 206
Registering a Program ... 207
Don't Lose the Original Program Stuff ... 207
Removing Installed Programs ... 207
Add/Remove Programs ... 208
Installing Missing Windows Components ... 209
Steps for Installing ... 209
Browsing the Components ... 210
Install/Uninstall Checkboxes ... 211
Removing a Windows Component ... 212
Installing New Fonts ... 212
Which Fonts Do You Have? ... 213
Steps for Installing Fonts ... 213
Using Fonts in Documents ... 215
Installing New Hardware ... 216
Doing It Yourself ... 216
If Windows Doesn't Get It ... 217
Add New Hardware Wizard ... 217
Summary ... 218

Part Three — Work and Play

9 Create Your Own Shortcuts ... 221
What Is a Shortcut? ... 222
Creating Desktop Shortcuts ... 232
Shortcuts to Menu Items ... 223
Rearranging Shortcut Icons ... 224
Shortcuts to Files and Folders ... 224
Shortcuts on the Quick Launcher ... 225
Making the Quick Launcher Visible ... 225
Adding the Shortcuts ... 226
Renaming Quick Launch Buttons ... 227
Other Quick Launcher Tricks ... 228

xiii

CONTENTS

Shortcuts in the Start Menu 229
Adding a Shortcut to the Start Menu 229
Rearranging Start Menu Items 230
Other Start Menu Changes 230
The Start Menu Folder 231

Creating a New Program Group 232
Make a New Folder 232
Drag In the Programs 232

Still More Ways to Create Shortcuts 234
The Create Shortcut Wizard 234

Summary 236

10 Performance, Maintenance, and Troubleshooting 237

Converting to FAT 32 238
Starting the Conversion 238
Wizard Warnings 239
Incompatible Programs 240
Backing Up 240
Completing the Conversion 241

Tuning Up Your Hard Disk 242
System Tools 242
Which One First? 243

Automating Maintenance Tasks 243
What Time of Day? 244
Changing the Schedule 245
Rescheduling a Task 246
Adding Other Maintenance Tasks 247

Troubleshooting 248

Keeping Windows Up to Date 249
Windows Update Site 249

Other Places to Nose Around 250
Looking Under the Hood 250
Printing a Hardware Record 251

Summary 252

11 Windows 98 Entertainment Features ... 253

Music, TV, and More ... 254

Playing Audio CDs ... 254
Windows CD Player ... 254
Using the Entertainment Menu ... 255
CD Player's Buttons ... 255
CD Player's Options ... 256

WebTV for Windows ... 256
WebTV Components ... 257
Starting Web TV ... 257

WebTV Configuration ... 258

WebTV Program Guide ... 259
Navigating the Program Guide ... 260
Searching for Programs ... 261
Coolest Feature! ... 262

Viewing the Banner ... 262

Favorite Banner ... 263

Leaving Program Guide ... 263

TV Viewer ... 263
Interactive TV ... 264
Need More Help? ... 264

Using WaveTop ... 264
Installing WaveTop ... 265
Running WaveTop ... 266
WaveTop Help and Information ... 266
Dismissing WaveTop's Window ... 266

Summary ... 267

Part Four — Cruising the Internet

12 Connecting to the Internet ... 271

Getting Connected ... 272

Choosing an ISP ... 272

Installing a Modem ... 273
Hooking up the Modem ... 273

CONTENTS

The Internet Connection Wizard 274
   What Do You Want To Do? 274

Signing Up with an ISP 275
   Logging On 275
   Picking the ISP 276
   ID and Credit Card Info 277
   Dial-in Access Number 277
   E-Mail Address 278
   Agreement and Confirmation 278

Testing the Connection 279

You're IN! 280
   Alan's Web Site 280

About Dial-up Networking 281
   Manual Dial-in 282

Disconnecting from the Internet 283

Summary 284

13 Doing Internet E-Mail **285**

What You Need for E-mail 286
   You Used the Internet Connection Wizard 286
   You Hired an ISP 286
   You're Online But Don't Have E-mail 286

Introducing Outlook Express 287
   About E-mail Servers 287

Logging On 288

View Options 289

Composing an E-mail Message 290

Sending an E-mail Message 291
   Using the Outbox 291

Checking Your E-mail 292

Reading Your E-mail 293

Replying to a Message 293
   The Reply Window 294

Forwarding a Message 294

Deleting a Message 295
   Deleted Items Folder 295
   Permanently Deleting Messages 295

CONTENTS

E-mail Attachments 295

Sending an Attachment 296

Reading an Attachment 297
Filename Extensions on Attachments 297
The Associated Application 298
Always Ask? 299

Saving an Attachment 299
About Zip Files 300

Personalizing Outlook Express 300

Using Your Address Book 301
Adding Names 301
Properties Dialog Box 302
Managing Addresses 303

Addressing E-mail to Contacts 304
Finding a Recipient 304

Printing Your Address Book 304

Manual Set-up of E-mail Accounts 305
Creating Your Account 306
Using Wizard Connection 307
Dial-up Connection for E-mail 308

More on Outlook Express and Address Book 309

Summary 310

14 Browsing the World Wide Web 311

Introducing Internet Explorer 312
Starting Internet Explorer 312
You Start Out at a Home Page 313

View Options 314

Home Pages and URLs 315
Domains 315
Your Default Home Page 316

Browsing the Web 316
URL Typing Tips 316
Other URL Quickies 317
The History Explorer Bar 318
Surfing in a Nutshell 318

xvii

CONTENTS

Using Links and Buttons 319
Toolbar Buttons 319

Searching the Web 319
Performing a Search 320
AltaVista Search Example 321
Coolnerds Mega Search 321
Popular Search Engines 322

Keeping Track of Favorite Sites 323

Downloading Files from the Web 323
Print Those Instructions! 324
It's Best To Save First 324
Note the Path and Filename! 324

Cool Download Sites 325

Protecting the Kids 326

Summary 327

15 Subscriptions, Channels, and the Active Desktop 329

Subscriptions 330
Subscribing to a Site 330
Browsing Offline 330
A Little Technical Stuff 331

How To Subscribe 331

Managing Your Subscriptions 332
Getting Ready 332
The Subscriptions Window 333

Make Your Schedules 333

Predefined Schedules 334

Modifying the Daily Schedule 335

Modifying the Weekly Schedule 336

Modifying the Monthly Schedule 336

Scheduling a Subscription 336

Changing Individual Subscriptions 337

Update Options 338
Update Notifications 338
Arranging for Dial-up 339
Manual Updates 339

xviii

CONTENTS

Checking Your Subscriptions ... 339
How To Browse Offline ... 340
Channels ... 341
Accessing the Channel Bar ... 341
Channels Explorer Bar ... 342
Subscribing to Channels ... 343
Organizing the Channel Bar ... 345
Scheduling Channel Updates ... 346
Channel Icons ... 346
Channel Updates ... 346
Channel Surfing ... 347
Active Desktop Items ... 347
The Active Desktop Layer ... 347
Active Desktop On/Off ... 348
Finding Active Desktop Items ... 348
Adding an Item ... 350
Schedule Updates, Too ... 351
Managing Active Desktops Items ... 352
Hiding the Regular Icons ... 352
Hiding Active Desktop Items ... 353
Customizing Active Desktop ... 353
Updates to Active Desktop Items ... 354
Manually Updating Items ... 354
Summary ... 356

Appendix A: Installing Windows 98 ... 357
What You Need ... 358
Performing the Installation ... 358
CD-ROM Installation ... 358
Floppy Disk Installation ... 359
Restart the PC ... 360

Appendix B: Keyboard Shortcuts ... 361
General Shortcuts ... 362
Windows Natural Keyboard ... 363
Dialog Boxes ... 363
My Computer and Windows Explorer ... 364

xix

Windows Explorer 364
Program Shortcuts 365
Drag-and-Drop 366
Accessibility Features 366

Glossary **367**
Index **377**

Read Me First

I have to confess that like many people, I subscribe to the "If all else fails, read the instructions" philosophy of trying to get things done. Even if the instructions are no more than a page long, I'll still try to wing it first without even glancing at the instructions. So, I suppose you could say I have some nerve writing book-length instructions for other people to read!

But the reason I wrote this book is because so often all else does fail, and I do have to read the instructions. I'm sure many of you are at that point with Windows 98—sort of hacking about and saying, I can do this if the instructions are clear, to the point, and very specific about telling me exactly what I need to know, and do. So that's been my goal here—to tell you exactly what you need to know to use your PC effortlessly and efficiently, without boring you to tears with irrelevant technical mumbo-jumbo.

Tutorial and Reference

You can use this book as a tutorial for learning Windows 98, as a reference for looking up information on-the-fly, or both. Using the book as a tutorial is simple. Start reading from page 1 and keep going. The book is organized such that you'll learn the most basic, fundamental skills first and then build on those skills to become ever more competent and savvy.

As a reference, this book offers many visual cues to help you find the answers you need quickly. First and foremost, of course, is the index at the back of the book. But in addition to that, just about every page offers these **visual cues** to help you scan the page for the information you need right now:

- Keywords and headings in the **outside margins** point out the main topic of each paragraph or passage.
- **Boldface** terms are used within paragraphs to call attention to additional keywords you might be searching for.

READ ME FIRST

What You Should Already Know

I assume you know nothing about computers

I think most tutorial books promise that anyone will be able to understand the book easily. Though, I can't tell you how many times someone has written to me about some so-called "bonehead-level" computer book that they purchased, and about how they were then severely disappointed in it. The usual cause is that the author assumes the reader is already hep to the many buzzwords used in the computer industry. In this book, I'm working from the assumption that you perhaps have never even touched a PC in your life. And I assume you may very well not know the difference between computer software and a turtle dove.

Other Book Features

Buzzwords and Glossary

While we're on the topic of jargon, let me tell you that any time I introduce a term that you might not have heard before, I'll define that term right there on the spot. Though, I'm well aware of the fact that many of you will jump around through the book looking for answers to questions as they arise. Not to worry. I've also defined all the buzzwords in a glossary at the back of the book. So when you come across a term that means nothing to you, all you have to do is look that term up in the glossary.

Icons

Occasionally you'll also come across some **icons in the margin**. One icon indicates tips—little tidbits of knowledge that are definitely worth remembering. The other icon indicates a warning—some action that if undertaken carelessly could lead to problems. (Fortunately, there aren't too many of those!). So anyway, here's what those will look like:

I'm a tip: Anything next to the icon at left is a tip. In keeping with that philosophy, I'll give you a tip right now. Don't plant corn in the dead of winter. (OK, so it's kind of a stupid tip. But I don't want to get too technical here).

I'm a warning: Warnings sport this icon. I suppose I need to give you a warning now, so that this really is a warning. So here goes. Don't run with scissors in your mouth.

So that pretty much covers it. Enough yakkin' about the book. Let's start talking about Windows 98 now. Though I feel compelled to just give you one more little tidbit of advice. If you really find you're having a hard time learning this stuff, do yourself a favor and stop trying to teach yourself. At least for a while. Let me take a shot at teaching you this stuff. Go hide somewhere, get all comfy and relaxed, and then just start reading from page 1 of this book. I know it sounds like a dreadfully boring thing to do. But in the long run you'll probably save yourself a lot of time. And you'll definitely save yourself a lot of frustration.

Enjoy, and best of luck to you.

Part One
Essential Basic Skills

Beginner's Basics

I recently spent about two hours on the phone explaining to someone how to download and print an income tax form from the Internet. Normally, such a job would only take about ten minutes. But the person I was talking to didn't understand a single word of computer terminology. So, for example, when I would say "Get back to the Windows desktop" he would ask "What's that, and how do I do it?" When I would say "Right-click the program's button in the taskbar and choose Close," he would ask "What's the taskbar, how do I right-click, what do you mean by 'choose'?" This went on for a couple of hours, rather than the few minutes it would have taken if he'd known at least the basic terminology.

1: BEGINNER'S BASICS

I know you're probably anxious to dive right in and start putting Windows 98 to work, right now. But if I don't explain some of the essential terms to you first, things will be difficult. So, in this chapter we're going to cover those absolute beginner's basics that you need to know in order to get anything done with your PC. Besides, not knowing the meaning of all those buzzwords—like *Ks* and *gigs* and *memory* and such—just makes things all the more intimidating. Getting rid of that intimidation will make your life at the PC easier, and much less scary.

And there's more than mere terminology in this chapter. You'll also learn some fundamental concepts and skills that will help you start putting Windows 98 to work for you, right now.

PC Basics

A PC (Personal Computer) system consists of **hardware** and **software**. The hardware is the stuff that you can actually see and feel. If you throw it out a second-story window, it will probably break.

Here's a quick summary of what each hardware component is for:

- **Monitor**: The part that looks like a TV. It probably has its own On/Off switch, as well as buttons for adjusting contrast, brightness, and other settings.

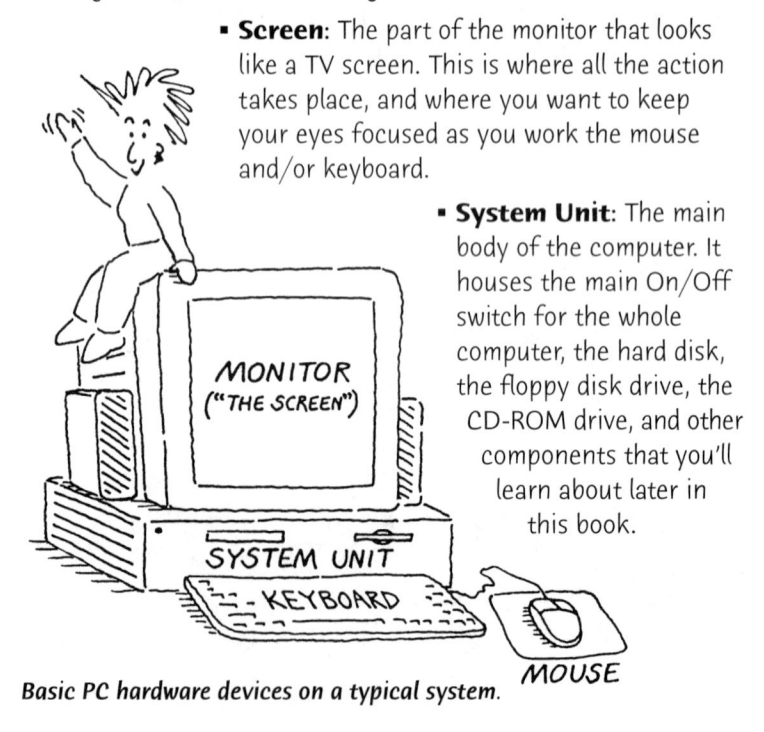

- **Screen**: The part of the monitor that looks like a TV screen. This is where all the action takes place, and where you want to keep your eyes focused as you work the mouse and/or keyboard.

- **System Unit**: The main body of the computer. It houses the main On/Off switch for the whole computer, the hard disk, the floppy disk drive, the CD-ROM drive, and other components that you'll learn about later in this book.

Basic PC hardware devices on a typical system.

- **Mouse**: Your main tool for using Windows and your PC. We'll talk about working with the mouse a little later in this chapter.
- **Keyboard**: Similar to a standard typewriter. Like the mouse, the keyboard lets you interact with the computer.

Have you ever heard or seen an ad selling a PC, promising "16 megs of RAM," a "3 gig hard drive," and stuff like that? If you're not familiar with computers, you might wonder what on earth these people are talking about, and whether you really want to spend your money on these "megs" and "gigs." Let's take a moment to talk about what all those buzzwords mean.

Ks, Gigs, and All That

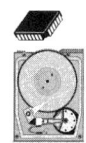

The first thing you need to understand is that inside your computer (inside the system unit, that is), information is stored in two different places. One place is the **hard disk**. The other place is called **RAM—Random Access Memory**, or just **memory** for short. Here's the difference:

- **Hard Disk**: Stores lots of information magnetically and can hold that information even while the computer is turned off. In a sense, the hard disk is your computer's filing cabinet, where everything is stored.
- **Memory**: RAM stores only whatever you are working on at the moment. RAM is *volatile*, meaning that when the power goes off, everything in RAM instantly disappears. In a sense, RAM is like your office desktop, where you keep only those things you're working on right now.

Why two difference types of memory? Well, RAM is very, very fast—much faster than a hard disk. That extra speed is great for doing work. But RAM's volatility means that it doesn't work for long-term storage. As soon as you turn off the PC, RAM gets cleaned out. So although it's good for getting work done, RAM is totally useless for *saving* that work.

To avoid losing all your work in RAM, you need to get in the habit of **saving** your work on the hard disk. This is a simple task that you'll learn to do in Chapter 2. But for now, just keep in mind that the hard disk is kinda like your filing cabinet, and memory (RAM) is kinda like the top of your desk.

Inside your PC, RAM memory just looks like little black chips. Your hard disk is in fact a disk—it spins around like a CD in a CD player. A little drive head moves across the spinning disk to find, and place, data.

1: BEGINNER'S BASICS

Those buzzwords you've probably seen or heard, like "megs" and "gigs," describe *how much* information can be held in memory and on the hard disk. The basic unit of measurement for data is a single character—like the letter *a* or the letter *b*. The amount of storage required to store one character is called a **byte**. Thus, it takes three bytes to store the word *cat* in a computer's memory or hard disk. Modern computers can store thousands, millions, even billions of bytes of information. Thus we measure the computer's storage capacity in **kilobytes** (about a thousand bytes), **megabytes** (about a million bytes), and so forth.

The following table lists all the buzzwords, their abbreviations, and the amount of storage each buzzword defines.

Buzzword	Abbreviations	Amount of Storage	In English
Byte		1	One
Kilobyte	K, KB	1,000	Thousand
Megabyte	M, MB, meg	1,000,000	Million
Gigabyte	G, GB, gig	1,000,000,000	Billion
Terabyte	T, TB	1,000,000,000,000	Trillion

What You Need for Windows 98 — Knowing *exactly* how much RAM and hard disk storage you need is, well, pretty much impossible. For a Windows 98 PC, you'd do well to get at least 16MB of RAM and at least 1GB of disk space. More is better in a couple of ways, actually. Lots of hard disk storage is good because it means you can put a lot of stuff on the computer. Lots of RAM is good because the more RAM you have, the faster things go. You don't need as much RAM as disk storage—for the same reason that you don't need to dump the entire contents of your filing cabinet onto your desk every morning. You only need to work with one or two things at a time, not everything in the filing cabinet at once.

On the other hand, you don't want to skimp on RAM either. That's because the more RAM you have, the faster your work goes. How does "more" equate to "faster"? Well, think of RAM as a dump truck. Now imagine you have a two-ton pile of dirt to move. A truck that can hold two tons of dirt could move all the dirt in one trip. A truck that holds one ton of dirt would have to make two trips. Obviously, the bigger truck gets the job done faster.

Don't Skimp! — So the bottom line is that you probably want to get as much RAM as you can afford. Any computer that comes with Windows 98 already installed has enough hard disk storage and RAM to get most jobs done. And that may be sufficient for you. If not, you can always upgrade later.

Processors and Megahertz

Another factor that affects the speed and cost of a computer is the **microprocessor**, which can also be called the **processor**, the **Central Processing Unit**, the **CPU**, or even just "the chip." It lives in the system unit of the computer. Unlike RAM and disk storage, which only store the information, the microprocessor does the actual work on that information. The faster the microprocessor, the faster the work flows.

> If you're interested in learning more about PC hardware, take a look at *The Little PC Book* by Lawrence J. Magid, also published by Peachpit Press. That book describes, in more detail, all the components that make up a PC.

You may have heard of some "brand name" microprocessors, like the 386, 486, Pentium, and Pentium II, all manufactured by a company named Intel. As I write this book, the Pentium II is the "latest and greatest" processor. Most new PCs sold these days have a Pentium, Pentium II, or some equivalent processor in them. The Pentium II has the advantage of **MMX (multimedia extensions) technology**. This makes it especially good at running multimedia programs that incorporate sound and video—which is to say, the games and educational titles you run on your PC will just plain work better.

The speed at which the processor does its work is measured in **megahertz** (MHz). The faster the processor, the more it costs. There is no minimum or maximum processor-speed requirement for using Windows. However, most modern programs—especially those with video and sound—work best with a processor running at 200MHz or better. A 300MHz or faster Pentium II processor can pretty much scream through even the most demanding jobs.

The Bottom Line

So the bottom line on all this terminology is that "more is better." Or, stated more simply, the larger the numbers used to describe a PC, the more impressed you should be. For instance, a computer with a 300MHz Pentium processor, 32MB (megs) of RAM, and 3GB (gigs) of storage is faster and more expensive than one with a 200MHz Pentium processor, 16MB of RAM, and 1.5GB of storage.

I realize that all these concepts are pretty vague if you don't have much computer experience. Don't worry about that—you don't need to be a buzzword guru to use a computer effectively. Having some sense of what these terms mean, however, is helpful—so you won't feel intimidated by them.

Software Basics Computer software, also called **applications** and **programs**, is the stuff you purchase to run on your computer. Even if you've never used a computer in your life, chances are you already have some experience with software. For example, when you rent a movie from the video store, the movie itself is actually software that's stored on the tape inside the videocassette. Music that you listen to on a stereo is also software, usually stored on a CD or a cassette tape.

Bundled vs. New A lot of computer software is already stored inside your computer on the hard disk. You never actually see that disk because it never comes out of the computer. New software that you buy will usually be on CD-ROM disks or floppy disks. Your computer has floppy disk and CD-ROM drives to accept and read these disks.

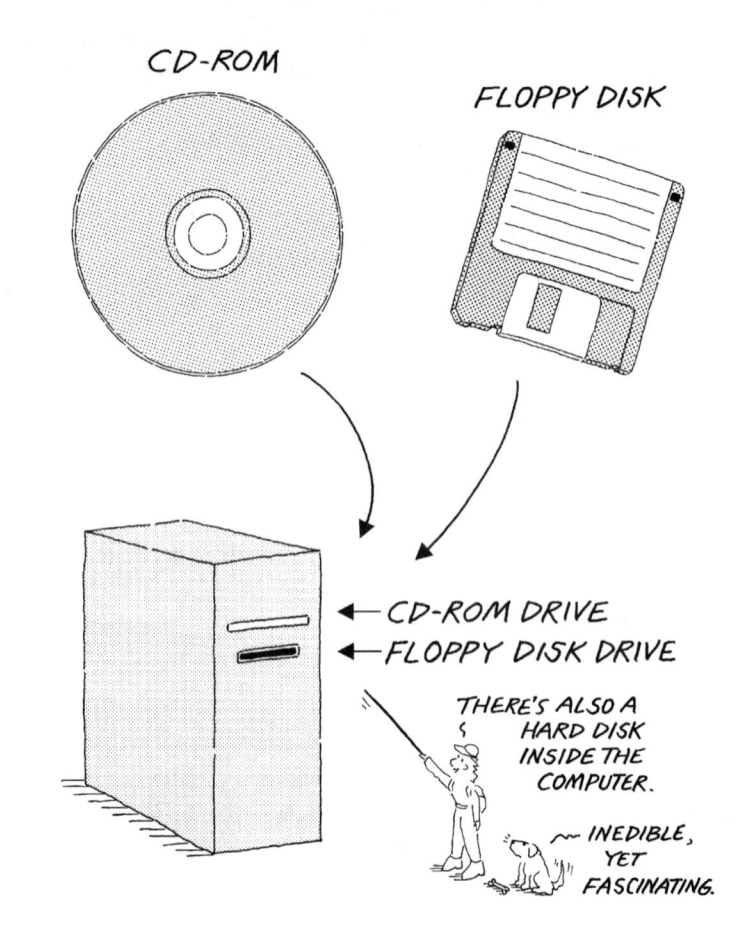

Some software is already stored inside your computer on its hard disk. New software often comes on CD-ROM or floppy disks.

To use a new program, you usually need to copy it from the floppy disk or CD-ROM onto your hard disk. That's called **installing** the software, and you'll learn how to do that in Chapter 8.

Just as a stereo can play many different kinds of music—classical, rock, jazz, and so forth—computer hardware can play all kinds of software—games, educational titles, graphics programs, word processing programs, Internet browsers, office aids, and more. If you really have no idea what kinds of programs are available for your PC, you should take a trip to your nearest computer store. Chances are you'll find programs dealing with everything from astrology to zoology.

Types of Programs

Windows 98 is a special type of software known as an **operating system**, often abbreviated *OS*. (By the way, it's pronounced with the emphasis on the first word rather than the second, like "*OP-erating system*" and not "*operating SYS-tem.*") Unlike most software programs, which are entirely optional, an operating system is mandatory. Your PC simply cannot run without an operating system installed.

So What Is Windows 98?

The operating system defines how you interact with your PC. Also, as you'll discover in the chapters the follow, you'll use the operating system every time you sit at the computer. Here are just a few common tasks you'll perform with the Windows 98 operating system:

- Start and use other programs
- Customize the appearance of the screen to your liking
- Move, copy, delete, and rename files
- Find stuff on your computer
- Perform routine maintenance and tune-ups

Because your PC cannot run without an operating system, there's a good chance that Windows 98 is already installed on your computer's hard disk. (We'll find out, one way or the other, in just a bit.)

An Operating System in Every PC

So now that we have some fundamental concepts and terminology under our belts, let's get to the meat of the thing—starting and using Windows 98.

How to Start | If Windows 98 is already installed on your PC (and we'll assume it is),
Windows 98 | starting Windows 98 is a simple matter: Turn on your computer to *boot up* from the hard disk, and then wait a minute or two. Follow these steps:

Your floppy disk drive looks something like this

- ▼ Make sure there is no disk in the floppy disk drive. To do so, push the little eject button on the front of the drive on the system unit. If a disk pops out, leave it out. If nothing pops out, the drive is probably empty, which is good.

- ▼ Turn on your monitor (if it has its own On/Off switch). If you have any other devices attached to your computer (such as a printer, modem, or scanner), turn those on too.

- ▼ Turn on the main power on the system unit.

- ▼ Wait a minute or so for your computer to boot up and start Windows 98.

Dialog Box | You'll probably see some technical-looking text whiz by on the screen. Depending on how your computer is set up, your screen might show a *dialog box*, asking you to type in a user name and password.

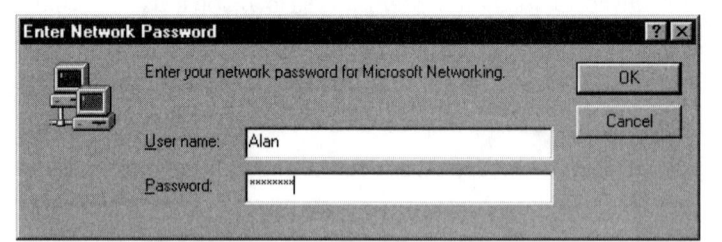

You may be asked to supply a user name and password while Windows 98 is starting.

What you do next depends on your situation:

- ▼ If nobody gave you a user name and password, you can ignore this dialog box. Just click OK or press the Enter key to move on.

Passwords
- ▼ If you're using this PC at work and your company's network administrator gave you a user name and password to log on to the network, type that information into the dialog box. To enter information into text boxes like these, just click on the box you want to type in, or press the Tab key until the cursor is blinking at you from the box. Then start typing. Notice that when you type your password, only asterisks (***) appear. This is to prevent people from looking over your shoulder and discovering your password. Click the OK button or press the Enter key to move on.

Once you get past that little log-on dialog box (if it came up at all), you'll be at the Windows 98 *desktop*. This is your "home base" for everything you do at the computer. So let's talk about some of the buzzwords that go along with the desktop

> If Windows 95 or some other operating system starts up, this book isn't going to do you any good until you install Windows 98, as discussed in Appendix A.

In your day-to-day use of the PC, most activity will take place through the Windows 98 **desktop**. Let's look at the various doodads on the desktop that you'll use to interact with your computer.

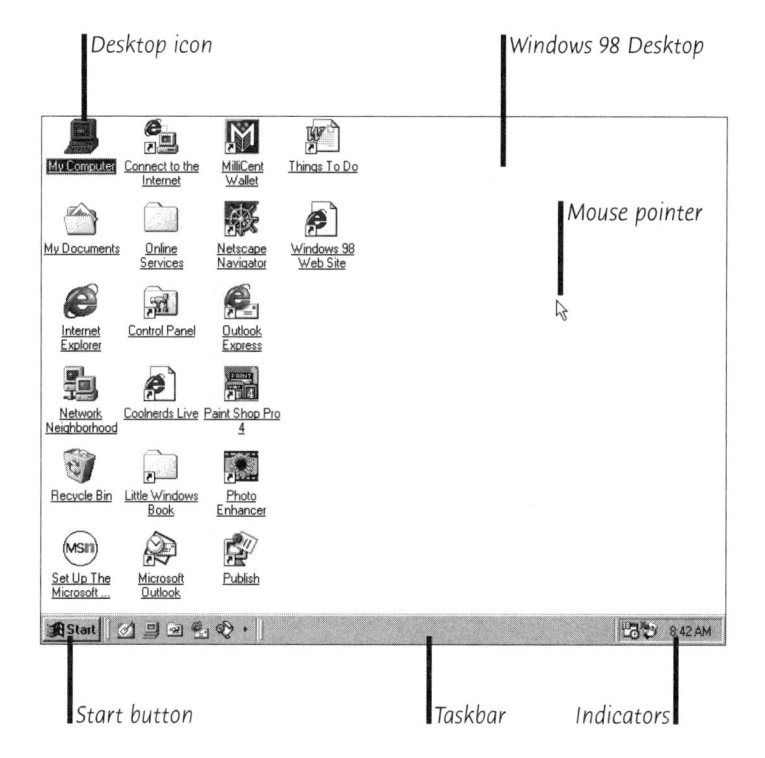

The Windows 98 Desktop

Things that appear on the Windows 98 desktop.

Your own Windows 98 desktop might look a little different, but it should have the same essential components, including the taskbar at the bottom and some desktop icons in the main area in the center.

It's a good idea to become familiar with all these doodads, because you'll come across them all the time in your work with Windows 98. Here's a quick overview. (If you come across a new buzzword while reading these descriptions, don't worry. I'll define all the terms in just a moment.)

1: BEGINNER'S BASICS

The mouse pointer

The Start button

Windows 98 Start menu.

- **Desktop (Windows 98 desktop)**: The large main area behind the icons and above the taskbar. This is your "virtual" desktop, where you do most of your work.

- **Mouse pointer**: As you roll the mouse around on your desktop, the mouse pointer (right now it's represented by an arrow on the desktop) moves in the same direction. You'll use the mouse and mouse pointer to tell the computer what to do.

- **Start button**: *Clicking* the Start button presents the Windows 98 Start menu. You use the mouse pointer to *point* to menu items. To see more, *click* on the menu items to open them.

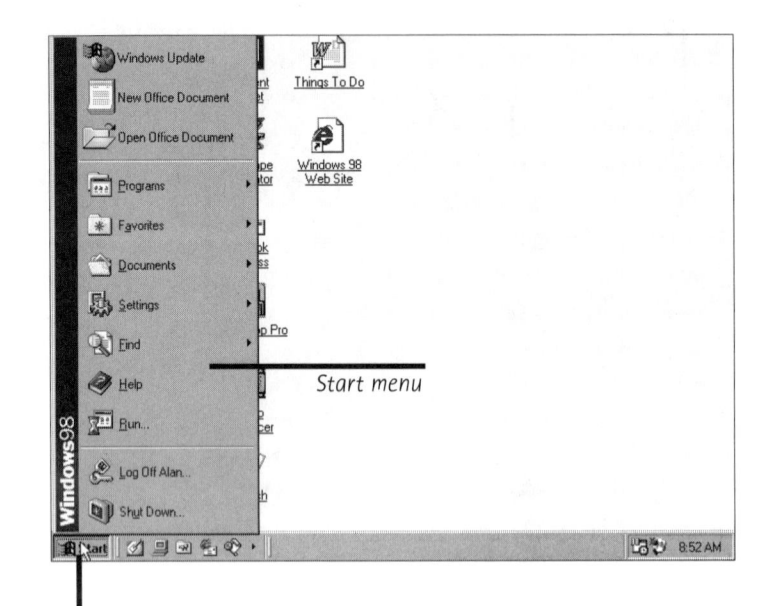

Start menu

Start button

A typical desktop icon

- **Desktop icon**: These are the little pictures with a label underneath. Each icon represents a *window* that you can open by clicking on the icon.

- **Taskbar**: The long gray bar along the bottom of the screen is called the taskbar, and you'll learn all kinds of tricks that you can do with it. By the way, the taskbar may be positioned along the top or edge of the screen on your computer (if someone moved it there). It may also be invisible at the moment. You'll learn how to make it visible shortly.

1: BEGINNER'S BASICS

- **Indicators:** The right end of the taskbar shows some indicators, such as the current time. You'll learn more about these later.

Indicators

So—armed with all this new knowledge, let's get down to business and talk about how you work the PC.

Working a PC is largely a matter of keeping your eyes on the screen as you use the mouse and keyboard to make selections, give commands to the PC, and so forth. In Windows, you'll probably use the mouse more often then the keyboard, so let's take a look at that now.

How to Work It

The first piece of hardware that you'll want to get comfortable with is the **mouse**. If you've never used a mouse before, here's all there is to know is the mouse:

Mouse Anatomy

The mouse has two buttons—a **primary mouse button** on the left and a **secondary mouse button** on the right.

Basic mouse anatomy.

WHEEL (OPTIONAL) USED FOR SCROLLING

PRIMARY MOUSE BUTTON (OR JUST "MOUSE BUTTON") USED FOR CLICKING, DOUBLE-CLICKING, & DRAGGING

SECONDARY (RIGHT) MOUSE BUTTON, USED FOR RIGHT-CLICKING & RIGHT-DRAGGING

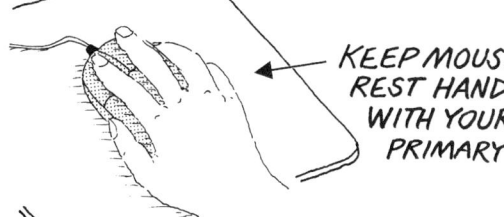

KEEP MOUSE ON DESKTOP OR MOUSEPAD, REST HAND COMFORTABLY ON THE MOUSE WITH YOUR INDEX FINGER OVER THE PRIMARY MOUSE BUTTON

13

1: BEGINNER'S BASICS

Holding the Mouse

Using the mouse is pretty simple. You leave the mouse on your desktop or mouse pad, and gently rest your right hand on the mouse. Rest your index finger over the primary (left) mouse button, but don't press on that button. The preceding illustration shows an example of a hand resting on a mouse.

As you move ("roll") the mouse around on your desktop or mouse pad, the mouse pointer on the screen moves in exactly the same direction. Here are some standard terms that go along with using a mouse. You'll want to become very familiar with these terms, because you'll see them again and again.

- **Mouse pointer**: As mentioned earlier, this is the little pointer on the screen, usually in the shape of an arrow, that moves in whatever direction you roll the mouse.
- **Point**: To move the mouse so that the mouse pointer is touching some object on the screen.
- **Click**: To point to an item, then press and release the primary (usually the left) mouse button.
- **Double-click**: To point to an item, then click the primary mouse button twice in rapid succession—click-click!
- **Right-click**: To point to an item, then press and release the secondary (usually the right) mouse button.
- **Drag**: To hold down the primary mouse button while moving the mouse.
- **Right-drag**: To hold down the secondary mouse button while moving the mouse.

If you're a lefty, you can customize the mouse so that the primary mouse button is on the right, and the secondary button is on the left. See Chapter 5 for more info.

If your mouse has three buttons on it, you can ignore the button in the middle for now. Windows 98 is very much geared toward two-button mouse operation. If your mouse has a little wheel in the middle, you can use that for *scrolling*, as discussed in Chapter 3.

Another piece of hardware you'll use to interact with your computer is the **keyboard**. It's laid out like a standard typewriter keyboard, for the most part. It does have a few special keys that you'll use often. Take a moment now to locate these keys and get to know what they do.

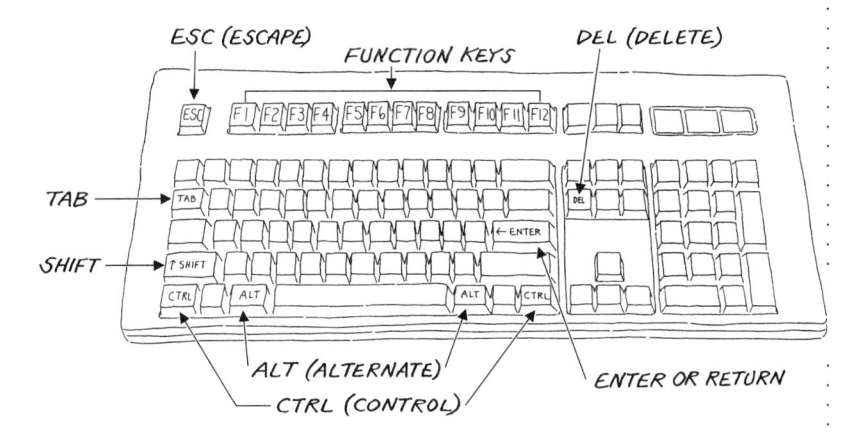

Pounding the Keyboard

Special keys on a computer keyboard.

- **Enter or Return**: Completes some action, like ending a paragraph or executing a command or leaving a text box.
- **Esc (Escape)**: Cancels out the previous command so you can "escape" from unfamiliar territory.
- **Del (Delete)**: Deletes something that's on the screen.
- **Function keys**: The function keys F1, F2, and so forth, play special roles, as you'll learn. For example, the key labeled F1 is the Help key, which you can press whenever you need help with a command, button, or other item.
- **Tab**: Often used to move from one item to the next on a screen that offers multiple options. Has other functions in various programs.
- **Ctrl (Control)**: Used as the first key in many *combination keystrokes*, such as Ctrl+A.
- **Alt (Alternate)**: Used as the first key in many combination keystrokes, such as Alt+Tab.
- **Shift**: Hold the Shift key down while typing a letter to make an uppercase letter. Also used in some combination keystrokes, such as Shift+Tab.

1: BEGINNER'S BASICS

Combination Keystrokes

Often, you'll type on the computer keyboard just as you'd type on a regular typewriter. But unlike a typewriter, a computer keyboard offers **combination keystrokes** that act as shortcuts for performing common tasks. You'll learn about the various shortcut keystrokes as we go along in this book. But first, you need to know how to type them.

*Combination keystrokes are usually shown in **key+key** format, as in these examples:*

Alt+F1
Ctrl+A
Shift+Tab
Ctrl+Alt+Del

Whenever you see a **key+key combination**, you need to *hold down* the first key, press and release the second key, and then release the first key. For example, to press Alt+F1 you hold down the Alt key, press and release the F1 function key, then release the Alt key. To press Ctrl+A you hold down the Ctrl key, press and release the letter A, and then release the Ctrl key.

The last example in the preceding list, Ctrl+Alt+Del, is a **triple key-press**. To do that one you have to hold down the Ctrl key *and* the Alt key, press and release the Del (or Delete) key, and then release the Alt and Ctrl keys.

About the Numeric Keypad

Today's keyboards have two sets of **number keys** and two sets of **arrow keys**.

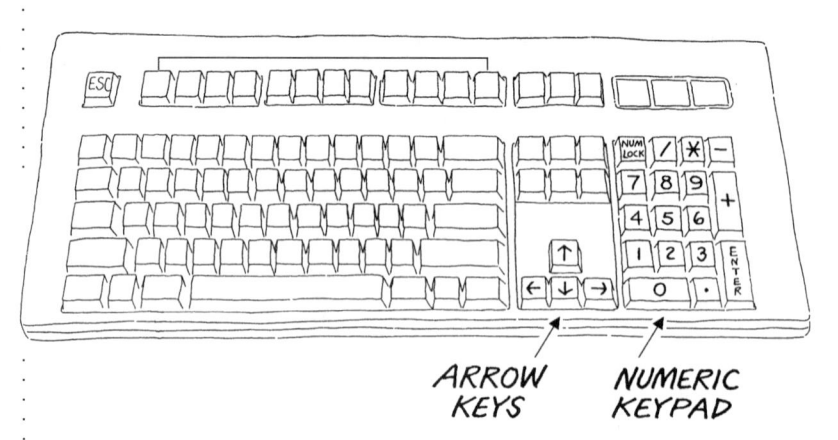

ARROW KEYS

NUMERIC KEYPAD

Special keys on a computer keyboard.

As you'll learn later, you use the arrow keys to move the **cursor** (the small blinking line) around the screen, and the number keys to type numbers.

Typing Numbers

The number keys across the top of the keyboard always work for entering numbers. So whenever you want to type a number somewhere, you can use those keys. And the arrow keys to the immediate right of the main keyboard also work all the time. When you get into a situation where you want to move things using the arrow keys, you can use those arrow keys.

On some keyboards, there's a second set of number and arrow keys on the **numeric keypad**, as shown in the preceding illustration. On the numeric keypad, the number keys are arranged like the keys on an adding machine. So if you're accustomed to using an adding machine, you might prefer to use this set of keys to type numbers. However, there's a catch to using these number keys: They only work when the Num Lock key is in the On position.

Arrow Keys

Notice that most of the keys in the numeric keypad contain arrows and other characters in addition to the numbers. When the Num Lock key is in the Off position, the arrows, Home, PgUp (Page Up), End, and PgDn (Page Down) functions work instead of the numbers. So in other words, you can use the numeric keypad to type numbers *or* to navigate using arrow keys, but not both at the same time. When Num Lock is on, the number keys type numbers. When Num Lock is off, the other functions work: the arrows, Home, PgUp, PgDn, and End instead of the numbers.

Num Lock

It's pretty easy to determine if the Num Lock key is on or off at any given time. If your keyboard has indicator lights, the indicator for the Num Lock key will light up on when Num Lock is on. (Try pressing and releasing the Num Lock key a few times to see if any such indicator lights up on your keyboard.)

When you get to a situation where you might want to use the numeric keypad, you can also find out the status of the Num Lock key just by trial-and-error. If you press a number key on the numeric keypad to type a number, but no number appears on the screen, then the Num Lock key must be turned on. If the cursor moves when you press one of those number keys, then the Num Lock key must be off.

Toggles

We say that the Num Lock key acts as a **toggle**. That is, you press it to turn it off if it's on, and you press it to turn it on if it's off. But the main thing to remember, right now, is that the numeric keypad is optional. You can always type numbers using the number keys across the top of the keyboard, and you can always use the group of arrow keys beside the main keyboard to move the cursor. You'll have an opportunity to play around with the arrow keys when we get to Chapter 2.

1: BEGINNER'S BASICS

Practicing What You'll Be Doing

Most of your work at the PC will involve opening and closing programs and documents. In fact, you'll do this dozens of times a day. Each program and/or document will appear in its own **window**, which you can close when you've finished with that program or document. To see how to do that, we'll practice using the icon labeled **My Computer**— it's near the upper-left corner of your desktop. Follow these steps:

Step 1. Click the My Computer icon. In other words, move the mouse pointer so that it's resting on the My Computer icon; then press and release the primary mouse button—usually the mouse button on the left.

Step 2. If the My Computer window opens, go to step 4 now.

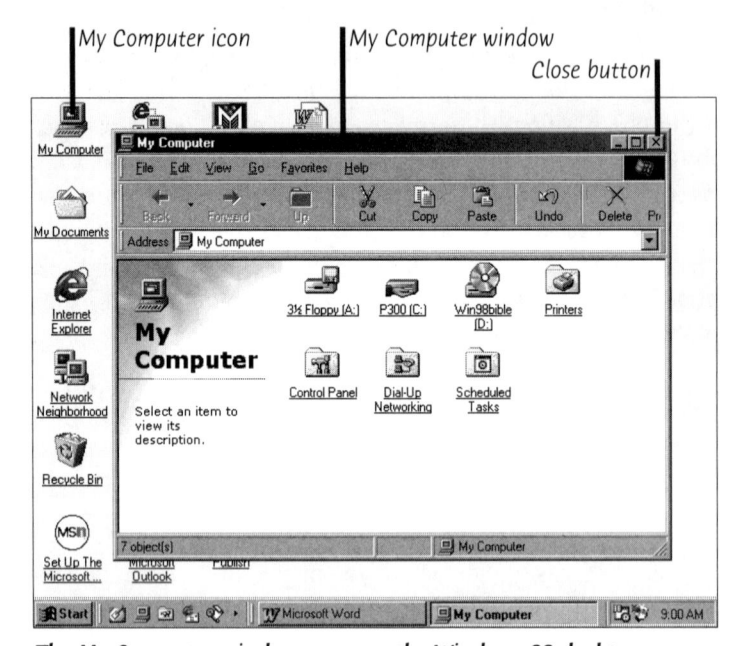

The My Computer window open on the Windows 98 desktop.

The strip along the very top of the My Computer window is called the **title bar**. Notice how the icon and name at the left end of the title bar resemble the icon and name used to open that window. Most windows that you open will have a title bar containing the program's icon and name. So if you're ever wondering what program is open in a window, just look at the upper-left corner.

18

Step 3. If My Computer didn't open in step 2, try double-clicking the desktop icon (rest the mouse pointer on the My Computer icon and, without moving the mouse, press and release the primary mouse button twice, as quickly as you can).

Step 4. Take a close look at the My Computer window, and notice the Close (X) button in the upper-right corner. To close a window, you just need to click (once) on that Close (X) button. Go ahead and do so now. The My Computer window closes and you're back to "home base," the Windows 98 desktop.

Really, that's what you'll be doing a lot of the time—opening icons into windows, and then closing those windows (using the little X button in the upper-right corner) when you've finished working. Think of "opening an icon" as being the equivalent of taking something out of the filing cabinet and putting it on your desktop so you can work with it. "Closing a window" is essentially the same thing as putting it back in your filing cabinet so it's out of the way, but still within reach when you need it.

As you'll learn throughout this book, there are many **keyboard shortcuts** that you can use as an alternative to using the mouse. Keyboard shortcuts are handy when your hands happen to be on the keyboard and you don't feel like reaching over and grabbing the mouse.

The keyboard shortcut for closing a window, for instance, is Alt+F4. Follow these steps if you want to try it out:

▼ Open that My Computer icon again, by clicking it (or double-clicking if single-clicking doesn't work).

▼ Instead of clicking on the Close (X) button to close the window, press the shortcut: Alt+F4. (Hold down the Alt key, press and release the function key labeled F4, and then release the Alt key.)

Pretty simple, no? So now you see that there are two ways to close a window—either by clicking on its Close (X) button, or by pressing Alt+F4. There is no right way or wrong way here—use whichever method is most convenient for you at the time.

You can choose between using single-clicks or double-clicks to open icons, as discussed under "To Click or Double-Click" a little later in this chapter.

Try a Keyboard Shortcut
I'm not sure why they call it a "keyboard shortcut." Really, it's only a shortcut if your hands happen to be on the keyboard rather than the mouse when you want to execute the command.

To Click or Double-Click?

As mentioned earlier, you may be able to open an icon by clicking it once. Or you may need to double-click it. To open icons with a single click, you need to set Windows 98 to work in **Web Style navigation**. This setting has this name because you can get virtually anywhere using a single mouse click, just as you can on the Internet's World Wide Web. If you prefer using the double-click method, you can set Windows to work with **Classic Style navigation**, so named because earlier versions of Windows offered only the double-click approach to opening icons.

To choose between Web Style or Classic Style navigation right now, follow these steps:

▼ Click on the Start button (usually down near the lower-left corner of the screen) to open the Start menu.

▼ Point to Settings on the menu, and rest the mouse pointer on Settings until a little submenu appears off to the right.

Submenus: When using menus, you may notice that some options menu have a little triangle off to the right. The triangle indicates that when you point to this item, a submenu will appear, giving more options.

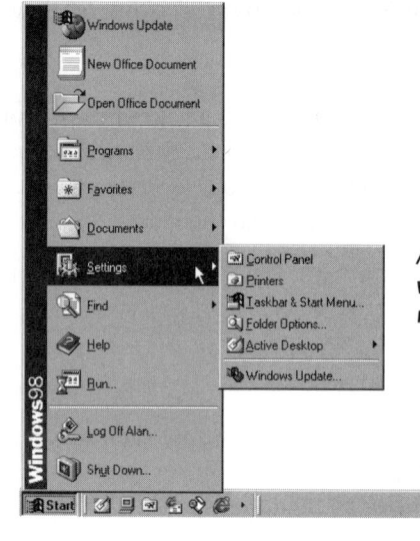

A little submenu appears when the mouse pointer is resting on Settings.

▼ Choose Folder Options by clicking it (move the mouse pointer to Folder Options on the submenu; then press and release the primary mouse button). The Folder Options *dialog box* opens up.

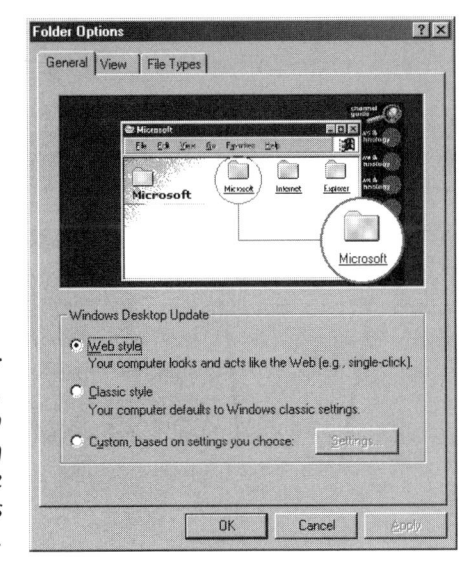

In this Folder Options dialog box, the General tab is open, showing that Web-style navigation is selected.

Dialog boxes *are so named because you carry on sort of a little dialog with them. The dialog box presents your options, you make your selections, and then click the OK button to close the dialog box and return to wherever you were before.*

▼ If your Folder Options dialog box doesn't look quite like this one, it's probably because a different page of the dialog is showing. Click on the General tab near the top of the dialog box to see the page of General options.

▼ Choose either Web Style or Classic Style navigation. If you don't really know which you want, choose Web Style for now, by clicking on that option so that the little button to its left is filled, as shown in the illustration.

▼ Click the OK button down near the bottom of the dialog box to activate your selection and close the dialog box.

Congratulations—you've just opened, used, and closed your first dialog box. In Chapter 2 you'll learn more about dialog boxes and what they contain.

Now that you've switched to Web Style navigation, I'd like to point out some new items that will appear on your screen in Web view.

Using Web View

You've already learned that one advantage to Web view is that you only have to click an icon—not double-click it—to open the icon into a window. However, Web view also provides some additional visual cues that the classic Windows navigation style does not. For one thing, "clickable" text tends to be underlined like links on the Web, as in the icon on the next page. Underlined text shows you it's something you can click on to get a result—known as **hot text**.

1: BEGINNER'S BASICS

Web view offers extra visual cues: Hot text is underlined, and the mouse pointer changes to a little hand when hovering over something you can click.

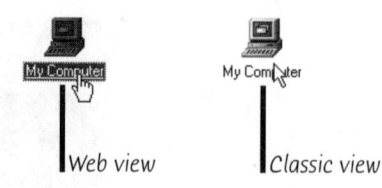

|Web view |Classic view

The Hand Pointer

Also, whenever the mouse pointer touches hot text, the pointer turns into a little hand. So if you're not sure whether or not something is clickable, you can just move the mouse pointer to that item and see if the mouse pointer changes to the little hand. If it does, just click the primary mouse button to see where that "hot spot" leads.

Should you decide you don't like Web view, you can easily go back to the Classic view at any time. Just repeat the steps presented earlier to get back to the Folder Options dialog box, but choose the Classic Style button rather than Web Style.

Taking the Guided Tour

The CD-ROM edition of Windows 98 comes with a Guided Tour that you can take to reinforce what you've learned here, and to learn more about Windows 98 in general. To take the Guided Tour, follow these steps:

▼ Insert the Windows 98 CD into your CD-ROM drive (with the label side facing up), and close the CD-ROM drive door.

▼ If this window pops up, close it by clicking the little Close (X) button in its upper-right corner.

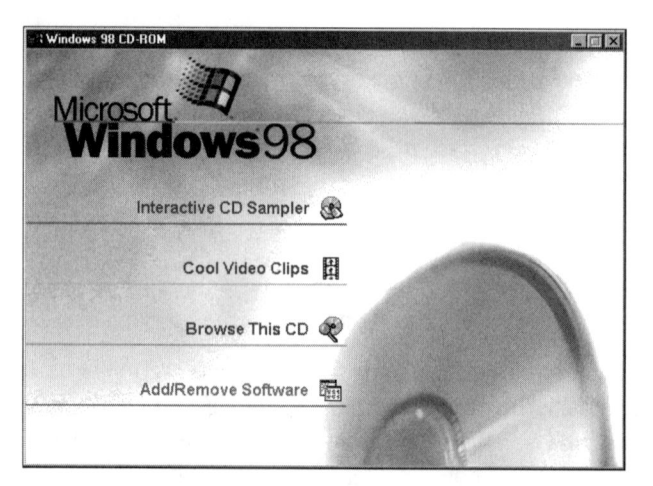

This screen may appear automatically a few seconds after you put your Windows 98 CD-ROM into your CD-ROM drive. Just close it.

▼ If you see an icon named Welcome to Windows on your desktop, open that icon by clicking (if you're in Web view) or double-clicking (if you're in Classic view).

If you don't see a Welcome icon, click the Start button and choose Run from the Start menu. Type the word **welcome** and click OK.

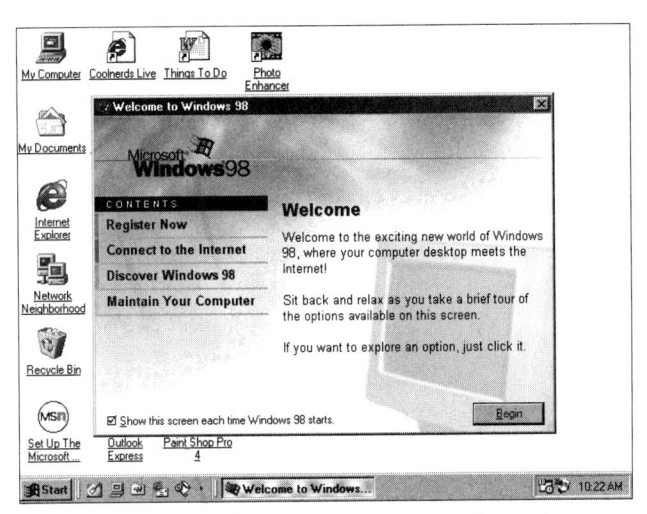

The Welcome to Windows program open on the desktop.

▼ To take the tour, click the Discover Windows 98 option in the Welcome window, and wait a moment. When you get to the Discover Windows 98 screen, you'll be ready to start the tour. Click Computer Essentials, and just follow the instructions that appear on the screen.

The Discover Windows 98 guided tour starts with this screen.

1: BEGINNER'S BASICS

Hands-on Review To review some of what you've learned in this lesson, I suggest that you take the first three lessons that appear after you click the Computer Essentials option. You'll be taken step-by-step through simple lessons in recognizing hardware, using your keyboard, and using your mouse. Whenever you want to quit the Guided Tour, follow these steps:

▼ Click the Contents icon down near the lower-left corner of the screen.

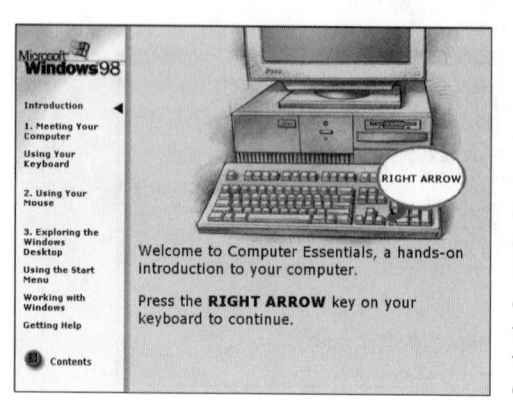

Click the Contents icon in the lower-left corner to get to the option to Close this Guided Tour.

▼ In the next screen that appears, click the Close button.

▼ When you see the message asking if you're sure you want to quit Discover Windows 98, click the Yes button.

▼ Now you have a couple of new choices. If you want that Welcome to Windows window to appear each time your computer starts, make sure the little checkbox next to "Show this screen next time Windows 98 starts" is checked. If you don't want to see the welcome window automatically, uncheck the checkbox.

💡 To check or clear a checkbox, just click it with your mouse.

▼ If you'd like to close the Welcome to Windows window right now, click its Close (X) button.

If you do close the Welcome to Windows window right now but want to get back to it later, just repeat the earlier steps for "Taking the Guided Tour" to bring that window back up. Have fun, and enjoy.

Shutting Down Your PC Shutting down your PC at the end of the day involves a little more than just hitting the Off button. It's always best to exit Windows properly before you turn off your PC. Doing so allows Windows to close any open programs and save any work in progress, before the power goes off and everything in RAM gets erased. To shut down your PC, follow these steps:

▼ Click the Start button and choose Shut Down from the Start menu.

▼ In the Shut Down dialog box, choose Shut Down by clicking on that option.

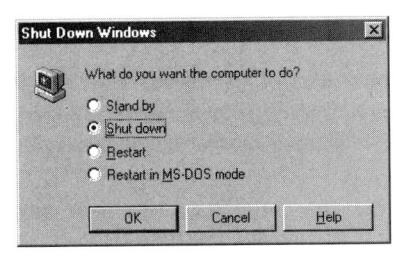

The Shut Down dialog box with the Shut Down option selected.

▼ Click the OK button.

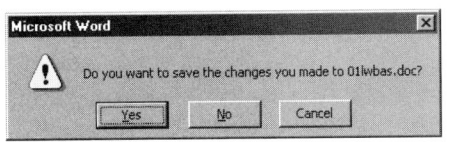

If you happen to see a message like the one illustrated here, that means you've left some unsaved work on your virtual desktop (i.e. in RAM). We won't be showing you the Save As dialog box until you actually start creating documents of your own. You'll learn more about that topic in Chapter 3.

▼ Click the Yes button if you want to save your work. This brings up the Save As dialog box, where you have an opportunity to save your work before the PC shuts down.

▼ When you see the message "It is now safe to turn off your computer," that's the time to switch off the monitor, the PC, and any other devices attached to your computer (such as your printer or an external modem).

To restart your computer at any time in the future, just repeat the steps presented earlier in this chapter under "How to Start Windows 98."

If your computer has the ability to shut itself off, you won't see the "It is now safe . . ." message. Don't worry about that though. It's just that the computer has shut itself down already, when it was safe to do so.

I suppose I should point out that it's not entirely necessary to shut down the PC each time you finish using it. The system unit uses very little energy when idle. So there's no harm in just leaving the PC on all the time. The monitor, on the other hand, does use up quite a bit of energy. So even if you leave your PC on all the time, you'd do well to at least shut off the monitor when you're not using the system unit.

If your PC supports a **sleep mode** or **Standby mode**, it may *never* be necessary to shut down your PC. Your PC may shut itself off, automatically, after you've been away for 15 minutes or half an hour. Let's talk about that alternative for a moment.

Standby Mode

Not all PCs have this Standby option

Some computers can go into Standby mode (also called "sleep mode") automatically when left idle for any length of time. You can also force such computers to go into Standby mode whenever you want, by repeating the shutdown steps in the preceding section and choosing Standby instead of Shut Down.

In Standby mode, everything on the PC seems to turn off and the computer is quiet. To wake the computer back up, you just have to move the mouse around a little, or press some key on the keyboard. It might take a few seconds for the monitor to warm up, but it's a lot quicker than starting up from scratch.

If your PC and/or monitor have the ability to go into Standby mode automatically, you can choose how long you want the computer to sit idle before Standby mode kicks in. You'll learn how to do that in Chapter 5.

Different PCs have different standby capabilities, so the instructions I've given you here may not be specific to your machine. If your PC does support a standby mode and you're having trouble using it, you'll need to refer to the manual that came with that computer to learn more. The ability to go into Standby mode is a feature of the PC itself—not really a feature of Windows. Windows just supports the option if it happens to be built into your PC.

Summary

You're off to a good start. In the next chapter you'll learn more Windows "basic skills" that will help you understand and use your PC better. Before we move on, though, take a minute to review the important concepts and buzzwords discussed in this chapter:

- Computer **hardware** is the stuff you can see and touch.
- Computer **software** is "invisible" stuff, stored on your computer's hard disk, or floppy disks, or CD-ROMs, that makes your computer perform a certain type of work.
- **Windows 98** is software. To be more specific, it's your PC's operating system (OS) software.
- **To start** Windows 98 on your PC, remove any disks from your floppy disk drive(s). Then turn on the monitor, the PC, and any other devices that are attached to your PC.
- Using your PC is largely a matter of **using the mouse** to move the mouse pointer onto some item you want to open, and then clicking (or double-clicking) that item using the primary mouse button.
- To choose between modern single-click **Web view** and the older double-click **Classic view** navigation style, click the Start button, point to Settings, choose Folder Options, and then make your selection from the General tab in the Folder Options dialog box.
- **To shut down** your PC at the end of the day, click the Start button and choose Shut Down from the Start menu.

Understanding Programs and Documents

There is really one, and only one, reason to buy a PC. And that's to run *programs*. Programs come in all flavors, including games, educational programs, word processing programs to help with writing, graphics programs to help with drawing, programs for doing e-mail, programs for browsing the Internet—the list goes on and on. Chances are you'll use some programs to create your own *documents*—things like letters, drawings, invoices, legal papers, photos, videos—whatever your profession, business, or hobby requires. In this chapter you'll learn all about using programs and about creating documents on your PC.

What Is a Program?

A computer **program** is generally something you purchase at a computer store and install on your PC. There are actually lots of different terms used interchangeably with the term *program*—including *software application, application program, software program, app, applet,* and just plain *software*.

As mentioned in Chapter 1, Windows 98 itself is a program. Other popular programs whose names you may have heard already include Microsoft Word, WordPerfect, Microsoft Excel, Lotus 1-2-3, Microsoft Internet Explorer, Doom, Tomb Raider, Myst, TurboTax, and Betty Crocker's Multimedia Cookbook—just to name a few!

Windows 98 is certainly not the only program you'll use on your PC. Chances are, you'll eventually learn to use many different kinds of programs to do various kinds of work. In this chapter I'd like to show you general techniques for starting whatever programs happen to be installed on your computer at the moment, so you can get a feel for what that's all about.

Starting a Program

To start a program, you just click its **icon**. For example, to start a program that has its own icon on the Windows 98 desktop, you just click that icon (or double-click if you're using Classic view). If the program you want to start doesn't have an icon on the desktop, you can probably find its icon somewhere in the **Programs menu**. To get to the Programs menu, just click the Windows 98 Start button and then point to Programs on that menu. The submenu that appears will contain a list of **program groups** (options that provide access to more programs), as well as some program names.

The exact appearance of the Programs menu depends on what programs are installed on your PC. Don't worry if your Programs menu doesn't contain the same options as the Programs menus shown in this book.

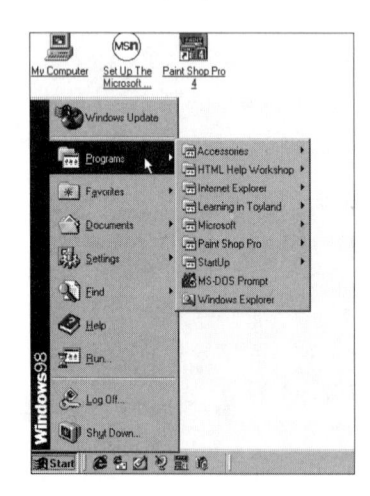

The Programs submenu appears after you click the Start button and point to Programs.

2: UNDERSTANDING PROGRAMS AND DOCUMENTS

If you want to run and use a simple program right now, follow these steps to run the **Calculator** program—one of several accessory programs that come free with Windows 98:

▼ Click the Start button in the Windows 98 taskbar.

▼ Point to Programs on the Start menu.

▼ In the submenu that appears, point to Accessories.

▼ In the next submenu, click on Calculator. A little calculator appears on your screen.

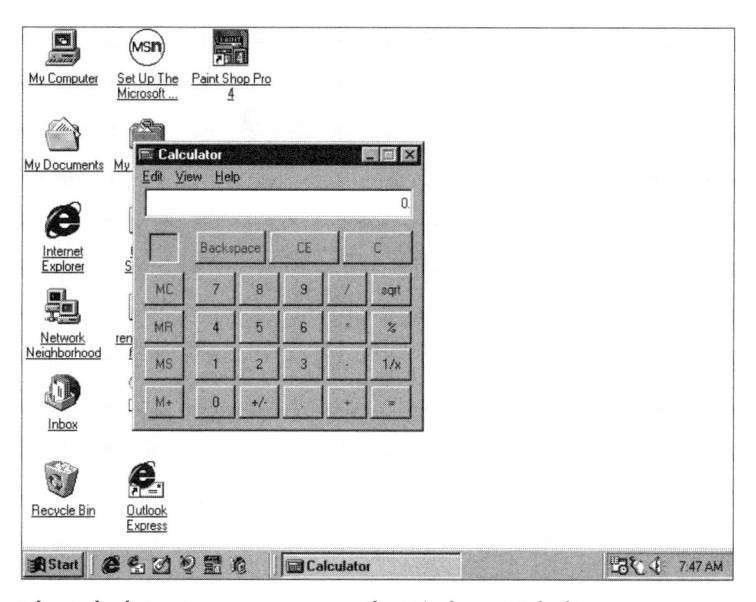

The Calculator program open on the Windows 98 desktop.

To use the calculator, click its buttons as you would with a normal calculator. For example, if you click 1, then +, then 1, and then =, you'll get the answer 2 because 1+1 equals 2. Click the C (clear) button to return to 0, and then maybe try a little math of your own.

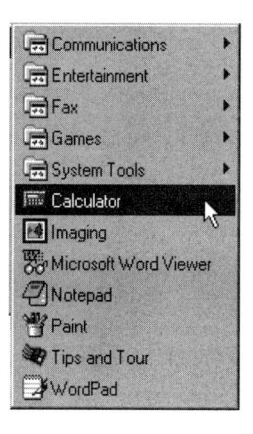

Note: *If the Calculator program isn't available on your computer, it just hasn't been installed. You can install it at any time by following the instructions under "Installing Missing Windows Components" in Chapter 8.*

31

2: UNDERSTANDING PROGRAMS AND DOCUMENTS

Using Menus in Programs

Most programs provide a set of options (also called "commands") that you can access via **menus**. A menu in a computer program is somewhat similar to a menu in a restaurant in that it provides a list of choices. In most programs, only the **menu bar** appears initially. Selecting one of the options in the menu bar, however, reveals a **pull-down menu** of more options.

Options on menus are also called commands, because choosing an option "commands" the computer to do something.

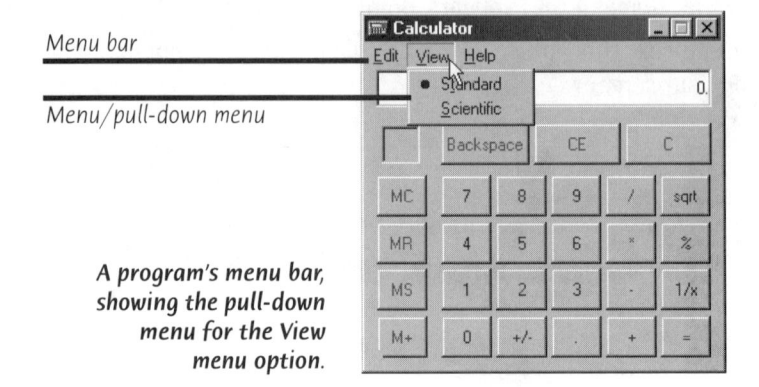

Menu bar

Menu/pull-down menu

A program's menu bar, showing the pull-down menu for the View menu option.

You can operate menus using either the mouse or the keyboard. To use the mouse, just click on an item when you want to use it. For example, if you click View in Calculator's menu bar and then click Scientific in the pull-down menu that appears, the Calculator expands into one of those major nerd-o-rama calculators.

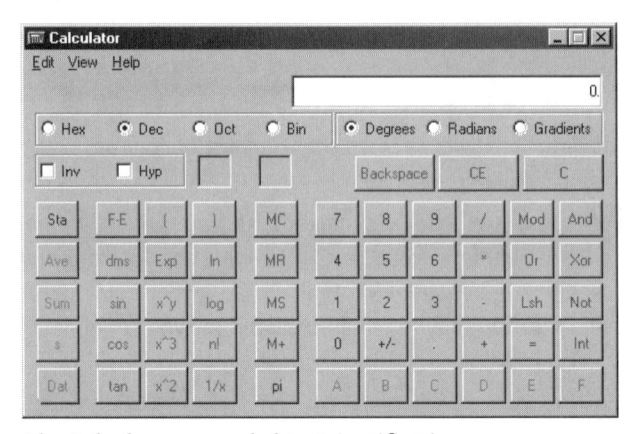

The Calculator expanded to Scientific View.

If your hands happen to be on the keyboard when you want something from the menus, you don't need to reach for the mouse. You can open a menu by holding down the Alt key and typing the underlined letter in the menu option. For example, to open the View menu, you press Alt+V. Notice the plus sign between the two keystrokes Alt and V; this plus sign creates a **key-combination**. For the key-combination Alt+V, you hold down the Alt key, press and release the V key on the keyboard, and then release the Alt key.

Holding down the Alt key is only necessary to select an option on the menu bar. When you're selecting an option from a pull-down menu, just type the underlined letter without messing with the Alt key.

When the View menu opens up, choose the Standard option. To to this, just type the letter **t**. The Calculator returns to the Standard view.

You can also use the keyboard arrow keys to navigate in pull-down menus. You need to first use the mouse or an Alt+key combo to pull down a menu. For example, in the Calculator program you could press Alt+E to open the Edit pull-down menu. Once any menu is pulled down, press the up-arrow and down-arrow keys to move the highlight up and down the menu, from command to command. Use the left-arrow and right-arrow keys to move left and right across the menu bar itself. To select the item that's currently highlighted on a menu, press the Enter key.

Don't forget that if you want to use the arrow keys on the numeric keypad, the Num Lock key must be turned off.

You can close any open program simply by clicking its Close button. For example, to close the Calculator program, just click the Close (X) button at the far-right end of the Calculator program's title bar. The Calculator program will close and disappear from the screen. To get back to the Calculator program again, just repeat the steps for "Starting a Program" presented earlier in this section.

Closing a Program

The Close button

You can also close a program by pressing Alt+F4 to close the program's window. This is handy if your fingers happen to be on the keyboard when you want to leave the program. It's also a quick exit when you want to close a game or some other program that takes over the entire screen and doesn't offer any Close (X) button or menu commands.

As we progress through the book, I'll show you more techniques for using programs. For now, however, just knowing how to open, recognize, and close a program is sufficient. Next, I'd like to explain to you what a document is and how to work with it.

2: UNDERSTANDING PROGRAMS AND DOCUMENTS

What Is a Document?

Whereas a program is generally something you buy and install on your computer, a **document** is something that you create yourself, using one of those programs. For example, as I write this chapter, it's really a document on my computer. Letters, budgets, balance sheets, memos, magazine articles, pictures and photographs, even business cards and greeting cards—virtually anything you might want to print on paper—are all examples of documents.

Saving a Simple Letter

To help you get a feel for what a document is, I'll take you through the steps required to create, print, and save a simple letter using the WordPad program that comes with Windows 98. WordPad is a simple word-processing program, meaning that it's primarily designed to help you work with words as opposed to numbers. WordPad is actually a watered-down version of Microsoft Word, a more sophisticated wordprocessing program that you can purchase and install separately, if you're so inclined.

Anyway, to try out WordPad and create your first document, you first need to start the WordPad program. Here's how:

▼ Click the Windows 98 Start button.

▼ On the Start menu, point to Programs and then point to Accessories.

▼ Choose WordPad, by clicking the WordPad item in the Accessories submenu. The WordPad program opens up in its own window.

If the WordPad program isn't available on your computer, it just hasn't been installed. You can install it at any time by following the instructions under "Installing Missing Windows Components" in Chapter 8.

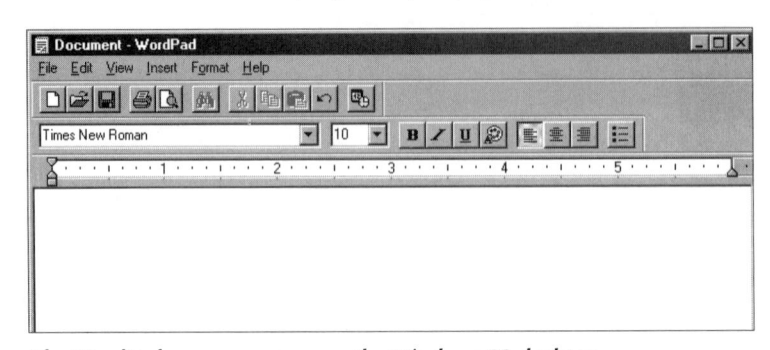

The WordPad program open on the Windows 98 desktop.

Notice that WordPad has its own title bar, showing the words "Document - WordPad." WordPad also has its own menu bar containing the options File, Edit, View, Insert, Format, and Help. One major difference between the Calculator program and the WordPad program is the giant white area occupying the main part of your screen. That area is actually a document—sort of like a blank piece of paper in a typewriter. To create a document in WordPad, you just type within that big white area.

2: UNDERSTANDING PROGRAMS AND DOCUMENTS

For example, let's suppose you want to type up a letter. You could just start typing, as though on a regular typewriter. After typing a short line, press the **Enter key** (like the Carriage Return key on a normal typewriter) to end the line and move down to the next line. To add an extra blank line, press Enter again. Here's a sample letter I typed up in WordPad:

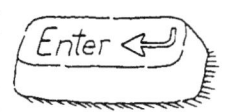

The Enter key on a keyboard usually has a bent arrow on it, like this one.

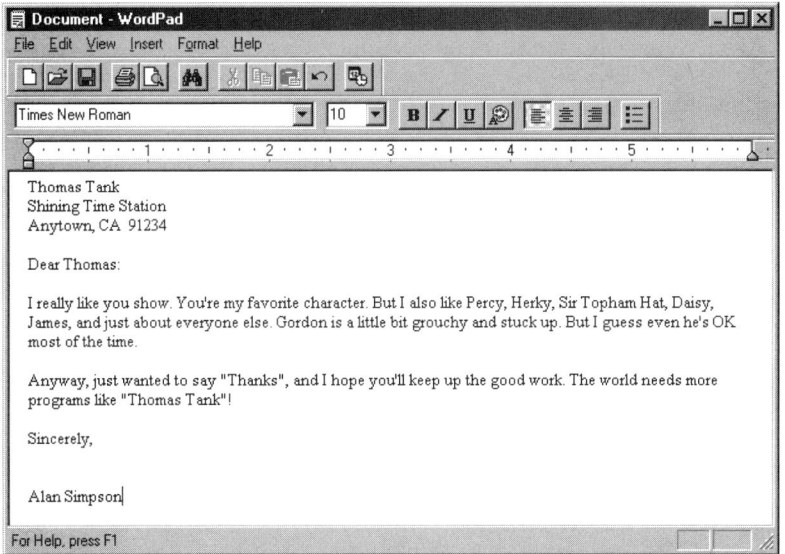

One difference between a computer and a regular typewriter is that you don't need to press Enter to break lines while typing a paragraph. For example, look at the bent arrows in the following screen. They show where I pressed the Enter key while typing my sample letter. Notice how each short line ends with an Enter keypress, and that each blank line was created by pressing the Enter key again. While typing the larger paragraphs, I had to press Enter only at the end of the paragraph, not at the end of each line.

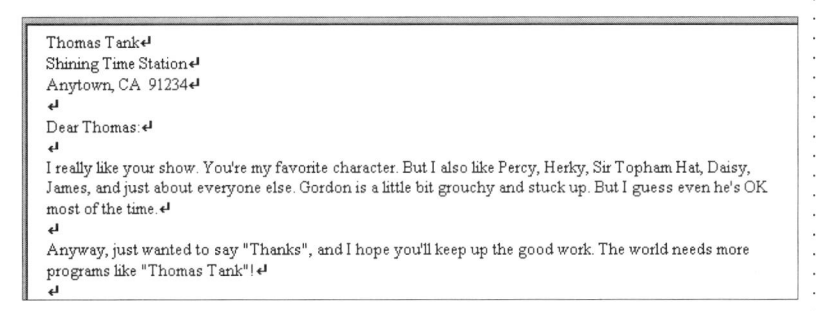

On a computer, you don't press Enter to end every line in a paragraph.

35

If you want to type up a similar letter of your own, go ahead and try it. Don't worry about mistakes—we're not really going to send this letter to anyone. But if you do want to correct a mistake, you can press the Backspace key to back up and erase whatever you just typed.

> The **blinking cursor**, *not* the mouse pointer, shows where the next character that you type will appear. If you want to type near the mouse pointer position, just click the primary mouse button to make the blinking cursor jump to where the mouse pointer is pointing.

The Cursor Click anywhere in the document where you want to make a change, and the blinking cursor moves to that location. (The blinking cursor always shows where any characters you type will appear in the document.) Once the blinking cursor is in place, you just type to insert new text. Use the Backspace key to erase characters to the left of the cursor, or press the Delete (Del) key to erase characters to the right of the cursor. But, as I said earlier, don't worry about getting it perfect. The purpose of this little exercise is just to show you an example of a document.

Printing a Document Any program that lets you create a document will also let you print that document. The steps to follow, in most programs, are simple:

▼ Choose (click on) the File command in that program's menu bar.

▼ Choose Print from the pull-down menu. A Print *dialog box* appears.

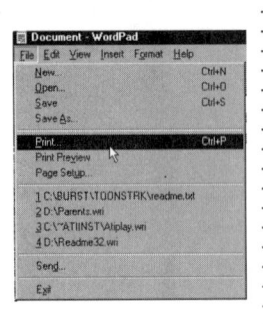

The Print dialog box, displayed when you choose File → Print from WordPad's menu bar.

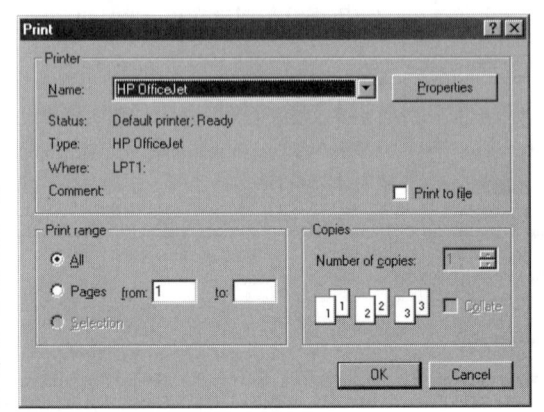

▼ You may be taken to a dialog box of more options, such as the number of copies you want to print. If you just want to print one copy, click the OK button to accept the suggested settings.

2: UNDERSTANDING PROGRAMS AND DOCUMENTS

Assuming that your printer is turned on and ready to go, the document should print just fine. If you have any problems, or want to learn more about the options in the Print dialog box, see the section "Notes on Printing" later in this chapter.

When you create a new document from scratch, that document exists only in RAM—the volatile memory from which things disappear when the computer is turned off. If you want to be able to access this document again in the future, you need to **save** it. That means giving it a name and putting a copy on the hard disk.

Saving a Document

The steps for saving a document are pretty much the same in all programs. For example, to save the letter in WordPad, follow these steps:

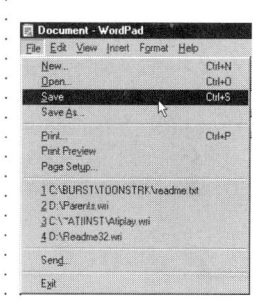

▼ Click on File in WordPad's menu bar.

▼ Choose Save from the File pull-down menu. A Save As dialog box appears.

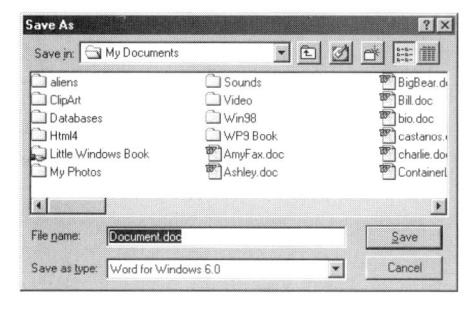

The Save As dialog box.

▼ Next, give the document a name. I've opted to name my document Thomas Letter.doc. I'll do this by replacing the suggested name that's in the File Name box (document.doc), with my own filename Thomas Letter.doc.

The filename you provide can be up to 128 characters in length. But it's a good idea to use a short, descriptive name that will be easy to remember in the future.

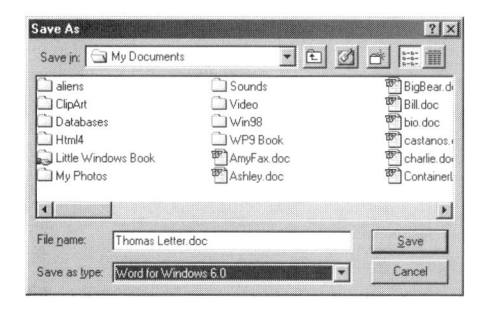

Saving this document as Thomas Letter.doc.

37

2: UNDERSTANDING PROGRAMS AND DOCUMENTS

If you have any trouble replacing the suggested filename (document.doc) with your own choice of filename, click on the text that reads "File name:" to select the existing filename. (The selected text turns to white letters on a blue background.) Then type the new name to replace the selected name.

▼ After typing your filename, click the Save button.

The characters ".doc" at the end of a WordPad filename are an example of a filename extension. Windows uses this extension to associate documents with programs. Just accept the .doc extension in whatever filename you give your document.

You won't notice any major change on the screen, except that the WordPad program's title bar now reads "Thomas Letter.doc - WordPad." That's because the document in that program is now saved and has a name. You now have two copies of that letter—one in RAM that's visible on the screen and another copy stored in the "filing cabinet": your PC's hard disk.

It's important to understand that when you save a document, you're saving exactly what's on the screen at the moment. If you then make more changes to the document, those changes are *not* saved automatically. You'll need to choose File → Save from WordPad's menu bar again to save those new changes. You won't have to enter a filename each time, though. Once you've saved a document and given it a name, choosing File → Save just saves the current version of the document to that same filename.

Closing a Document

When you've finished with a document for the time being, you can easily close it, and also close the program you used to create that document, all in one fell swoop. Here's how:

▼ Choose File from the program's (WordPad's in this example) menu bar.

▼ Choose Exit from the File pull-down menu.

If you've made any changes to the document since the last time you saved it, you'll see a dialog box like this one:

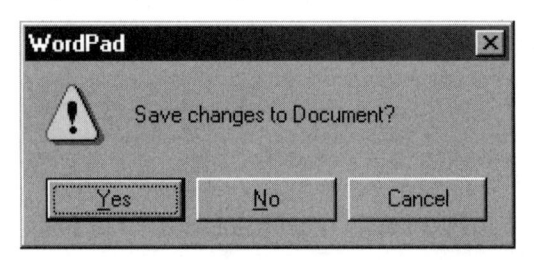

Last chance to save a document before closing it.

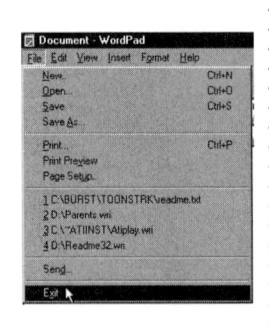

38

▼ In most cases, you'll want to choose Yes in this dialog box, to save all your work up to the very last minute. The only reason you wouldn't want to save current changes to a document would be if you've somehow made a real mess of things and don't really want to save that mess. If you go ahead and choose (click) Yes now, both your document and the WordPad program will close and disappear.

So now you've created a document, perhaps printed it, and saved it. Suppose that you now want to reopen that document, perhaps to make some changes and reprint it. How do you go about finding that document? Well, there are actually several ways to go about reopening a document, but let me just show you a couple of easy ways right now.

One way is to restart the program that you used to create the document in the first place (WordPad), and use that program's File menu to open the document. Follow these steps:

▼ Click the Windows 98 Start button, and choose Programs → Accessories → WordPad once again to open the WordPad program.

▼ Click on the File option in WordPad's menu bar. The File menu offers several options, including the names of some of the documents you've recently saved.

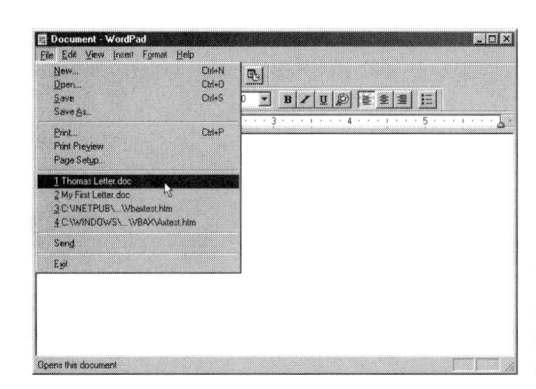

The File menu in WordPad lists recently saved documents.

▼ Click on the name of the document you want to open (in this example, Thomas Letter.doc). The document comes back into WordPad, looking just as it did the last time you saved it.

If you wanted to make any changes to the document right now, you could just click wherever you want to make a change and start typing. Remember, however, that any changes you make will not be saved unless you explicitly save the document again.

Reopening a Document

Opening from Within a Program

But rather than work any more with this sample document now, I'd like to show you another way that you can open a recently edited document. So follow these steps to close WordPad and your document, and then we'll take a look at this second technique.

- ▼ Close the WordPad program by clicking its Close (X) button or by choosing File → Exit from the WordPad menu bar.
- ▼ If you made any changes to the document while it was openend, you'll be asked if you want to save those changes. Choose Yes.

Now you're back to the Windows 98 desktop, with no sign of the WordPad program or your document.

Next, I'll show you a quick and easy way to open a document, and a program to work with that document, in one step.

Opening a Document from the Documents Menu

Windows 98 does a good job of keeping track of documents that you've recently saved. It lists them in the Documents menu, which you can get to from the Start menu. To open your Thomas Letter.doc document right from the desktop, without first opening WordPad, follow these steps:

- ▼ Click the Windows 98 Start button.
- ▼ Point to Documents.
- ▼ Click on the name of the document you want to open (Thomas Letter.doc in this example).

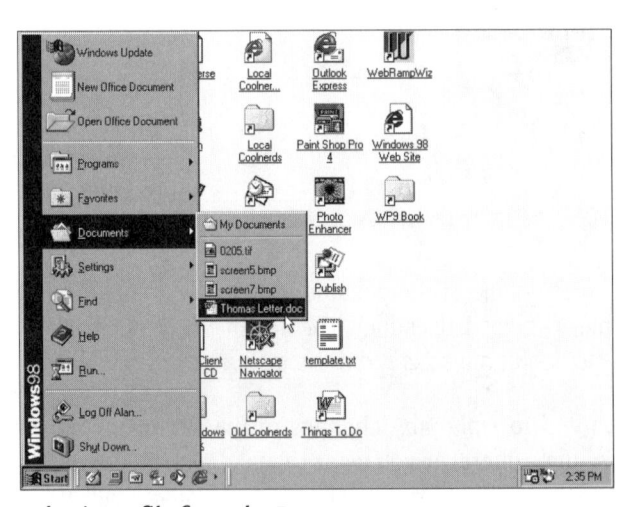

Selecting a file from the Documents menu.

The Thomas Letter.doc opens on the screen in either the WordPad program or the Microsoft Word program, if you happen to have that one installed on your computer. For the moment, don't worry about which program your document opens in—we'll get into all of that later. The important thing to gain from this little exercise is the fact that you can usually reopen any previously saved document along with its creating application, just by clicking the Start button, pointing to Documents, and then clicking on the name of the document you want to open.

If you are actually following along on your computer right now, you can close the Thomas Letter.doc document and whatever program it's in, by choosing File ➔ Exit from that program's menu bar or by clicking the Close (X) button in that program's title bar.

Each type of printer offers its own unique capabilities, which makes it impossible for me to tell you how best to use your particular printer. Here, I'll describe features that are common to most printers. But to take full advantage of your printer, you'll want to read the manual that came with it.

Notes on Printing

The first point we need to cover here concerns how you load paper into the printer. Most modern printers are **sheet fed**, meaning that when you load the printer, you generally put a stack of individual sheets of paper into some kind of bin on the printer. **Tractor-fed** printers, on the other hand, don't accept individual pages. Instead, you get sort of one super-long continuous sheet of paper, with pages separated by perforations. After printing on the continuous paper, you tear the sheets at the perforations to get individual sheets of paper.

Sheet-Fed vs. Tractor-Fed Paper

Watch That Perf! An important trick to using tractor-fed paper is understanding that the moment you turn the printer on, you're telling the PC that the printer is at the top of a new page. If, in truth, the paper is positioned so that printing will start in the middle of a page, then you'll get this weird situation where the page perforations are all in the wrong place rather than at the top of each page. To prevent this problem, you should always turn off the printer, and then position the paper in the printer so that there's a page perforation just above the print head. *Then* turn on the printer.

The print head is the part of the printer that moves back and forth and does the actual printing when the printer is working. It's usually visible only on tractor-fed printers.

If you need to manually crank some paper through the printer, *always* turn the printer off before you move the paper. Crank as much paper as necessary through the printer, and then perhaps crank a little more

2: UNDERSTANDING PROGRAMS AND DOCUMENTS

until the next page perforation is just above the print head. *Then* turn the printer back on to tell the PC, once again, that the printer is now poised to start printing at the top of a new page.

> Manually cranking paper through a printer while the printer is turned on can actually damage the printer! You should always turn off the printer before adding new paper and before repositioning the paper that's already in the printer.

With sheet-fed printers, you don't have to worry about any of that. The printer should always just start printing at the top of a new page whenever you start printing.

The Print Dialog Box

As mentioned earlier in this chapter, when you're using a program that lets you view or create documents, you can choose File ➔ Print from that program's menu bar (or press the Ctrl+P shortcut) to print whatever document you're viewing on the screen at the moment. Before the printing actually begins, however, you'll see the Print dialog box, which will look something like this:

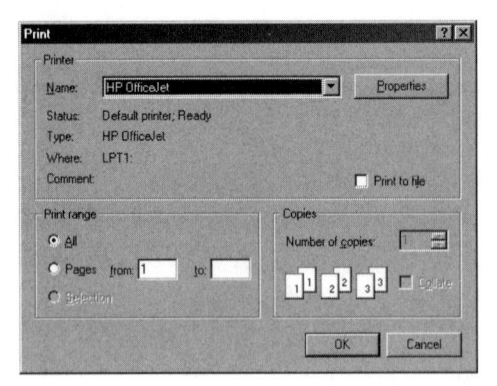

An example of a Print dialog box.

Before you actually start printing, you can make selections from this dialog box to specify exactly how you want to print.

> Don't worry—If you don't know how to make selections in the Print dialog box, you can skip all that for now. You'll learn more about choosing dialog box options in Chapter 4.

42

For example, if you have two or more printers attached to your computer, you can use the Name drop-down list to select which printer you want to use to print the current document.

Using the Print Range options, you can choose to print the entire document (All), or just certain pages, such as pages 1 to 3. If the Number of Copies option is enabled (not grayed out), you can choose how many copies you want to print.

If you do print multiple copies, you can check the **Collate checkbox** to tell the print program to collate your copies. For example, if you print three copies of a five-page document and collate them, the printer will print one copy of all five pages of the document, then a second copy of all the pages, then a third copy. But with the Collate checkbox turned off (unchecked), the printer will print three copies of page 1, then three copies of page 2, and so forth, until all the pages were printed. You would then need to collate those pages yourself.

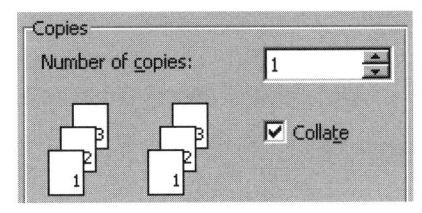

Usually, the only advantage to printing without collating is that the print job goes faster. Whether or not that time savings makes up for the amount of time required to collate all the pages after printing them depends on what you're printing at the moment. Chances are, you'll find it easier to just print everything with the Collate option turned on.

The **Properties button** in the Print dialog box calls up another dialog box that lets you change the properties (characteristics) of whatever printer is currently selected. (The "currently selected" printer is the one whose name appears in the Name field of the Print dialog box. Unfortunately, I can't tell you what you'll find in your printer's Properties dialog box, because it depends on the printer you happen to be using at the moment. You can check the written documentation for that particular printer, and you'll be able to find out what those settings are all about.

2: UNDERSTANDING PROGRAMS AND DOCUMENTS

You can continue to use your PC while the printer is printing. You don't have to wait for the print job to finish first.

When you are actually ready to print, just click the OK button (or the Print button, in some programs). The printer might not start up right away, because it takes a little time for the PC to get everything together and sent to the printer. This is especially true when you're printing pictures (as opposed to text) and when you're printing in color. So be patient!

There may be times when you want to print a "snapshot" of the computer screen, much like many of the illustrations you see in this book. This kind of printing is sometimes called a "screen dump." There are actually two steps to this type of printing: First you have to take the snapshot. Then you have to paste the snapshot into some program that's capable of displaying that snapshot, and then print the snapshot from within that program.

▼ To get started, first make sure your screen looks the way you want the printout to appear. Then do either of the following:

- To take a snapshot of the entire screen, press the Print Screen (Prnt Scrn) key on the keyboard.

- **Or,** if there's an open window on the screen and you want to print just that window, press Alt+Print Screen (hold down the Alt key then press and release the Prnt Scrn key).

If Paint isn't included on your Accessories menu, you can install it at any time. See "Installing Missing Windows Components" in Chapter 8 for more information.

Nothing will seem to happen at first. Behind the scenes, however, Windows 98 has stored a snapshot of the screen (or window) in an area of the computer's memory known as the Windows Clipboard. To print the snapshot, you need to paste it into a graphics program. You can use Microsoft Paint, if you wish, by following these steps:

▼ Click the Start button and choose Programs ➔ Accessories ➔ Paint.

▼ When the Paint program's window opens up, choose Edit ➔ Paste from its menu bar.

▼ If the screen presents a message asking if you want the bitmap enlarged, just click the Yes button. The snapshot appears inside Paint's window.

▼ To print the snapshot, choose File ➔ Print from Paint's menu bar. Then click the OK button in the Print dialog box. Again, be patient. It might take a while for the printer to actually start printing the snapshot.

▼ If you want to save this snapshot, just choose File ➔ Save from Paint's menu bar, and give the snapshot a file name.

▼ You can exit Paint as you would any other program. Click its Close (X) button, or choose File ➔ Exit from its menu bar, or press Alt+F4.

Summary

As I said at the beginning of this chapter, much of the time you spend at the computer will be spent opening, using, and closing programs. Also, if you use your computer for anything other than games, there's a good chance you'll be creating documents on your computer as well. In this chapter you've learned the basic techniques for opening and closing programs and documents. Let's take a moment to review the important stuff:

- A **program** is something that you *use*, as opposed to something you *create*.
- **Windows 98** is a program, and it comes with additional programs such as Calculator and WordPad that you can open and use to do work.
- Programs that are installed on your computer are in most cases accessible through the **Programs menu** (click the Start button and point to Programs).
- Each program has its own **title bar** that shows the name of the program. In addition, each program has its own **menu bar**, which provides options for using that program.
- Some programs allow you to create **documents**. Think of a document as being anything that you can print on paper, be it a letter, memo, photo, drawing, or whatever.
- When you create a document, it's important to **save** your work so that you can reopen the document again in the future to make changes or corrections.
- To save a document, you generally choose File ➔ Save from the menu bar that's just above the document you're creating.
- To **print** a document, you generally choose File ➔ Print from the menu bar that's just above that document.
- To **close** a document and the program used to create that document, click the program's Close (X) button, or choose File ➔ Exit (if available) from the program's menu bar. If prompted to save your work, remember to choose Yes unless you're certain you don't ever want to access this version of the document again.
- To **reopen** a document, click the Windows 98 Start button, point to

Documents, and then click on the name of the document you want to open.

▼ You can also open a document by first starting the program that you originally used to create that document. Then open the File menu in that program's menu bar and click on the name of the document you want to open.

Icons, Windows, and the Taskbar

3

In Chapter 2 you learned how to run programs using the Start menu. You also learned how to create, save, and reopen a document. So to this point you've been exposed to some icons, windows, and other goodies in Windows 98—but these elements deserve some further attention and explanation. In this chapter, I'll teach you a whole lot more Windows "basic skills" that are sure to come in handy often in your day-to-day work with your PC.

Using Icons

Imagine, if you will, a futuristic desk where everything can be reduced to the size of a pea just by touching it. You can shrink your stapler, in-box, out-box, computer, telephone, sheets of paper—whatever—to some size so small that the item hardly takes up any space at all. When you need the item, you just touch it and it expands to full size so that you can work with it. Keeping such a desk tidy would be easy because anything you're not using at the moment could be made very tiny and very manageable.

The Windows 98 desktop is like that futuristic desk, and all those temporarily tiny things are called **icons**. Each icon represents some object that can be made larger just by clicking it (or double-clicking it). Once the object is enlarged, or "opened," you can use it for as long as you want. When you're done, you click its Close button to shrink it back down to a little icon. Then it's within easy reach but not wasting any space on the screen.

You've already seen many icons. There are icons on the Windows 98 desktop, icons in the Start menus, and there may even be some icons down in your taskbar.

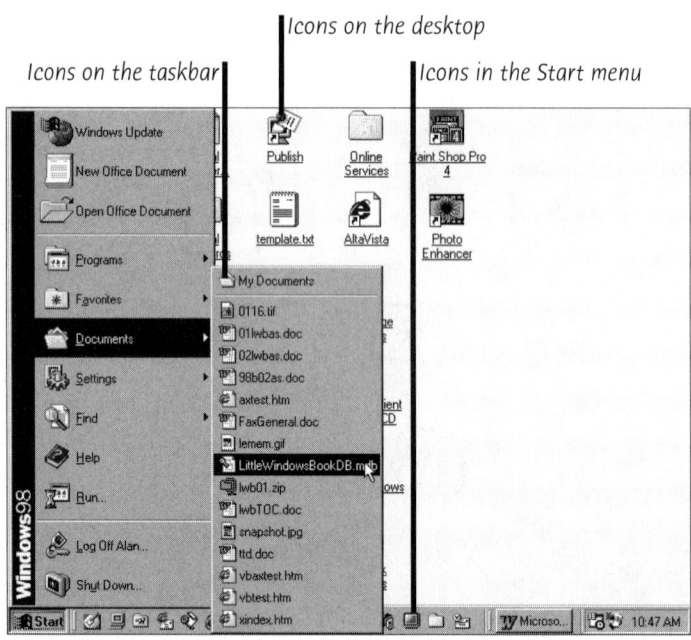

Icons appear in many places, including the desktop, Start menu, and taskbar.

The purpose of an icon is to give you a clue as to what will appear when you open the icon. Some icons represent programs, some represent documents, and still others represent *folders* that contain yet other icons. The following table describes some of the icons similar to those that you'll come across in your day-to-day work with Windows 98.

Icon	Role
	Opening an icon with this symbol displays a group of program icons. You can click the program icons to start programs.
	An icon with a logo or picture usually opens a program.
	Opening this icon on the Start menu displays a list of recently saved documents.
	Icons that resemble a sheet of paper folded over at the upper-right corner usually open into documents.
	When you open a folder icon, you see the contents of that folder (which is likely to be more icons).
	A book and/or question mark icon generally provides help when opened
	A folder or other icon with a little arrow in the lower-left corner is a shortcut to something else. You'll learn about shortcuts in Chapter 9.

You've already learned the basics of opening and closing icons in Chapters 1 and 2. But since it's an important basic skill and something you'll do many times a day, every day, let's just quickly review what that's about.

To open an icon, you usually just have to click it (unless you're using the Classic view rather than Web view, in which case you'll need to double-click desktop icons to open them). And you also know that the clicked icon opens into a window.

Opening and Closing Icons

3: ICONS, WINDOWS, AND THE TASKBAR

Perhaps you didn't notice, however, that whenever you open a window, a little button for that window appears in the taskbar. As you'll learn in this chapter, that little taskbar button can be a handy tool for making a "buried" window jump to the forefront.

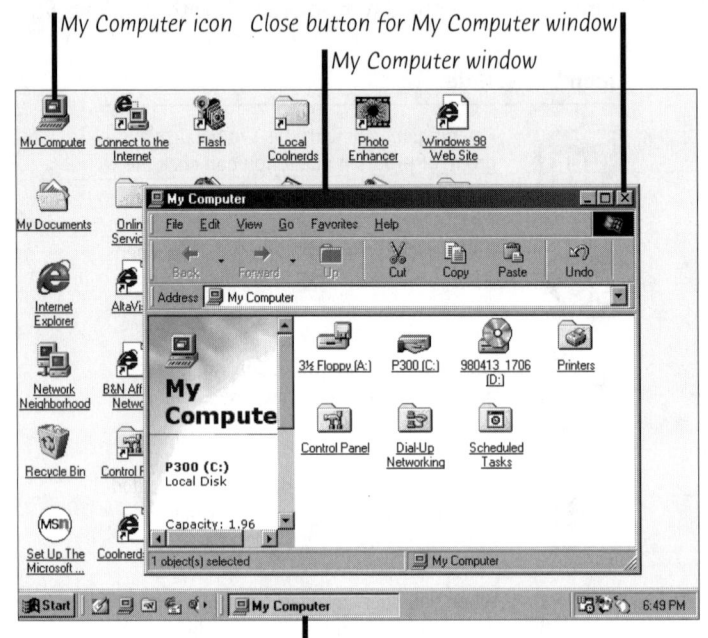

My Computer icon   *Close button for My Computer window*
My Computer window

Taskbar button for My Computer window

There are lots of ways to close a window. None of these is particularly better than the others, so feel free to use whichever technique seems handy at the moment:

- Click the window's Close (X) button, located at the far-right end of the window's title bar.
- **Or,** press Alt+F4 on the keyboard.
- **Or,** if you're working with a program that has a menu bar inside the window, you can choose File -> Exit from that program's menu bar.
- **Or,** right-click the window's taskbar button and choose Close. (There's more on this approach later in this chapter.)

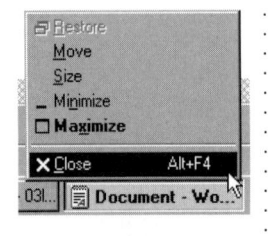

Remember that if you created or changed a document while using a program, when you close it you'll see a dialog box asking if you want to save your work (as explained in Chapter 2). Be sure to choose Yes and save the document unless you're absolutely sure you want to trash the current version of the document.

When a window closes, it no longer consumes any space on the screen. (It's also removed from RAM, making more room there for other programs.) The only way to reopen the window is to repeat whatever steps you used to open it in the first place.

Many icons have labels associated with them, to tell you more about what the icon will display when opened. You've seen these labels under all the desktop icons and many of the other icons you've seen illustrated so far in this book.

Many buttons sport tooltips, too.

Tooltips and Shortcut Menus

Some icons don't have labels. Eventually, you'll learn what those icons do just by experimenting with them and using them in your work. However, many icons offer tooltips, which are similar to labels. But the tooltips only appear after you rest the mouse pointer on the icon for a couple of seconds. For example, the large letter e graphic here is an icon with a tooltip:

This icon's tooltip identifies it as the icon to start Internet Explorer.

Pointing to that icon for a couple of seconds produces the tooltip that says "Launch Internet Explorer Browser." You might want to try resting the mouse pointer on some other icons on your own screen, just to see which ones offer tooltips.

You can do more with icons than just open them, as you'll learn in a moment. Different icons offer different options. But you can always find out just what kinds of options an icon has to offer by *right-clicking* the icon. A little **shortcut menu** will pop up next to the icon.

3: ICONS, WINDOWS, AND THE TASKBAR

To right-click something, you rest the mouse pointer on it and then press and release the secondary mouse button, which is typically the button on the right-hand side of the mouse.

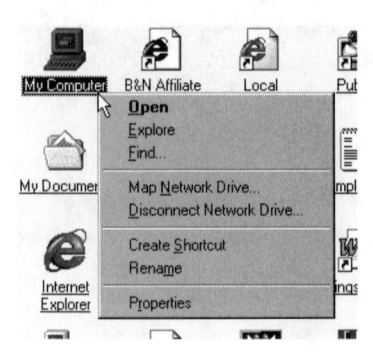

Many icons display a shortcut menu when you right-click them.

You can make a selection from the shortcut menu by moving the mouse pointer to the option you want and then clicking on it. If there's nothing particularly interesting on the shortcut menu and you just want to get rid of it, you can either

- Click somewhere outside the menu
- **Or,** press the Escape (Esc) key on your keyboard.

The shortcut menu disappears, and you're back to where you were before you right-clicked the icon.

It's never absolutely necessary to use either tooltips or shortcut menus. But since both these elements provide additional information and/or options associated with the icon, it's good to know that they're available to you.

Moving Icons

You can move desktop icons around on the screen to put them wherever seems convenient at the moment. To move an icon, just drag it to a new location. It's easy:

▼ Move the mouse pointer until it's resting on the icon you want to move.

▼ Press and *hold down* (rather than click) the primary mouse button.

▼ Without releasing the mouse button, move the mouse until the little "ghost image" of the icon is placed where you want the icon to be.

▼ Release the mouse button.

The icon jumps to where the ghost image was, and you're done. (If it doesn't, chances are your Auto Arrange feature is turned on. Not to worry—I'll show you how to turn that on and off in just a moment.)

52

3: ICONS, WINDOWS, AND THE TASKBAR

If you change your mind while moving an icon, press the Esc key while you're still holding down the mouse button. Then release the mouse button and Esc key.

If your desktop icons get disorganized, you can easily tidy up by following these simple steps:

▼ Right-click in a neutral area of the desktop. (By "neutral area" I mean somewhere *other than* on an icon or the taskbar. Choose some part of the blank space between icons on the desktop.)

▼ When this menu appears, point to **Arrange Icons**. As you can see by the triangle beside Arrange Icons, there's a submenu available.

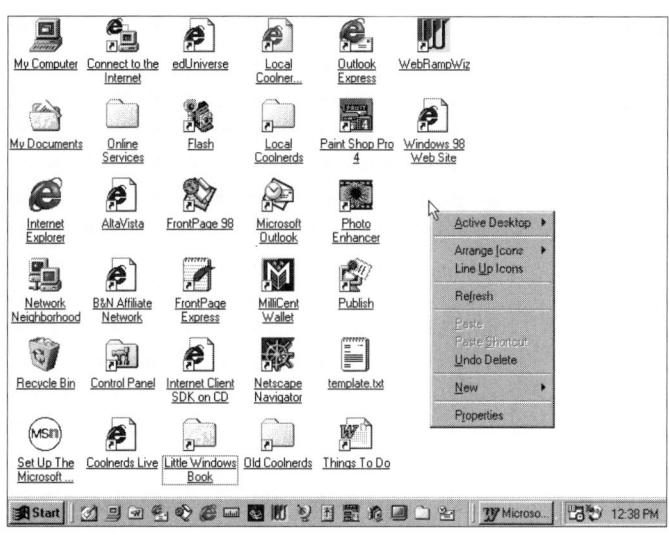

Arranging Desktop Icons

The shortcut menu for the desktop appears when you right-click in a neutral area of the desktop.

▼ In the Arrange Icons submenu, choose (that is, click) By Name or any other option that looks interesting. (But leave Auto Arrange alone for now.)

Now the icons arrange themselves neatly according to your selection, starting at the upper-left corner of the screen. Be aware that some icons, like My Computer, Recycle Bin, and perhaps others (depending on your PC setup) will always be listed first, starting at the upper-left corner. For instance, even if you choose the By Name arrangement to put the icons into alphabetical order by name, those "permanent" icons will always be listed first in their predefined order. The other icons on your desktop will be alphabetized below and to the right of those permanent icons.

53

Using Auto Arrange

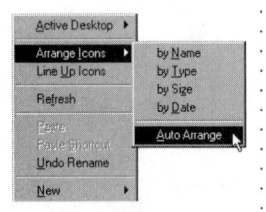

Auto Arrange option

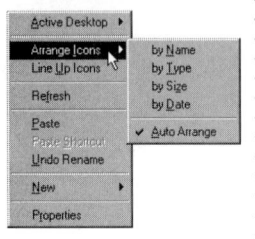

Auto Arrange is already activated on this PC.

Arranging Icons in the Start Menus

Now let's see what that Auto Arrange feature does. If you find that your icons often get messed up, you can turn on **Auto Arrange**. This feature forces any icons you've moved, right back into their original position. It keeps your icons neatly arranged at all times. (However, you can't reposition icons by dragging them when this feature is on.)

Anyway, if you want to turn Auto Arrange on or off, follow these simple steps:

▼ Right-click in a neutral area of the desktop.

▼ Point to Arrange Icons and take a look at the Auto Arrange option that appears on the submenu. Then . . .

If the Auto Arrange option has a check mark on it, then the option is already turned on.

If the Auto Arrange option does not have a check mark next to it, it's turned off.

▼ If you want to keep the current setting, click somewhere *outside* the shortcut menu. If you want to change the Auto Arrange setting from on to off or from off to on, click on the option in the menu.

You cannot rearrange icons on the Start menu, but you can on its submenus. For example, here's an example of my Programs submenu before playing around with its icons. Notice that the program groups and program icons are in no particular order. And, in fact, with my Programs menu arranged this way I'll often have to look through the whole menu to find a particular icon.

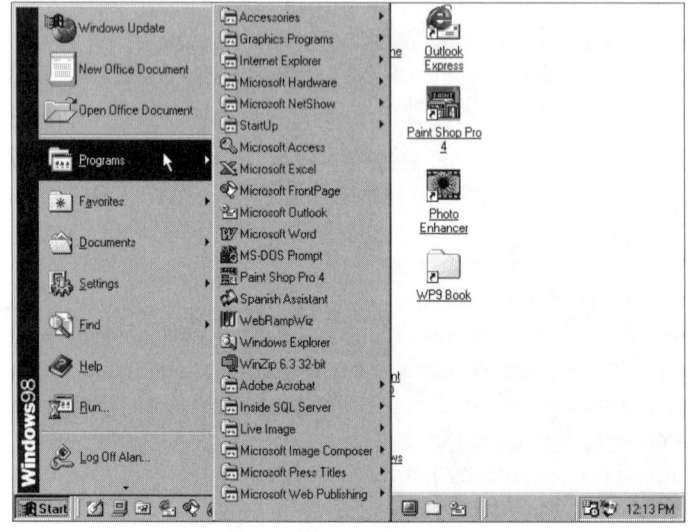

My Programs menu, before I rearranged its icons.

To rearrange the icons in a Start submenu, do the following:

▼ Click the Start button to open the Start menu.

▼ Point to the item whose submenu you want to rearrange (Programs, in this example).

▼ When the submenu opens up, move the mouse over to it. Then . . .

▼ To move an item on the submenu, just drag it up or down. A horizontal black line will follow the mouse pointer. To drop the icon where the black line is, just release the mouse button. The icon will move to its new position.

▼ To delete an item from the menu, right-click the item you want to delete, and choose Delete from the shortcut menu. Choose Yes when you're asked for confirmation.

Here's my Programs menu after dragging some icons to new locations, and deleting a few icons.

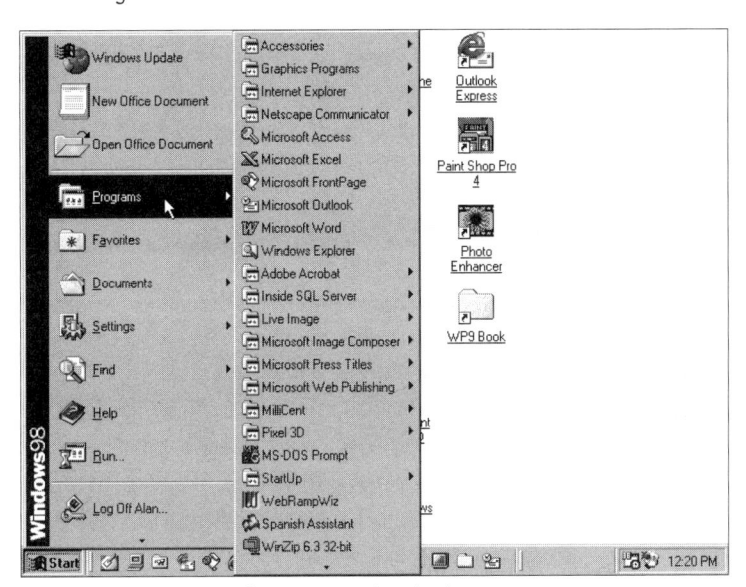

My Programs menu after rearranging its icons.

I suppose it might not look much better to you, but there's a method to the madness. I put the program *groups* that I access most often in alphabetical order at the top of the menu. Beneath those, I put (again, in alphabetical order) the *individual* programs I access most often. Next come the program groups and program icons I use *least* often. So now when I open up my Programs menu, I have some idea of where to look for whatever it is I'm looking for.

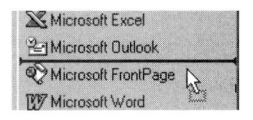

As mentioned in Chapter 2, a "program group" is group of program icons that are all accessible from a single menu item.

3: ICONS, WINDOWS, AND THE TASKBAR

Dragging icons around on the Programs menu, and deleting those icons, is just one way to personalize your Start menus. You'll learn more customization techniques in Chapter 9. For now, it's sufficient to know that you can drag icons around on the Start submenus just as you can drag icons around on the desktop.

> To make a *desktop shortcut* to something on a menu, right-drag any icon from the menu onto the desktop. After you release the mouse button and the shortcut menu appears, choose Create Shortcut(s) Here. For more detailed instructions and examples, see "Creating Desktop Shortcuts" in Chapter 9.

Things That All Windows Do

You've already seen a couple of examples of windows: the window housing the My Computer program, and the one for the WordPad program (back in Chapter 2). If you looked *really* closely at the borders, you probably noticed a whole lot of similarities. In fact, you'll discover that most windows have all, or at least some of the doodads shown here:

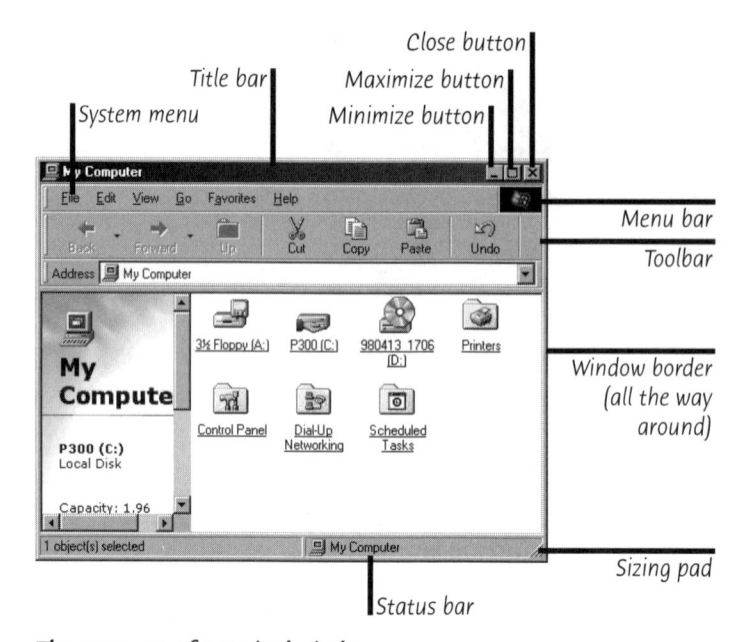

The anatomy of a typical window.

56

In this section, you'll find out the names of the various doodads that make up a window. Also, I want you to be aware that those doodads are actually *controls* that let you control the size, shape, and position of the window. The table below provides a quick overview of what each item is for:

Window Elements

Window Element	Function
Title bar	Shows the name of the program that's inside the window. You can drag the title bar to move a window. Double-click the title bar to maximize the window (expand the window to full-screen size), or to restore it to its previous size after maximizing.
Minimize button	When clicked, reduces the window to a button in the taskbar, without actually closing the window.
Maximize button	When clicked, expands the window to full-screen size. At that point, the Maximize button turns into a Restore button, which you can click to return the window to its previous size.
Close button	Closes the window, leaving only its icon on the desktop.
Menu bar	Presents options that are relevant only to the program inside the window. You can click on any item in the menu to see the entire pull-down menu.
Toolbar	Contains shortcut buttons to the most frequently used menu options, just to save you from having to go through all the menu options to perform that task.
Window border	Drag any side of the border around the window to change the size and shape of the window.
Sizing pad	Drag the sizing pad around on the screen to resize and/or reshape a window.
Status bar	Occasionally provides instructions and other information about the program that's inside the window.
System menu	Lets you move and size the window using your keyboard rather than the mouse. Also has an option to close the window.

Both the Title bar and the Maximize button allow you to expand a window to full-screen size. Neither method is "right" or "wrong"—feel free to use whichever method seems convenient at the moment.

Now let's look more closely at some of these window elements and find out all the things you can do with any open window.

Sizing a Window

When you first open a window, it's usually the same size as when you last left it. But you're not stuck with any particular size. You can, for instance, expand the window to full-screen size to devote all of your screen to that one program, as in the example here on the left. You can also make a program's window smaller so that you can still see some of the Windows 98 desktop in the background, as in the window here on the right.

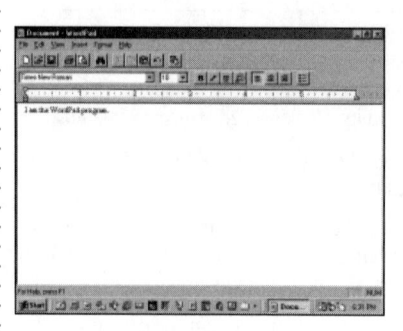

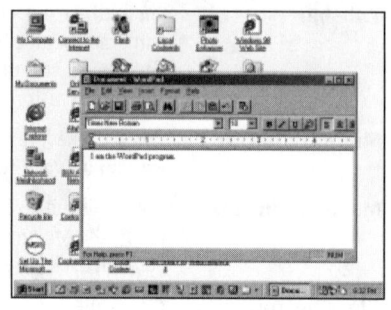

A maximized window at left, and the same window "restored" on the right.

If you want to try the techniques described in the sections that follow, just open any sizable window. Your My Computer window will do, as will the WordPad program described back in Chapter 2. (The tiny Calculator program's window isn't sizable.)

To change the size of any open window:

- To switch between full-screen size and a "windowed" view, as you saw illustrated just above, double-click the window's title bar.

- Another way to expand a window to full-screen size is to click its Maximize button (the one with the large square in it).

- To restore a maximized window to its previous smaller size, click the Restore button. The Restore button replaces the Maximize button after you've maximized the window. It's the button with the short, straight vertical bar.

- To size a window more precisely, drag the sizing pad in the lower-right corner of the window in any direction. (If the window is maximized, you'll need to minimize it to a smaller size in order to get to the sizing pad.)

- Another way to resize a window is by dragging the left or right border horizontally across the screen, or by dragging the window's top or bottom border up or down vertically on the screen. (Again, if the window is maximized, you'll need to minimize it to a smaller size to make the borders accessible.)

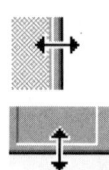

To **drag** something means to rest the mouse pointer on that item, and then hold down the primary mouse button as you move the mouse in the desired direction.

When you place the mouse pointer on a window's border or sizing pad, the pointer changes to a two-headed arrow, as in the examples below. The arrow is a visual cue reminding you that if you drag the mouse pointer in one of the directions indicated by the arrows, the window underneath will expand or shrink in that direction.

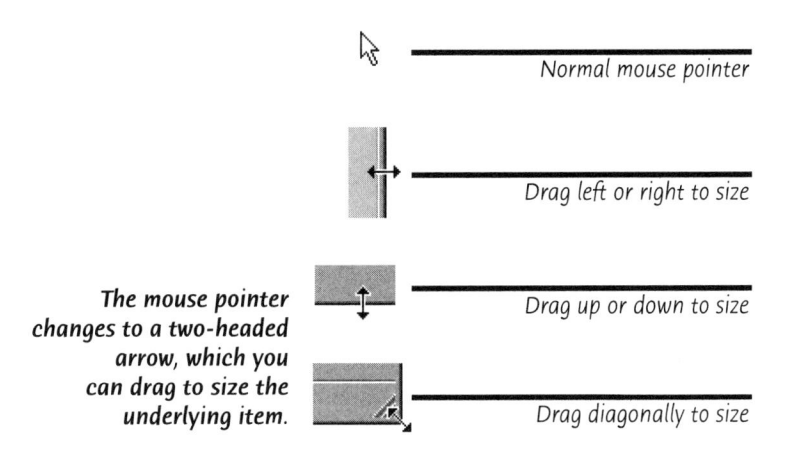

Normal mouse pointer

Drag left or right to size

The mouse pointer changes to a two-headed arrow, which you can drag to size the underlying item.

Drag up or down to size

Drag diagonally to size

Moving a window is even easier than sizing one. Here are the steps:

▼ If the window you want to move is maximized, first shrink it by clicking its Restore button or by double-clicking its title bar.
▼ Rest the mouse pointer on the title bar of the window that you want to move.
▼ Hold down the primary mouse button and drag the window (or the ghost image of the window) to some new location on the screen.
▼ Release the mouse button to drop the window in place.

> **Multiple Monitors**: If you have more than one monitor attached to your PC, you can use these same steps to drag a window to any active monitor on the PC.

When you drop the window in place, it jumps to the mouse pointer position. Anything that was in that place before will now be covered by the window. Which brings us to our next topic . . .

Bringing a Window to the Forefront

Take a minute to visualize a desk with a bunch of papers scattered on top. Chances are, many of the sheets of paper overlap one another. Windows that you open on your Windows 98 desktop are similar to those sheets of paper—the more of them you open, the more likely they are to overlap. Here's my Windows 98 desktop with three windows open: My Computer, Calculator, and WordPad. The My Computer window is "on top of the stack" so to speak, so you can see all of it. The WordPad and Calculator windows are partially covered by the My Computer window.

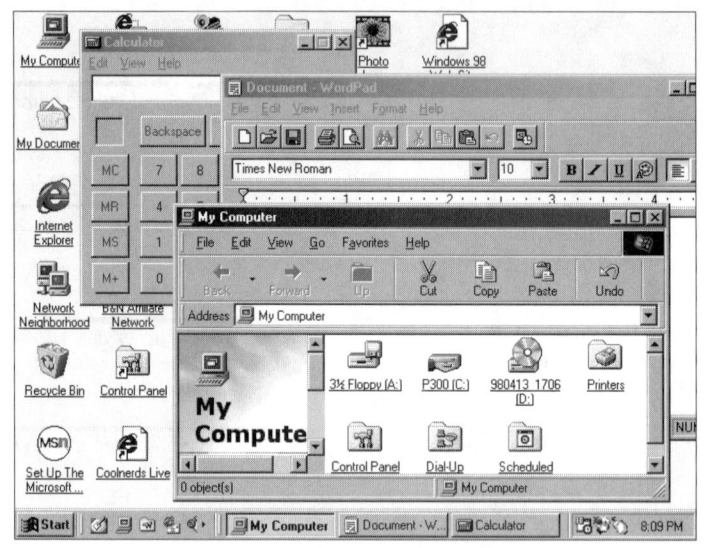

The My Computer window, on the top of the stack, is partially covering the Calculator and WordPad windows.

With the windows arranged like this, suppose I want to do something with the Calculator. How do I get its window to the top of the stack, so I can see the whole thing?

To bring a window to the top when several windows are open:

- Click in any visible part of the window that you want to bring to the top of the stack.
- **Or,** click the window's taskbar button (down in the taskbar).
- **Or,** if your hands happen to be on the keyboard, you can press Alt+Esc repeatedly until the window you want is shuffled to the top.
- You can also press Alt+Tab to get to a particular window among several that are open—but this is a little more intricate.

To use the Alt+Tab method of bringing a window to the forefront, you need to Hold down the Alt key and press the Tab key, and watch the window that appears in the center of the screen. Keep pressing Tab until the the icon of the window that you want is surrounded by the blue frame. Then release all keys. The window instantly jumps to the top of the stack.

For example, here I've brought the Calculator window to the top of the stack. Calculator is now the active window, which conveniently brings us to our next topic.

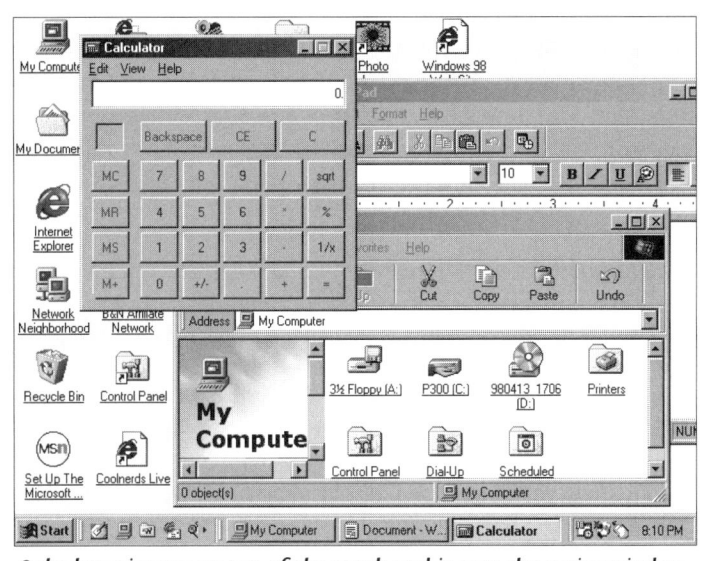

Calculator is now on top of the stack and is now the active window.

When you have two or more windows open on the screen at once, only one of those windows is the **active window**. The active window is the only one that responds to keypresses. So if you were trying to, say, type a letter in WordPad while Calculator or My Computer happened to be the active window, your keystrokes would seem to go nowhere!

How can you tell if a particular window is the active window? There are a couple of major clues right before your eyes:

- The title bar of the active window is colored differently than the other windows.
- The active window itself is on top of the stack (there are no other windows covering it).
- The active window's taskbar button is the only one that looks like it's pushed in.

The Active Window

3: ICONS, WINDOWS, AND THE TASKBAR

Even though the figures in this book aren't in color, you can verify all three of these characteristics of active windows by looking back at the last two illustrations, where My Computer and Calculator are the active windows.

And when you do want to make any open window on your screen the active window, just bring it to the top of the stack, using any of the techniques described in "Bringing a Window to the Forefront" a few paragraphs back.

Hiding and Showing Open Windows

When you maximize a window to full screen, or even if you just have a few smallish windows open, you'll not be able to see the Windows 98 desktop. This is a bummer if you're trying to get to something that's *on* that desktop. Fortunately, clearing the clutter off your Windows 98 virtual desktop is a whole lot easier than clearing the papers off your real desktop.

What we're about to do is roughly the equivalent of taking your forearm and sweeping all that paper into an open desk drawer, then closing the drawer. To sweep your windows away, temporarily, just do either of the following:

- Click the Show Desktop button in the taskbar. (If you don't see a Show Desktop button in your taskbar, don't worry about it. I'll show you how to make it appear when we talk about the Taskbar in just a moment.)

- **Or,** right-click a neutral area of the taskbar (not on a button) and choose Minimize All Windows from the taskbar's shortcut menu. In the image just to the left of this paragraph, the little space to the left of the indicators is a neutral spot on the Windows 98 taskbar.

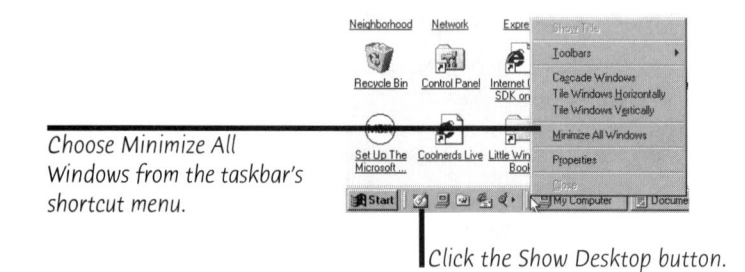

Choose Minimize All Windows from the taskbar's shortcut menu.

Click the Show Desktop button.

Two ways to unclutter your desktop in a hurry.

62

You're back to a nice clean desktop. But you haven't closed any windows. All your open windows are still open—they're just not visible on the screen at the moment. Notice that their taskbar buttons are still visible in the taskbar. To bring the inactive open windows out of hiding . . .

- Click the Show Desktop button in the taskbar again.
- **Or,** right-click a neutral area of the taskbar again (not on a button) and choose Undo Minimize All from the shortcut menu.
- **Or,** if all you want is to see just one or a few of those windows, click the taskbar button of whichever window(s) you want to see.
- **Or,** if you prefer to use the keyboard, hold down the Alt key and press the Tab key until the blue frame surrounds the icon for the window you want to open; then release all keys.

Using the mouse is probably the easiest way to move and size windows on the desktop. But if you do want to move or size a window using the keyboard, you can use the System menu. Follow these steps:

▼ Make sure the window that you want to move or size is the active window.

▼ Press Alt+Spacebar to open the System menu in the upper-left corner of the active window.

▼ Choose an option by typing its underlined letter: Restore, Move, Size, Minimize, Maximize, or Close.

▼ If you are using the Move or Size command, press the arrow keys to resize or reposition the window, and then press Enter.

Note that you can select only enabled options in the System menu (or any other menu, for that matter). Any menu option that is unavailable (disabled) for any reason will look grayed out or faded; that means it cannot be selected. An option is grayed-out when it would make no sense to select the option. For example, if a window is already maximized to full-screen size, the Maximize option on the System menu will be disabled. Why? Because there's no need to maximize a window that's already maximized!

In Chapter 4 we'll talk more about general techniques for using menus and about disabled options.

Moving and Sizing with the Keyboard

Disabled/Enabled Options

3: ICONS, WINDOWS, AND THE TASKBAR

Arranging Open Windows

When your screen becomes cluttered with lots of open windows—and it happens more often than you might think—you might want to try *cascading* or *tiling* them.

If you cascade your windows, they'll be stacked neatly, like a stack of paper. The active window is fully visible, but you can pretty much see only the title bars of the inactive windows. Tiled windows, on the other hand, are sized equally and placed side-by-side like tiles in a tile floor. You can tile horizontally or vertically.

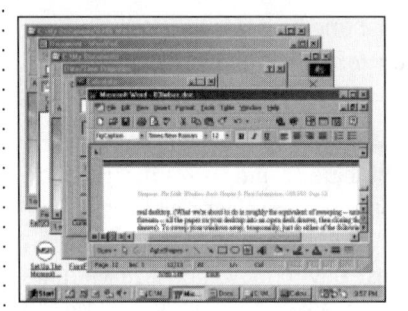

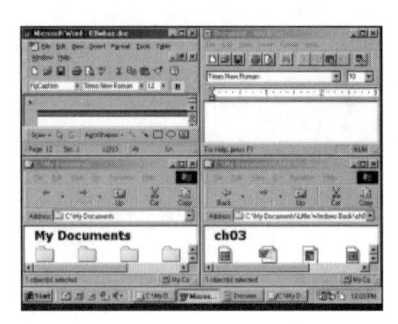

Cascaded windows on the left, tiled windows on the right.

To tile or cascade two or more open windows on your desktop follow these steps:

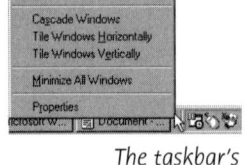

▼ Right-click a neutral area (not on a button) of the taskbar to pop up its shortcut menu.

▼ Choose (click on) Cascade if you want to cascade the windows, or choose one of the two Tile options.

The taskbar's shortcut menu.

Horizontal or Vertical? Whether or not there's any difference between tiling horizontally and tiling vertically depends on how many windows are open. But if you have, say, three windows open when you choose Tile Horizontally, then the windows will be stacked horizontally. Choosing Tile Vertically stacks the windows in a vertical manner.

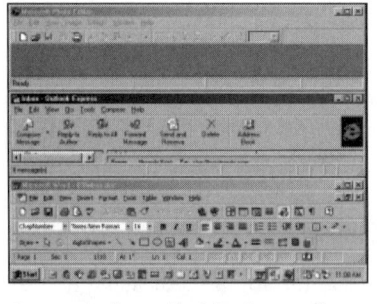

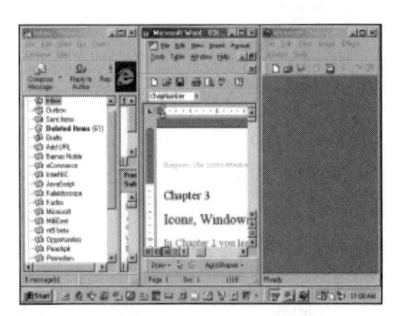

Open windows tiled horizontally on the left, vertically on the right.

64

Well, the taskbar sure has reared its virtual head a few times in this chapter, as well as the previous chapters. I guess it's time we really got down to . . .

You've probably already figured out that the **taskbar** stretched along the bottom of the screen is a really handy tool. As you know, it contains that important Start button. And it also displays a button for every open window on the desktop. When you're hard at work and the screen is cluttered with lots of open windows, the taskbar makes it easy to bring a particular window to the forefront, or to sweep all the open windows off the desktop. And there's more. In this section, you'll learn about all the neat tricks that the taskbar can do.

Using the Taskbar and Toolbars

Normally, the taskbar remains visible no matter how many windows are opened on the screen, because the taskbar's default setting is "always on top," meaning that nothing ever gets on top of it and covers it. However, it is also possible to hide the taskbar, move it, and so forth. For starters, I'd like to show you how to control exactly where and when the taskbar appears.

Setting Taskbar Visibility Settings

To set up the visibility options for the taskbar, you need to adjust some of its settings. Here's how:

- ▼ Right-click a neutral area of the taskbar (not on a button) to bring up its shortcut menu.
- ▼ Choose (click) Properties from that shortcut menu. The Taskbar Properties dialog box appears on the screen.

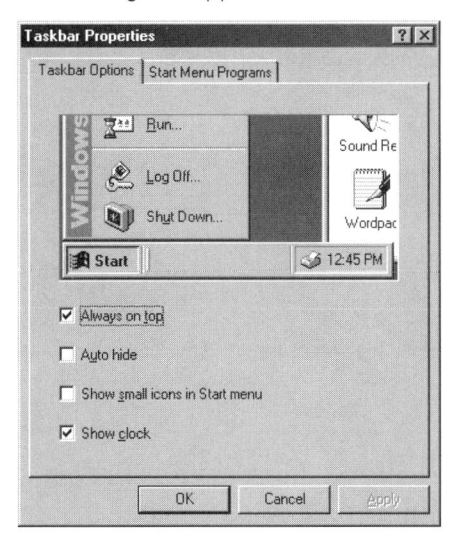

The Taskbar Options tab in the Taskbar Properties dialog box.

Keep the Taskbar Handy
If in doubt about how to set up your taskbar, I suggest matching your settings to the ones shown here. They'll keep the taskbar always visible and within easy reach on your Windows 98 desktop.

▼ Click on the Taskbar Options tab at the top of the dialog box, so that yours looks like the one shown here. Make your selections by clicking on the little checkboxes next to the options presented. To turn an option on, click so that its checkbox is checked. To turn an option off, click until its checkbox is empty. Here are your choices:

Taskbar Options	Description
Always on top	When checked (the recommended choice), this option ensures that the taskbar will never be covered by other open windows. When this setting is turned off, the taskbar can be covered by open windows.
Auto hide	If this option is checked, the taskbar when it's not in use will shrink to a tiny gray bar along the bottom (or some other edge) of the screen. To bring the taskbar out of hiding you must rest the mouse pointer on that thin gray strip. When Auto hide is turned off (the recommended setting), the taskbar is always visible on the desktop and never shrinks to a tiny strip.
Show small icons in Start menu	Even though this option lives in the Taskbar Options list, it actually controls the appearance of the Start menu rather than the taskbar per se. When it's selected (checked), the icons in the Start menu are small, like the icons in submenus. Using this setup is handy only if your Start menu is so crowded that it doesn't even fit properly on the screen, or if you prefer to keep the Start menu small so there's less mouse movement required to go from one option to the next.
Show clock	Turn this one on if you want the current time to appear in the indicator section at the right end of the taskbar.

▼ After making your selection, click the OK button in the Taskbar properties dialog box to activate the settings and close the dialog box.

There's no rule that says the bottom of the screen is where you *have to* display the taskbar. You can attach it to any edge of the screen just by dragging it there. For example, I've dragged the taskbar shown here over to the right edge of the screen. I've also widened it there.

Positioning and Sizing the Taskbar

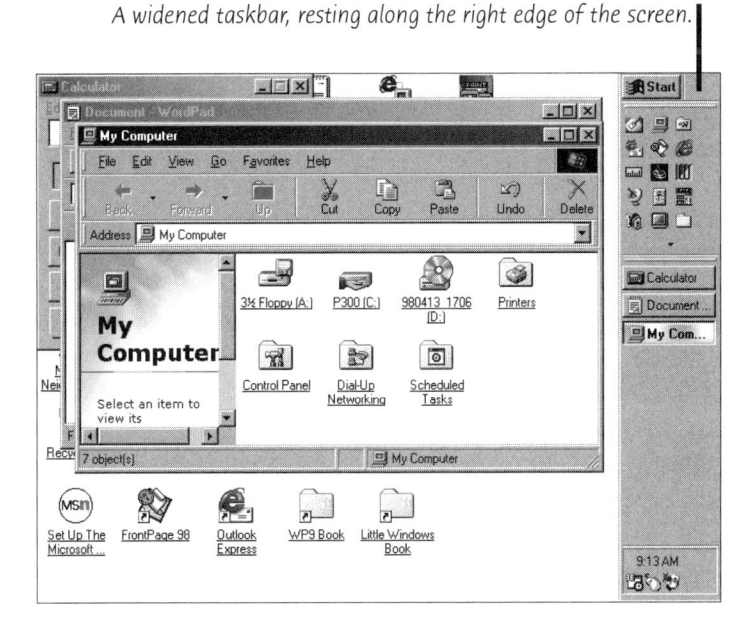

A widened taskbar, resting along the right edge of the screen.

To move and/or resize the taskbar:

▼ Rest the mouse pointer on a neutral area of the taskbar (not on a button or icon).

▼ Hold down the primary mouse button and drag the ghost image of the taskbar to any edge of the screen.

▼ When the ghost image is in the location where you want to put the taskbar, release the mouse button.

▼ To make the taskbar wider or narrower, place the mouse pointer on the edge of the taskbar that is nearest to the center of the screen. When the mouse pointer is positioned correctly, it turns into a two-headed arrow. Drag that edge of the taskbar in either direction indicated by the arrows to widen or narrow the taskbar.

And that's all there is to that.

Taskbar Toolbars

A **toolbar** is a little strip of icons or buttons that provide easy one-click access to frequently used programs and documents. The taskbar is capable of displaying several toolbars. You can follow these steps to decide which toolbars you want the taskbar to display:

▼ Right click a neutral area of the taskbar to bring up its shortcut menu.

▼ Point to Toolbars on the shortcut menu, and notice the list of toolbar names that appear. Toolbars with check marks next to them are already being displayed in the taskbar. The others (the unchecked ones) are not visible in the taskbar.

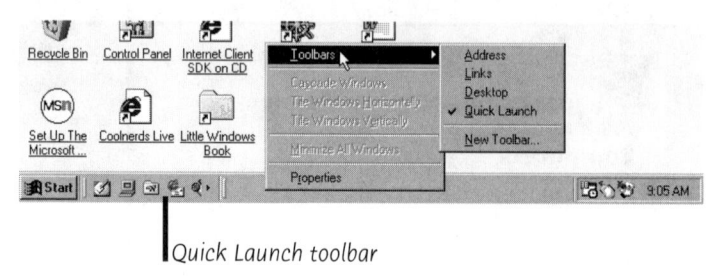

|Quick Launch toolbar

Only the Quick Launch toolbar is checked, so it's the only one visible in the taskbar.

▼ To hide or display a toolbar, simply click its menu option to turn it on or off.

▼ Repeat these steps for each toolbar that you want to hide, or display.

Your options for taskbar toolbars are described in the following table.

Toolbars Available in the Taskbar	Function
Quick Launch	Provides one-click access to frequently used programs.
Desktop	Presents a button for each desktop icon.
Address	Provides a box for entering local paths and Internet addresses (discussed in more detail in Chapter 14).
Links	Provides quick access to popular Web sites on the Internet (discussed in Chapter 14).

The appearance of the toolbars in the taskbar depends on how many of them you have open, and how large a screen area you have to work with. If you open all four toolbars, you may be able to see only the titles of some of them.

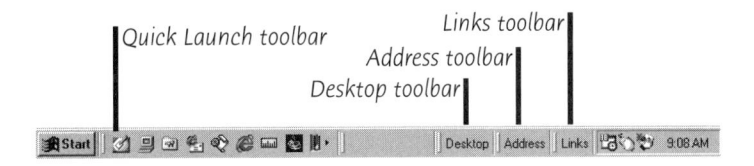

Quick Launch toolbar
Links toolbar
Address toolbar
Desktop toolbar

Notice how each toolbar has a thin, raised vertical line at its left. As we'll discuss next, you can use that little bar to size and move each toolbar independently.

There are a number of things you can do to control the appearance of your open toolbars. Many of these techniques involve using that thin vertical bar at the left edge of each toolbar. When you rest the mouse pointer on that bar, the pointer turns into a two-headed arrow, and you can do any of the following things:

- To expand the toolbar to its maximum size on the taskbar, double-click the thin vertical bar.
- To widen or narrow the toolbar, or move it, drag the thin vertical bar in either direction indicated by the two-headed arrow.
- To move the toolbar off of the taskbar and onto the desktop, just drag the thin vertical bar off of the taskbar and onto the desktop.

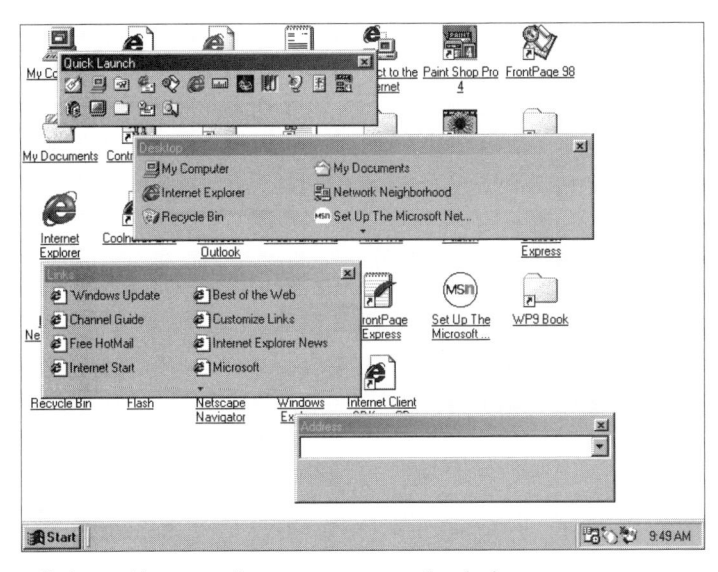

All the taskbar's toolbars are open on the desktop.

Managing Toolbars

3: ICONS, WINDOWS, AND THE TASKBAR

Once the toolbar is on the desktop, you can drag it around by its title bar. You can also size it by dragging any of its borders. If you want to put it back into the taskbar, just drag it by its title bar right back into the taskbar, and drop it there.

Changing the Appearance of Toolbars

The various toolbars all offer their own options. But in general, you can adjust the appearance of a toolbar by right-clicking its thin vertical bar (if it's in the taskbar) or by right-clicking a neutral area in the toolbar. The options presented to you will depend on the toolbar in use and whether it is currently *free-floating* (on the desktop) or inside the taskbar.

When the toolbar's shortcut menu appears, you'll be able to choose some of the options described in the following table:

Toolbar Option	Description
View → Small icons	Icons in the toolbar are small.
View → Large icons	Icons in the toolbar are large.
Show Text	Text labels appear next to icons. (Normally, these labels appear only in tooltips when you rest the mouse pointer on the icon.)
Show Title	Displays the toolbar name to the left of the icons when the toolbar is in the taskbar.
Always on Top	If the toolbar is free-floating, this option ensures that no open windows will ever cover the toolbar.

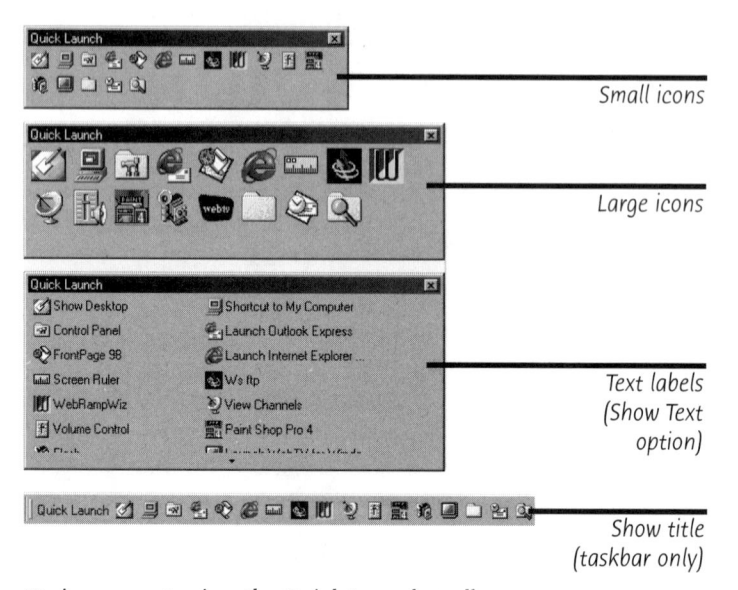

Small icons

Large icons

Text labels (Show Text option)

Show title (taskbar only)

Various ways to view the Quick Launch toolbar.

70

Which Toolbars Do You Need? With so many options to choose from, it may be hard to decide which set of toolbars and which toolbar options are best for you. My own personal preference is to keep only the Quick Launch toolbar on display, using small icons, in the taskbar. In Chapter 9 I'll show you how to customize that toolbar to give yourself quick one-click access to the programs that you, personally, use more often.

Sometimes a window, toolbar, or menu has more stuff in it than can be displayed in the space available on the screen.

When a window contains more than what's visible at the moment, scroll bars appear at its bottom, right, or both borders.

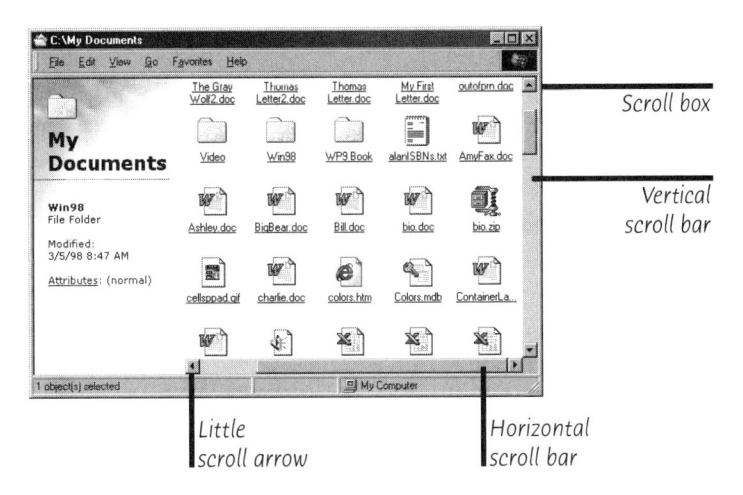

Examples of scroll bars and a scroll arrow.

The size of the scroll box within the overall scroll bar gives you some indication as to how much is *not* being displayed within the window at the moment. For example, if 50% of the window's content is being displayed at the moment, then the scroll box will be half (50%) the size of the entire scroll bar. If the window is only showing about 10% of the entire window's contents, then the scroll box will be about one-tenth the size of the entire scroll bar.

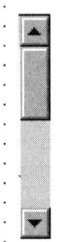

Remember, scroll bars appear automatically whenever they're needed. If a particular window is showing all of its content, then the scroll bars won't appear at all.

There are several ways you can scroll through the contents of a window using its scroll bars:

- To scroll in small increments, click the little arrow buttons at the ends of the scroll bar.
- To scroll gradually, you can drag the scroll box along the scroll bar.
- You can click anywhere on the scroll bar itself to move the scroll box one "screenful" in that direction. Sort of like thumbing through a book—but rather than going page-by-page, you go screen-by-screen.
- If the scroll bar is in the active window, you can also scroll using the arrow keys on your keyboard, and the Page Up (Pg Up) and Page Down (PgDn) keys.
- If your mouse has a wheel on it, and if the active window has a vertical scroll bar at its right edge, you can turn the mouse wheel to scroll up and down.

Scroll Arrows: When a toolbar or menu contains more items than can fit, a tiny triangle appears. The tiny down-pointing triangle at the bottom of the Start menu indicates that there is more stuff under the Log Off Alan option. And in the cutout from the Quick Launch toolbar, the right-pointing triangle at the right end indicates that there are more buttons to the right.

Those tiny arrows allow you to scroll over to see what's missing from the current view of that toolbar or menu. To work these tiny triangular arrows, simply click them to scroll in the direction indicated by the arrow. On some menus, you can just rest the mouse pointer on the little arrow to scroll automatically. Scrolling stops when you move the mouse pointer off the arrow.

Reinforcing What You've Learned

Many of the topics discussed in Chapter 2 and in this chapter are also covered in the Discover Windows 98 tutorial. If you purchased Windows 98 on CD-ROM, you can use it to review some of the skills and concepts covered in these last two chapters. Here's how:

▼ Get back to the Welcome to Windows dialog box, as discussed in "Taking the Guided Tour" back in Chapter 1.

▼ In the Welcome to Windows dialog box, click on the "Discover Windows 98" option, and wait a moment.

▼ In the next screen to appear, click on "Computer Essentials."

▼ In the next screen, click on "3. Exploring the Windows Desktop" and then follow the instructions as they appear on the screen.

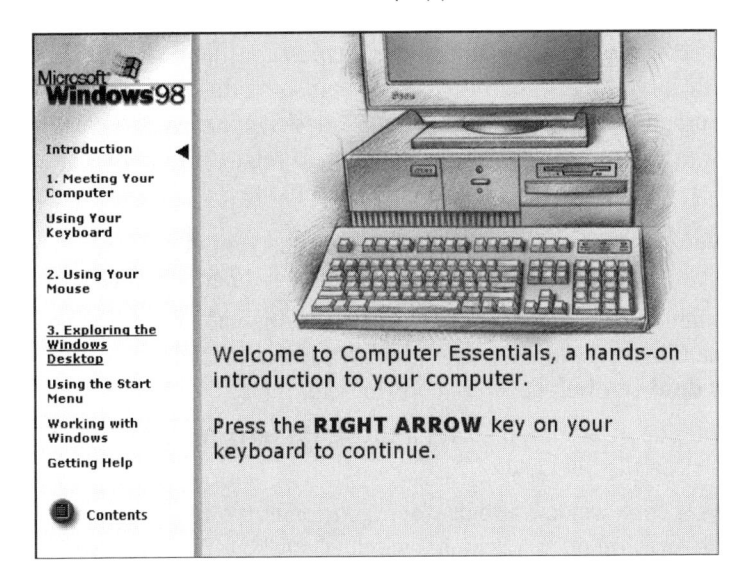

You should be able to just follow the instructions on the screen to take the tutorial lessons. At this point in the book, I recommend you try out the lessons "Exploring the Windows Desktop," "Using the Start Menu," and "Working with Windows." When you've finished, you can click take the quick exit route by pressing Alt+F4 and choosing Yes when asked for confirmation.

Summary

We've covered a lot of ground in this chapter, teaching you more of those critical basic skills—in this case, for managing the general appearance and organization of your Windows 98 desktop. Before we move on to the next chapter, let's take a moment to review the most important topics and techniques described in this chapter:

- ▼ Every **icon** on the desktop, in your menus, and in the taskbar represents some larger object that you can open into a window.

- ▼ In general, you can just **click** an icon to open it. However, if you use the Classic navigation style (discussed back in Chapter 1), you need to **double-click** desktop icons to open them.

- ▼ Every open window displays a **Close (X) button** that you can click to close that window.

- ▼ Every open window also displays a button in the **taskbar**. If multiple windows are open, clicking a window's taskbar button brings that window to the top of the stack, and makes that window the active window.

- ▼ You can move any open window by dragging its **title bar**.

- ▼ You can **size** most open windows by dragging any border or the sizing pad in the lower-right corner of the window.

- ▼ To quickly **tidy up** icons on your desktop, right-click a neutral area of the desktop and choose Arrange Icons → By Name.

- ▼ To adjust taskbar settings, right-click some neutral area of the taskbar and make selections from the **shortcut menu** that appears.

- ▼ To control toolbars, right-click a neutral area of the taskbar, point to the **Toolbars option** on the shortcut menu, and click on the name of the toolbar that you want to view or hide.

- ▼ To control the appearance of a toolbar, right-click the thin vertical bar at the left edge of the toolbar (if it's in the taskbar). Or you can right-click a neutral area of the toolbar (not on an icon or button) and make your selections from the shortcut menu.

- ▼ **Scroll bars** appear along the edges of windows that contain more stuff than is currently visible. You can click in the scroll bar, or drag the little scroll box inside the scroll bar, to move to other parts of the window's content.

▼ When a menu or toolbar contains more icons than can be displayed in the space available, a tiny triangle appears at one or both ends. Click that triangle to scroll through the menu or toolbar.

Dialogs, Menus, and Help

4

Throughout the first three chapters of this book you've been exposed to some of the Windows 98 dialog boxes and menus. In this chapter, I want to teach you the basic skills required to work *all* menus and dialog boxes. Then we'll get into one of the most important basic skills of all—getting instant help.

4: DIALOGS, MENUS, AND HELP

What Is a Dialog Box?

A **dialog box** is something that opens up on your screen, like a window. But rather than displaying an entire program or file, a dialog box generally just presents a limited set of options and/or settings for you to choose from. It's called a dialog box because you sort of carry on a dialog with it. It presents options to you, and you make your choices from those options.

You've already seen a couple of examples of dialog boxes, including the Folder Options dialog box shown back in Chapter 1 and the Taskbar Properties dialog box in Chapter 3. If you were to right-click a neutral area of your Windows desktop (not on an icon) right now and choose Properties from the shortcut menu, you'd come to the Display Properties dialog box.

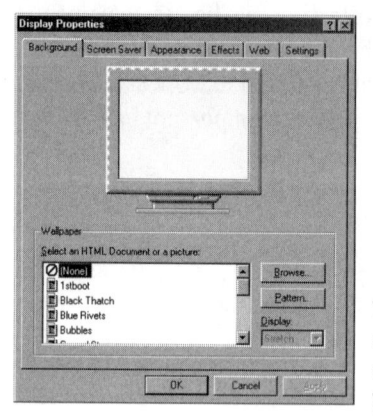

The Display Properties dialog box lets you adjust settings for your screen display.

No two dialog boxes look exactly the same, but most share a common set of controls that you use to make your selections. The controls in dialog boxes are similar to controls on everyday machines like dishwashers, radios, cars, and so forth. But rather than working the dialog box's controls directly with your hands, you use the mouse (or keyboard) to operate them.

How can you tell when a control is selected? Look for a dotted frame surrounding it.

As a rule, it's easiest to work a dialog box using your mouse. You just click whatever option you want. If you prefer to use the keyboard, it's important to keep in mind that you can only operate one control at a time. You can press the Tab key to move forward from one control to the next, and Shift+Tab to move backward. When the little outline surrounds the control you want to work with, then you can use the keyboard to make your selection.

I'll describe other techniques for using the keyboard within a dialog box a little later. For now, in the sections that follow, I'd like to briefly explain how to work all the different kinds of controls you're likely to come across in as you encounter dialog boxes in your day-to-day use of Windows.

Some dialog boxes contain more controls than can actually fit into the box. In that case, the options are split up into two or more **tabs**. For example, the Display Properties dialog box shown just above contains six tabs. They're labeled Background, Screen Saver, Appearance, Effects, Web, and Settings. To select a tab:

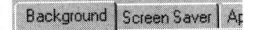

Tabs

▼ Click the tab you want.

That part's simple enough.

Most dialog boxes contain two or more **buttons** that you "push" to make something happen. Buttons you're likely to encounter in nearly every dialog box include the following:

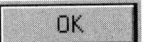

Buttons

- **OK**: Clicking the OK button activates any selection you made in the dialog box and then closes the dialog box.
- **Cancel**: Clicking the Cancel button closes the dialog box *without* activating any settings you made (just in case you change your mind).
- **Apply**: If a dialog box offers an Apply button, you can make your selections and then click the button to apply them, and leave the dialog box open so you can make more selections.

As you may have guessed, to "push" a button you just click it with your mouse.

You can also use the keyboard in lieu of the buttons. The button with the darkest border around it is called the **default button**. In most dialog boxes, it is the OK button. As an alternative to clicking on the default button with the mouse, you can just press the Enter key on the keyboard to activate that button. As an alternative to clicking on the Cancel button, you can just press the Escape (Esc) key to close a dialog box without activating any settings.

Using the Keyboard

4: DIALOGS, MENUS, AND HELP

Closing a dialog box by clicking its Close (X) button is the same as Canceling the box. The dialog box closes without activating any of your current selections.

You can also access buttons from the keyboard. Just hold down the Alt key and press and release the key that's underlined in the button's label. For example, to activate the Pattern button in the Background tab of the Display Properties dialog box, you can press Alt+P instead of clicking that button with your mouse.

Dimmed (Disabled) Controls

In any dialog box, one or more controls may be dimmed or grayed out, because the control isn't relevant at the moment. For example, the Apply button in the Display Properties box shown earlier is disabled, because clicking that button makes no sense until you've actually made some kind of selection that you *can* apply.

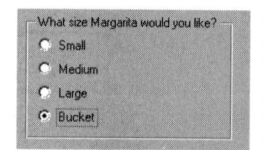

Those disabled controls will not work at all, no matter how many times you click them. However, if the situation changes and the control becomes relevant, then it will immediately become "undimmed" and clickable again. For example, if you were to choose some options in the Display Properties dialog box that can be applied to the screen, then the Apply button will instantly be enabled and you can click it normally to apply your settings.

The Little Help Button

As an added convenience, many dialog boxes have a little **Help button** up in the title bar. The button just has a question mark on it, and shows the tooltip "Help" when you rest the mouse pointer on it.

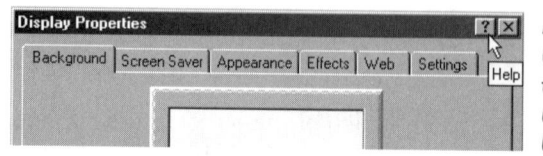

Many dialog boxes have their own little Help (?) button.

That little button is worth its weight in diamonds when you need it. And it's simple to work. Whenever you have a question about some item that appears in a dialog box, just follow these simple steps:

▼ Click the Help (?) button. A question mark is added to the mouse pointer and will move right along with the pointer.

▼ Move the pointer to any control inside the dialog box that you're curious about, and click.

A brief descriptive help message appears.

▼ After reading the message you can just click it, or anywhere outside of it, to return the mouse pointer to normal.

You'll find much more detailed help on most dialog box options through the Windows 98 online help system, which we'll discuss later in this chapter.

When a dialog box presents a set of mutually exclusive options to you—where you can only select one of several options—you'll see a group of **option buttons** (also called **radio buttons**). To choose one of these option buttons, just click the one you want.

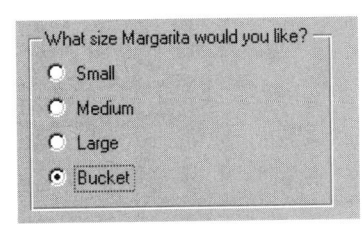

Option (Radio) Buttons

Option buttons are used to display a set of mutually exclusive options.

Checkboxes are sort of like option buttons, but the options they represent aren't mutually exclusive. That is, when you see a set of checkboxes, you can choose none, one, some, or all of those options. Here's an example, in the Effects tab of the Display Properties dialog box:

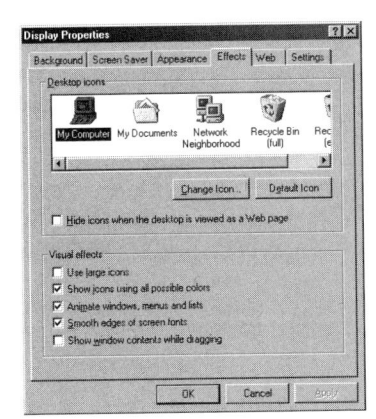

Checkboxes

In this dialog box, the Visual Effects options are displayed as checkboxes.

When a checkbox contains a check mark, we say that option is **selected** or **activated** or **turned on**. When a checkbox is clear (it contains no check mark), the corresponding option is not active. To check a checkbox, or clear it if it's checked, just click it once with your mouse.

Sliders

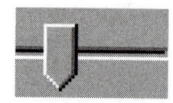

Sliders let you adjust settings by moving a little tab along a slide bar. For example, the Screen Area control in the Settings tab of the Display Properties dialog box is a slider control.

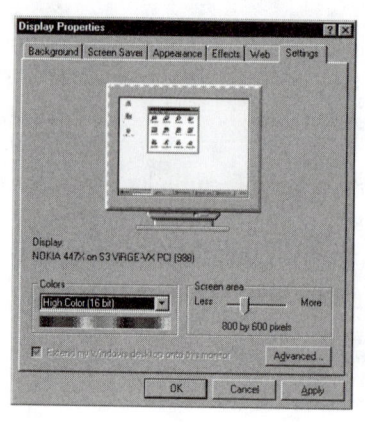

The Screen Area control is a slider.

To work a slider control, rest the mouse pointer on the little sliding tab and drag it left or right (or up and down, if you happen to be working with a vertical slider control).

Drop-Down Lists

A **drop-down list** (also called a **combo box**) is a control that initially appears as a single text box, with a little down-pointing arrow button. Clicking that little button opens the drop-down list so you can see all of its contents.

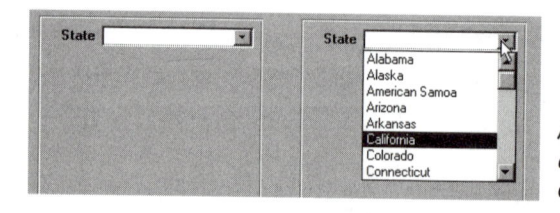

A drop-down list closed (left) and opened (right)

The simplest way to work a drop-down list control is simply to click the little arrow button to see the list of available options. If the list is long, the opened drop-down list may have a little scroll bar on it, like the right-hand example shown just above. You can scroll up and down through the list using the scroll bar, or by pressing the up- and down-arrow keys on your keyboard. When you see the option you want, click it. That text then fills the box, and the list disappears. If you change your mind about the option you selected, just open the list again and make another choice.

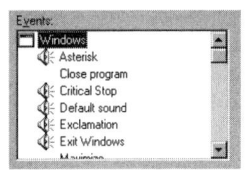

In a **list**, or **list box**, of options, you can choose an option by simply clicking on it. If the list has a scroll bar next to it, you can use that scroll bar to view options that aren't visible because they're farther up or down in the list.

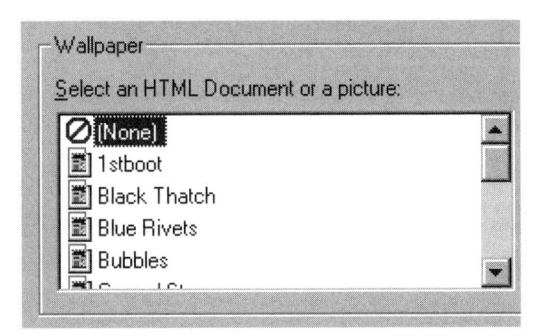

List Boxes

List box controls.

Multiple Choice List Boxes: Some list boxes allow you to choose more than one item. You can use the Ctrl+Click and Shift+Click to select multiple items from such a list; these techniques are described under "Selecting Files and Folders to Manage" in Chapter 7.

If your mouse has a wheel, you may be able to use it to scroll up and down through a list. In addition, you can use the up- and down-arrow keys on the keyboard to scroll. To jump directly to the bottom of a list, press Ctrl+down arrow. To jump back up to the top of the list, press Ctrl+up arrow.

Text boxes let you type in text or numbers. Some text boxes are small and only "expect" a single line of text. Here, the Name and Wait fields are both single-line text boxes:

Text Boxes

Text box controls

Other text boxes, like the Address field shown here, can hold several lines of text. Some text boxes, particularly those that expect you to type in a date or a number, have little **spin buttons** next to them. The Wait field shown on the preceding page has these spin buttons.

To type text into a text box, you must first move the blinking cursor into the text box. Otherwise, whatever you type will end up in some other text box, or perhaps nowhere. There are two simple ways to get the blinking cursor into a text box:

- Click anywhere inside the text box.
- **Or**, press Tab or Shift+Tab repeatedly until the cursor lands in the text box.

Once the cursor is on a text box, you can just type your entry using the standard typewriter keys. Use the Backspace and Delete keys on the keyboard to make corrections, as necessary, while you type. If you need to change some text that's already in the text box, and you want to move the cursor to a specific character, you can use the arrow keys to move the cursor.

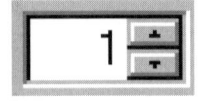

What About Those Spin Buttons? The spin buttons are available in text boxes that accept numerical entries. By clicking the buttons, you can quickly increase or decrease the number entered in the accompanying text box. Clicking the button on top, with the up-pointing triangle, increases the number; and clicking on the down-pointing triangle decreases the number.

There are actually a lot of ways to edit (change) text on computers. Text boxes support all those techniques. So let's take a moment now to discuss all the different ways you can work with text on your computer screen.

Changing Text

The first thing you need to realize about working with text on a screen is that the spot where you put the mouse pointer has nothing to do with the spot where the typed text will appear. It's the **cursor**, not the mouse pointer, that shows you where the next character you type will appear.

In general, you can move the cursor to any chunk of text just by clicking the spot where you want to type. Let me say that another way: If you just *point* to where you want to type, that won't work. But if you **point and click** that spot, then the blinking cursor will jump to that spot, and anything you type will wind up where the cursor is.

Here are some simple editing techniques you can use to change text in a text box (or in a word-processing document, or any other place where you're allowed to type text):

- To delete the character to the right of the cursor, press the **Delete (Del) key**.
- To delete the character to the left of the cursor, press the **Backspace key**.
- To insert new text, just start typing (*after* you've positioned the cursor in the right spot!).
- To choose between insert and overwrite modes, press the **Insert (Ins) key**.

Let me take a moment to show you the difference between *insert* and *overwrite* modes when it comes to typing with a computer. Let's say you've already typed something into a text box, like the name "Roscoe Hooligan." Then let's say you click between the two names to position the blinking cursor there, as demonstrated by the vertical bar (|) character in this text:

Roscoe| Hooligan

If you were to press the Spacebar (to type a blank space) and type the name **Mindy** and you were in insert mode, the new text would be *inserted into* the existing text, starting at the current cursor position. So in this case the result would be

Roscoe Mindy Hooligan

Now, had you typed the blank space and the name **Mindy** while in overwrite mode, the new text would *replace* the text that was already there. So the result would be

Roscoe Mindygan

The **default** (most common) setting for typing on a computer is insert mode. It's a good idea, though, to try to keep your eyes on the screen as much as possible when typing changes and corrections, so you'll know right off the bat if your new text is being added to existing text or if that new text is replacing existing text. As I said earlier, the usual method for switching from one mode to the other is to press the Insert (Ins) toggle key on your keyboard.

Insert vs. Overwrite

Selecting Text If you need to delete or change a big chunk of text, you can save a lot of work by first **selecting** the text you want to delete or replace. The selected text will be highlighted, typically as white letters against a blue background.

Here are your options for selecting text:

- Drag the mouse pointer through the text you want to select.
- **Or,** position the blinking cursor at the start or end of the text you want to select. Then hold down the Shift key and press the arrow keys to extend the selection.
- In some cases, you can select all the text in a text box just by clicking on the label that's next to the text box.
- You can select a single word by double-clicking that word.

Once you've selected a chunk of text, you can

- Press Delete (Del) to delete the selected text.
- **Or,** just start typing new text. As soon as you start typing, the selected text disappears and is replaced by whatever you type.

A very handy way to change what you type

Don't miss the importance of this last little technique—it can save you a whole lot of keystrokes. To illustrate, I'll use the Address text bar of a **Web browser,** which is a program used to explore the Internet. (You'll learn all about Web stuff in Chapter 14. For now, I just want to use the Address text box as an example of editing text inside a text box.) Let's say the text in the Address text bar currently reads http://www.microsoft.com/, which happens to be the URL (address) of Microsoft's site on the World Wide Web. It looks like this:

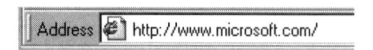

[Address http://www.microsoft.com/]

Let's say you want to cruise over to my Web site, which is at http://www.coolnerds.com.

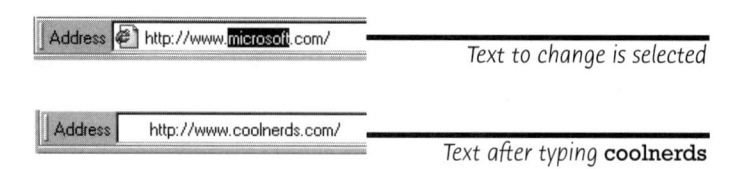

[Address http://www.**microsoft**.com/] — Text to change is selected

[Address http://www.coolnerds.com/] — Text after typing **coolnerds**

Selecting and replacing a chunk of text.

One way to change the Web address would have been to completely delete the existing address and type in the new one. But, since both addresses start with **http://www**. and end with **.com**, it's way easier just to change the one part of the address that's different.

To do that, you drag the mouse pointer just through the **microsoft** portion of the current URL, as shown just above. Then just type **coolnerds**. The newly typed text instantly replaces the selected text, and you're done. That's quite a bit easier than retyping the entire address (and taking a chance on making mistakes) or using the Backspace and Delete keys to delete characters and retype them.

Dialog boxes are designed to be easily worked with the mouse. But if your hands happen to be on the keyboard, you can get by with the keyboard. The main thing to remember when using the keyboard is that you must first choose the control you want to work with, by pressing the Tab and Shift+Tab keys until the dotted frame is around the control you want to change.

Using the Keyboard in Dialog Boxes

To do this in a dialog box...	Press these keys:
Move from one option to the next.	Tab (to go forward) and Shift+Tab (to go backward)
Move through the tabbed "pages" of the dialog box.	Ctrl+Tab, Ctrl+Shift+Tab
"Click" the corresponding command.	Alt+underlined letter
Activate the current button or option (that is, to "click" a button, check/clear a checkbox, or choose an option button).	Spacebar
"Push" the selected (dark-framed) button.	Enter
"Push" the Cancel button.	Escape (Esc)
Open a drop-down list (if it's the current control).	Alt+Down Arrow
Move the cursor through text or a list.	Arrow keys
Move the cursor to the start of a line in a text box, or to the first item in a list.	Home
Move the cursor to the end of a line in a text box, or the last item in a list	F4
Scroll through a list	Up and Down arrow keys, Page Up (PgUp) and Page Down (PgDn)

Remember, the keyboard is entirely optional in most cases. The only time you really need to use the keyboard is when you need to type text or a number into a textbox.

4: DIALOGS, MENUS, AND HELP

Using Menus

You've already seen examples of some menus. There's the **Start menu** that pops up when you click the Windows 98 Start button. And individual programs that you typically run often have their own **menu bar** and **pull-down menus**. Here are some examples of menus:

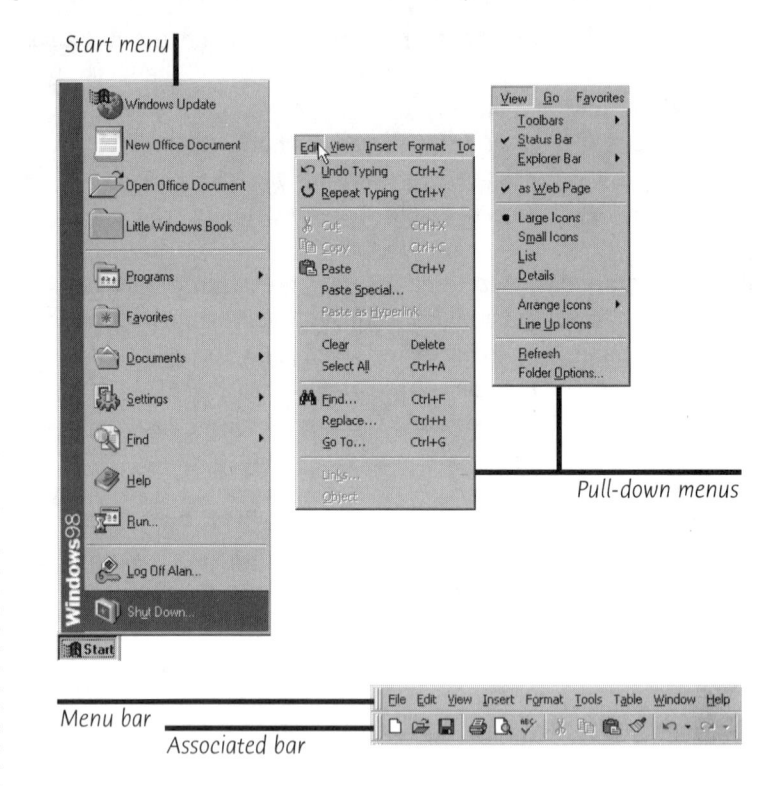

Start menu

Pull-down menus

Menu bar
Associated bar

One of these examples is a menu bar with an **associated toolbar**. Many programs offer such toolbars as alternatives to going through the menus to get to an option.

Using Menus and Toolbars

You already know the basic techniques for selecting options from menus. To review:

- To open a pull-down menu from the menu bar, just click that item in the menu bar. **Or,** hold down the Alt key and press the underlined letter—for example, pressing Alt+F opens the File menu, if one is available in the current window.

- To choose an option from an open pull-down menu, just click the option you want. **Or,** press the underlined letter for that option (there's no need to hold down the Alt key once the menu is open).

- Once a pull-down menu is open, you can use the up, down, left, and right arrow keys to move from option to option. The options will be highlighted as you navigate among them. To select the currently highlighted option, press the Enter key. To close a menu without making any selections, click somewhere outside the menu, or press the Escape (Esc) key.

Some frequently used menu options have **toolbar button equivalents**. The symbol on the toolbar will match the symbol to the left of the option on the pull-down menu. For example, the Undo Typing option on the Edit menu is represented by a curved arrow. That same icon is used to identify the Undo button on the toolbar, as at left. The toolbar button performs exactly the same task as the menu option—it "undoes" your most recent action. The toolbar just provides quicker, one-click access to that same menu option.

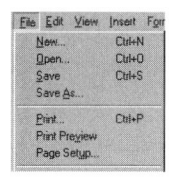

Toolbar Button Equivalents

Some menu options have **shortcut key equivalents**. For example, the shortcut for the Save option on the File menu is Ctrl+S. As a quick alternative to opening the menus, you can just press Ctrl+S at the keyboard to save a document.

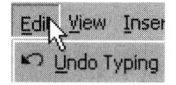

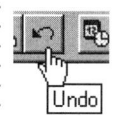

Menu Keyboard Shortcuts

Some menu options are **toggles**, which means they can either be "on" or "off." If such an option is on, it has a check mark next to it, like the Status Bar option in the View menu. Choosing one of these toggle options, either by clicking or using the keyboard, always changes it to the opposite setting (from on to off, or from off to on).

Menu Symbols

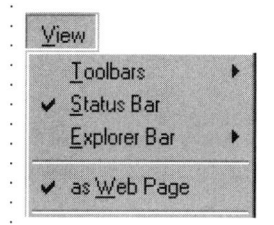

You already know that the little right-pointing triangle at the right side of a menu option indicates that a submenu with more stuff will appear if you select that option. (You've seen these submenus open up from the Start menu.) Typically, you just have to point to (not click) such an option to view its submenu. As in dialog boxes, menu options that are dimmed or grayed out are not relevant at the moment and therefore cannot be selected.

> **Practice Makes Perfect**: Most people feel a little klutzy at first while they're getting the hang of working menus and dialog boxes. However, with a little practice it will all become second nature to you. The mouse is always the easiest way to make selections in dialog boxes and menus, because all you have to do is point-and-click. Whether or not you ever use the keyboard for such actions is entirely a matter of personal preference.

4: DIALOGS, MENUS, AND HELP

Getting Instant Help

If there's anything a beginner needs, it's lots of help. Fortunately, in Windows 98 there's always plenty of help just a few mouse clicks away. Follow these simple steps:

▼ Click the Windows 98 Start button.

▼ In the Start menu, click Help to get to the Help window.

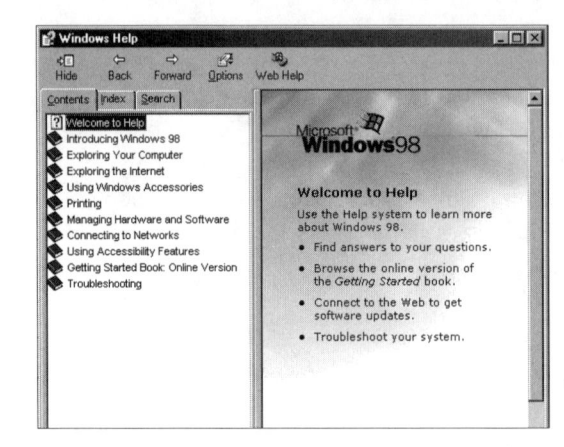

The Windows 98 Help window.

Notice that the title bar for the help window reads "Windows Help." It's important to understand that the help available to you from the Windows 98 Start button is for the Windows 98 program only. Other programs that you use will probably offer their own help, usually available from the Help option of that specific program's menu bar. For example, here's the Help pull-down menu for the WordPad program:

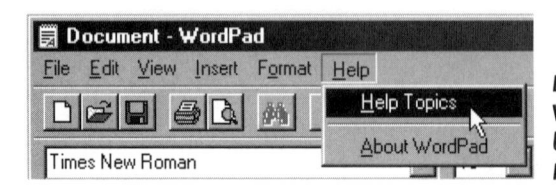

Like most programs, WordPad's menu bar includes a Help option.

Clicking the Help Topics option on that menu will open up a windows similar to the Windows Help window, except that the title bar would read "WordPad Help." The information it offers is relevant only to the WordPad program.

Once you have opened the Help window for Windows 98 or any other Windows program, you can use the techniques described in the sections that follow to look for the information you need.

90

Finding Information Using Tabs

If you look at the top of the left pane in the Windows Help window, you'll notice three tabs, named Contents, Index, and Search. The first two tabs are similar to the table of contents at the front of a book and the index at the back of a book.

The Contents Tab

The **Contents tab** usually displays a list of little book icons, each representing some major topic of information. To open a book, just click it. Then you'll see icons for individual pages, more books, or both.

For example, opening the Introducing Windows 98 book in the Windows help screen will reveal more books, including one titled How to Use Help. Opening that book will reveal several individual help topics, including Find a Topic, Get More Out of Help, and so forth.

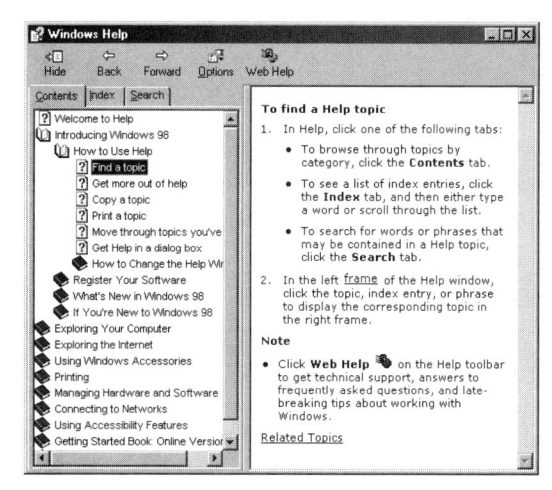

The Introducing Windows 98 book contains a How To Use Help book, which offers more specific topics.

As you can see, when you click a Help topic (the items with a little page-and-question-mark icon), the text of the topic appears in the right-hand pane of the Help window.

The Index Tab

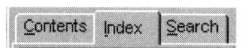

The Index tab in a Help window gives you access to the Help's index which, as I mentioned, is like the index at the back of a book. You can use the scroll bar at the right side of the index to scroll up and down through topics. Or, you can start typing the word or phrase you're looking for. If that topic is included in the index, you'll automatically move to that part of the index. For example, let's say you're looking up the word *save* or *saving*. Type **sav,** and by the time you press the V key you'll instantly be taken to that section of the index.

4: DIALOGS, MENUS, AND HELP

When (and if) you find the index entry you're looking for, to get your Help text you need to click that entry and then click the Display button down at the bottom of the list. Optionally, you can just double-click the topic you want. Or, you can use the arrow keys to move the highlight to the option you want and press Enter to select that topic.

The "sav" section of the Help window's index.

The Help text, as always, appears in the right-hand pane of the window. In a few cases, you may come to a separate dialog box, named Topics Found (illustrated here), that lists several related topics. But the same basic rule applies. You just click any topic and then the Display button, or double-click the topic, to see the corresponding Help page.

The Search Tab

The **Search tab** offers yet a third technique for accessing Help. Rather than offering you a precise Table of Contents or Index, the Search tab lets you search for any word or phrase. After clicking on that tab, just type in a word or phrase and click the List Topics button. All topics that contain that word or phrase will be listed in the Topic list. To read a topic, click the topic and then the Display button; or double-click the topic. The right-hand pane will show the requested Help page, and the specific word or phrase you searched for will be highlighted.

The first time you use Search, you may have to wait a moment while Windows builds a list of all the occurrences of your search words in the Help pages. But it only takes a few seconds to do that.

For example, let's say I type "Time Zone" as the topic to search for. When I click the List Topics button, only one topic appears: "To change your computer's time zone." When I double-click that topic, I see the corresponding Help page on the right. Notice how the phrase "Time Zone" is highlighted throughout the page.

92

Using the Search tab is a more flexible technique that is helpful when you're not quite sure what you're looking for.

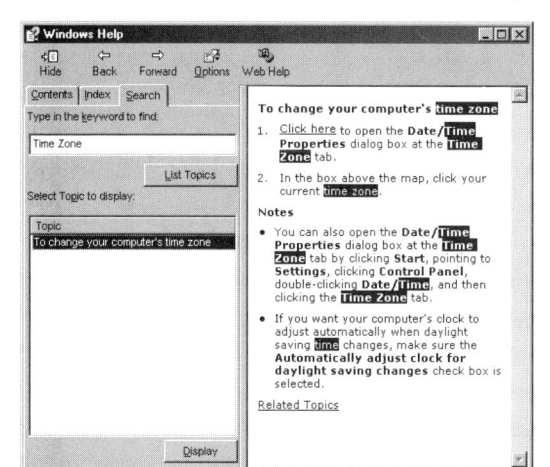

Results of searching the Help pages for "Time Zone."

The **Help windows** have some of their own unique navigation capabilities. The toolbar near the top of the dialog box contains the following options:

- **Hide/Show**: Hides the left pane of the Help window. When the left pane is hidden, the Hide button changes to Show, which you can click to bring the left pane back out of hiding.

- **Back**: After you've scrolled through several pages of Help, the Back button takes you back to previous pages.

- **Forward**: After you've scrolled back through several pages, the Forward button takes you back to the pages you backed out of.

- **Options**: Clicking this button presents numerous options for controlling the appearance of, navigating through, and printing Help screens. (Feel free to open the menu and experiment on your own.)

- **Web Help**: If you have access to the Internet, the Web Help button takes you to Microsoft's Technical Support Web site, where you can ' search for more information, recent updates, and other information.

Like any other window, you can move the Help window by dragging its title bar. You can also resize it by dragging any border or by clicking the Minimize, Maximize, and Restore buttons in the upper-right corner.

Navigating the Help Window

4: DIALOGS, MENUS, AND HELP

Closing a Help window is no different from closing any other window. Just click the Close (X) button in the upper-right corner of the Help window that you want to close.

Uncovering Help

Because Help is displayed in a window, there's always a chance that some other window on the desktop will cover all or some of the Help window. You can bring the Help window to the forefront at any time using any of the usual techniques:

- Click any visible part of the Help window.
- **Or,** click the Help window's button in the taskbar.
- **Or,** press Alt+Esc repeatedly until the Help window is on top.

Other Ways to Get Help

There are several other methods of getting help with whatever you're working on in Windows 98. You've probably already noticed the Help option on the Windows 98 Start menu. In addition, most programs' menu bars contain a Help choice. Here are a few other kinds of help available to you as well:

- The Help key (F1) is a fairly universal tool, but it works only for the active window. For example, if you're using the WordPad program and you press the F1 key, you'll get to the Help window for that program.

- Any underlined word or phrase in a Help screen can be clicked to get more information. In some cases, you'll be taken elsewhere, to another window. In other cases, you'll just see the definition of that term pop up on the screen.

- Earlier in this chapter I told you about the question mark (?) button that appears in the upper-right corner of most dialog boxes. You can click that button and then click any option in the dialog box to see a brief description of that option. In addition, the dialog box may contain a specific Help button that you can click to get to the program's complete online Help.

Help is readily available from within many dialog boxes.

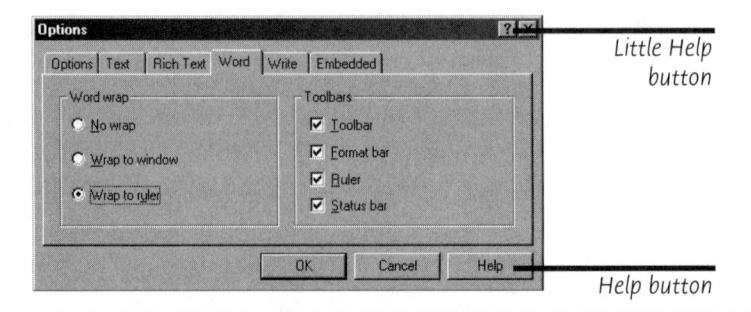

Little Help button

Help button

94

Finally, don't forget those **tooltips** I mentioned back in Chapter 3. When you see some mysterious button or icon, often you can identify it just by resting the mouse pointer on it for a couple of seconds. If there's a tooltip, it will display the name or description of that item.

> Shortcut menus can act sort of like help, because they give you an idea of what you can do with a particular item. You know what to do: Just right-click the item to see if it has an associated shortcut menu.

Summary

If you've been reading directly through this book since Chapter 1, without skipping over too much material, you now actually have *all* the basic skills required to use Windows, and virtually all your Windows programs! In Part II of this book, coming up next, you'll have a chance to put those skills to work in getting Windows and your PC to do the things you want it to do. Before we move on, though, let's review the most important skills and concepts covered in this chapter:

- ▼ A **dialog box** is similar to a window, but generally offers a more specific set of options.

- ▼ Most dialog boxes offer some combination of **common controls**, such as text boxes, drop-down lists, checkboxes, option buttons, and so forth. You can just click any control to make a selection.

- ▼ The **OK button** near the bottom of a dialog box activates any selections you've made and then closes the dialog box.

- ▼ The **Cancel button** closes the dialog box without applying any selections you might have made.

- ▼ To get to **options** in menus, just click whatever option you want.

- ▼ To get help with Windows 98, click the Windows 98 Start button and choose Help from the Start menu.

- ▼ To get help in a particular program other than Windows 98, choose Help (if available) from that program's menu bar.

Part Two
Have It Your Way

Personalizing Your PC 5

It's time to start putting all your new skills to work, starting with an exploration of all the different ways you can personalize Windows and your PC to your own needs and tastes. In this chapter you'll learn how to set your PC's clock, how to customize your screen, mouse, and keyboard to your liking, and more. We'll start by getting acquainted with the Control Panel, which is sort of like "Dialog Box Central" for personalizing your PC.

The Control Panel

You're about to meet the Control Panel, where all the settings for personalizing Windows 98 are conveniently grouped together. To get to the Control Panel, follow these simple steps:

▼ Click the Windows 98 Start button.

▼ Point to Settings on the Start menu.

▼ Choose (click) Control Panel. The Control Panel window opens up.

You can also open Control Panel by clicking the My Computer icon, then opening the Control Panel icon inside that window.

Your Control Panel may not have the exact same set of icons as the ones shown here. However, you probably have the most important ones, which include Date/Time, Display, Keyboard, and Mouse.

Most icons in the Control Panel open up into dialog boxes that contain the options you need for personalizing the appearance and behavior of Windows. Now that you know how to work dialog boxes, it should be pretty easy (and fun, in fact) to adjust things the way you want them. Let's start with the simplest dialog box of all, the Date/Time Settings.

Setting Date/Time

Your PC has a built-in clock that keeps track of the date and time. It does so even while the computer is turned off, thanks to a tiny battery that keeps the clock running. Like any clock, though, the one inside your PC needs to be set once in a while to be accurate.

To adjust the date and time in your PC:

▼ Open the Control Panel (click the Start button and choose Settings → Control Panel).

▼ Open the Date/Time icon to reveal the Date/Time Properties dialog box. If you don't see the clock and calendar shown here, just click the Date & Time tab.

You can also get to the Date/Time Properties dialog box by double-clicking the time indicator (if any) at the far right side of the taskbar.

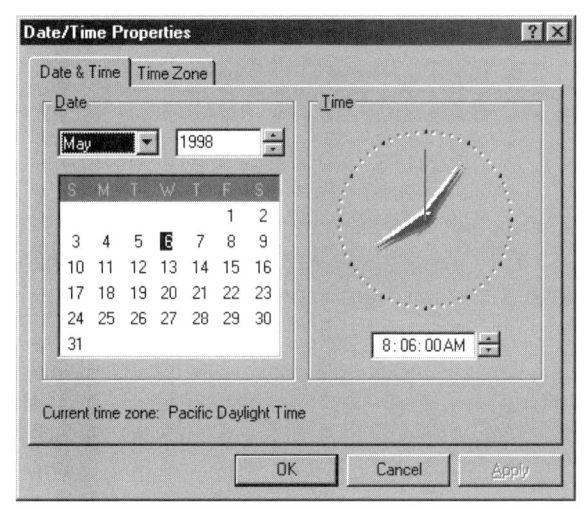

Adjusting your PC's internal clock.

▼ Once you're in the Date/Time Properties dialog box, adjusting the date and time is simple. Use the drop-down boxes under Date to select the current month and year. Then click today's date within the little calendar.

▼ To adjust the time, you can type in the current time using the format **hh:mm:ss AM/PM**.

Or, click to highlight a part of the current time, such as the hour, and use the spin box to adjust the number up or down.

5: PERSONALIZING YOUR PC

Time Zones
- ▼ To tell the clock what time zone you're in, click the Time Zone tab to reveal the time zone map and its options.

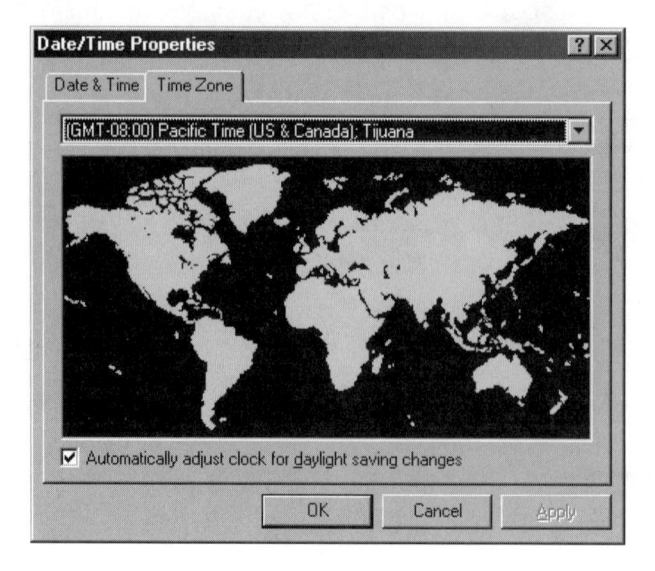

- ▼ You can choose your time zone from the drop-down list above the map, or you can click on your location in the map (which is more fun). If you're in an area that uses Daylight Saving Time, check the Automatically Adjust Time For Daylight Saving Changes checkbox. Doing so will automatically adjust your computer's clock at the start and end of Daylight Saving Time in your time zone.
- ▼ To save your changes and close the dialog box, click the OK button at the bottom.

Taskbar Clock
If you want the current time to be visible in the taskbar (or, if you *don't* want the time to be visible in the taskbar), follow these steps:

- ▼ Right-click a neutral area of the taskbar (not on a button).
- ▼ Choose Properties from the shortcut menu.
- ▼ If you want the time displayed in the taskbar, choose (check) the Show Clock checkbox. If you don't want the time to be visible on the taskbar, clear that checkbox.
- ▼ Click the OK button to save your changes and close the dialog box.

Pretty easy, no? Now let's take a look at the umpteen different ways you can customize the appearance of your Windows 98 desktop.

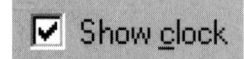

102

There are lots of ways to make your Windows 98 desktop look and act just the way you want it to. All of them are accessible through the Display Properties dialog box. There are two ways to get to that dialog box:

- Right-click a neutral area of the desktop (not an icon) and choose Properties from the shortcut menu.
- Or go to the Control Panel (Start → Settings → Control Panel) and open the Display icon.

Your Own Desktop

Display

The Display Properties dialog box will open. (If yours doesn't look like this one, click the Background tab.)

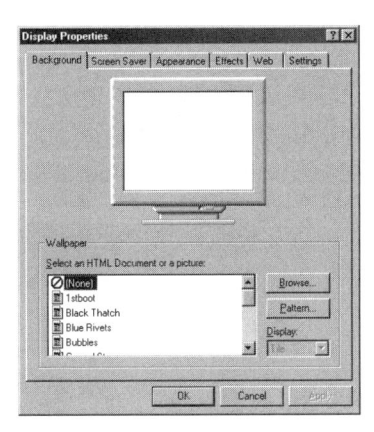

The Display Properties dialog box, with the Background tab on top.

The Background tab in the Display Properties dialog box lets you choose a **wallpaper**, behind the desktop icons. Wallpaper is basically just a picture or pattern or picture used as a background for your Windows 98 desktop.

Your Own Wallpaper

To experiment with the available wallpapers and find one you like:

▼ Click any wallpaper displayed in the Wallpaper list.

▼ To try out that wallpaper right now, click the Apply button.

▼ You might also want to take time now to experiment with the options in the Display drop-down list. (For most wallpapers, the Tile option works best.)

To try another wallpaper, click its name in the list and then click the Apply button. You can keep doing so until you find a wallpaper that you like. Keep in mind that wallpaper is entirely optional. If you decide against using wallpaper, choose None from the top of the Wallpaper list and click the Apply button once again.

103

Your Screen Saver — Computer screens (and TV screens in general) can suffer from a malady known as burn-in, which occurs when an unchanging image is left on the screen for too long (say, several hours). The result of burn-in is a loss of clarity on the screen. There are two ways to avoid burn-in:

- Use a **screen saver**, which is a changing pattern that kicks in when the screen has been idle for a while (perhaps because you're out to lunch or whatever).
- Use an energy savings feature to have the monitor turn off automatically when left unattended for a long time.

All PCs support screen savers. Only newer monitors with special power supplies, however, can use the energy-saving features. If you want to use a screen saver, follow these steps:

▼ If you've exited the Display Properties dialog box, reopen it now, by going through the Control Panel or by right-clicking the desktop and choosing Properties.

▼ Open the Screen Saver tab.

▼ To try out a screen saver, first choose one from the drop-down list under Screen Saver. A preview of that screen saver appears in the sample screen at the top of the dialog box.

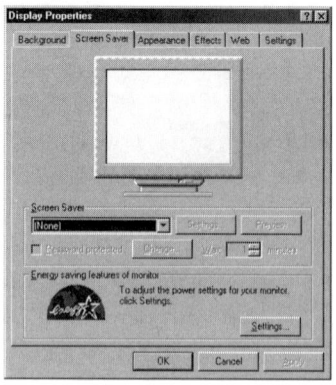

Screen Saver Options — To adjust settings for your chosen screen saver, click the Settings button and make your selections from the dialog box that appears. (I can't give you much more direction than that because each screen saver offers its own unique set of options. Don't worry—you'll be presented with familiar controls such as checkboxes and radio buttons.)

Setting the Wait time — One thing you'll want to set is the amount of time the PC needs to sit idle before the screen saver kicks in. Use the Wait text box and spin buttons to specify the number of minutes the computer must sit idle before the screen saver clicks in. After your settings are established, click the Preview button to see how the screen saver will look when it kicks in. The screen saver will fill the whole screen. When you're ready to return to your normal desktop, just move the mouse or click some area of the screen to turn off the screen saver.

Your screen saver can act as a "lock" to keep others from using your computer while you are away from it. To use the screen saver in this manner, you first need to think up a short password that will allow you in and keep others out.

Screen Saver Password

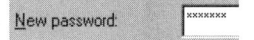

> **Be careful**: Be sure to use a password that you'll easily remember. If you forget the password, you'll end up locking yourself out of your PC!

Anyway, to password-protect your system, first choose your screen saver as described above. Then, within that same dialog box:

▼ Choose (check) the Password Protected checkbox.

▼ Click the Change button.

▼ In the New password text box, type your password. Each character you type will turn into an asterisk (*), to prevent people from looking over your shoulder to see your password.

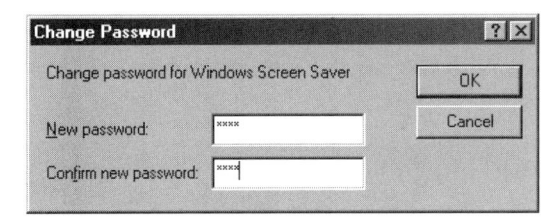

The Change Password dialog box for a password-protected screen saver.

▼ Type the password a second time in the Confirm New Password text box. Again, you'll just see asterisks.

▼ Click the OK button.

If you messed up when typing your password the second time, you'll see a message box telling you there's a problem. You'll need to click the OK button in that message box and then retype your password, twice, into the Change Password dialog box.

Once you have typed your password correctly, clicking the OK button at the bottom of the Display Properties dialog will show you a message to that effect. Just click OK in that box to dismiss it. You can then close the Display Properties dialog box, too, by clicking on its OK button.

5: PERSONALIZING YOUR PC

Want to See What It Looks Like?

The screen saver won't kick in until the computer has been sitting idle for however many minutes you specified in the Wait option of the Display Properties dialog box. If you want to test your screen saver and/or password right now, you can follow these steps to activate the screen saver at any time:

▼ Get back to the Display Properties dialog box, either by right-clicking the desktop and choosing Properties, or by opening the Display icon in Control Panel.

▼ Click the Screen Saver tab.

▼ Click Preview to see the screen saver, and then don't move the mouse or touch the keyboard (or you'll instantly turn the screen saver off).

▼ When you're ready to return to the desktop, just move or click the mouse, or press and release any key (to tell the screen saver that you're back, and ready to get to work again).

▼ If you password-protected your screen saver, you'll now see a small dialog box in which you must type your password. (It will appear as asterisks again.) Click OK to turn off the screen saver and get back to reality.

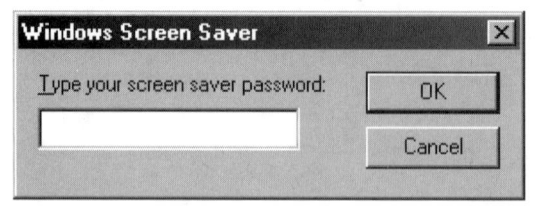

Dialog box that appears when a password-protected screen saver turns off.

Want to Turn Passwords Off?

If you change your mind about password protection and decide you don't want to use the feature anymore, you can easily turn it off. Just open the Screen Saver tab of the Display Properties dialog box, and uncheck the Password Protected check box. That's all there is to it. You won't need a password to turn off the screen saver anymore.

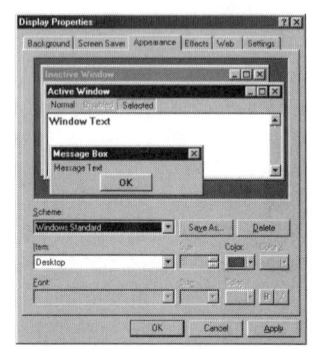

If your computer supports modern energy-savings features, you'll have additional options for protecting the screen and creating your own password. See "Using Energy Saving Features" later in this chapter for more information.

106

Screen Colors

If you're not too crazy about the color scheme that Windows 98 uses on your desktop, you can easily change it. Here's how:

▼ If you closed the Display Properties dialog box after setting up your screen saver, reopen it now via the Display icon in Control Panel or My Computer.

▼ Click the Appearance tab to get to those options.

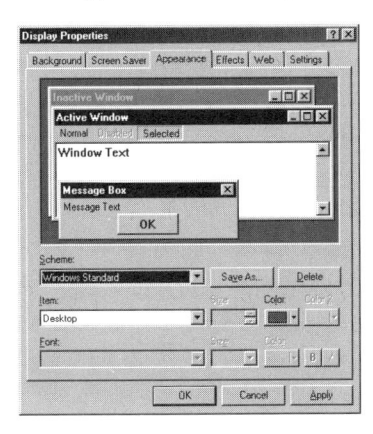

The Appearance tab lets you choose screen colors for the various elements of your screen.

The sample items inside the window (those things named Inactive Window, Active Window, Message Box, and so forth) act as a preview of a **color scheme.** When you choose a new color scheme, the preview instantly takes on the newly selected color scheme. So you can see at a glance how the real screen will look when applied to the actual desktop. If you change an item that's not represented by the Preview window's item, that change won't become apparent until you click the Apply button.

The easiest way to work this dialog box is simply to experiment with the existing, predefined color schemes. You might try, for instance, the first color scheme from the Scheme drop-down list. Select (click) it, and the preview will change colors to illustrate that color scheme. Optionally, you can click the Apply button to see how the color scheme will *really* look.

> When the Scheme drop-down list is active, you can just press the up-arrow and down-arrow keys to preview various color schemes.

When you find a color scheme you like, just click OK to save that setting and close the Display Properties dialog box. The color scheme immediately takes effect in the Windows environment.

Your Own Desktop Design

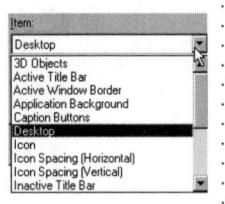

You can create your own custom color scheme by choosing colors for the various components that make up your Windows 98 desktop, such as one for the Windows 98 desktop, and another for menu bars. Use the Item drop-down list in the Appearance tab to access the things you can color.

Some desktop items, like Icon Spacing, have nothing to do with color. The following table lists the desktop items that you can customize, gives an example or two of that item, and indicates which characteristics of that item you can change.

Desktop Item	Examples	Size	Color	Font	Font Color
3D Objects	Dialog boxes, taskbar	No	Yes	No	Yes
Active Title Bar	Any open, active window	Yes	Yes (2)	Yes	Yes
Active Window Border	Any open, active window	Yes	Yes	No	No
Application Background	Background of open program	No	Yes	No	No
Caption Buttons	Minimize, Restore, Close buttons	Yes	No	No	No
Desktop	Entire desktop	No	Yes	No	No
Icon	Any desktop icon	Yes	No	Yes	No
Icon Spacing (Horizontal)	Horizontal space between desktop icons	Yes	No	No	No
Icon Spacing (Vertical)	Vertical space between desktop icons	Yes	No	No	No
Inactive Title Bar	Any open window that's not in use at the moment	Yes	Yes (2)	Yes	Yes
Inactive Window Border	Any open window that's not in use at the moment	Yes	Yes	No	No
Menu	Any program's menu bar	Yes	Yes	Yes	Yes
Message Box	Any message that pops up on the screen	No	No	Yes	Yes
Palette Title		Yes	No	Yes	Yes
Scroll bar	Any scroll bar	Yes	No	No	No
Selected Items	Text you dragged the mouse pointer through	Yes	Yes	Yes	Yes
Tooltip	Tiny message that appears when you point to a button	No	Yes	Yes	Yes
Window	Open space inside a window	No	Yes	No	Yes

To change any individual appearance item in the Item drop-down list, first select the item you want to change. The various controls that you can change, such as Size, Color, Color 2, Font, and so forth, will adjust to the selected item. For example, if you want to change the appearance of title bars in active windows, select Active Title Bar from the Items list. The **Appearance tab** allows you to change the Size (height) and Color (active title bars can be displayed as a color gradient with two colors). You can also change the font used to display text in active title bars. The Font, Size, and Color options can all be enabled; you can even apply **boldface** (the **B** button), *italics* (the *I* button), or both to that font.

Changing Appearance Items

> Two-colored gradients appear in title bars only when the color's depth (discussed a little later in this chapter) is set to High Color (16-bit) or higher.

Let's say, on the other hand, you decide to change an item like Icon Spacing (Horizontal). In this case, only the Size option is enabled, which allows you to choose how many pixels (tiny screen dots) you want between icons. The Color and Font options are dimmed and unavailable, because there is no color or font involved in the spacing between icons. Also, since the Preview example shows no icons, you cannot see the effect of a change to Icon Spacing until you click the Apply button and get to where you can see the icons on your desktop (or in a folder).

As an example of changing just one item, let's suppose I want to use the Windows Standard color scheme, but I want the desktop to be off-white rather than dark cyan. To make that happen, I choose Windows Standard as my scheme and then select Desktop from the Item drop-down list. I use the Color button to switch from the desktop's original dark teal to an off-white.

My favorite color scheme

> You can use the Other button from the little color palette that appears to create your own custom color.

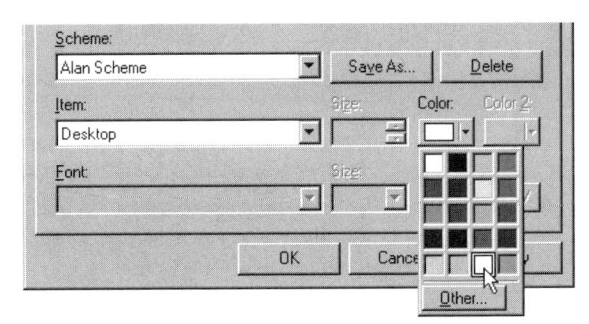

Changing the color of the desktop.

109

5: PERSONALIZING YOUR PC

Save your custom scheme As soon as you change any item in the current color scheme, you create a new color scheme which initially has no name. To give your custom color scheme a new name, click the Save As button and make up a name (I named mine Alan Scheme, as you can see). When you're done playing around with colors and such, click the OK button to save your settings and close the dialog.

Effects Tab The **Effects tab** of the Display properties dialog box lets you choose different icons to replace those "permanent" icons like My Computer, My Documents, and so forth, on your desktop. You can also use the Effects tab's options to activate or deactivate special visual effects. To get to the Effects tab, open the Display Properties dialog box, as usual, and click the Effects tab.

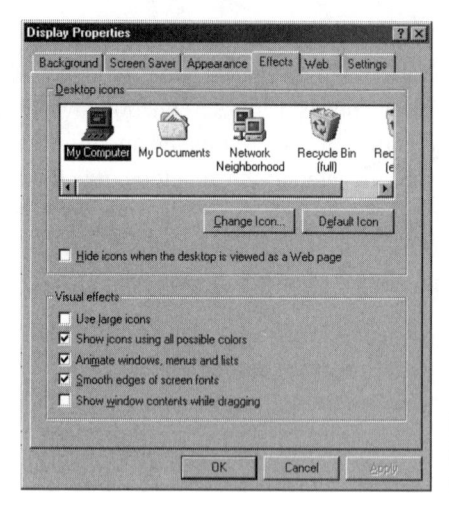

The Effects tab of the Display Properties dialog box.

Changing Icons To change any of the Desktop icons, click it and then click the Change Icon button. A new dialog box appears, showing several icons to choose from. Just click the one you want to use, then click OK. You can change as many or as few icons as you wish. (Your selections won't be carried over to the real desktop, however, until you click either Apply or OK after you return to the Display Properties dialog box.)

The checkbox option for Hide Icons When the Desktop Is Viewed as a Web Page has the rather peculiar effect of making all your desktop icons invisible when you use the Active Desktop feature. We'll discuss that feature in Chapter 15. For now, your best bet is to leave that checkbox turned off.

Visual Effects

The visual effects listed at the bottom of the Effects tab are things you'll generally want to use. Be aware, however, that on older PCs (with a 486 or 386 processor), using those effects might slow things down and become irritating. (On most Pentium computers, the slowdown is so insignificant it's practically unnoticeable.) If you're not sure how your computer will handle these settings, just try them out. If your computer seems sluggish after activating these features, you can go back and clear some, or all, of the options until your computer acts like it's back to its normal speed.

The following table gives a quick overview of what each of the visual effects has to offer. After making your selections, click the OK button to activate them and return to the Windows desktop. Remember, if your PC seems sluggish, you can go back and disable some (or all) of those visual effects to bring things back to normal speed.

Check it out for yourself

In a way, you don't really need this table, because it's easy enough to research these effects for yourself—just click the little question-mark Help button near the upper-right corner of the Display Properties dialog box, and then click any setting you're curious about. Some explanatory text will appear near the mouse pointer.

Visual Effects Setting	Description
Use large icons	Enlarges desktop icons, making them easier to see on small monitors.
Show icons using all possible colors	Uses a broader range of colors to display icons, making them "prettier."
Animate windows, menus, and lists	Some programs use animations, which can slow things down on some computers. Clearing this checkbox disables those animations.
Smooth edges of screen fonts	Because a screen is composed of tiny little squares of light, the edges of letters and numbers on the screen can look jagged (a phenomenon known as "the jaggies"). Check this option to help smooth out those jagged edges.
Show window contents while dragging	When this option is selected, dragging a window across the screen leaves the window intact. Without this option enabled, dragging a window shows only a ghost image of the window.

111

5: PERSONALIZING YOUR PC

Web Tab — The Web tab in the Display Properties dialog box allows you to choose **Active Desktop** features. Those features, however, may not be of much interest to you unless you're an Internet user. If you are, read Chapter 15 for more information on using the Active Desktop.

Settings Tab — The Settings tab of the Display Properties dialog box provides important options for choosing a screen area and color depth, and for managing multiple monitors attached to a single PC. To get to the Settings tab, just open the Display Properties dialog box (if it isn't already open), and click the Settings tab.

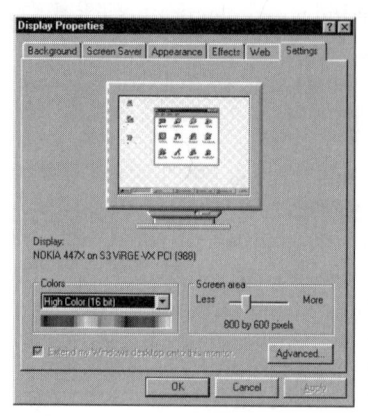

The Settings tab for your computer will look pretty much like this one.

Choosing the Screen Area — The Screen Area setting defines the **resolution** of your screen. Or, stated another way, it defines how many **pixels** (little dots of light) are visible on your screen. The more pixels there are, the more stuff you can cram onto the screen. However, as you increase the pixel count, everything on the screen also gets smaller—as demonstrated in these examples:

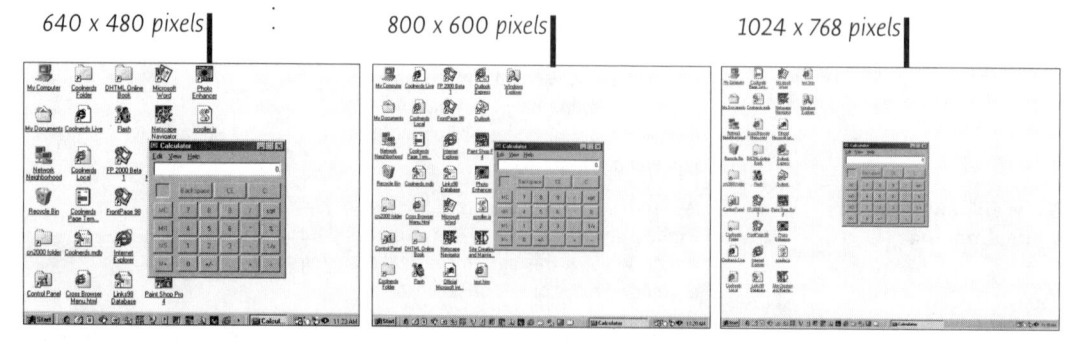

640 x 480 pixels

800 x 600 pixels

1024 x 768 pixels

Examples of three different screen resolutions. As you can see, the higher the resolution, the more space there is on the screen. And the cost is that everything becomes smaller.

112

Screen Area Options

Before you experiment with the screen area settings, be aware that the range of options available to you depends on your PC's display card. You may not have the option to go as high as 1024x768, for instance. Or, your card may have an even higher capability. You'll find out what your limits are when you go to change the setting, because Windows will only offer you whatever options your display card can support.

The question of how high you should go is really a matter of personal preference. If you have a large monitor and/or good eyesight, you might prefer 1024x768. If you have a tiny monitor, like that of a laptop, you may want to stick with a smaller resolution. The best way to find out what works best for you, of course, is just to try out different resolutions. Here's how:

▼ In the Settings tab of the Display Properties dialog box, drag the little Screen Area slider to the left or right until you see the resolution you want to try (640x480 or 800x600 or some other setting, as allowed by your system).

▼ To apply your selection, click the Apply button.

What happens next also depends on your display hardware. You may be asked to restart your computer (by clicking a simple button). Or, you may just see a message indicating that you can resize the desktop just by clicking an OK button. Or, you may be given the option to apply the new setting with or without restarting your computer. Whatever the case, you should be able to proceed on your own from here on out just by following the instructions that appear on the screen, and by clicking a button or two in response to each message.

> After you change the screen area, you might want to rearrange your icons to better fit the screen area. To do that, just right-click a neutral area of the desktop and choose Arrange Icons ➔ By Name from the shortcut menu.

Choosing a Color Depth

The Colors drop-down list in the Settings tab lets you choose the number of colors that can be displayed on your screen. This option is sometimes called **color depth**. As a general rule, the higher the color depth, the richer and more lifelike the colors on your screen will look. However, a higher color depth consumes more resources. So if your computer seems to slow way down after going to a higher color depth, you might want to back up and return to a smaller depth.

5: PERSONALIZING YOUR PC

Note: Most Pentium computers can handle even the highest color depth without noticeably compromising the speed at which the screen redraws.

To choose a color depth:

▼ Get back to the Settings tab of the Display Properties dialog box (if you're not already there).

▼ Choose an option from the Colors drop-down list. Options are listed from lowest (least resource-consuming) to highest (most resource-consuming). The exact options presented to you depend on the capabilities of your PC's display card and monitor. (The rainbow bar gives you an idea of how many colors your screen will be able to show.)

▼ After making your selection, click the Apply button to see how the color setting looks.

▼ You may be prompted to restart your computer. Just follow whatever instructions appear on your screen.

Feel free to experiment—you can't do any harm. The goal is to find a color depth that looks good without slowing down your computer substantially.

Desktop Themes

A **desktop theme** is a predefined collection of desktop settings—such as wallpaper, colors, icon size and font, and so forth—that you can apply with a simple mouse click. It's called a theme because all the settings will center around some idea or motif. For example, here is my desktop after choosing the theme named "The 60's USA." (If you could see it in color you'd see that the background wallpaper is a tie-dyed pattern.)

"The 60's USA" theme on my Windows 98 desktop.

114

To choose a desktop theme for your own PC, follow these simple steps:

- Open the Control Panel (Start → Settings → Control Panel, or open My Computer and click the Control Panel icon there).
- Open the Desktop Themes icon.
- Choose a desktop theme from the Theme drop-down list near the top of the dialog box.

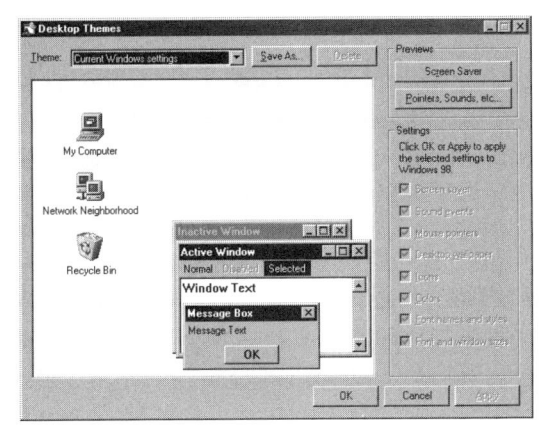

When you select a desktop theme, you get a coordinated collection of screen appearance settings.

If you have only a few desktop themes to choose from, you can install more via the Windows Setup tab of Add/Remove Programs. For more information see "Installing Missing Windows Components" in Chapter 8. The optional Windows 98 Plus! product, which you can purchase separately, also contains several desktop themes.

The large area in the center of the dialog box gives you a preview of how your desktop will look when your selected theme is applied. The Settings checkboxes at the right side of the dialog box show you all the different aspects of the screen that will be affected by the theme. You can apply the theme to as many, or as few, screen elements as you wish just by turning these settings on and off. You'll instantly see the results of your settings in the preview window.

In the Previews section:

- The Screen Saver button lets you see the screen saver that the currently selected theme will use.
- The Pointers, Sounds, etc., button lets you preview (and change, if you want to) the mouse pointers, sound effects, and other visuals associated with this theme.

Desktop Themes

Previewing Theme Settings

***A Very Cool Option**: If you choose the Rotate Theme Monthly checkbox (available through the Pointers, Sounds, etc., button), Windows will automatically apply a different desktop theme each month!*

115

When You Like It, Apply It

As always, you can apply the selected theme to your real desktop by clicking the Apply button or by clicking OK, which applies your settings and closes the dialog box.

Changing a Theme

If you find that you like some aspects of a desktop theme but not others, you can change individual components of the theme. For starters, you need to go back to the Desktop Themes dialog box.

You might find it easiest to first choose the Windows Default scheme from the drop-down list, and then apply it to the actual desktop by clicking the Apply button. Then, clear the checkboxes of any theme components that you don't like. For example, let's say you don't care for the settings of the Colors element and the Font Names and Styles element of the theme. After clearing the checkboxes to turn these components off, choose your preferred theme again and reapply it. The components you turned off won't be applied. Whatever settings are defined in the Display Properties dialog box, discussed earlier in this chapter, will be applied instead.

Saving Your Theme

When you're happy with the changed theme, click OK to apply the new theme to the desktop and close the dialog box. Your theme will be applied, and you can see all of its features. Should you decide you want to save these new settings as your own custom theme, reopen the Display Properties dialog from within the Control Panel. The name of your theme will be "Current Windows Settings." To save those settings as a theme, click the Save As button and give the current theme a new name.

Removing a Theme

If you find that a desktop theme is slowing down your computer considerably, or if you just get sick of looking at that particular theme, it's easy enough to get rid of it. Just follow these steps:

▼ Go to the Control Panel once again.

▼ Open the Desktop Themes icon.

▼ Choose Windows Default from the Themes drop-down list near the top of the dialog box. (Though, of course, you can choose any theme you like.) The preview window gives you an idea of your choice.

▼ Click the OK button.

If by removing a desktop theme you lose a custom color scheme that you particularly liked, you can easily reapply just those color settings. Go back to the Display Properties dialog box (the Display icon in Control Panel), open the Appearance tab, and choose the color scheme you want from the Scheme drop-down list. Then click OK.

Even though the theme you've removed is no longer being applied to your desktop, it still exists as one of the available options in the Themes drop-down list. To reapply it in the future, just select it there.

Deleting a Theme

To remove a theme from the list altogether, you first need to select the theme from the Themes drop-down list. Then click the Delete button just to the right of that list.

Your Own Keyboard

You can control the typematic delay and rate of your keyboard using the Keyboard Properties available through Control Panel. The term *typematic* refers to the capability of holding down a key to make that key repeat itself, as though you were actually tapping away madly on that key. These settings affect the Delete and Backspace keys in addition to the letter and number keys.

- The **typematic delay** is the amount of time you have to hold down the key before it starts repeating itself.
- The **typematic rate** is the key's rate of repetition once it gets going.

To get to the Keyboard Properties dialog box:

▼ Go to the Control Panel (Start → Settings → Control Panel, or open My Computer and open the Control Panel icon in that window).

▼ Open the Keyboard icon.

Once the Keyboard Properties dialog box is open, experiment with different settings until you find just exactly the arrangement that works best for you. Adjust the Repeat Delay and Repeat Rate slider bars to any setting. Then click inside the text box below the sliders and hold down a letter key, such as X or Z. One character will appear in the text box. Then, after a short delay (as determined by the Repeat Delay setting), that character will keep appearing until you release the key.

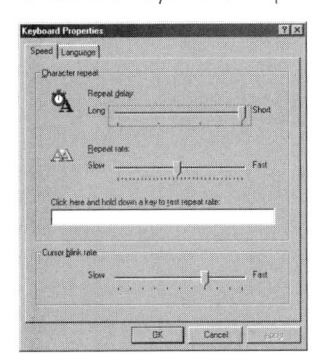

Keyboard

117

5: PERSONALIZING YOUR PC

As long as you've already got a bunch of characters in the text box, you might also want to experiment with holding down the Delete (Del) and Backspace keys to see how your settings affect your ability to erase characters. You'll need to position the cursor first, though. The Delete key deletes characters to the *right* of the cursor; the Backspace key deletes text to the *left* of the cursor. (The Home key moves the cursor to the start of the line, and the End key moves the cursor to the end of any text in the text box.)

Cursor Blink Rate The Cursor Blink Rate option at the bottom of the dialog box does exactly what it says: It determines how fast the cursor blinks. I'm not exactly sure why this option even exists, but I suppose different people in different areas might prefer different speeds. You know, like in New York maybe they *so* like that cursor blinking *really* fast. Here in San Diego, and perhaps in places like Hawaii, people like their cursor to be more relaxed—like, laid back.

To adjust the cursor blink rate to your own locale (or biorhythms or whatever), just move the slider bar left and right and watch the speed of the sample blinking cursor. When you're happy with your selections, click the OK button, as usual, to apply those settings to the desktop and close the dialog box.

Your Own Mouse The Control Panel also contains a **Mouse icon** for customizing the behavior of your mouse. Of course, the options available in Mouse Properties dialog box will depend on the make and model of your mouse. Even though I can't give you exact instructions on how to personalize your mouse, I can point out some options that apply to most mice. And by now, you can probably experiment with your own mouse and find the settings that work best for you. I think you'll find that the options available to you are pretty self-explanatory.

So, to get to the Mouse Properties dialog box on your PC, you'll follow the same simple steps you take to access all of the Control Panel's icons:

▼ Open the Control Panel.

▼ Open the Mouse icon.

Mouse

118

5: PERSONALIZING YOUR PC

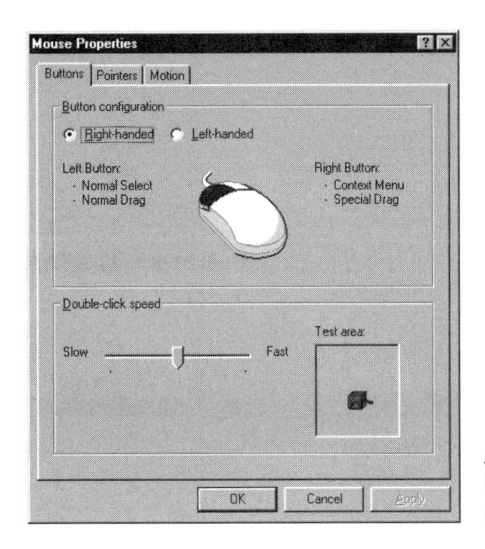

An example of a Mouse Properties dialog box (yours may be different).

The Buttons tab of the Mouse Properties dialog box lets you choose between a **left-handed mouse** and a **right-handed mouse**. If you switch to a left-handed mouse, the primary and secondary mouse buttons will be reversed. That is, the button on the right (the one that's under your index finger when holding the mouse with your left hand) becomes the primary mouse button. The mouse button on the left becomes the secondary mouse button; this is the button you'd use for right-clicking and right-dragging.

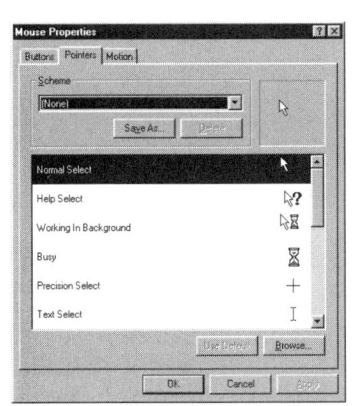

Southpaws, Take Note!

The **Double-Click Speed** option lets you determine how long a delay is allowed between the two mouse clicks of a double-click. "Slow" means even if the two mouse clicks are pretty far apart, they'll still count as a double-click. "Fast" means that you have to make those two keypresses really quickly to get your computer to recognize it as a double-click. If your Buttons tab offers an option similar to the one shown in the Mouse Properties example shown here, you can adjust the slider bar and then double-click the image in the test area. If the computer recognizes your two clicks as a double-click, the jack-in-the-box will pop up (or back down). If the two clicks aren't close enough together to count as a double-click, the image in the test area won't change at all.

Need Slower Double-Clicks?

119

Choosing a Mouse Pointer

The Pointers tab in the Mouse Properties dialog box lets you choose a mouse pointer, or a set of mouse pointers. The options available to you will depend on how many mouse pointers are installed on your PC. But switching pointers is an easy task.

For starters, you can choose a set of pointers from the Scheme drop-down list. The sample pointers in the main list of the dialog box will change to show you the pointers in the currently selected theme.

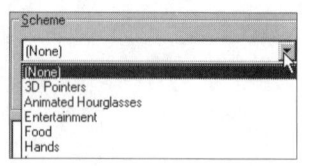

You can also change any one type of pointer. Select it in the main list and click the Browse button. A window containing the available mouse pointers will appear. Click the pointer you want to use, and click OK. To revert to the original (default) pointer that Windows uses, click the Use Default button.

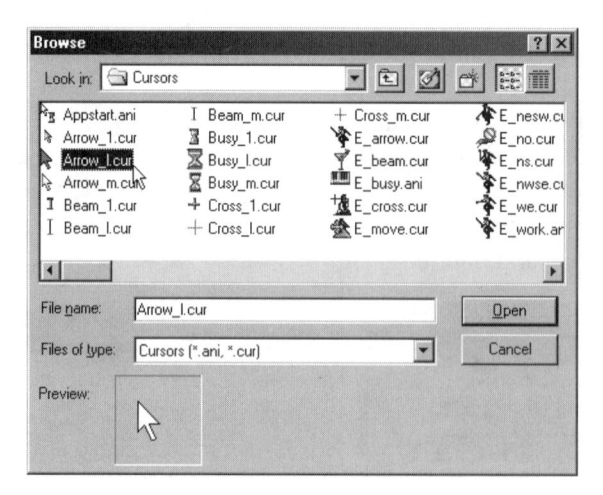

Let's look at an example of choosing just one custom mouse pointer. Say you're having a hard time seeing the mouse pointer that's used for normal selection of items on your screen, and you want to go to a larger pointer. You click the Normal Select pointer and then the Browse button. In the next dialog box that appears, click the cursor named Arrow_l.cur (watch out; that's a letter el following the underline character, *not* the number one). Click the Open button, and you now have a larger cursor. You can do the same with any of the other cursor options. As always, to apply your current selection(s) to the real mouse pointer, you'll need to click the Apply or OK button at the bottom of the dialog box.

Once you're happy with your mouse pointers, you can save the entire selection as a scheme. Just go back to the Mouse Properties dialog box, click the Pointers tab, click the Save As button, then enter a name for your scheme.

Want More Mouse Pointers?

If you find that you don't have a whole lot of mouse pointers to choose from, you might want to install more from the Windows 98 CD-ROM (or floppy disks). To do that, you use Control Panel → Add/Remove Programs and open the Windows Setup tab, as discussed under "Installing Missing Windows Components" in Chapter 8. You can also install desktop themes from that same dialog box. Doing so will add the mouse pointers from that theme to your current collection of mouse pointers.

The Mouse Motion

The Motion tab in the Mouse Properties dialog box lets you control how fast the mouse pointer moves in relation to how fast you're moving the mouse. The farther you move the Pointer Speed slider bar toward the Fast end, the more quickly the mouse pointer will move across the screen as you roll the mouse.

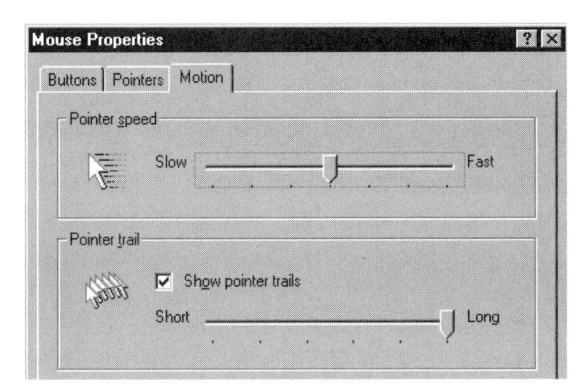

Using trails to make the mouse pointer more visible

As its name implies, a **pointer trail** is a little trail, like the trail of a comet, that follows the mouse pointer around the screen. This trail is very valuable on slow-response laptop computers, and when you're giving a presentation from your computer, and just to make it generally easier to see the mouse pointer when it's moving on your screen'. To activate pointer trials, just select (check) the Show Pointer Trails checkbox. You can make the trail as long or as short as you wish. (Chances are, you'll want to use the longest trail.) As always, apply your selection by clicking the Apply or OK button.

If you don't see a Motion tab or Pointer Trails option in your dialog box, look around in the other tabs of the Mouse Properties dialog box. The trails option might be on the Visibility tab or on some other tab in your particular collection of mouse properties.

Mouse Wheel If your mouse has a **wheel** on it, then your Mouse Properties dialog box will probably include a Wheel tab:

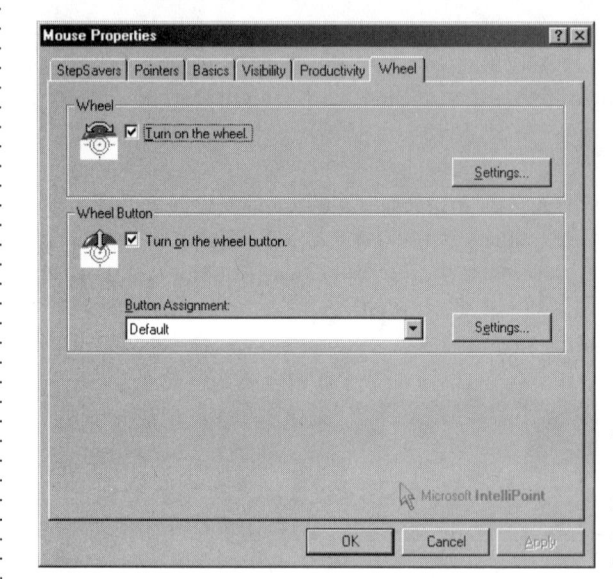

The Wheel tab is available in some Mouse Properties dialog boxes.

The wheel won't work at all unless the Turn On The Wheel checkbox is selected (checked). When the wheel is enabled, you can use the Settings button near the checkbox to define how the wheel operates. For example, after you check the Turn On The Wheel checkbox, you can click the Settings button just to the right of that option. Then you can decide how fast you want the wheel to scroll through the document. The larger the number of lines scrolled through with each mouse wheel notch, the faster your wheel scrolling will go.

You can also use the mouse wheel as a third button that you can click like a regular mouse button. For that to work, you need to make sure the Turn On The Wheel Button checkbox is checked. You can then define what happens when you click the mouse wheel, by choosing an option from the Button Assignment drop-down list. Here's a list of your options:

Wheel Button Assignments	Result
Default	Lets the wheel click function be determined by whatever program you're using at the moment. Also allows you to scroll by holding down the mouse wheel button and moving the mouse. The Settings button to the right determines the speed of that type of scrolling.
Double-click	Clicking the wheel once will have the same effect as double-clicking the primary mouse button.
Help (F1)	Clicking the wheel button will bring up the online Help for the current program.
Windows Explorer	Clicking the wheel button will open the Windows Explorer program, discussed in Chapter 6.
Start Menu	Clicking the wheel button will open the Windows Start menu.

After making your selections, you can just click the OK button to apply your choices and close the dialog box.

Computers consume electricity, and they also produce heat. If the computer is turned on but sitting idle, all that energy is really going to waste. And the heat rising from millions of computers around the world actually contributes to the problem of global warming, some scientists claim.

Managing Your Computer's Power

To reduce power waste and excess heat, the U.S. EPA (Environmental Protection Agency) has come up with guidelines for computer manufacturers to follow. Most manufacturers have abided by those guidelines for the last few years. So if your computer is fairly new, chances are it has power-saving capabilities built into it. Windows 98 gives you some flexibility in deciding how you'll use those energy-saving features.

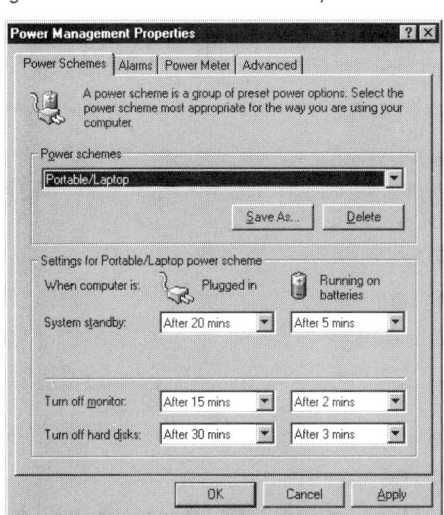

EPA Guidelines

All the settings for energy savings are in the Power Management Properties dialog box.

Your Power Settings

The specific options available to you for power management will, of course, depend on your specific PC. For example, if you're using a laptop computer that's capable of running on batteries, your options will look something like those shown in the example just above. If battery power isn't an option for your PC, then the options having to do with battery settings won't be there.

As is the case for other computer customization tasks, I can't show you exactly how the Power Management Properties dialog box on your PC will look because it all has to do with what kinds of power management capabilities your machine has. The Power Schemes and Advanced tabs are the ones you're most likely to encounter, so those are the features I'll discuss here.

To get to the Power Management Properties dialog box:

- Open the Control Panel; then open the Power Management icon.
- **Or**, if you happen to be in the Screen Saver tab of the Display Properties dialog box, you can click the Settings button down near the bottom of that dialog box.

Power Management

The easiest way to use the Power Management dialog box is to start with the Power Schemes tab. From the drop-down list under Power Schemes, choose one of the following setups:

Choose a power scheme that matches your most typical situation

Power Scheme	Typical Environment
Home/Office Desk	You use your computer several hours a day and usually turn it off at night.
Portable/Laptop	This is the preferred setting for any laptop or portable computer.
Always On	You always leave the computer turned on, never shutting it down.

After you select a power scheme, Windows adjusts the System Standby, Turn Off Monitor, and Turn Off Hard Disks options accordingly. Let's look at the settings for Portable/Laptop, for example. As you can see in the dialog box shown earlier, the System Standby option has been automatically set for the PC to go into Standby mode after 20 minutes of sitting idle, when the computer is plugged in. (*Idle* means no mouse or keyboard activity.) When the computer is running on batteries, it will go into Standby after just five minutes of sitting idle—to conserve battery power. You can change either setting just by choosing a new one from the drop-down lists.

Your PC's monitor consumes a lot of energy and produces a lot of heat. You can use the Turn Off Monitor options to determine how long the computer can sit idle before the PC automatically turns off the monitor to prevent wasted energy and heat. After the PC shuts down the monitor, all you have to do to bring it back to life is move the mouse pointer slightly, or press a key, and then wait a few seconds for the monitor to warm up.

Your hard disk also consumes a little power while spinning. You can have that shut off, as well, if the computer has been sitting idle for a while. If you set this option, you might notice some pretty serious slowing down of your machine after an idle period, because it takes longer to get stuff off the disk if it's not already spinning when a request is made.

> If you have any problems with power management, you may need more information from the documentation that came with your computer. Your PC may have power options that override the Windows 98 options.

The Advanced tab in the Power Management dialog box lets you adjust some other power-related settings relevant to your computer. Here you see the two options available on the computer I happen to be sitting at right now.

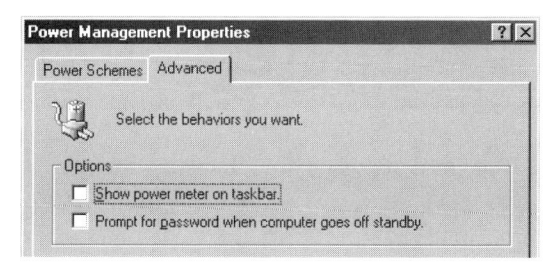

Advanced Power Settings

Options on the Advanced tab of the Power Management dialog box on one of my computers.

- **Show Power Meter On Taskbar**: When you turn this option on, a little icon shows in the Indicators section of the taskbar. The icon is a battery when the computer is running on batteries, or a power cord when the compouter is plugged into the wall.

- **Prompt For Password When Computer Goes Off Standby**: Turn on this option, and the computer will ask for a password before leaving Standby mode and returning to the Windows 98 desktop. The password you'll need to enter is the one you define in the Passwords dialog box, discussed in the upcoming section "Protecting Your Privacy."

When you click the OK button to save your Power Management settings, don't expect much to happen. The power-savings features don't kick in until the computer has been sitting idle for the time(s) specified in the dialog box.

Forcing Standby Mode

If you know you're going to be away from your computer for a while and don't want to wait for the Power Management options to kick your computer into Standby mode, you can easily put it into Standby mode yourself. (Of course, this only works on PCs that *have* a Standby mode.)

To put your computer in Standby mode:

▼ Click the Windows 98 Start button and choose Shut Down on the Start menu.

▼ Select (click) the Standby option, and click OK.

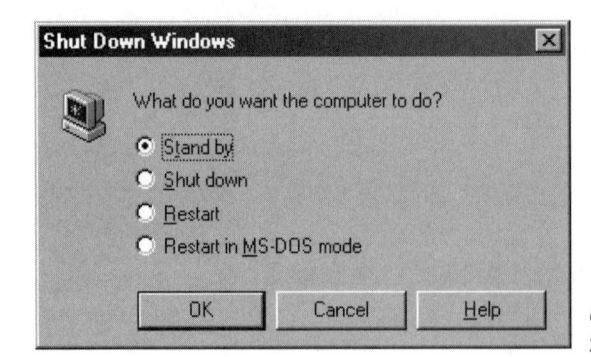

Going into Standby mode.

The screen will go dark (eventually), and stay that way until you bring the computer back up to speed. To do this, just move the mouse or press and release any key on the keyboard. You'll need to wait half a minute or so for everything to warm up. If you enabled password protection in the Power Management dialog box's Advanced settings, you'll be prompted to enter that password before you can get back' to the Windows 98 desktop.

Protecting Your Privacy

Don't forget your password!

To prevent other people from using your computer while you're away, you can give yourself a password. Just *make sure* to come up with a password that you won't forget. Otherwise, you'll end up locking yourself out of your own computer! (To play it safe in case you do forget, you might want to write your password down on paper and file it someplace where you can find it again when you need it.)

Never, *ever*, just "goof around" with the password dialog boxes. If you casually enter a password that you don't remember later, you'll end up locking yourself out of your own PC. I'm not kidding about this!

When you've decided on a password, follow these steps to password-protect your PC:

▼ Click the Windows 98 Start button and choose Settings → Control Panel.

▼ Open the Passwords icon, and if necessary, click the Change Passwords tab to open it'.

▼ In the Passwords Properties dialog box, click the Change Windows Password button.

▼ In the dialog box that appears next, leave the Old Password text box empty (unless you've previously assigned a password, in which case you'll need to type that old password in before you can continue).

▼ Type your new password in the New Password text box. It will show up as asterisks, like the sample entry shown here, to thwart nosy passersby from peeking over your shoulder to see your password.

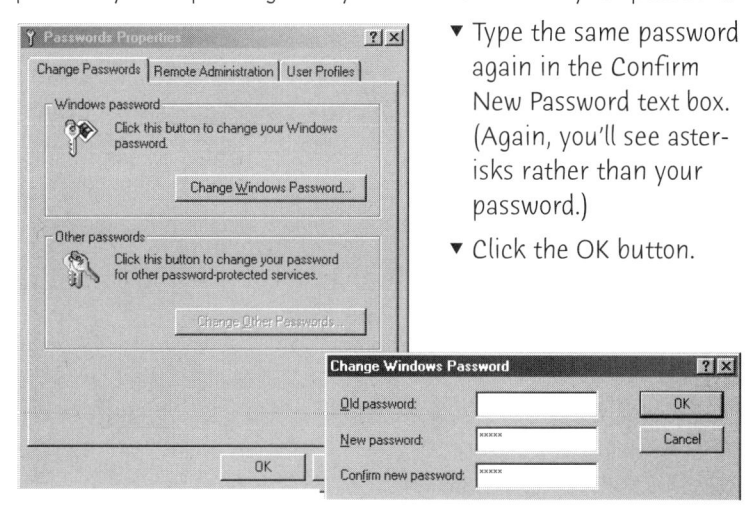

▼ Type the same password again in the Confirm New Password text box. (Again, you'll see asterisks rather than your password.)

▼ Click the OK button.

You'll see a message telling you that the password has been changed (unless the "new" and "confirm" passwords don't match, in which case you'll be directed to type them in again).

▼ Click the OK button at the bottom of the Password Properties dialog box to save your selections.

Using the Password Nothing much will seem to happen. However, from now on, any time you start (or restart) your computer, you'll see a Welcome to Windows dialog box that requires a user name and a password.

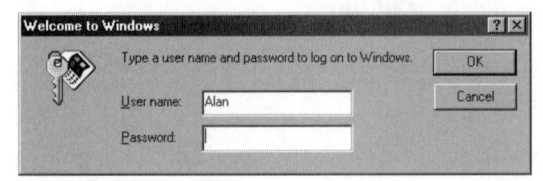

The Welcome to Windows dialog box prompts you for a user name and password.

You'll need to type in a **user name** (which can be your own first name), and then type in your password and click OK. You won't be able to get to the Windows 98 desktop until you enter the correct password.

Note that your password *won't* be required to get back to the desktop after the computer has gone into Standby mode, unless you activate that setting for "Prompt For Password When Computer Goes Off Standby" as described earlier in the "Advanced Power Settings" section.

Warning for Networked Users: If your computer is part of a network of computers in an office or other group environment, you'll also be prompted for a network user name and password. These items are not necessarily the same as your Windows user name and password. Your company's network administrator may give you a separate user name and password for accessing resources on the network.

Changing/Removing a Password To change your password or to remove password protection, you *must* know the existing password. Then you can just follow the same steps you used to create the original password. Here's the exact procedure:

▼ Open Control Panel, and open the Passwords icon.

▼ In the Passwords Properties dialog box, click the Change Passwords button.

▼ Type the existing password into the Old Password text box. Then . . .

▼ If you want to remove password protection altogether, leave the New Password and Confirm New Password text boxes empty.

Or, to change the existing password, type a new password into the New Password text box and retype it in the Confirm New Password text box.

▼ Click the OK button.

The effects of your change will be apparent next time you start the computer. If you removed password protection, you won't be prompted for a password. If you changed the password, you'll need to enter the new one to get to the Windows 98 desktop.

Controlling Sound

If your computer has a sound card and speakers, there are a number of things you can do to control the volume of that sound. This job can be a bit tricky, however. That's because there are three separate controls for volume—in the speakers, your taskbar, and the Programs menu.

- The speakers themselves have **volume controls**. (If your speakers are built into your monitor, the volume controls will probably be on the monitor).
- You may have a volume control in the indicators section of your taskbar. Its icon is a speaker; its tooltip is "Volume."
- A **Master Volume Control** is accessible through the Programs menu.

The Lowest Setting Wins

All three of these controls in combination affect how loud your speakers are. The lowest setting rules. For example, suppose the Master Volume and the volume control (in the taskbar) are both cranked up full blast. But the volume controls on the speakers are turned down all the way. In this case, the speaker volume (the lowest setting of the three) controls the volume; so you end up with no sound. Likewise, if the Master Volume is cranked up to the max, and so are the volume controls on the speakers themselves, but the taskbar control is turned down all the way, you will get no sound. That's because the lowest setting rules.

It might help to think of the sound traveling from your PC to your speakers as water running through a pipe. Along this pipe are three faucets. If you want the water to run full blast, you must turn all the faucets up full blast. If you want to decrease, or stop, the amount of water coming through, you only have to crank down one faucet. Any one of the three faucets would do.

I know it's kinda confusing. But the purpose of having several controls is really just to give you the option of controlling your speaker volume with either the speaker buttons themselves, or the mouse. Obviously, if your speakers are out of reach while you're sitting at the PC, using the mouse to control speaker volume would be a lot easier. The mouse is your *only* option if your speakers don't have their own volume control buttons.

129

5: PERSONALIZING YOUR PC

Easy Volume Control

To demystify the whole volume-control situation, I suggest that you decide which control you want to use on a day-to-day basis. Crank up everything *except* that volume control. Get your computer making some noise, and then adjust the volume through your preferred method.

Mystified about sound controls? Try these steps.

To control the volume for your computer:

Step 1: Go to the Master Volume Control, either by double-clicking the speaker indicator in the taskbar, or with Start ➔ Programs ➔ Accessories ➔ Entertainment ➔ Volume Control.

> **Easy-Access Volume Control:** You can make the Master Volume Control accessible from the desktop or Quick Launch toolbar. Just right-drag the option right out of the Entertainment menu, and drop it onto the desktop or the Quick Launch toolbar. Choose Create Shortcut(s) Here from the little menu that appears. You'll learn more about shortcuts in Chapter 9.

Step 2: Look carefully at the title bar of the window that opens. If it reads "Volume Control," go to Step 3 right now. If the title bar reads "Recording Control," choose Options ➔ Properties from Recording Control's menu bar. Then choose the Playback option and click OK. The title bar will now read "Volume Control."

Step 3: Center all the Balance sliders, clear all the Mute checkboxes, and crank all the Volume sliders up to max volume, as in the example just below. If you do *not* plan to use this Volume Control dialog box as your day-to-day volume control, go to Step 4 below right now. If you *do* plan to use this Volume Control dialog box as your regular volume control, slide the leftmost Volume slider way down.

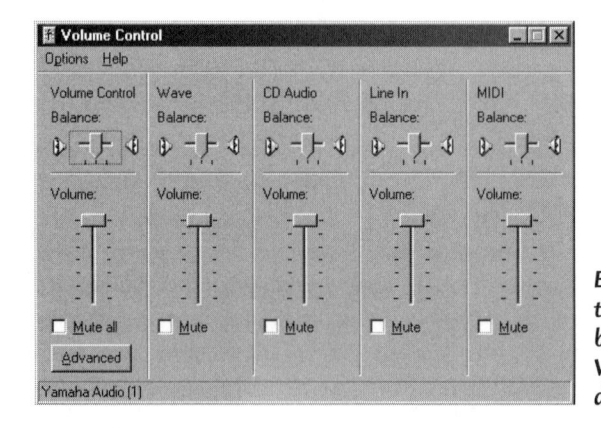

Everything turned up full blast in the Volume Control dialog box.

130

Step 4: Close the Volume Control dialog box.

Step 5: If you do *not* have a speaker indicator in your taskbar, go to Step 6 right now. Otherwise, click your speaker indicator, and in the volume control make sure the Mute checkbox is unchecked. If you *do* want to use this as your day-to-day volume control, crank the Volume slider way down. If you do *not* want to use this as your regular volume control, crank the Volume slider way up. Click anywhere outside the volume control to close it.

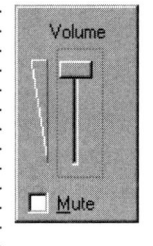

Step 6: If your speakers do *not* have their own volume control buttons, go to Step 7 right now. Otherwise, if you plan to use the control buttons on your speakers as your day-to-day volume control, crank the volume down pretty far. If you do *not* plan to use the speaker buttons as your regular volume control, turn them up as far as you like.

Step 7: At this point, you have a situation like the water pipe metaphor: two faucets on full blast, and a third faucet turned way down. You can now get some sound going and use your preferred volume control device to turn up the volume to a comfortable level.

> **One More Volume Control?** Much as I hate to complicate things even further, be aware that your PC may have yet *another* volume control of its own—like the Packard Bell Navigator program, for instance. That control figures into the equation, too, acting as yet another faucet on our imaginary water pipe. If you know of such a volume control on your own PC, make sure it's not muted or cranked down too far. Otherwise, your speakers won't have any sound, no matter how high you adjust the other volume controls.
>
> **Be Careful with Your Headphones**: If you use headphones to adjust your volume control, be careful to hold the headphones a little distance from your ears when getting started. Otherwise, if the volume suddenly jumps to superloud, you might damage your eardrums.

Now you need to get your computer to make some sound, so that you can test your new day-to-day volume settings. You can use an audio CD (the kind of CD you usually play in your sound system or CD player), if your PC has a CD-ROM drive.

Test It Out

Put the audio CD into the CD-ROM drive, and wait a few seconds. If a new button titled CD Player appears in your taskbar, the CD is playing.

You can now slowly crank up your day-to-day volume control to a comfortable setting.

If your audio CD didn't play automatically, you can probably play the CD manually. I can't get into all of that right here, but if you want to take a shot at it, you can read the section titled "Using Windows 98's CD Player" in Chapter 11.

No CD? If playing a CD isn't an option for you, perhaps you can find a game or some edutainment-type program to run. Most of those play sounds. If all else fails, you may have to wait until we get to "Changing Sound Effects" later in this chapter to finish adjusting your day-to-day volume control.

When You're All Set Up . . . Now you've got everything set up the way you want it. So, in the future, whenever you need to adjust your speaker volume, try to remember to use the day-to-day volume control you've worked so hard to figure out! Then you can just forget about the other volume controls. You know they're turned up to the max and therefore aren't hindering anything.

Put a Cap on It: You can put a cap on the loudness of your day-to-day volume control just by cranking down either of the other volume controls a little. This might be handy if you need to keep youngsters from turning the speakers up to a deafening roar.

The Volume Control Dialog Box I suppose that some of you are wondering what all those sliders in the Volume Control dialog box were for. In fact, you might have noticed that your own dialog box has more (or fewer) volume controls than the one shown above—as in this one, for instance:

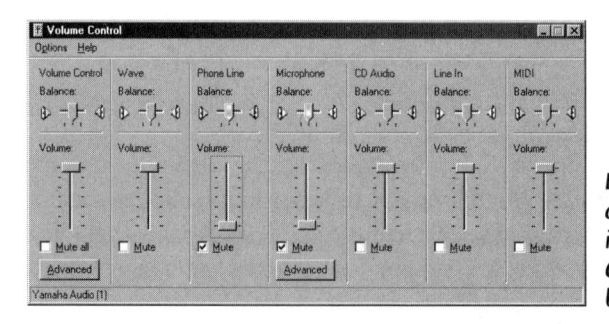

Lots of volume control panels in this Volume Control dialog box.

The main control on the far left determines how much sound gets through to the speakers. The remaining panels determine the relative volume of various types of sound your computer can play. Here's a quick summary of what each type of sound is:

Volume Control Panel	What It Controls
Wave	The loudness of your computer's sound effects. Wave files store sound. These sound files are generally used as small sound effects. Wave files stored on your PC all have the filename extension .wav.
Phone Line	The volume of your PC's built-in phone or speaker phone, if it has one.
Microphone	The volume of your PC's microphone. If you plug a microphone into your PC's sound card and start talking into it, you can hear your own voice coming right through the speakers. The Advanced button contains options that are relevant to your own microphone. Feel free to take a peek.
CD Audio	The volume when you play an audio CD in the CD-ROM drive.
Line In	The loudness of a stereo or other sound-system device that's plugged into your sound card's Line In port.
MIDI	The volume at which your computer's music files are played. MIDI stands for Musical Instrument Digital Interface, which is the file format that is used to store most computer music. Any time you run a program or visit a Web page that has background music, you can bet it's probably MIDI music. These files have the filename extension .mid, .midi, or even .rmi.

Which Volume Controls Do You Want?

To determine which sliders appear in your Volume Control dialog box, choose Options → Properties from the Volume Control's menu bar. In the dialog box that appears, make sure the Playback option button is selected. Then, in the list near the bottom of the dialog box, check each item that you want included in the Volume Control dialog box. Clear the checkbox if you want to remove that panel.

Remember that if you check the Mute checkbox in any Volume Control panel, that sound will not ever make it to the speakers. So that sound will not be heard, ever, no matter how high up you turn the volume controls.

Use the sliders, moving them up and down, to control any of the sound elements represented in the Volume Control's panels. For example, if you find everything's fine except that the sound effects are too loud, you can lower the Wave volume control. If you want to put a damper on how loud the kids can crank up their audio CDs, move the CD Audio volume down a tad.

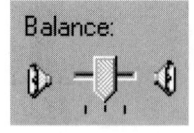

The horizontal Balance sliders work just like the balance controls on a regular sound system: They control the relative volume of the left and right speakers. If your computer is positioned so that its speakers are not equidistant to your ears, you might want to adjust the Balance slider on the main Volume Control panel. Or, should you need to for any reason (I can't think of any, myself), you can adjust any of the Balance sliders for just that type of sound.

Saving the Settings

There's no OK button in the Volume Control dialog box. To save your setting and exit, just click the Close (X) button in the dialog box, or press Alt+F4.

Changing Sound Effects

If your computer has a sound card and speakers, you've probably noticed little bells and beeps and other sounds from time to time as you interact with your PC. That's because Windows 98 has a small collection of sound effects built into it. The various desktop themes also have their own unique collections of sound effects. You can change the sound effects that occur on your system by using the Sounds dialog box in Control Panel. Here's how:

▼ Click the Windows 98 Start button and choose Settings → Control Panel.

▼ Open the Sounds icon to reveal the Sound Properties dialog box.

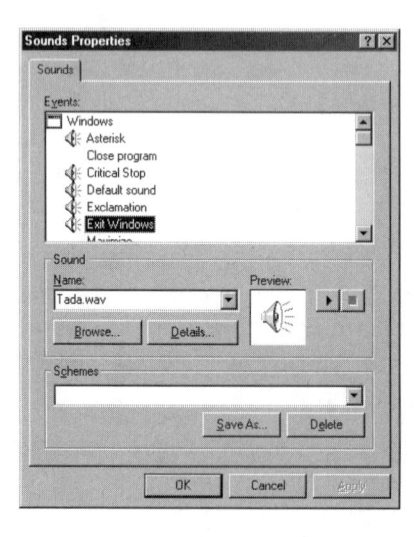

The Sounds Properties dialog box lets you pick and choose your system's sound events.

134

Sound Schemes

Your PC may already have some predefined **sound schemes** stored in it, for you to use as you like. You can select one of these schemes from the Schemes drop-down list near the bottom of the dialog box. If there are no predefined schemes, you can still play around with the individual sound events listed in the scrollable Events list.

> **More Sounds**: You may be able to add more sounds and sound schemes to your current collection. To do that, install the Multimedia Sound Schemes and Sample Sounds from your Windows 98 CD-ROM or floppies, as described in "Installing Missing Windows Components" in Chapter 8.

Sound Events

The Events list shows **events**—things that happen—on a PC, to which you can tie sound effects. The little speaker icon to the left of the item in the Events list indicates that there's a sound effect assigned to that event. For example, the Asterisk event occurs whenever Windows puts up a noncritical message box, like the "Information" message shown here.

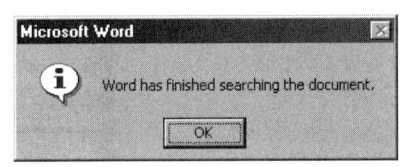

The Close Program event, on the other hand, has no sound effect assigned. This event occurs whenever you close a program's window.

Sounds are part of desktop themes

If you selected a desktop theme for your PC, as discussed earlier in this chapter, the sounds in the Events list will be from that desktop theme. Any changes you make here, however, will override the desktop theme.

Changing the Sounds Properties

You can listen to and, optionally, change or delete the sound effect associated with any event. You can also remove the sound effect from any event. And, of course, you can assign a sound effect to any event that currently has no sound.

First, you need to click the event that you want to hear or change. That will show you the name of the wave file (sound effect), if any, that's currently assigned to that event. With the event selected, you can do any of the following:

- To listen to the sound effect, click the Play button (the right-pointing triangle next to the Preview box).

    To adjust the sound effect's volume to a comfortable level, increase or decrease your day-to-day volume control, as discussed in the earlier section. Then play the sound again, and keep adjusting until the volume is satisfactory.

- To choose a new or different sound effect, click the Browse button and then click any sound file that appears. (You can then press the Play button to listen to that sound.)

- To remove the sound event that's currently assigned to the event and thereby make the event quiet, choose (None) from the top of the Name drop-down list.

- To see copyright and other information about the currently selected sound file, click the Details button.

Saving a New Sound Scheme

If you come up with a set of sounds you're particularly fond of, you can save them as a new sound scheme. Just click the Save As button and give the scheme any name you like. Then click OK, as usual.

When you're happy with all your individual selections, you can save them and close the dialog box by just clicking the OK button. Remember, you won't actually hear your sound effects until the events associated with those sounds occur. You can trigger some sound events yourself. For example, you can hear the Close Program sound by starting any program and then closing its window. Other events, like the ones associated with various kinds of message boxes, you'll just have to wait for.

Your Locale Settings

Chances are, your Windows 98 program is already set up to use the date, time, number format, and currency format of the country you're in. But if your system needs to have these things adjusted, you can easily adapt Windows 98 to a particular country's conventions.

To adapt your computer's setting to a specific locale:

▼ Open the Control Panel (click the Start button and choose Settings → Control Panel).

Regional Settings

▼ Open the Regional Settings icon.

▼ In the Regional Settings Properties dialog box, use the drop-down list on the Regional Settings tab to select your country.

▼ Click OK to apply your selection and close the dialog box.

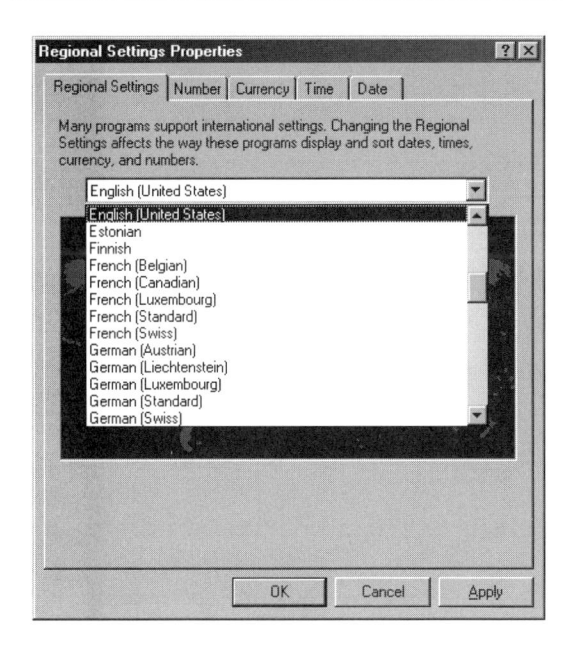

Selecting a region provides all the formats needed for your geographic locale, including number and currency formats, date, and time.

Chances are, that's all it will take to get the correct formats for your country. However, if you need to adjust individual items such as the currency symbol, you can. Just reopen the Regional Settings Properties dialog box and click one of the tabs at the top to see the Number, Currency, Time, or Date format settings.

One of the best new features of Windows 98 is Multiple Display Support—the ability to use multiple monitors on a single PC. Unfortunately, *installing* a second monitor is a complex task that goes beyond the scope of this book. But chances are, if you call any computer store or repair shop and tell them you want to add a second monitor to your Windows 98 PC, they can tell you exactly what it will cost and will also do the work for you. The labor charges will probably be small, but the cost of a second display card and monitor can run into a couple thousand dollars or more. So make sure you know what you're getting into before you commit to adding a second monitor.

If you do have two or more monitors, it's important to understand that each monitor is an extension to your Windows 98 desktop. You won't see the desktop icons and taskbar on each monitor. However, you will be able to drag any icon, open window, toolbar, or whatever onto the second monitor (and any additional monitors), just as though all the monitors were just one big monitor.

Multiple Monitors

Multiple Display Support

5: PERSONALIZING YOUR PC

For example, here's a fairly common situation where I've opened the WordPad program (in back) and its Help window (on top) in the same monitor. The Help window is overlapping most of the WordPad program's window.

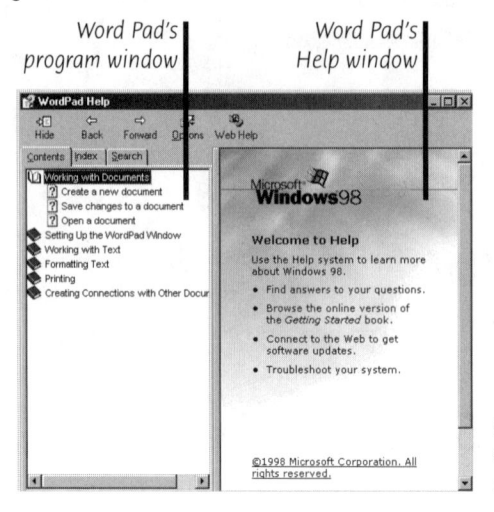

Word Pad's program window

Word Pad's Help window

Multiple windows overlapping on a single monitor.

The advantage to having two monitors attached is that there's plenty of room to see more than one program window without their overlapping. You just drag one window or the other over to the second monitor. For example, here I've dragged the Help window over to the second monitor, thereby making the WordPad program's window completely visible.

Two monitors, one desktop

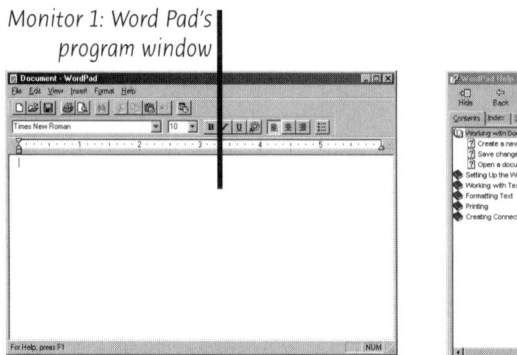

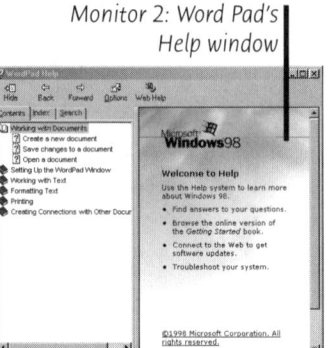

Monitor 1: Word Pad's program window

Monitor 2: Word Pad's Help window

With two monitors attached, I can drag some windows over to the other monitor.

Keep in mind that the example shown in these illustrations is *just* an example. With two or more monitors attached, you can drag anything, anywhere on any monitor. That's because each additional monitor just extends the size of your Windows 98 desktop. Let's see how this works.

If you have two or more monitors attached to your PC, the Settings tab of the Display Properties dialog box will include a picture for each one. Here's the Settings tab of the Display Properties dialog box for my dual-monitor PC.

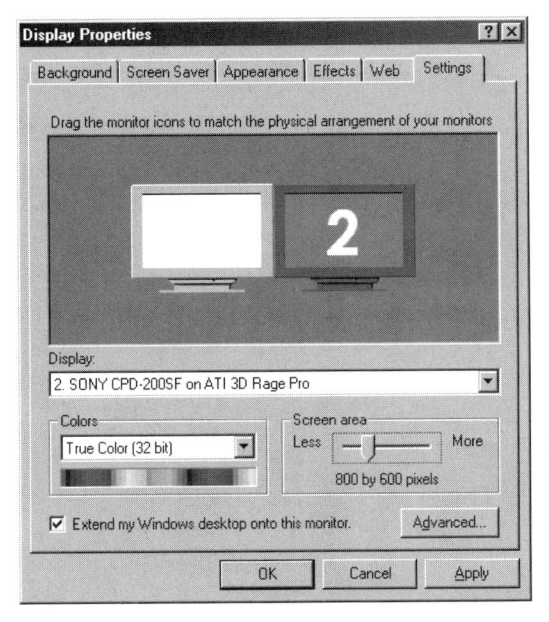

The Settings tab of the Display Properties dialog on a PC with two monitors attached.

Arranging Multiple Monitors

If you can't remember where you saw this Display Properties dialog box, you can get to it by right-clicking a neutral area of the desktop and choosing Properties from the shortcut menu. Or open the Display icon in Control Panel.

The first step to using multiple monitors is to arrange the little monitor pictures so that they match the actual arrangement of your monitors. Start by determining which is Monitor 1 and which is Monitor 2. To do that, move the mouse pointer to either monitor image, and hold down the mouse button for a few seconds. A large 1 or 2 appears on the actual monitor to show you which is which.

Then drag the monitor pictures inside the dialog box so that they match the actual physical layout of the monitors. On my desktop, for example, Monitor 2 sits just to the right of Monitor 1. Therefore, I've arranged the monitor pictures so that Monitor 2's picture is to the right of Monitor 1's picture.

Once your monitors are represented, you can adjust the color depth and screen area of each monitor independently. Just click on whichever monitor you want to adjust (or choose a monitor from the Display drop-down list). Then choose your color depth and screen area for your monitor. You might find it easiest to give both monitors the same settings, but that decision is entirely up to you. You *can't* give each monitor its own wallpaper, however, nor its own color scheme or any other setting that affects the entire Windows 98 desktop. And no matter how many monitors you attach to your PC, you still have only one Windows 98 desktop. (Potentially a very *large* desktop, but just one desktop nonetheless.)

If you need help with the Colors and Screen Area settings, see the "Screen Colors" and "Settings Tab" sections earlier in this chapter.

Once you've arranged the monitor pictures and chosen any necessary settings, you can close the Display Properties dialog box (with the OK button, as usual). Then, when you're back to your Windows 98 desktop, you can drag things between one monitor and the other, wherever the two monitor images touch.

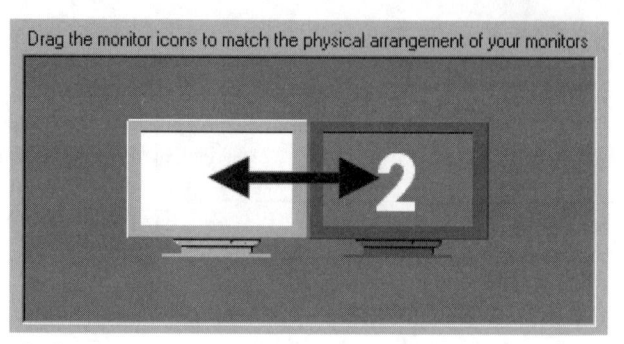

The large arrow indicates the point where I can drag from one monitor to the other, because their images touch along the one side.

Multiple Monitors: Some Guidelines

If you are fortunate enough to have multiple monitors attached to your PC, there are a few "gotchas" that you need to keep in mind.

For one, you cannot drag a maximized (full-screen) window from one monitor to the other. You'll need to shrink that window a little (by clicking the Restore button near the upper-right corner of the window) before you can drag it.

Remember that multiple display support is new to Windows 98, and it may not be supported by all of your programs. Let's say you're working on a document. It's always a good idea to save your work often, but this is especially true before you try to drag that document's program window from one monitor to another.

Finally, be aware that if the two monitors aren't set to the same screen area size, the monitor images will be sized accordingly. The monitor with the larger screen's picture will look bigger than the monitor with the smaller screen area's picture. For example, take a look at this next illustration, in which I set Monitor 1 to a screen area of 1024x768 and Monitor 2 to 800x600.

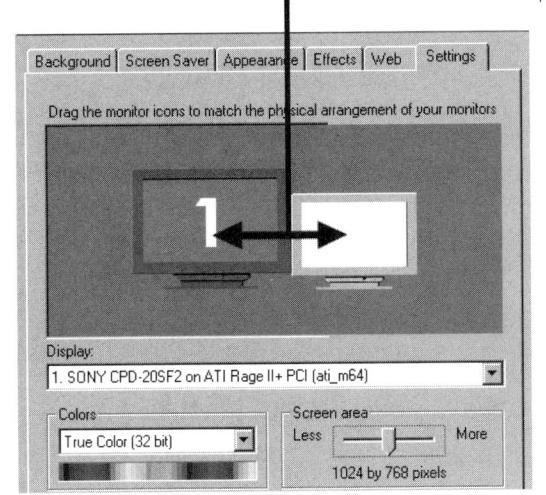

On the real monitors, you can't drag across right here because monitor the pictures don't touch

The trick to using an arrangement like this is to understand that you can drag things across the real monitors *only* at those places where the two monitor pictures actually touch. For example, I wouldn't be able to drag something from the top of Monitor 1 straight across to Monitor 2, because the two monitor pictures don't touch there. I would need to drag the item on Monitor 1 downward a little ways before I could drag it to the right, over to Monitor 2.

Summary

In this chapter you've learned umpteen different ways to personalize the Windows 98 environment to your own tastes and needs. Yes, we've covered a lot of ground—but it all boils down to this: When you want to change some kind of setting, open the Control Panel first. Chances are, the icon you need is there. More specifically:

- Most options for customizing Windows 98 are in the **Control Panel,** which you can open by clicking the Start button and choose Settings → Control Panel.
- There's also a **Control Panel icon** inside the My Computer window. You can open whichever icon is most convenient at the moment.
- To set your computer's date and time, use the **Date/Time icon**.
- To change the appearance of your screen, use the **Display icon** to work with the Display Properties dialog box. You can also get to the Display Properties dialog box by right-clicking a neutral area of the desktop and choosing Properties from the shortcut menu.
- To apply or remove a desktop theme, use the **Desktop Themes icon**.
- To personalize the behavior of your keyboard, use the **Keyboard icon**.
- To control the properties of your mouse, use the **Mouse icon**.
- If your PC has modern energy-saving features built in, you can adjust those through the **Power Management icon**.
- To password-protect your PC and your privacy, use the **Passwords icon**.
- If your computer has a sound card and speakers, you can adjust the **volume** in three ways: (1) Using the buttons on the speakers themselves or on your monitor, (2) using the volume control that appears when you click the little speaker indicator in the taskbar, and (3) using the Volume Control program that comes with Windows (Start → Programs → Accessories → Entertainment → Volume Control).
- To make Windows use a particular country's currency signs, date and time formats, and so forth, use the **Regional Settings icon**.

Exploring Your PC

6

In earlier chapters I've drawn a comparison between your computer's hard disk and a filing cabinet. Everything that's "in the computer," so to speak, is actually stored on the computer's hard disk. In this chapter you'll learn how things are organized on that hard disk and learn some valuable techniques for finding things inside that structure. The same techniques can be used to explore the contents of floppy disks and CD-ROMs. But in this chapter we'll focus on the hard disk, because that's where all your "important stuff" is.

6: EXPLORING YOUR PC

Disk Drives

Although you were introduced to the hard disk and the disk drives of your computer in Chapter 1, here in this chapter we're going to take a much closer look. First and foremost, you need to understand what a **disk drive** is. A disk drive in your PC is a gadget that can spin a disk around, read information from it, and in most cases write information to that disk as well. Your floppy disk drive can read the stuff that's on floppy disks. Your CD-ROM drive can read ("play") stuff that's on CDs. And the hard disk can both read from and write to the hard disk that's inside the hard disk drive.

Hard disk

Unlike the floppy disk drive and CD-ROM drive, there is no little door on your PC for inserting and removing a hard disk. That's because the hard disk is sealed up tight inside its drive and cannot be tampered with. For this reason, the hard disk is sometimes referred to as a **non-removable**, or **fixed, disk**. In contrast, floppies and CD-ROM are often called **removable media**, because you can remove the disk from its drive and replace it with another disk.

Even though you can't, physically, yank the hard disk out of its drive, there are plenty of things you *can* do with it. You can explore it, to see what's on there already. You can add stuff, delete stuff, rename stuff, and so forth. Basically, you have a pretty free rein with it.

Your PC's Drives

To see exactly what disk drives are available on your computer, just open the My Computer icon on your desktop. The first few items shown will be icons for your disk drives. For example, the My Computer window shown here has icons for three disk drives: a floppy disk drive (drive A:), a hard disk (drive C:), and a CD-ROM drive (drive D:). There may be other icons inside your My Computer window. But for now, we're just concerned with the disk drives.

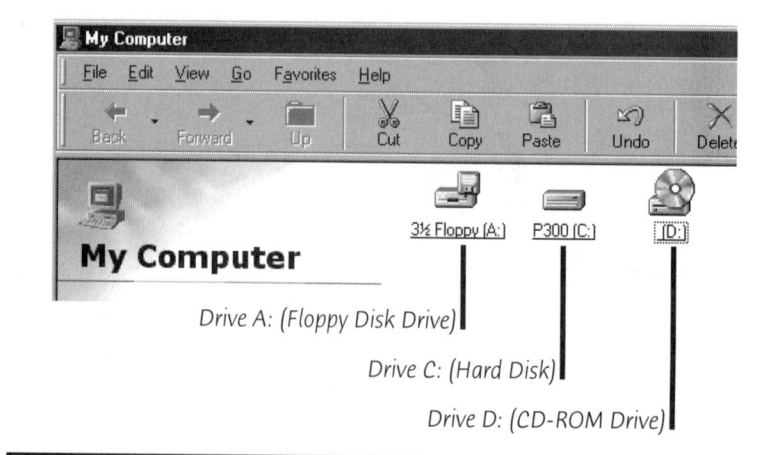

Drive A: (Floppy Disk Drive)
Drive C: (Hard Disk)
Drive D: (CD-ROM Drive)

144

To see what's on a particular disk, open its icon right there in My Computer. Since the hard disk is always in its drive, you can open that icon at any time.

The floppy disk drive and the CD-ROM drive might be empty of disks. If you try to open one of those icons while the drive is empty, you'll get an error message like the one shown in the margin. (If that message were written in normal English, it would probably say "I can't show you the contents of the disk in that drive, because there *is* no disk in that drive!" But we're stuck with this technical gibberish about the device not being "accessible," and "not ready.") The solution to this problem is simple: Put a disk into the appropriate disk drive and click the Retry button. If the disk is indeed readable, its contents will appear in the My Computer window.

Your hard disk can hold many thousands of **files**. A file is a single unit of storage. For example, when you create and save a document, that document is saved as one file. When you install a new program on your PC, the files that make up that program are also stored on your hard disk.

Files and Folders

Because a hard disk can contain many thousands of files, you're allowed to create **folders** to organize those files in whatever manner suits you best. In a sense, a folder is like a drawer in a file cabinet (there's that file cabinet metaphor again). The folder, like the drawer, holds its own unique set of files. The folder on a hard disk is different, however, because it can contain still more folders, as well as some files.

Allowing you to put folders inside of other folders lets you organize your files hierarchically, sort of going from the general to the specific. For example, you might decide to put all the documents you yourself create into your My Documents folder. But if you have thousands of documents, as most of us do, you'll probably want to break them down into smaller groups. For example, inside the My Documents folder you can have **subfolders** with names such as Photos, for photographs; Letters, for letters you've written; and Resumes, for the various versions of resumes you've composed.

Folders are arranged hierarchically

You'll see several examples of various ways to organize information into folders as we progress through this chapter. For now, the important thing to remember is that a disk stores files. The files on any disk might then be grouped into folders. A folder can contain any number of files, and can also contain folders of its own (subfolders).

145

6: EXPLORING YOUR PC

As your collection of files grows, creating folders will help you think of ways of organizing your files so that they're easy to find later. For example, you might not remember the exact filename of a recipe that you stored in a file on your hard disk. But if you put all your recipes in a folder named Recipes, it should be pretty easy to find the exact recipe within that group of files.

The Root Folder

Every disk has a **root folder** (also called a **root directory**) which is named simply \ (a backslash). The reason for this short name stems back to the early years of computers, before mice, when computer users had to communicate with the computer by typing *everything* at the keyboard. To minimize typing in those days, programmers tried to think of very short names for things. Since the backslash character (\ ) wasn't used for much else, someone decided to use that one character as the name of the root folder. So, the correct way to refer to "the root folder of my hard disk" is simply this: **C:**

Here the **C:** is the name of the drive, and the backslash (\) refers to the root folder.

Be careful: Don't confuse the backslash (\ ) with the forward slash (/)—they are not the same character. A backslash leans *back* on the character that precedes it. A slash leans *forward* on the character that comes after it.

Changing the Label on Your Hard Drive

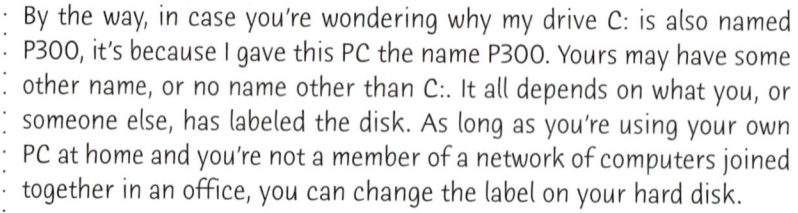

P300 (C:)

By the way, in case you're wondering why my drive C: is also named P300, it's because I gave this PC the name P300. Yours may have some other name, or no name other than C:. It all depends on what you, or someone else, has labeled the disk. As long as you're using your own PC at home and you're not a member of a network of computers joined together in an office, you can change the label on your hard disk.

LAN Users Beware: If you're using a computer at work, and your computer is part of a network, *don't* change the label on your C: drive. Other people on the LAN may not recognize that drive if you change its label.

Label: P300

To change the label, all you need to do is right-click the C: drive icon and choose Properties. In the Label textbox on the General tab, type any label up to 11 characters in length. (Not very lengthy, I know). Then click OK. When you get back to the My Computer window, your new label should appear within a few seconds. If it doesn't, choose View → Refresh from My Computer's menu bar.

The folders within the root folder are likely to have more meaningful names than a backslash. For example, if I open the icon for the C: drive on my PC, I immediately see a list of the contents of the root folder (\ ) for that drive immediately. Here's what it looks like:

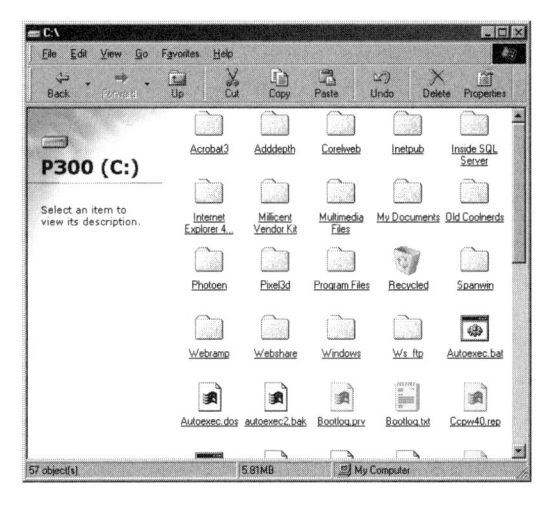

This window appears when I open the C: drive icon; it lists the contents of my PC's C: drive root (\ ) folder.

Other Folders under Root

As you can see, the root folder on my C: drive contains quite a few folders (these are the icons that look like manila file folders). And C: also contains some files, represented by icons other than file folders. (As you'll learn later, a file's icon gives you a clue as to what's inside that file.)

Windows 98 offers several tools for exploring the contents of disks. My Computer is one of them. The other two are Windows Explorer and Find. Of the three, Windows Explorer provides the best view of all the folders and files on a disk. So let's start there.

As its name implies, Windows Explorer is designed to help you explore the contents of your PC. More specifically, this handy program is your gateway to the contents of any disk that happens to be in your PC at the moment. When you first open Windows Explorer, however, it usually jumps right to the root folder of drive C:, because that's where most people prefer to begin their searching.

Windows Explorer

There are a couple of ways to start Windows Explorer. Feel free to use whichever one is most convenient at the moment:

- Click the Windows 98 Start button and choose Programs → Windows Explorer.

147

6: EXPLORING YOUR PC

- **Or,** if you happen to be in the My Computer window, you can right-click any drive's icon and, in the shortcut menu, choose Explore to explore that disk.

Shortcuts to Explorer: If you find yourself using Windows Explorer a lot, you might want to create a shortcut to it and put it right on your desktop and/or the Quick Launch toolbar. That'll give you easy access to Explorer at any time. You'll learn how to create shortcuts in Chapter 9. In a nutshell, all you need to do is right-drag the Windows Explorer option right off the Programs menu and drop it onto the Windows 98 desktop or the Quick Launch toolbar. In the shortcut menu, choose Create Shortcut(s) Here.

Your Guide to the Hard Disk

The Windows Explorer window opens, looking something like the example shown here.

The My Documents folder on your computer might not contain any folders or files at all. That's just because you haven't put anything in that folder yet, so don't worry about it.

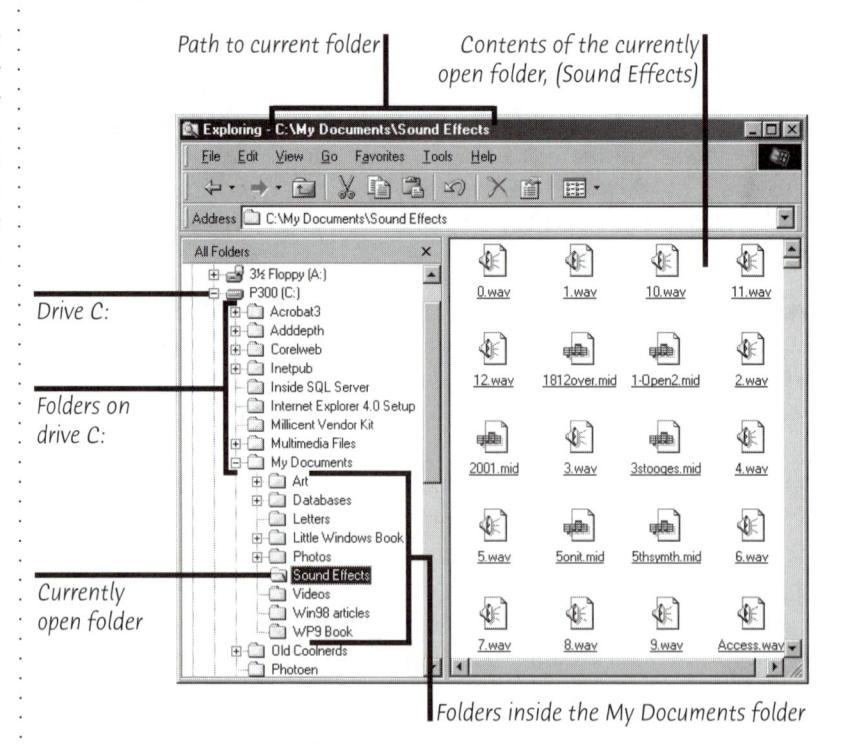

Path to current folder

Contents of the currently open folder, (Sound Effects)

Drive C:

Folders on drive C:

Currently open folder

Folders inside the My Documents folder

Windows Explorer, showing the contents of my C:\My Documents\Sound Effects folder.

148

Your own Explorer window won't look exactly like this, of course, because Explorer will show you the contents of *your* hard disk. However, it should show two panes just like this one. There's a bunch of folders in a hierarchical-style list in the left-hand pane, and a bunch of icons in the right-hand pane.

If you want to tweak your Explorer window to look more like mine, follow these steps:

▼ From Windows Explorer's menu bar, choose View → Explorer Bar → All Folders.

▼ Again from Explorer's menu bar, choose View → Large Icons.

That should be sufficient to see what you need to see right now.

Here, in a nutshell, is how you work the Windows Explorer window:

- Use the left pane to choose a disk drive to view, by clicking that drive's icon.
- Beneath the icon you clicked, and indented a little, you'll see all the folders and files on that drive.
- To see the contents of one of these folders, click the folder's icon. The little folder icon turns into an open folder, and the right-hand pane shows just the contents of that one folder.
- If a folder has a plus (+) sign next to it, that means it has still more folders inside.
- To see the folders inside such a folder, click the plus sign. The subfolders now appear under the folder, indented a little more.

For example, let's see how all of this has worked in my computer's Explorer window shown in the preceding section. I clicked the icon for my hard disk (C:). Then I clicked the plus sign next to My Documents. I can still see all the folders on C: listed in the left-hand pane. But I can also see the folders inside the My Documents folder listed in the right-hand pane. Then I clicked on the Sound Effects folder within My Computer, and that folder's icons are revealed in the right-hand pane. So in the Exploring window shown in the preceding section, you can see the contents of the Sounds Effects folder only.

Notice that when you open a folder that contains still more folders, the plus sign next to that folder changes to a minus sign (–). You can click that minus sign to "collapse" the folder, once again hiding the list of folders within that folder. The minus sign turns back to a plus sign.

Note: *The title bar for Windows Explorer says "Exploring" rather than the program name, Windows Explorer.*

Explorer in a Nutshell

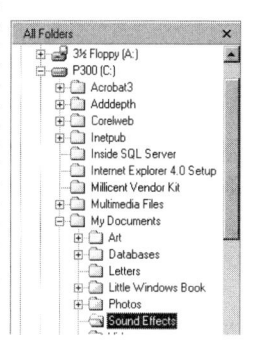

6: EXPLORING YOUR PC

Remember that the right-hand pane shows *only* the contents of the current folder (the folder you clicked on most recently). There are two ways to tell, at a glance, which folder is currently open:

- The little file folder icon is open.
- The **path** to the open folder is displayed in the Address Bar (and perhaps in Explorer's title bar, as well). We'll be learning about paths in the upcoming section.

If your Windows Explorer doesn't show an Address bar, choose View ➔ Toolbars ➔ Address Bar from Explorer's menu bar.

As you click around from folder to folder, the right-hand pane instantly redraws itself to show you the contents of whatever folder you just clicked on. And the Address bar instantly shows the path to the folder you just opened.

We'll return to the Explorer window a little later to see some options available to you for viewing its information. But first let's look further into this concept of **paths**, which you'll come across often in your work with your PC.

Paths

3stooges.mid

A **path** is sort of a roadmap to a particular file on a computer. For example, if you look inside the right-hand pane of my computer's Explorer window, you'll see that one of the Sound Effects files there is named 3stooges.mid. (It just so happens that this file contains the musical notes required to play the theme song from the old *Three Stooges* movies. But that's certainly not important at the moment.)

Parts of a Path

If I want to tell someone in everyday language how to get to that sound file, I can say "Go to drive C, open the My Documents folder, then open the Sound Effects folder. In that folder open 3stooges.mid." Computers, however, don't like big long sentences with lots of words in them. Here's how the computer describes the exact location and name of that file is:

C:\My Documents\Sound Effects\3stooges.mid

This is the path to the 3stooges.mid file. The path is a sequence of the various components of the route to this file, separated with backslashes (\ ) rather than words. The PC "knows," from this path, that in order to find a file named 3stooges.mid, it needs to go to drive C, then to the My Documents folder, and then to the Sound Effects folder inside My Documents.

150

All the paths you come across will follow this same format, going from the general (the drive letter C:) to the specific (the file named 3stooges.mid). Here's another example: A file named MyLetter.doc that's in the My Documents folder of drive C (not a subfolder) could be referred to as C:\My Documents\Myletter.doc.

General to specific

A couple of other buzzwords that you might hear in relation to folders are **parent** and **child**. A folder that contains subfolders is said to be the parent of those subfolders. The folders inside a parent folder are the **children** of that folder. Hence in this next illustration the My Documents folder is the parent to the folders named Art, Databases, Letters, and so forth, all the way down to the WP9 Book folder. Those folders are all children of the My Documents folder. Folders at the same level are said to be **siblings** of one another.

Parents and Children

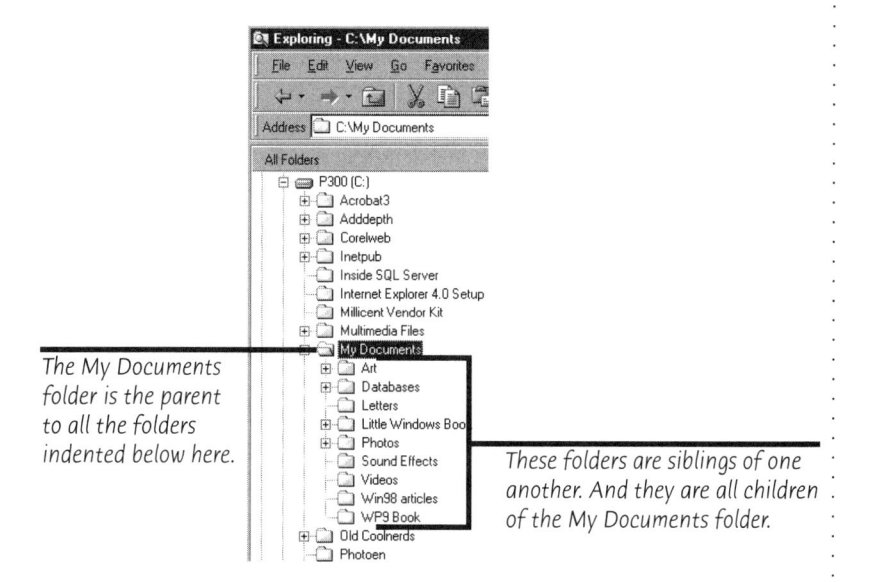

The My Documents folder is the parent to all the folders indented below here.

These folders are siblings of one another. And they are all children of the My Documents folder.

Before we get any deeper into this stuff, you might be wondering why your brand-new PC already has a zillion folders and files on it. The reason there are so many folders and files on most PCs is that the programs stored on the PC's hard disk occupy folders, just like anything else stored on the PC. And each program might actually consist of dozens or even hundreds of files, separated into any number of folders. You don't need to know anything right now about what's in those files and folders; in fact, you may *never* need to know much about

Why So Many Folders?

151

6: EXPLORING YOUR PC

them. The programs that use them do so on their own with no help needed from you.

Stay Away From Program Files: As a general rule you never, ever want to mess with the files that make up a program. You can browse around and look, but don't touch! There's really never any need to alter or reorganize the files that a program uses. When you **install** a new program (as we'll discuss in Chapter 8), the program will automatically create whatever folders it needs and will automatically copy the files it needs into the appropriate folders. If you ever remove (uninstall) the program, those folders and files will be deleted for you automatically.

For the most part, you only need to think about where you want to store the documents and other files that you create. We'll get to that shortly. For now, let's continue our exploration of your PC with Windows Explorer.

Explorer View Options

Now that we've completed our *most* thrilling discussion of paths, I'd like to get back to the subject we were discussing before the diversion: Windows Explorer. You've learned already that the idea behind that helpful program is simply this: You click on any icon in the left pane to see the contents of whatever that icon represents, which will appear in the pane on the right.

There are several different ways to view the contents of that right-hand pane. And you can choose any view that's helpful to you, from the View pull-down menu or from the View button in the toolbar. Your options are as follows:

- **Large icons**: Each folder or file is represented by a fairly large icon, as in the earlier Explorer window showing the Sound Effects files.
- **Small icons**: Each folder or file is represented by a smaller icon. This allows more items to be displayed within the pane. Take a look at the following group of illustrations.

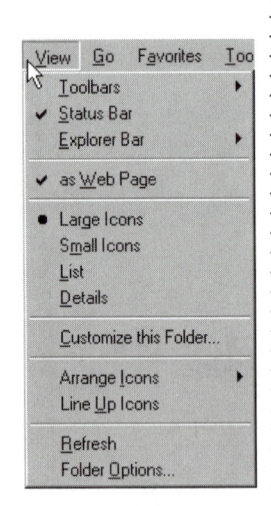

152

Small Icons view

List view

Details view

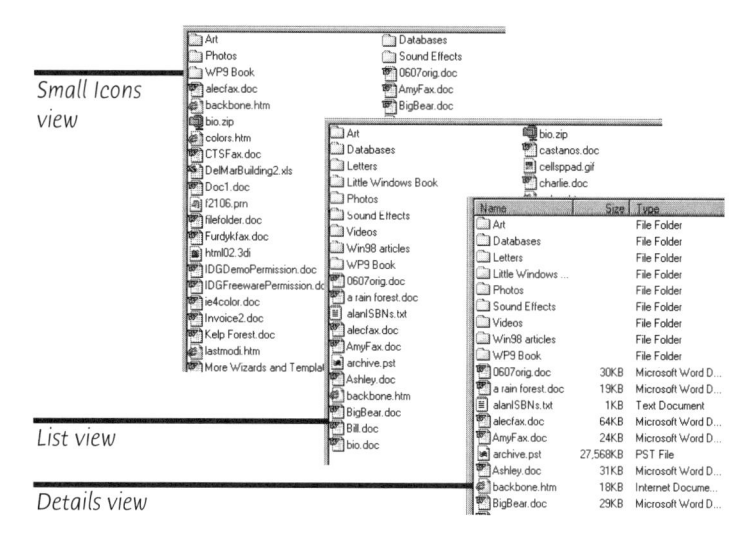

Various ways of viewing information in the right-hand pane of Windows Explorer.

- **List**: This view is similar to Small Icons view, but the folders and files are listed in alphabetical order down columns. Folders are listed first, followed by files.
- **Details**: This view offers lots of details about each folder and file, including name, size, type, and date last modified.

The Details view in Explorer is particularly handy because it gives you a lot of choices in determining how the information is displayed. For starters, you can adjust the width of any column simply by dragging one of the lines that separate the column heads. When the mouse pointer is correctly in position to drag, the mouse pointer changes into a two-headed arrow.

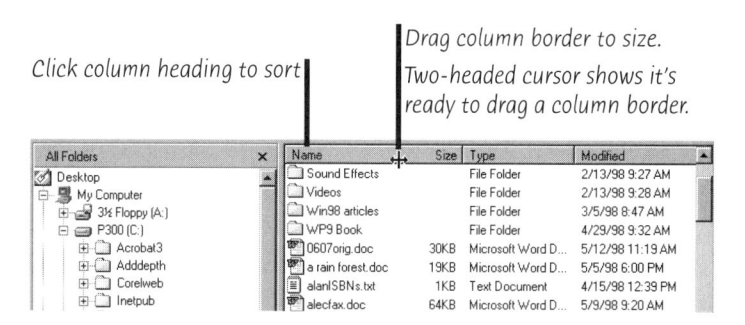

Using the Details View

Click column heading to sort

Drag column border to size.
Two-headed cursor shows it's ready to drag a column border.

In Details view you can adjust the width of each column.

You can also alphabetize or sort the information displayed in the pane, in either ascending or descending order. The following table shows how each order affects what you see.

Explorer Column Heading	Ascending Order	Descending Order
Name	Alphabetized A to Z	Alphabetized Z to A
Size	From smallest file to largest	From largest file to smallest
Type	Alphabetized A to Z	Alphabetized Z to A
Modified	Oldest to newest	Newest to oldest

As an example of how this detailed information could be useful, suppose you want to see which files in a particular folder are hogging the most disk space. All you need to do is sort the Size column in descending order so that the files are listed from largest to smallest. Then scroll to where you can see the first few files listed, and you'll be able to see which ones are the largest.

Maybe you need to see the newest files in a particular folder. You can sort the Modified column into descending order. Then the newest files in the folder will be listed first, on down to the oldest file.

You can also use the Arrange Icons menu option on Windows Explorer's View menu to organize icons by name, size, type, or date, regardless of which view you're using. I won't go into a lengthy discussion of all these options here, and I suggest you just experiment with Explorer's various configurations until you're familiar with them. You can't do any harm, and you may have some fun in the process. As with any other window, when you're finished with Windows Explorer, you can close it by clicking its Close (X) button.

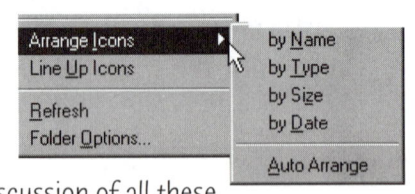

Exploring with My Computer

Like Windows Explorer, My Computer is a program that lets you browse around your system to see what's where. About the only difference between Windows Explorer and My Computer is that My Computer has only one pane. There is no left-hand pane showing all folders hierarchically.

When you first open My Computer, it displays one icon for each disk drive in your PC, as well as a few folders that we'll discuss later in this book. Here's an example using my PC:

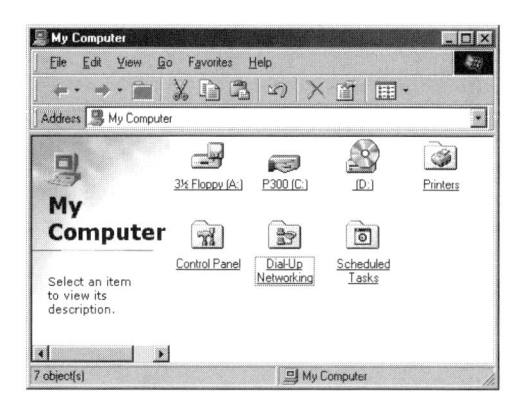

Levels in My Computer
First level

A sample My Computer display.

To view the contents of a drive or folder, just open its icon. For example, when I open the icon for my C: drive in My Computer, the window shows me the contents of the root folder of just drive C: (C:\):

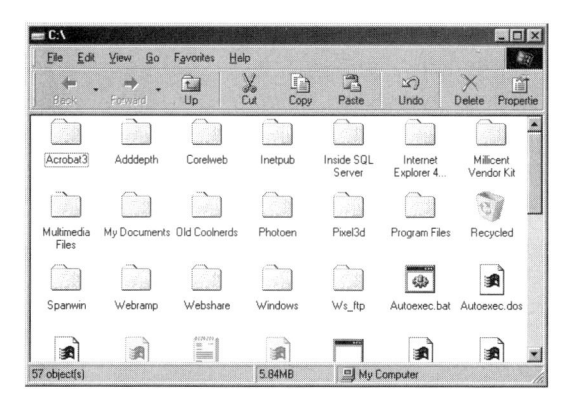

Next level

My C:\ folder.

If I click on the My Documents folder in this window, My Computer shows me just the contents of that folder.

Next level

If you find you've drilled down too deep in My Computer, you can return back to the parent folder, one level at a time, using any of the following techniques:

- Click the Up button in My Computer's toolbar.
- **Or**, choose Go → Up One Level from My Computer's menu bar.
- **Or**, just press the Backspace key.

Going Backward Up the Hierarchy

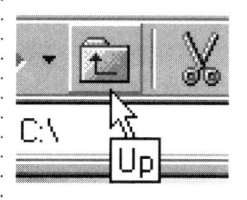

6: EXPLORING YOUR PC

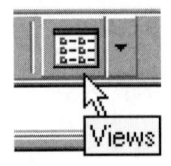

Views

My Computer offers all the same viewing options that are available for the right-hand pane of Windows Explorer. As in Explorer, these options are available from the View option in the menu bar, as well as from the View button in the toolbar. Again, I won't bore you with all the details of how those options work. You're far enough along in your basic skills that you can just experiment on your own.

Saving Your Stuff

Knowing how to use Windows Explorer and My Computer to browse around your hard disk and find things is a good skill to have. But the most important challenge for beginning computerists is keeping track of the files that you create and save. I can't tell you how many times people have told me that "the computer ate my file!" Truth is, computers don't eat files. In most cases, the person just didn't pay attention to *where* they saved the file. Or, in some cases, people forget what they named a file—another way for a file to get lost.

The trick is to get in the habit of storing all your documents in one folder, such as My Documents, or perhaps in a subfolder within My Documents, if you consistently work with a large number of files. You decide *what* to name a file, and *where* you're going to put it, when the Save As dialog box appears (right after you save the file). Let's look at an example.

Suppose I start up WordPad (Start → Programs → Accessories → WordPad). Within the WordPad program, I type up the letter shown here.

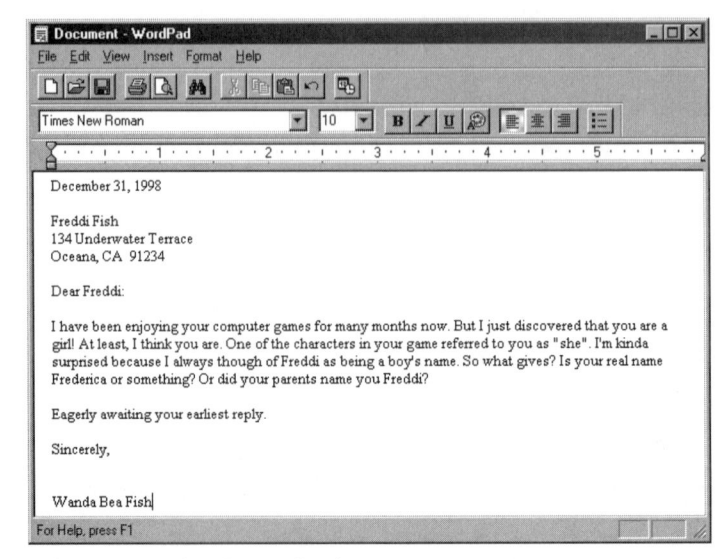

A letter I typed up in WordPad.

156

Now, let's say I want to save this letter so I can work on it later, or for future reference, or whatever. The way to save a document in virtually all Windows programs that allow you to save a document is to choose File ➔ Save from the program's menu bar (WordPad's menu bar in this example). Doing so brings up the Save As dialog box.

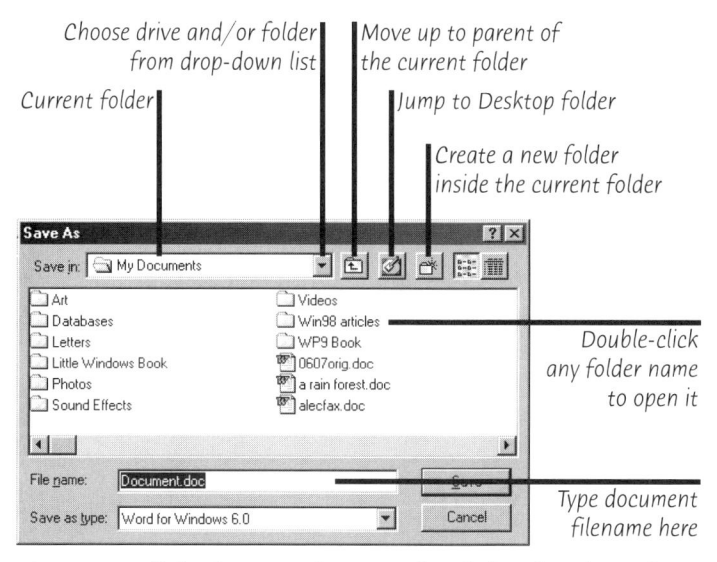

The Save As Dialog Box

Choose drive and/or folder from drop-down list
Current folder
Move up to parent of the current folder
Jump to Desktop folder
Create a new folder inside the current folder
Double-click any folder name to open it
Type document filename here

Note: *The Save As dialog box also appears when you download files from the Internet. It's important to keep track of those files too!*

The Save As dialog box contains several tools for choosing a drive and folder in which you want to save your file.

Whenever you see this Save As dialog box, it's time to stop and think a moment. Think about where you want to put this file, as well as what you want to name it. To specify where you're going to save it, you need to enter the appropriate path in the Save In text box. Let's see how to do this.

Choosing a Path

In the Save As dialog box shown just above, the current Save In folder is the folder named My Documents. If, indeed, you want to save the file in that folder, then you don't need to mess with the Save In text box at all. You can skip right to the next section, "Naming Your Files."

If you *do* want to choose another folder for the file you're about to save, you must **navigate to** (that is, work your way to), and open, the appropriate folder. You can use the tools I've pointed out in the sample Save As dialog box to navigate to the folder in which you want to store this document. As you navigate about, the Save In text box will automatically be updated to refer to whichever folder is open at the moment. Your goal is to get that Save In text box to specify exactly the drive and folder name where you want to store the current document.

Navigating to a Folder

157

Saving to the Desktop

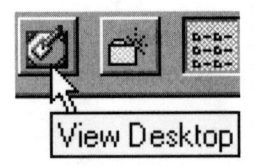

To save your file onto the Windows 98 desktop, where its icon is plainly visible along with all your desktop icons, click the View Desktop button, or choose Desktop in the Save In drop-down list (it's up at the top of the list). This might seem odd, but the truth of the matter is that your Windows 98 desktop really is just a folder on your hard disk, like any other folder. The path to the folder is C:\Windows\Desktop. The only thing that makes that folder different from any other is that you can see and change its contents right from the desktop. You don't need to navigate to the C:\Windows\Desktop folder first.

Naming Your Files

After you've selected *where* you're going to save this file, you need to come up with a name for the file. Try to think up a name that will be easy to remember, or easy to identify in the future.

- The filename can be up to 128 characters long.
- It can contain blank spaces.

Forbidden characters in filenames

- However, it cannot contain any of the following characters:

forward slash	(/)	question mark	(?)
backslash	(\ )	quotation mark	(")
greater than sign	(>)	pipe symbol	(|)
less than sign	(<)	colon	(:)
asterisk	(*)	semicolon	(;)
period	(.)		

Filename Extensions

A **filename extension**, which is added to the main part of the filename, consists of a period followed by one or more characters (usually three). Although you can add an extension to a filename if you wish, it's important to realize that the extension helps Windows keep track of which program was used to create the document. If you don't assign your own extension to the filename, the program you're using probably will. The extension assigned by the program will be the correct one for associating that document to the current program. So your best bet is probably *not* to type an extension. Just type a filename.

Hints for Filenames: I suggest you keep filenames short and put the most important word(s) at the start of the name. Take my letter to Freddi Fish, for example. I wouldn't want to name this document "A letter to Freddi"—mainly because later, when I view a list of filenames, this name would be alphabetized under A. A better name would be simply "Freddi" or "Freddi Letter."

Some programs will give you a choice of multiple formats for saving your document. Your best bet, however, is to just use whatever file type is already selected in the Save As Type drop-down list. That's the default (normal) format for the type of document you're saving. You'd only want to select one of the other formats shown if you need to export the document to some other program, and that program can only accept files stored in one of the other formats listed.

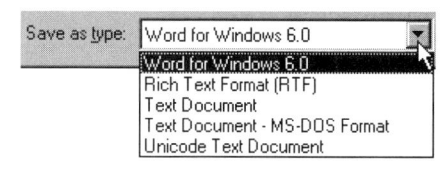

File Types

So now let's say I decide to save this document in my My Documents\Letters folder. Here are the steps I would follow:

Steps to Save a File

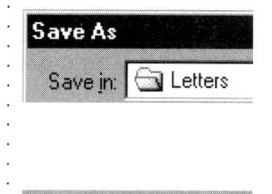

- First, I need to open the Letters folder by double-clicking its name in the Save As dialog box. The Save In text box will then read Letters, because that's the open folder at the moment. There aren't any files in the folder yet, so the large area in the main part of the Save As dialog box is empty.
- Next, I type **FreddiLetter** into the Filename text box.filename. I don't bother entering a filename extension.
- I leave the Save As Type as is, which means my letter will be saved as a .doc file.

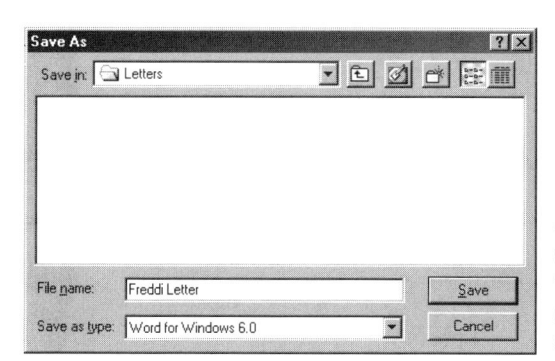

Ready to save this document as "Freddi Letter" in the Letters subfolder of C:\My Documents.

- Finally, I click the Save button to save the file. It takes a second or two for the computer to save the file in the place I've indicated. Then the Save As dialog box disappears, and I'm back to WordPad and my document.
- I can close WordPad now by clicking its Close (X) button or by choosing File → Exit from its menu bar.

6: EXPLORING YOUR PC

Overwriting Files: No two files in the same folder can have the same name. If you see a warning box indicating that the file you're about to save is going to overwrite (replace) an existing file with the same name, don't do anything until you're *sure* about the filename you've specified. If you are certain that it's OK to overwrite the existing file, you can choose Yes to proceed with the save. If you have any doubts at all, choose No and give the current document some other filename.

Opening a Saved Document

There are many ways to open a document you've saved. Using my new Freddi Letter document as an example, let's open a file using three different techniques.

From the Documents Menu

You already know about the Documents menu, which automatically keeps track of recently saved files. So you'll probably find your document listed there, and you can open both your document and the WordPad program from there. Click the Windows 98 Start button, point to Documents, and then click on the name of the file you want to open. I would click on Freddi Letter.doc, as shown here:

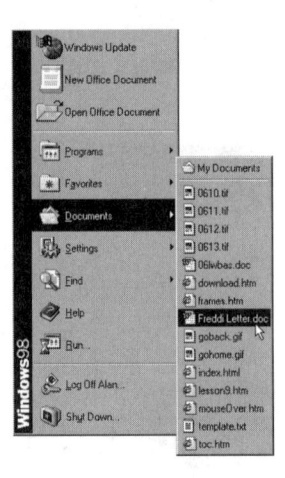

The Documents menu provides quick access to recently saved documents.

From Explorer or My Computer

If I had saved this file some weeks ago, it would no longer be appearing on my Documents menu. But I still have plenty of other options for opening that file. For example, I could browse to and open the \My Documents\Letters folder on my C: drive, using either Windows Explorer or My Computer. Once that folder is open, I can just click (or double-click) on Freddi Letter (or Freddi Letter.doc) to open that document and the WordPad application.

160

Windows Explorer showing the contents of the C:\My Documents\Letters folder.

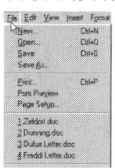

If I am in the WordPad program rather than the Windows 98 desktop when I need the Freddi Letter file, I can open the letter right from within WordPad. Like many programs, WordPad keeps track of recently saved documents right on its File menu. Just click File in WordPad's menu bar, and choose Freddi Letter.doc in that menu's list of most recently opened files.

From a File Menu

If Freddi Letter isn't in the list of most recently opened files on the File menu, then I have to go looking for it. In WordPad, and virtually all Windows programs that allow you to work with documents, choose File → Open from the menu bar and look for your file in the Open dialog box.

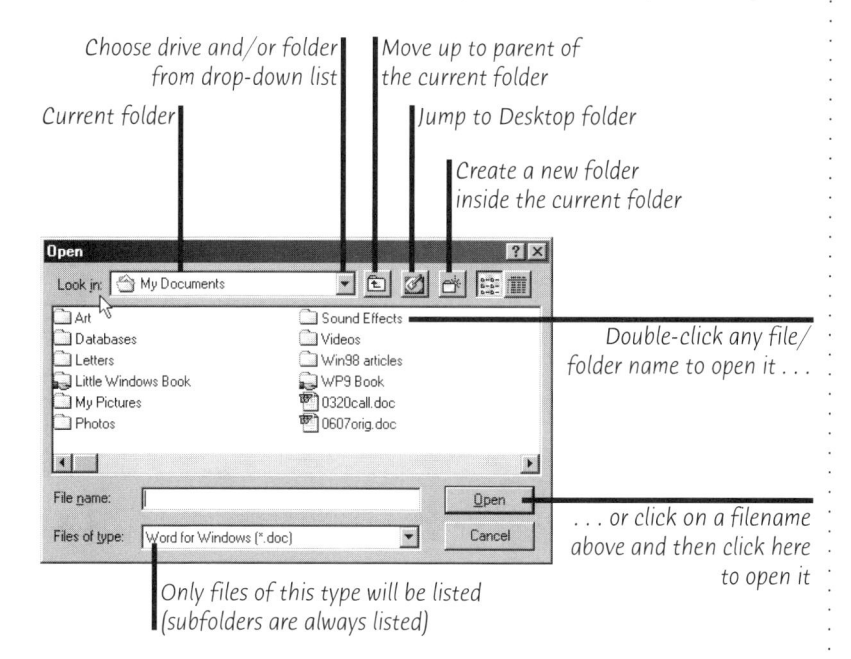

From the Open Dialog Box

Choose drive and/or folder from drop-down list
Current folder
Move up to parent of the current folder
Jump to Desktop folder
Create a new folder inside the current folder
Double-click any file/folder name to open it . . .
. . . or click on a filename above and then click here to open it
Only files of this type will be listed (subfolders are always listed)

161

In the Open dialog box, you need to first open the folder that contains the document you want to open (if that folder isn't open already). You can use the same basic tools offered in the Save As dialog box to look around here in the Open dialog box. More specifically:

- The Look In drop-down list always shows the name of the current folder.
- You can use the Look In drop-down list to navigate to another drive or folder.
- You can open any folder or file that's visible in the large main file list area, simply by double-clicking that folder or file.
- You can use the Up One Level button in the toolbar to move up to the parent folder of whatever folder is open at the moment.
- To jump to the Desktop folder, click the View Desktop button or choose Desktop from the top of the Look In drop-down list.
- To limit the filenames displayed to those of a certain type, choose a type from the Files of Type drop-down list. Or choose All Files (*.*) to view all files in the current folder.

Once the appropriate folder is open, an icon representing your document will appear. For example, here I've navigated to the My Documents\Letters folder on my C: drive, and you can see the icon for Freddi Letter right there in the dialog box.

If there are a lot of files in the folder, scroll bars will appear, and you can use them to look around further within the folder. When you find the file you want to open, click it once and then click the Open button. It's even faster to double-click the filename. The document will open in the current program.

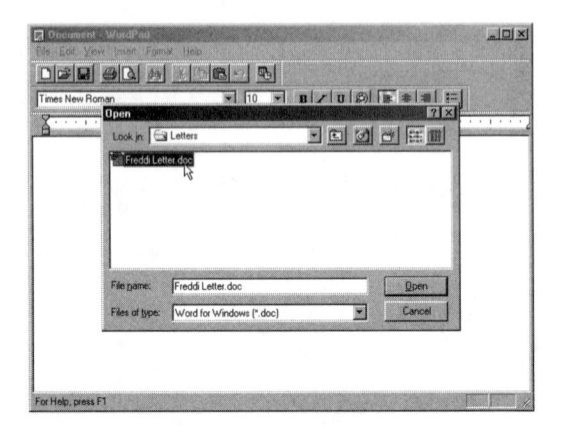

Let's take a moment to summarize all of this discussion about files and folders. The "logic" of it all goes something like this:

- Everything that's "in your computer" is actually stored as a file on hard disk, drive C:.
- Like any disk, your hard disk can be divided into folders, where each folder holds its own unique set of files.
- As a beginning user, your main concern is keeping track of what you name your files and where you save them.
- The Save As dialog box that appears when you first save a document will help you navigate to any drive and folder.
- You'll always want to navigate to the drive and folder where you plan to put the document—*then* click the Save button to save the file in the selected folder.

Once you've saved a document, reopening it is usually a simple matter:

- If you saved the document recently, it will probably be available for selection from the Documents menu item. Click the Start menu, point to Documents, and click the name of the file you want to open.
- If the file you want to open isn't in the Documents menu item, you can use My Computer, Windows Explorer, or Find (discussed a little later in this chapter) to locate the file.
- You may want to start the program that you originally used to create the file (WordPad, for instance). Choose File from that program's menu bar. If the name of the file that you want to open is right on the File menu, click that name to open the file. Otherwise, choose Open from the File pull-down menu, navigate to the document's filename, and then click that filename to open the document.

Now, even if you are very good about keeping track of where you save your files and remembering their names, there's a good chance you'll still lose track of a file now and then. Maybe more often than now and then, especially if you need to open some document that you haven't worked with in months. For those situations, there's the Windows Find program, which will obligingly search far and wide for any file you ask it to. That's our next topic.

What You've Learned

Finding Stuff

Both My Computer and Windows Explorer are sometimes referred to as "browsing" programs, because they let you browse around and see what's on a disk. But browsing isn't always the best way to find something that you need. For example, suppose you save a document as MyLetter.doc. When you go to reopen it, it's not where you were expecting it to be. Did someone delete the file? Perhaps. But the more likely event is that you've simply forgotten which folder you put MyLetter.doc in when you saved it. So before you go hollering at a coworker or a family member, you'd do well to check all the folders on your hard disk to see where that missing file might be.

Checking every folder on your hard disk using My Computer or Windows Explorer would be a tedious job. Wouldn't it be better if you could say to Windows, "Bring me my MyLetter.doc file—I don't care what folder it's in." Well, you can. That's exactly the kind of command the Find program lets you bark at your computer.

There are a couple of ways to get to Find:

- Click the Windows 98 Start button and choose Find ➔ Files or Folders
- **Or,** if you happen to be in My Computer, you can right-click on the icon of the disk you want to search and choose Find from the resulting shortcut menu.

Either way, you'll end up at the **Find dialog box**, which will look something like the one pictured here. The rest is pretty easy, but once again, you do need to think and pay attention to what you're doing.

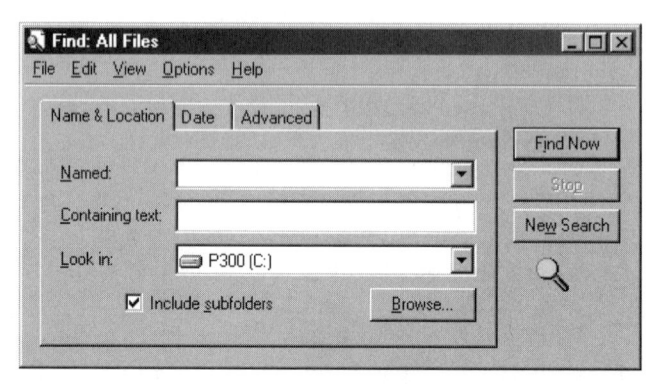

The Find dialog box lets you search an entire disk, or even several disks, to find a file or even several files.

The first step to using Find is telling it *where* you want to search. You do that by choosing a path from the Look In drop-down list. For example, if you want to search your entire hard disk, then make the Look In text box refer to C:, and check the Include Subfolders checkbox.

Where to Search

> **Include Subfolders Checkbox**: Don't overlook this important option when you're defining a search. If you *don't* select the Include Subfolders checkbox, Find will search only one folder—the current one—which may not be adequate to find what you're looking for.

If you know all or even part of the filename of the document you're looking for, you can type that information into the Named text box. For example, let's say I've forgotten where I saved my Freddi Letter.doc file and want to search for it now. I can type any part of that filename into the Named text box—say, **Freddi**—and then click the Find Now button. The Find program searches the disk and eventually lists all the filenames containing the word Freddi, like this:

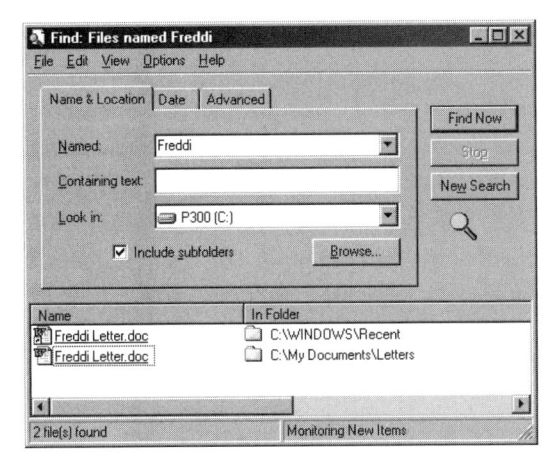

Searching for a Filename

Find located Freddi Letter.doc when searching for files with Freddi in the name.

As you can see, Find actually found two files named Freddi Letter.doc. One is in a folder named C:\WINDOWS\Recent. The other is in C:\MyDocuments\Letters. You'll often end up with what appears to be two copies of the same file, because Windows keeps track of recently saved files in a folder named C:\WINDOWS\Recent.

Real Files vs. Shortcut Files

However, if you look really closely at the icon for that version of the file, you'll see that it's really just a shortcut. (There's a little curved arrow in the lower left-corner of the icon). You want to open the *actual* file—not its shortcut. So in this example, if I want to open Freddi Letter.doc right now, I click (or double-click) the file that's in C:\My Documents\Letters.

6: EXPLORING YOUR PC

Need a closer look?
Remember, if you want to take a closer look at the icons inside Find, or in any other window that displays icons, choose View → Large Icons from the menu bar.

Opening the Containing Folder: Once Find locates a file for you, you may want to open its parent folder—the folder that contains the file you have found. Perhaps you need to see what other files are stored near that one. To accomplish this, you need to click on the file whose folder you want to inspect. Then choose File → Open Containing Folder from Find's menu bar.

Searching for Content

Suppose you forget not only where you put a file, but also what you named that file. Don't worry, all is not lost. If you can remember something that's in that document, you can still search for it using the Containing Text option in the Find window. This lets you search the contents of files, not just their names.

Be aware that this approach can take some time, because it takes a while to read the contents of every file on your hard disk.

Techniques for narrowing the search and speeding it up

You can speed things up considerably by narrowing the search down to a particular set of folders. In the Freddi letter example, I would search just folders that contain documents (since the file I'm searching for is a document).

Then, in the Containing Text text box, type whatever it is you remember about the contents of the file. For example, let's say I remember that I started the Freddi letter off with "Dear Freddi." So I can fill in the File window's Containing Text and Look In text boxes as shown just below. Now when I click the Find Now button, I get a list of all documents on the computer that contain "Dear Freddi."

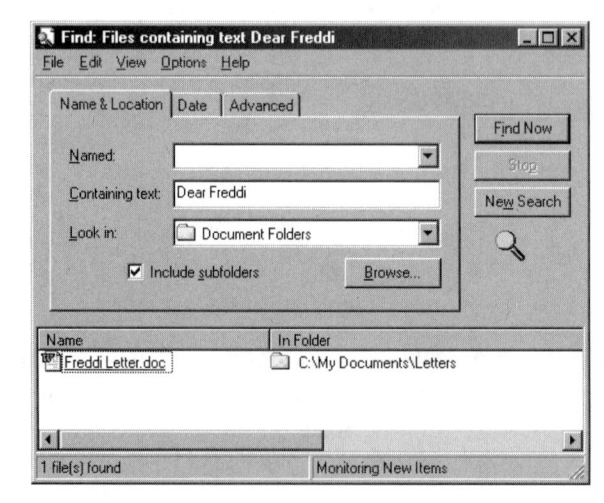

Results of searching for document files with "Dear Freddi" in them.

166

From these results I can see that one file, named Freddi Letter.doc, contains the words "Dear Freddi." I can see that the file is in C:\My Documents\Letters. And, I can open that file right now by clicking it (or double-clicking it).

You can also search for files based on when they were last saved. This can come in handy when you save some file without paying any attention at all to where you put it or what it was named. (This will probably happen to you a lot when you download stuff from the Internet.) Maybe all you can recall is that you saved the file today or on some other particular date. With Find, you can display the names of all files that were last saved on a given date, or within a range of dates.

Searching by Date

To use this approach:

▼ Start up Find in the usual manner.

▼ Be sure to define the scope of your search in the Look In textbox (for instance, drive C: if you want to search the entire hard disk, or C:\My Documents if you want to limit your search to the My Documents folder).

▼ Leave the Named and Containing Text text boxes empty.

▼ Then click the Date tab to reveal the options for searching by date.

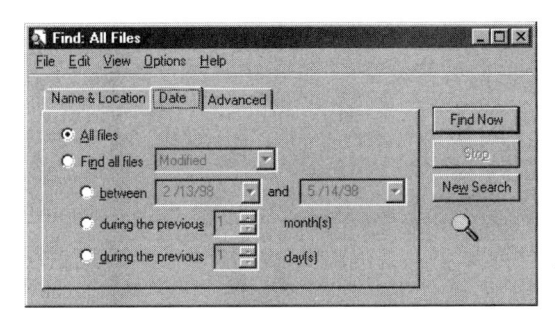

Here, I'm telling Find that I want to search all files by date.

Next you need to specify the calendar dates you're interested in. Keep in mind that Windows keeps track of three dates for every file you create: the date the file was created (first saved), the date the file was last modified, and the date the file was last accessed (opened) whether it was modified then or not. All this saved information means you can search for files that were created, modified, or opened on a particular date or within a range of dates.

Specify the Calendar Date

What day, or during what range of days?

6: EXPLORING YOUR PC

A Range of Dates

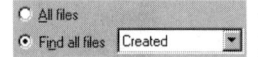

If you click the button for All Files option, the Find operation will list any file that was created, modified, or last opened within the range of dates you specify. To narrow things down, you can limit the search to the date the file was modified, created, or last accessed. For example, let's say I choose Created in the Find All Files drop-down list. Then I search for files dated 12/15/98. The files found will be only the files that were actually created on that date. Files that were modified or last accessed on that date won't be listed (unless they also happen to be created on that same date).

To specify a range of dates:

- To search for files dated between two dates, choose the Between button and fill in the range of dates to search for, using the m/d/yy format (for example, 6/1/99 or 12/15/99).

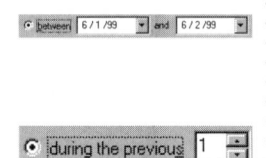

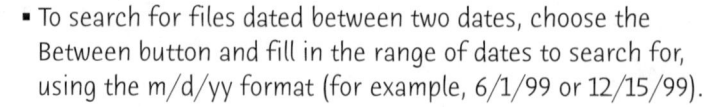

- To limit the search to files dated this month, and perhaps back a few months, too, choose the button for During The Previous 1 Month(s). Then set the number 1 to however many months back you want to search.

- To limit the search to files dated today, and perhaps a few days back, choose During The Previous 1 Day(s). Then set the number 1 to however many days back you want to search.

Here's a completed example: In this next Find window, I've opted to search for files that were accessed today—that is, "during the previous 1 day(s)." When I click the Find Now button, I get the the list of files that fit the date criteria I've entered.

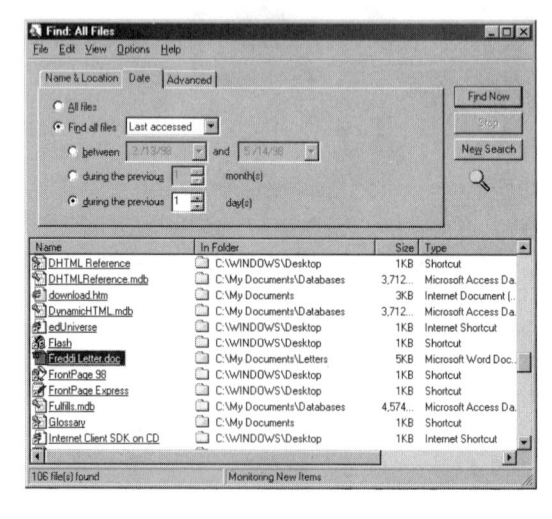

The results of a search for all files that were accessed today.

168

As it turns out, I've accessed quite a few files today, so the list is long. To simplify things, I can sort the list into alphabetical order by filename just by clicking the Name column heading. Scrolling down the list reveals that our trusty Freddi Letter.doc file has been found in this search.

You can also search for all files of a given **type**. For example, you can search for all files that you created with Microsoft Word, or all files that you created with Microsoft Access, or some other application. You can even search for files that are some exact **size**, or files that are less than or greater than a particular size. This option might come in handy if all you remember about a file is that it was especially large (say, greater than 5MB) or unusually small (say, less than 1K). Or, you might just want to see which files on your computer are taking up the most space.

Searching by Type or Size

▼ To get started, open the Find dialog box as usual and define the scope of your search using the Name & Location tab (as discussed earlier).

▼ Then click the Advanced tab and search by type or size. Here's how:

- To search by file **type**, choose the type of file you're interested in from the Of Type drop-down list. Click the Find Now button to find all the files that match your request.

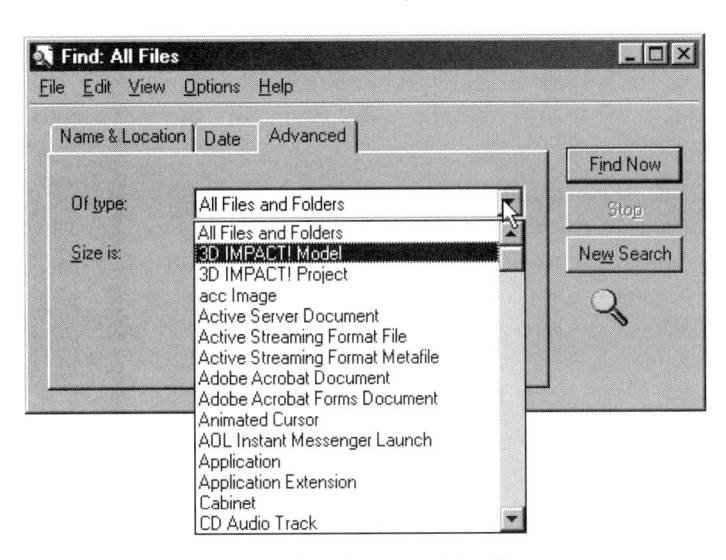

Using the Advanced tab of Find to search by file type.

- To search by file **size,** use the Size Is options on the Advanced tab of Find. Here I've asked Find to list all files that are 1MB (1024K) or larger.

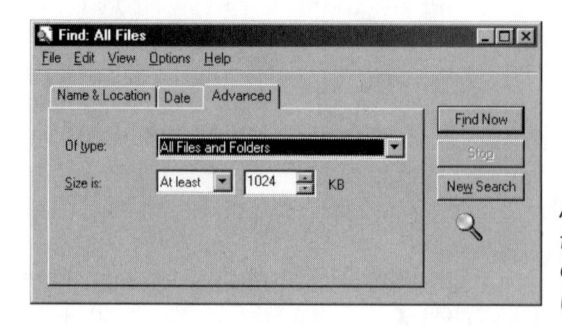

A search for files that are at least 1MB (1024K) in size.

Search Results Are Cumulative

Once you open Find, *each search you perform will be based on the results of the previous search.* For example, let's say you use Find to search all of drive C: for files that have the letter z in their filenames. When you click the Find Now button, the program produces that list of filenames for you.

If you do a subsequent search, it will be performed *only* on those files that are currently listed in the Find dialog box. For example, if after you've found your z files, you then search for files that were created today, you'll end up with only those files created today *and* that have the letter z in their filenames. That's because the second search is performed only on those files already listed in Find.

To remove the effect of cumulative searches and ensure that you're doing the broadest possible search, click the New Search button in the Find dialog box *before* you click Find Now. Doing so clears out the list of filenames already in Find and extends your search to the entire hard disk (or to whatever scope you've chosen in the Name & Location tab).

Summary

Whew! We've covered a lot of important stuff in this chapter. But understanding things like drives, folders, and files is critical to getting along with your computer and harnessing its power. Let's review the most important points:

- Each **disk drive** in your PC has a one-letter name followed by a colon. For example, your floppy drive is A: and your hard disk is C:. You may have additional drives, such as a CD-ROM drive named D:.
- A single unit of storage on a disk is a **file**. Each file has its own **filename**.
- Groups of files can be organized into **folders** on a disk.
- The Windows Explorer and My Computer programs help you browse through the folders and files on any disk.
- When you create your own documents using a program, you'll use the File ➔ Save options from that program's menu bar to **save** your work.
- The **Save As dialog box** that appears the first time you save a new document provides a place for you to give the document a filename and choose which folder you want to store that file in.
- Remembering where you stored a file is just as important as remembering what you named that file.
- You can **open** a previously saved document from the Documents menu, or from within My Computer or Windows Explorer, or from the results listed in the Find program's window.
- You can also open a document from within the program that you used to save the document. Just open the File menu and click on the name of the file to open. Or, if the filename doesn't appear on the File menu, choose Open from that menu and use the Open dialog box to look for and open the document.
- Whenever you lose track of a file, you can use the **Find program** to search the entire disk to find it, using whatever search characteristic you think will help identify the file you're looking for.

Copying, Deleting, and All That

7

In Chapter 6 you learned the basics of drives, folders, and files, and some fundamental skills for getting around your PC using My Computer, Windows Explorer, and Find. Here in this chapter you'll expand on those skills and learn to do what some people call "housekeeping tasks" on your PC—which means you learn how to copy, move, rename, and delete folders and files. How often you'll need to perform these tasks is entirely up to you. But they are the kind of tasks most PC users have to perform from time to time, so it's good to know the procedures.

TO ECONOMIZE ON DISK SPACE, ANYONE WHO'S OBSOLETE MAY BE ASKED TO JOIN OUR FRIEND, MR. RECYCLE BIN.

7: COPYING, DELETING, AND ALL THAT

Folder Options

Throughout most of this chapter you'll be learning how to create, copy, delete, and rename folders and files. The programs you'll use to do these things are the same programs you learned about in Chapter 6: Windows Explorer, My Computer, and Find. But first things first: Before we get into specifics, you need to consider the adjustment of some general **folder options** that influence the behavior and appearance of those three programs.

To set these folder options the way you want for all three programs, you need to start from the Start button, not from within a specific folder. Here are the exact steps:

▼ Click the Windows 98 Start button.

▼ Point to Settings.

▼ Click Folder Options.

Pretty simple, no? Here's the Folder Options dialog box, with the General tab open:

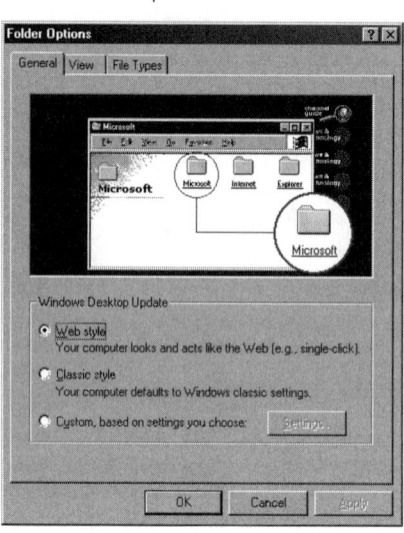

You first met up with the Folder Options dialog box when we discussed Web-style and Classic-style navigation, way back in Chapter 1 (under "To Click or Double-Click?"). Recall that in Web-style navigation, you can open icons with a single mouse click. In Classic-style navigation, you have to double-click icons to open them. Make sure you have chosen the setting you want.

Custom Settings for Folders

The third option on the General tab, Custom, lets you further refine the appearance and behavior of icons and such. Click the Custom option, then the Settings button, and you'll come to the Custom Settings dialog box. Following are brief descriptions of what each custom setting offers.

174

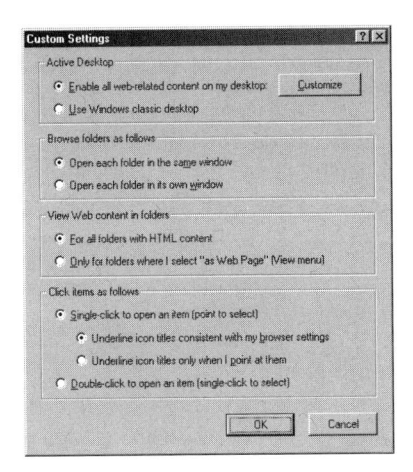

Custom Settings	Description
Enable All Web-related Content on My Desktop	Turns on the active desktop, as discussed in Chapter 15.
Use Windows Classic Desktop	Turns off the active desktop.
Open Each Folder in the Same Window	Windows Explorer and My Computer will display folder contents in one window.
Open Each Folder in Its Own Window	My Computer will create a new window for each folder icon you open, allowing you to view the contents of several folders at once.

If you opt to turn on the last folder option, to open each folder in its own window, here's a good trick to know: If you hold down the Shift key while clicking the Close (X) button on the currently open window, you'll close that window and all the windows that led up to it!

You might think **Web content** is a strange name for that stuff that appears in a folder. The term "Web" refers, of course, to the World Wide Web on the Internet. However, the Web content in a folder really doesn't come from the World Wide Web at all. The only thing that's similar about Web content on the Internet and Web content in a folder is that both types of content are formatted using a technology known as HTML.

Settings for Web Content

But there's no reason for you to understand HTML now—there are many other important things to discover in your expedition through Windows 98. When we get to Chapter 15, you'll learn more about how you can link up your Windows active desktop with information that really does come from the Internet's World Wide Web.

Let's look at the Web content settings:

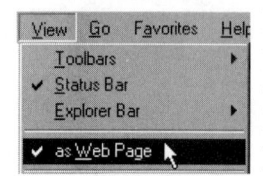

7: COPYING, DELETING, AND ALL THAT

View Web Content in Folders...	Description
For All Folders with HTML Content	Makes Web content visible in every window that offers such content. The content varies from folder to folder, but usually appears at the left edge of the window.
Only for Folders Where I Select "As Web Page" (View menu)	Makes Web content invisible in all folders, unless you specifically choose View→As Web Page from that folder's menu bar.

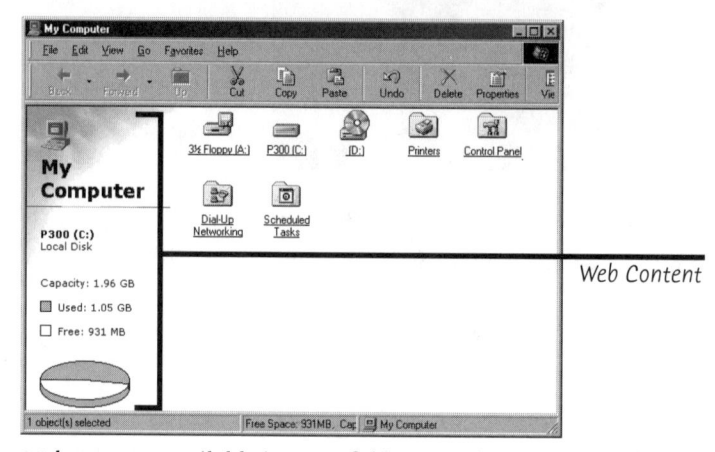

Web content, available in some folders, can be visible or hidden.

Settings for Mouse Clicking

Custom Settings	Description
 **Single-click to Open an Item (Point to Select)**	Lets you open icons by clicking them once, and to select by pointing ("selecting" is discussed later in this chapter).
 **Underline Icon Titles Consistent with My Browser Settings**	When you turn on the Single-click setting, you can choose this option to make icons on your desktop look like hyperlinks in Web pages (for consistency).
 **Underline Icon Titles Only When I Point at Them**	When you turn on the Single-click setting, you can choose this option to remove underlining from icon titles, if you want. The underlines won't appear until the mouse pointer is actually touching the icon or its label.
 **Double-click to Open an Item (Single-click to Select)**	Enables "Classic" Windows clicking scheme; you double-click icons to open them, and single-click icons to select them ("selecting" will be discussed a little later in this chapter). **Note:** Turning on this option disables the two Underline settings just above.

176

7: COPYING, DELETING, AND ALL THAT

You're welcome to choose whatever options seem most comfortable to you for working with folders in Explorer, My Computer, and Find. If you want your desktop to look and act like mine, choose the settings shown in the preceding illustration of the Custom Settings dialog box. Then click OK to return to the Folder Options dialog box.

The View tab of the Folder Options dialog box contains a long list of settings, as described in the following table. If you're not sure which options to choose, just choose the same ones as shown in the View tab illustrated here — they will work fine for you until you get more familiar with your own needs.

View Tab

Don't forget about that little question-mark button near the upper-right corner of the dialog box. You can click that little button and then click any Folder setting to get more information on that setting.

Settings for Files and Folders	Description
Remember Each Folder's View Settings	If you change the View settings within a particular folder window, those settings will be "remembered" on future visits to that folder. Clearing this check-box prevents Windows from remembering View settings you apply to individual folders on-the-fly.
Display the Full Path in Title Bar	Shows the full path to a folder (e.g., C:\My Documents\Letters) in the folder window's title bar, rather than just the name of the current folder (e.g., Letters).
Hide File Extensions for Known File Types	Hides file name extensions (like .doc and so forth) on most files. I prefer to leave this option turned off. But if you find those little filename extensions intimidating or irritating, you can choose this option to hide them.
Show Map Drive Network Button in Toolbar	Only relevant if you're an active member of a local area network of computers. Don't worry about it unless you're familiar with network drives and want a toolbar button to map network drives.
Show File Attributes in Details View	Shows file attributes such as Read-only and Hidden when you're using the Details view of Explorer, My Computer, or Find. We'll discuss these and other file attributes a little later in this chapter.

Settings for Files/Folders

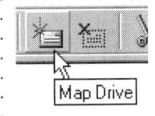

177

7: COPYING, DELETING, AND ALL THAT

Settings for Files/Folders (cont.)	Show Pop-up Description for Folder And Desktop Items	If you disable this option (by clearing its checkbox), you'll no longer see those little tooltips that appear on the Windows 98 desktop when you point to icons.
	Allow All Uppercase Names	Whenever you create filenames in all capital letters (MYLETTER.DOC), Windows automatically converts them to lowercase with initial caps (Myletter.doc), just for consistency. If you have a major hankerin' for all-caps filenames, you can choose this option.
Settings for Hidden Files	This next batch of settings is for hidden and system files. **Hidden files** have had their Hidden attribute (discussed later in this chapter) turned on. **System files** are files that Windows absolutely, positively must have to even get your computer started. These three options let you decide how much you want to protect those files by keeping them hidden from view.	

Settings for Hidden Files	Description
Do Not Show Hidden or System Files	The safest setting. Keeps all system files and Hidden files from appearing in Windows Explorer, My Computer, and Find.
Do Not Show Hidden Files	Keeps vital system files from view, but makes Hidden files visible in Windows Explorer, My Computer, and Find.
Show All Files	Least safe setting. All files on the disk are visible.

Visual Settings	Some of the visual setting options were described under "Customizing Icons and Screen Effects" in Chapter 5. In the context of our discussion here, they apply to the Windows Explorer, My Computer, and Find programs rather than to the screen as a whole.

Visual Settings	Description
Hide Icons When Desktop Is Viewed as Web Page	Be careful—choosing this option makes all your desktop icons invisible when you're using the active desktop (discussed in Chapter 15). I recommend leaving this option turned off.
Smooth Edges of Screen Fonts	If you have a reasonably fast computer (Pentium, Pentium II), enable this option to get rid of "jaggies" on screen fonts displayed in folder windows.
Show Window Contents While Dragging	If you have a fast computer, enable this option to have your screen show the actual window that you're dragging, rather than just a ghost image of that window.

As always, you can just click the OK button at the bottom of the dialog box to save the Folder Options/View settings and close the dialog box. The settings you chose will be applied to the current work session, and all future sessions, unless you specifically change the settings again in the future.

Finding the Files You Need

Much of this chapter is about managing files. By *managing files*, I mean doing things like deleting old files you don't need any more, to make room for new files. Or making copies of files to keep as extra backups. In order to do any of these file-management tasks, you first need to **find** the files you want to work with. And then, if you want to do something to a whole bunch of files, you need to **select** those files first.

To find the files you want, you can just browse to the file's folder using My Computer or Windows Explorer. If the files aren't all in one folder, or you're not sure which folder the files are in, you can use Find to locate all files of a specific type, or files with certain characters in the filenames. In short, you can use any techniques described in Chapter 6 to get to the files you want to manage.

With My Computer

Let's say I want to find a file from Chapter 6 of this book. I know that the path to the Chapter 6 files is **C:\My Documents\Little Windows Book\ch06** because I created that folder and put those files there. So, to get to those chapters I could open My Computer, then open the icons for drive C:, then My Documents folder, then Little Windows Book folder, and then ch06 folder. Or I could take the shortcut and open My Documents from its icon on the Windows 98 desktop. Then from there, I could open the Little Windows Book and ch06 folders. Either way, I end up viewing the files I created while writing Chapter 6.

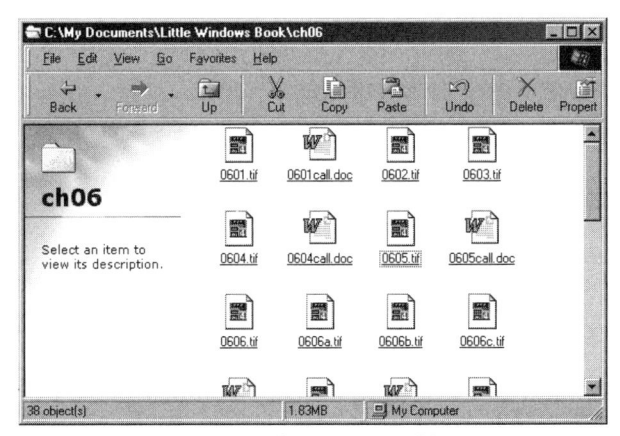

The My Computer view of Chapter 6's files.

7: COPYING, DELETING, AND ALL THAT

With Explorer Another way to go is to use Windows Explorer (Start ➔ Programs ➔ Windows Explorer). In Explorer's left-hand pane, I could open the My Documents, Little Windows Book, and ch06 folders to get to my Chapter 6 files. I'd end up in the Windows Explorer view of these same files.

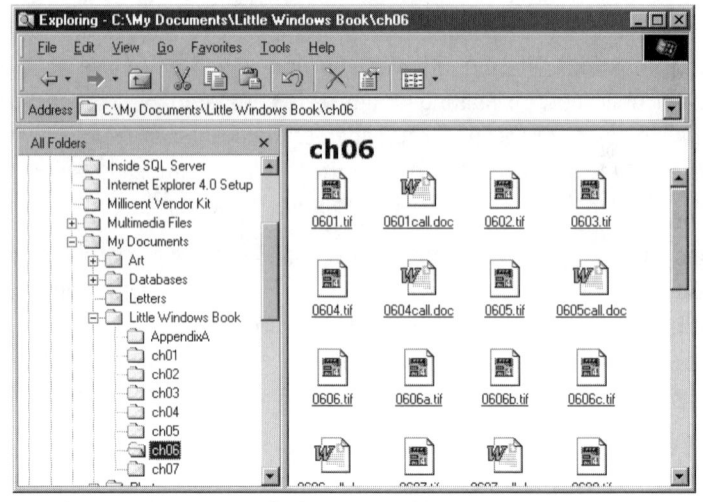

Windows Explorer view of Chapter 6's files.

With the Find Program Or, since I named all those files consistently, with the first two characters 06, I could use Find to locate all files with 06 in their filenames. In the resulting view, I could sort on the Name column (by clicking that column heading) to put the files into alphabetical order by name. Or I could click the heading of the In Folder column, to get all the files clumped together by folder. Then I'd just scroll down to where the files from C:\My Documents\Little Windows Book\ch06 files are stored.

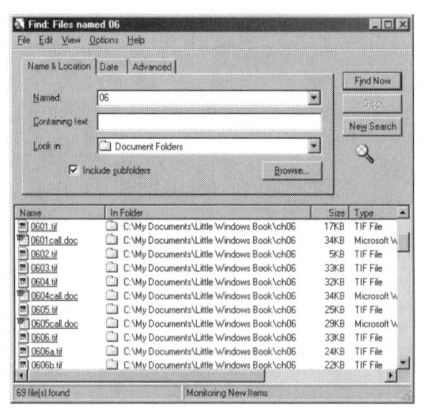

Find's view of Chapter 6's files.

180

Once you see the icon for the file you want—it doesn't matter if you got there via Windows Explorer, My Computer, or Find—there are a couple of things you can do right off the bat to manage that file:

- Right-click the icon to view the shortcut menu—a quick route to many of the tasks you need when working with files and folders.
- To open the file, click it (or double-click it in Classic-style windows navigation).

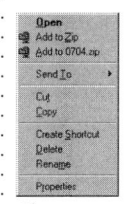

Shortcut menu

In many cases, you'll want to manage several files and/or folders in one fell swoop. For example, you might want to delete several files from a folder. Or you may want to copy a bunch of files from your hard disk to a floppy disk. In those situations you can use any of the following **selection techniques** to select two or more files. Notice that the table describes both forms of these file-selection techniques: one for Web-style navigation and one for Classic-style.

Selecting Files and Folders

Action to Select Files/Folders	Web-Style Navigation	Classic-Style Navigation
Select file/folder, deselect others	Point	Click
Select file/folder without deselecting	Ctrl+Point	Ctrl+Click
Deselect selected file or folder	Ctrl+Point	Ctrl+Click
Extend selection to this file/folder	Shift+Point	Shift+Click
Extend selection without deselecting any selected files or folders	Ctrl+Shift+Point	Ctrl+Shift+Click

Note that most file-selection techniques involve holding down one or more keys on the keyboard while you point or click with the mouse.

When you select a file or folder, its name and icon are highlighted in some manner. For example, here the selected files all have their names shown as white letters against a black background:

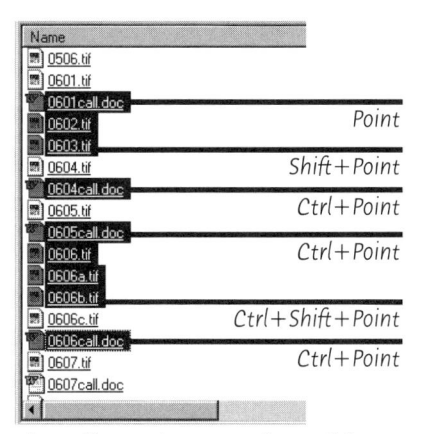

Point
Shift+Point
Ctrl+Point
Ctrl+Point
Ctrl+Shift+Point
Ctrl+Point

The callouts show you what I did to select these files.

7: COPYING, DELETING, AND ALL THAT

Steps for Selecting   Here are the steps I followed to select these files (using Web-style navigation):

▼ I started by selecting (pointing to) the topmost selected file, 0601call.doc.

▼ Then I held down the Shift key and pointed to 0603.tif. This selected 0602.tif, as well.

▼ Then I held down the Ctrl key and pointed to 0604call.doc and then 0605call.doc.

▼ Then I held down both Ctrl and Shift and pointed to 0606b.tif. All the files in between were selected.

▼ Finally, I held down Ctrl and pointed to 0606call.doc.

Keep That Key Held Down! The main thing to remember when selecting files in a file list is that if you point or click *without* holding down the Shift or Control key on the keyboard, you instantly deselect all files that you've already selected. Generally, you don't want this to happen when you're trying to select multiple files!

Lassoing Files and Folders   As an alternative to using the keyboard and mouse, you can select files by dragging a **frame**, or **lasso**, around them. That technique might work well, for instance, when you're using the Large Icons view in My Computer.

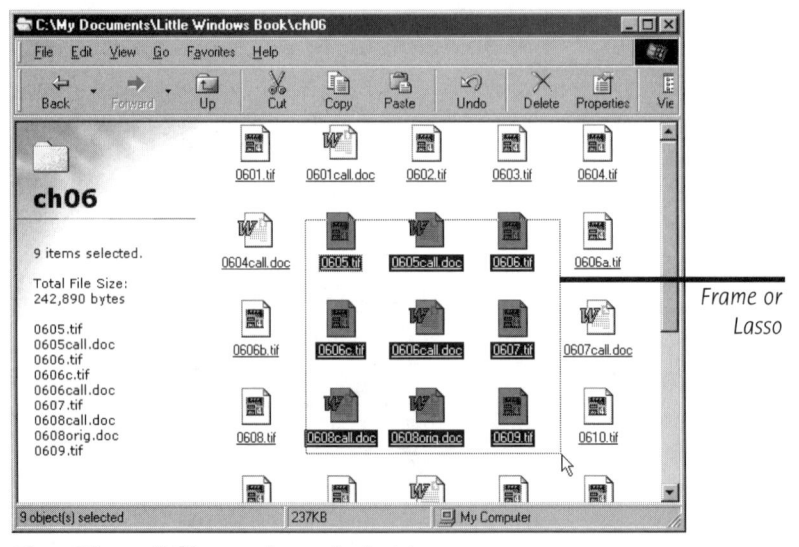

Frame or Lasso

These "framed" files can be worked with as a group.

182

To use the **lasso technique**, follow these steps:

▼ Move the mouse pointer so it's touching just outside the top-left corner of the *first* icon you want to select.

▼ Hold down the primary mouse button and drag the mouse pointer toward the *last* icon you want to select.

▼ When all the files and/or folders you want to select are highlighted, release the mouse button.

> You can combine the lasso and Ctrl+click techniques to refine your selection. For example, if you lasso too few or too many files, you can hold down the Ctrl key to increase or decrease the selection. Then point to selected files you want to deselect, or point to unselected files you want added to the selection.

To select all the file and folder icons within a folder, choose Edit → Select All from that window's menu bar. Or press Ctrl+A. Every icon will be selected (highlighted). If necessary, you can deselect some files by holding down the Ctrl key as you click the items you want to deselect. To instantly deselect all the icons, just click a neutral area within the window, perhaps just next to a selected item.

Selecting All Icons
Ctrl+A is the shortcut for Edit → Select All

If you're viewing files in the Details or List view, and your hands happen to be on the keyboard rather than the mouse, it may be easier or faster for you to **use the keyboard to select files**. (The keyboard doesn't offer as much flexibility as the mouse, however.) To move the selection highlighter from one file's icon to the next, use the arrow keys. To select multiple files, hold down the Shift key as you move from file to file with the arrow keys.

Selecting with the Keyboard

So now that you've added a few more basic skills and concepts for working with your files, let's look at the specifics of renaming, deleting, copying, and moving those files.

Sometimes you might want to change the name of some file or folder you've created. **Changing the name** of a file or folder doesn't affect its contents at all. You're only changing the label that appears next to or under its icon. (The computer uses this name, of course, to identify the file.)

Renaming a File or Folder

You can rename any folder or file on your hard disk, or on floppy disk. Be careful, however—if you don't know what's inside a file, you shouldn't rename that file. You cannot rename anything on a CD-ROM, because CD-ROM disks are read-only.

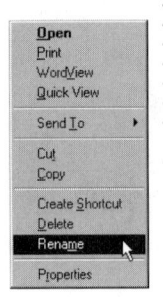

When you do want to rename a file you created earlier, follow these steps:

- ▼ Use Windows Explorer, My Computer, or Find to get to the icon for the file/folder that you want to rename.

- ▼ Right-click the file/folder's icon, and choose Rename from the shortcut menu. The current name is highlighted, and the blinking cursor appears next to that name.

- ▼ Start typing the new name, and it will replace the old one. Or you can use the standard text-editing techniques to change the existing name to the new name. (By "standard text-editing techniques," I mean the Backspace and Delete keys, the arrow keys, etc.) Don't change the filename extension, the part after the dot. That part of the name tells Windows which program you used to create that file. If the file currently has no visible extension, don't add one.

- ▼ Press the Enter key, or click anywhere outside the file or folder's icon to save the new name.

- ▼ If, after renaming a file or folder, you want to reorganize icons by name, choose View ➔ Arrange Icons ➔ By Name from the current window's menu bar. (Or, if you're in Details view, click the Name column heading.)

That's all there is to that. To sum up: Just right-click the file you want to rename, type in the new name, and then click anywhere outside that icon to save the new name.

Deleting Files and Folders

Deleting a file means removing it from your hard disk. Permanently. About the only reason to delete a file is to get rid of it to make space for new files. Returning to our good ol' filing cabinet metaphor, deleting a file on your hard disk is roughly equivalent to taking a file out of your real file cabinet and throwing it in the trashcan.

You want to be very, very careful when deleting files and folders. Most of the files on your computer belong to programs, and those programs won't work anymore if you delete their files. As a general rule, you don't ever want to delete a file unless you know *exactly* what that file is, whether it's used by other programs or people, and you are absolutely certain you and they can live without that file.

184

Deleting a folder is just as easy as deleting a file. However, the results can be far more devastating. When you delete a folder, you delete all the files and subfolders within that folder. That could be *hundreds* of files, wiped out with just a few mouse clicks. This is not a mistake you ever want to make. Before you delete a folder, make sure you know *exactly* what subfolders and files are in that folder. And make sure you can live without those files and folders.

Given that little lecture, here are the steps for deleting a file or folder:

Steps for Deleting

▼ Use Windows Explorer, My Computer, or Find to locate the files/folders you want to delete. (You can't delete files from a CD-ROM.)

▼ If you want to delete a single file or folder, right-click its icon, choose Delete from the shortcut menu, and click Yes when asked for confirmation. You can then skip the next two steps.

▼ If you want to delete several files or folders, use the selection techniques described earlier in this chapter to select the icons of the files and folders you're *sure* you're ready to part with.

▼ When the icons for the files/folders that you want to delete are selected—make sure *only* those icons are selected—you're ready to delete. Right-click any selected icon, choose Delete, and click the Yes button when asked for confirmation.

The files will be deleted, and no longer visible in the folder.

In addition to right-clicking an icon and choosing Delete from its shortcut menu, you can also delete all the selected files and folders using either of these techniques:

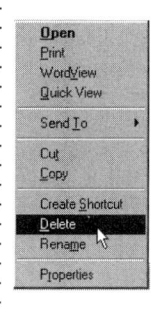

Other Ways to Delete

   • Drag the selected files/folders onto the Recycle Bin icon on the desktop, and drop them there (explanation of Recycle Bin coming right up).

   • **Or,** simply press the Delete (Del) key.

The end result is the same: The files are deleted from their folders. If you deleted folders, the files within are deleted.

When you delete files from your hard disk, they aren't irrevocably deleted; they are actually just moved to a special folder called the Recycle Bin. Which brings us to our next topic . . .

7: COPYING, DELETING, AND ALL THAT

Using the Recycle Bin

The Windows 98 **Recycle Bin** is sort of a safety net for files you delete from your hard disk (but not from floppy disks; see the Warning coming up). It gives you a second chance to change your mind before permanently deleting a file from your hard disk.

> The Recycle Bin does *not* keep copies of files deleted from floppy disks and other removable media. It works only with nonremovable hard disks inside your computer. Be *extra* cautious when deleting files from floppy disks, zip disks, and so forth, because there is *no* safety net for these!

The only problem with the Recycle Bin is that it grows and grows. In fact, when you delete a file from your hard disk, you really don't recover any disk space at all (well, not just yet, anyway). That's because you really just moved the file from its current folder to the Recycle Bin's special folder. To truly recover the space used by those deleted files, you must delete those files permanently. That means getting them out of the Recycle Bin.

Recycling Your Disk Space

To open the Recycle Bin, click the Recycle Bin icon on the Windows 98 desktop. In the Recycle Bin window, icons in the right-hand pane represent "deleted" folders and files that haven't truly been removed from the hard disk yet.

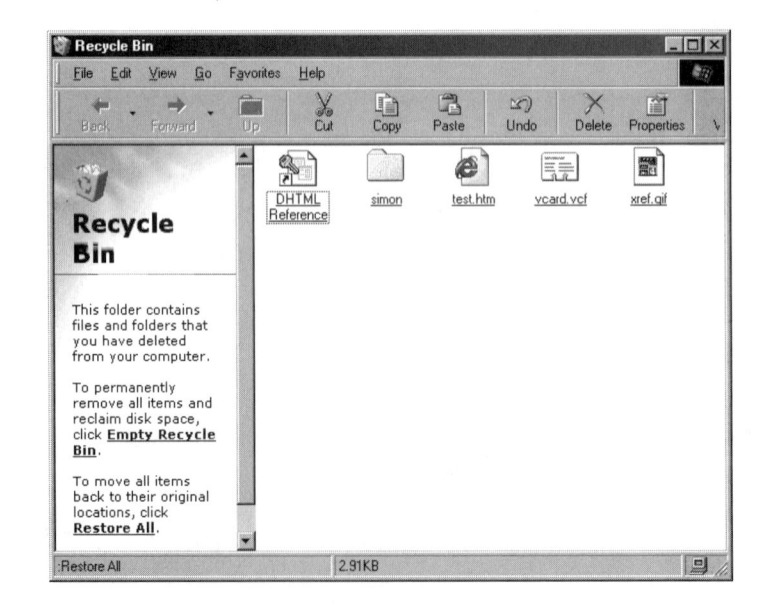

186

There are two operations you can perform in the Recycle Bin:

- **Empty it**: When you empty the Recycle Bin, you essentially "nuke" its contents. Files and folders in the bin are permanently deleted from the hard disk, and the space they consumed is freed up. From this point, you cannot change your mind and undelete.
- **Restore files**: To restore something in the Recycle Bin essentially means to "undelete" it. When you restore a file, for example, that file is taken out of the Recycle Bin and moved back to its original location. It won't be nuked next time you empty the Recycle Bin.

"Undeleting" Deleted Files

Whether you happen to discover some files or folders in your Recycle Bin that you *don't* want to delete after all, or whether you've made the trip here explicitly in hopes of recovering something you've mistakenly deleted, you can restore any files or folders that are represented by icons in the Recycle Bin. Use any of the following techniques:

- Right-click the folder or file you want to restore, and choose Restore from the shortcut menu.
- **Or**, select a group of files and folders you want to recover, right-click any one of them, and choose Restore from the shortcut menu.
- **Or**, select all the files and folders you want to save from extinction and choose File → Restore from Recycle Bin's menu bar.

Nukin' the Trash

When you're absolutely, *positively* certain that you really want to get rid of *all* the folders and files in the Recycle Bin and recover the disk space they're consuming, follow these steps:

▼ Choose File → Empty Recycle Bin from the Recycle Bin's menu bar.

▼ When you see the confirmation message, remember that this is absolutely your last chance to change your mind. If you are certain you want to destroy all the folders and files in the Recycle Bin, click the Yes button. If you have any doubts, click the No button.

*Really and truly the **last chance** to change your mind before permanently deleting items in the Recycle Bin.*

If you choose Yes, the files and folders are all deleted and their icons disappear from the Recycle Bin window. They're gone for good. If you choose No, nothing will be deleted from the Recycle Bin. Either way, you can then close the Recycle Bin by clicking its Close (X) button.

Moving and Copying Files/Folders

Occasionally, you might want to move or copy a file, or even an entire folder, to some new location. The difference between moving and copying on a computer is pretty much the same as moving and copying with real files in real filing cabinets.

Moving vs. Copying

For example, if I pull the file for "The Johnson Account" out of my filing cabinet and put it in Jane Doe's filing cabinet, I've **moved** that file from my filing cabinet to Jane's.

If, on the other hand, I pull the Johnson account file out of my filing cabinet, make photocopies of everything in that file, put the originals back in my filing cabinet, and place the copies in Jane Doe's filing cabinet, both Jane and I end up with copies of the the Johnson account file in our filing cabinets. In other words I **copied**, rather than moved, the Johnson file from my filing cabinet to Jane's.

Reasons to copy files

On a PC, you typically copy files to make **backups**—extra copies of a file in case the original gets destroyed somehow. Or you might need to copy a file to a floppy disk so you can take it home and work on that file. Or perhaps to mail the floppy disk to someone else.

Reasons to move files

On a PC, you typically move a file to put it in a better spot. For example, perhaps I have a photo in a file named MyPhoto.jpg and currently it's in the My Documents folder. I might decide that a better place to keep that photo, so it's easy to find later, would be in the My Documents\My Photos folder that I set up for just that purpose.

Another reason to move a file is to make an **archive** copy—a copy of the file that exists *off* the hard disk. For example, in the process of writing a book like this one, I create a lot of files that consume a lot of disk space. When the book is finished, I really don't need to keep all those files on my hard disk. However, I might want to keep an archive copy around on floppy disks or a CD-ROM, for future revisions and editions.

Moving and copying files always involves two folders, or perhaps two drives: the **source** and the **destination**. The difference is as follows:

- **Source**: This is the drive and folder where the files you want to move/copy are currently located.
- **Destination**: This is the drive and/or folder to which you want to move or copy the files.

A Note About CD-ROMs: You cannot move or copy files *to* a CD-ROM disk. You can, however, *copy* files *from* a CD-ROM to your hard disk. You cannot *move* files from a CD-ROM to another disk, though, because that would require changing the contents of the CD-ROM, which is not allowed.

Source and Destination

The general procedure for moving or copying files always goes something like this:

Steps for Moving/Copying

▼ Use My Computer or Windows Explorer to open the destination drive or folder. Size that window so you can see the open drive or folder but still have plenty of room on your desktop.

> **Running Two Instances of One Program**: You can use two instances of the My Computer or Windows Explorer to display files. For example, after opening My Computer and navigating to a specific folder, you can open My Computer's desktop icon again. Use that second My Computer window to navigate to another folder.

▼ Next, use My Computer, Windows Explorer, or Find to locate the files or folders you wish to move or copy. Size that window so you can see its contents, as well as the other window showing the destination drive or folder.

▼ If you want to move or copy more than one file, select the files/folders you want to move or copy, using the selection techniques described near the beginning of this chapter.

▼ Move the mouse pointer to the file/folder you want to move or copy (or to any one of the group of selected folders/files).

▼ Right-drag the selected icons to the destination drive or folder.

> **Change Your Mind?** If you start dragging icons for a copy or move operation and then change your mind, you can cancel the whole operation by pressing the Escape (Esc) key and then releasing the mouse button.

Steps for Moving/Copying
(cont.)

▼ When the mouse pointer is inside the destination window, release the mouse button. You'll see a special shortcut menu. In the example shown here, the shortcut menu appears because I'm about to drop some files into the window showing the contents of the floppy disk in drive A.

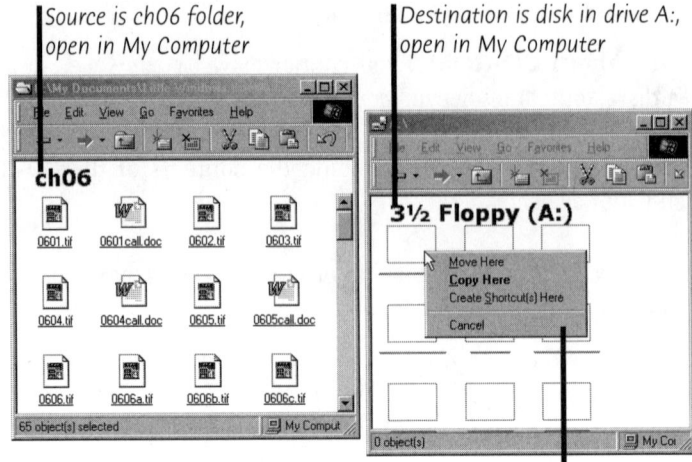

Source is ch06 folder, open in My Computer

Destination is disk in drive A:, open in My Computer

Right-drag and drop displays this shortcut menu

▼ If you are copying the files to this new location, choose Copy Here from the shortcut menu. If you are moving the files to this new location, choose Move Here.

That's it, you're done. If you moved or copied lots of files you might need to wait a few seconds for the job to complete. But once the job is done you should be able to see icons for the moved or copied files inside the destination window.

Using Disks and Other Media

One of the most common reasons for moving and copying files is to put items on **removable media**, such as a floppy disk or "zip" disk, either to transport the copy to another computer or to save the copy as a backup or archive. When you're working with these other media, here are a couple of things to be aware of:

- Floppy and other removable disks often need to be **formatted** before you can copy stuff to them.
- A floppy disk can hold only about 1.2 megabytes of data, which really isn't a whole lot. It might take several floppies to hold even just a few files from your hard disk. (That's why zip disks, which hold a lot more, are so handy.)

Never, ever format a disk that already has files on it. Doing so will permanently delete the files that are currently on that disk!

Let's look in more detail at the steps for copying some files from a hard disk to a floppy disk.

Copying to Removable Media

▼ First, put a blank, formatted floppy disk in drive A.

▼ Open My Computer and, in its window, open the icon to floppy drive A:.

If the floppy disk in drive A: is formatted but empty, opening the A: drive icon will display a window for the drive that contains no icons. If the floppy disk is *not* already formatted and ready to use, you'll get a message to that effect, along with the option to format the disk right now. Go ahead and format the disk, if necessary, by following the instructions on the screen.

▼ Use another instance of My Computer, or use Find or Windows Explorer to locate the files you want to copy.

▼ If you want to copy more than one file, select the files you wish to copy.

The status bar at the bottom of the window in which you're selecting files shows how much disk space the selected files require. In the example here in the margin, the selected files require 1.17MB, which is small enough to fit on one floppy disk. Otherwise, I would have to select fewer files and then copy them to one floppy. Then I'd have to use another floppy for additional files.

▼ Release the mouse button and choose Copy Here from the shortcut menu.

If you're copying a lot of files, or a very large file, a progress indicator will appear to keep you posted on the copy's progress. Don't remove the floppy disk from drive A: until the copy procedure is finished.

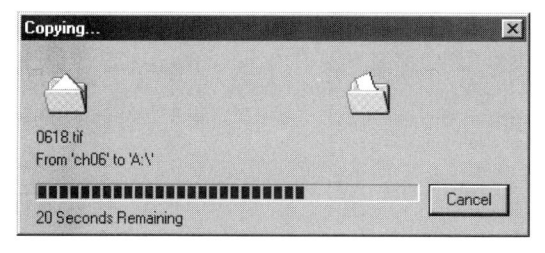

Progress indicator appears when you move/copy lots of files.

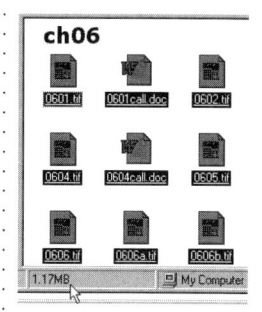

191

When You Need Multiple Disks

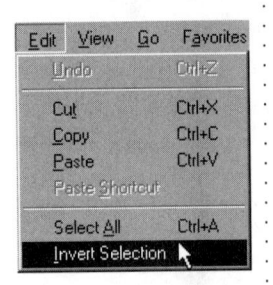

As mentioned earlier, in some cases you might need to use several floppies to make copies of files on your hard disk. For example, let's say that when you select all the files that you want to copy, the status bar says that you have selected 2MB worth of files. That means you'll need more than one disk. And, you'll have to copy some of the files on one floppy disk, the rest of the files to another floppy disk.

Here's a trick that makes copying to two floppies easier. Let's say you want to copy about half the files from a folder onto one floppy, and the other half of the folders to another floppy. Then select the first group of files you want to copy, and copy them to a floppy disk. Remove that disk when the copy is complete, and put in a second, blank floppy disk.

Then, **invert** your selection—that is, deselect the first group of files and select the *unselected* files. There's a command made especially for this operation: choose Edit → Invert Selection from the menu bar just above the selected files. Windows instantly reverses the selection so that the files that were selected *aren't* selected anymore, and the files that weren't selected *are* selected. Now you can copy the currently selected files over to that second floppy disk.

Inverting your selection of files or folders

A Quick Summary

So, to sum up so far, the basic procedure for moving or copying files is

- ▼ Select the files.
- ▼ Open a destination folder.
- ▼ Right-drag the files from the source folder into the destination folder.
- ▼ Drop the files into the destination folder.
- ▼ Choose Copy Here or Move Here in the shortcut menu.

Label Those Floppies! While we're on the topic of floppy disks, I should point out that most floppies have a paper label stuck on them, or come with blank stick-on labels you can use. It's always wise to jot down on that label—now, before the phone rings again—some description of what you've put on that disk. Otherwise, a few weeks down the road you may end up with a bunch of unlabeled floppy disks and no idea what's on them.

Copying within a Folder

You're not limited to copying folders and files to another drive or folder. You can store two or more copies of a folder or file within a single folder, provided you give them different names. This might come in handy if, say, you've just put a lot of time into a document. You want to make some changes to that document. But just to play it safe, you want to make a copy of the original in the same folder, in case you make a mess of things while you're revising.

A simple way to perform this sort of copy is to right-drag the icon (or selected icons) to some neutral place within the same window (not onto another icon). After you release the right mouse button, choose Copy Here from the shortcut menu.

Presto—icons for the newly created files appear. They have the same filename as the original files, but with the words "Copy of" tacked onto the front. For example, the name of the copy of Freddi Letter.doc will be Copy of Freddi Letter.doc. You can rename those copies, if you wish, using the basic renaming technique described earlier in this chapter.

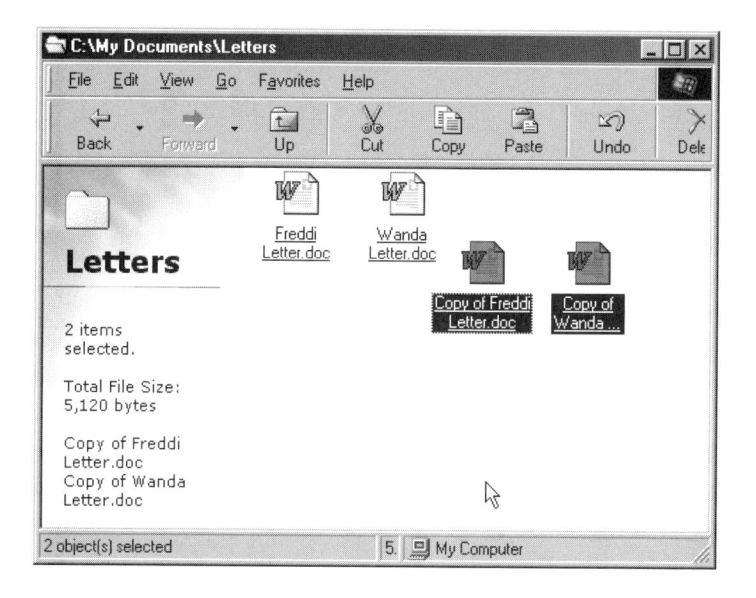

Moving/Copying with the Clipboard

As an alternative to dragging files from a source to a destination folder, you can use the **Clipboard**. To do this, you move or copy files in the source window to the Clipboard. Then you navigate to the destination folder and paste the files or folders from the Clipboard into that new folder. This technique is especially handy when you don't feel like navigating to two separate windows, such as when you're just moving or copying files to some nearby folder.

About the Clipboard: The Clipboard is sort of an invisible, temporary storage place in your PC's RAM. (I briefly mentioned the Windows Clipboard back in Chapter 2.) You can't see the Clipboard or what's in it, so you have to sort of keep a mental image of what's in there. Also, you need to remember that the Clipboard can hold only one thing at a time (and a selection of many files or folders counts as "one thing"). Therefore, whenever you copy or move something to the Clipboard, you want to always remember to Paste that thing (that is, copy it *out* of the Clipboard) *before* you move or copy something else into the Clipboard.

Steps for Using the Clipboard: So, the exact steps for moving or copying files using the Windows Clipboard are as follows:

▼ Use My Computer, Windows Explorer, or Find to locate the files you want to move or copy.

▼ If you want to move/copy several files, select all those files now.

▼ Right-click the file that you want to move or copy (or any file in the selected group), to view its shortcut menu. Then . . .

  ▪ If you want to move the files, choose Cut. (The icons go dim.)

  ▪ If you want to copy the files, choose Copy. (The icons remain unchanged.)

  Remember: Don't try to "add on" more files after you've chosen Cut or Copy in the shortcut menu. Come back and get them after you've finished this Cut/Copy and Paste operation. If you try to Copy or Cut more files before you Paste the ones you already have, those new files will *replace* the existing files you're moving or copying, not be added to them!

▼ Navigate to the destination folder—the one to which you want to move/copy the selected files—using any means you like.

▼ Right-click on (or within) that folder, and choose Paste from the shortcut menu.

If you pasted into an open folder, you should see the icons for the moved/copied file(s) after a brief wait. If you just pasted to the folder's icon without opening it first, you'll see the icons next time you open that folder.

Don't Forget the Arrange Icons Command: As always, if the folders are out of order after your Cut/Copy Paste operation, you can right-click a neutral area and choose Arrange Icons ➔ By Name from the shortcut menu.

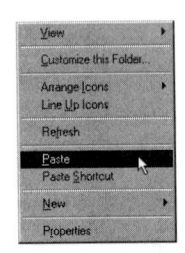

Undoing a Recent Action

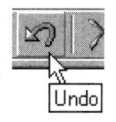

You've already seen a couple of examples, in earlier chapters, of how Windows (and most Windows programs) almost always gives you the option to undo your most recent action. The Cut, Copy, and Paste commands are no exception; you can undo these operations, as well. The Delete command is a little stickier, but you can undo it, too.

You can *only* undo the thing you just did, though. For example, if you delete some files and then rename a file, you can only undo the rename operation, because that was your most recent action. (To "undo" the deletion at this point, you'd need to open the Recycle Bin and restore the deleted files from there.)

To undo your most recent actions:

- Choose **Edit → Undo** from the menu bar of the window in which you performed the action you want to undo. The Undo command on the Edit menu will change to reflect your last operation. For instance, it might say "Undo Paste" or "Undo Bold."
- **Or** you can press **Ctrl+Z**, which is the shortcut key for the Undo command.
- **Or**, if you see an **Undo button** in the current window, you can just click that button.

Uncutting

As mentioned, when you use Edit → Cut to move files to the Clipboard, the icons for those files go dim. If you change your mind and want to "uncut," *you can't use Undo*—it just doesn't work for that. You can, however, press the Esc key to cancel the Cut operation. Doing so will turn all the icons back to their original undimmed appearance.

If pressing Esc doesn't work, you can right-click within the same folder from which you cut the files, and choose Paste from the shortcut menu. Then you may see a message indicating that you can't move the Clipboard files into the current directory. All you've done, then, is put the files back into the same folder you originally cut them from.

Creating a New Folder

As your collection of documents and other files grows, you might get the urge to create some new folders to better organize your collection. Creating a folder is easy.

Start from either the Explorer or My Computer window

▼ In either Windows Explorer or My Computer, navigate to the drive and folder that you want to contain the folder you're about to create.

For example, if you want to put the new folder in the root folder of drive C:, you can open My Computer and then click Drive C:'s icon.

Or, if you want to create a subfolder inside the My Documents folder, you'd want to open the My Documents folder, get the mouse pointer inside that folder's window, and then . . .

▼ Right-click a neutral area near the existing folders and files. The shortcut menu will appear, as usual.

▼ Choose New, and another submenu will pop up. Choose Folder from that menu.

▼ A new folder named New Folder appears. You can type in a new name for the folder right now. Or, if you decide to name the folder later, you can just right-click it and choose Rename.

The new folder is like any other folder in your disk—except that it's empty because it's brand new. You can, of course, move or copy any files you like into the new folder, now or later.

Creating a New Document

The techniques for creating a new folder also allow you to create a brand-new document. Unlike folders, however, which are all the same, documents come in many different kinds of formats. You already know that the three-letter extension added to the file's name tells Windows what kind of information is in the file. For example, the .doc (document) format is used on files you type using WordPad or Microsoft Word. Pictures are stored in other formats, such as bitmap (.bmp), Graphics Interchange Format (.gif), and others. So to use this method for creating a new document, you first need to know *which* kind of document you want to create.

Don't Let This Confuse You: Of course, if you don't know what kind of document you want to create, you can ignore this whole approach to creating a new document. Instead, just open whatever program you want to use to create the document. Then create and save the document as you normally would. The program you use will automatically add the correct three-letter extension to whatever filename you give the document when you save it.

Let's go ahead and take a look at the steps for creating a new, empty document right now, on-the-fly, from within Windows Explorer or My Computer. Just follow this procedure:

▼ Use Windows Explorer or My Computer to open the folder in which you want to put a new, blank document.

▼ Right-click a neutral area within that folder and choose New from the shortcut menu that appears.

▼ From the submenu that appears, click on the type of document you want to create. The options available to you will depend on what programs are installed on your PC.

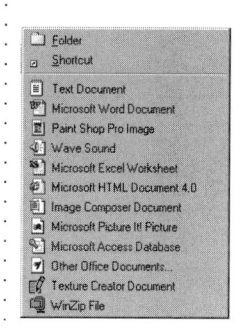

A new icon appears, with the name New . . . followed by a description of the type of file you created, as well as the appropriate extension for that type of file. For example, if you've opted to create a new text document, the new file will be named "New Text Document.txt."

You can rename the new file in the usual manner: Right-click and choose Rename. To open the new, blank document file, just click it (or double-click it, if you're using Classic-style navigation). The appropriate program for creating and editing that type of document will open, with your new blank document at hand and ready for action.

Every file on your PC has certain **properties** or **attributes** that you can tweak, as necessary.

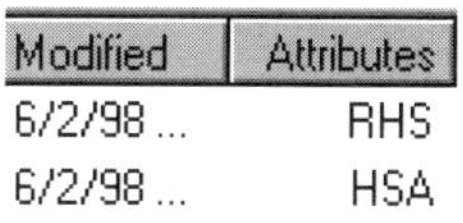

File Attributes

Usually, the only time you see these attributes is when you're viewing files in Details view, and you have the Show Attributes in Details View option turned on (as discussed earlier in this chapter). The Attributes column of the Details view shows the first letter of any attribute that's turned on. For example, a file with the attributes RHS has its Read Only, Hidden, and System attributes turned on.

In addition to the Details view, however, you can take a look at any file's attributes, at any time, by viewing the file's properties. Here are the steps:

Looking at Properties

▼ Navigate to the file's icon via Windows Explorer, My Computer, or Find.

▼ If your goal is to check/change the attributes of multiple files, select all those files now.

▼ Right-click the file's icon (or any one of the icons in the group of selected files). That now-familiar shortcut menu will appear; choose Properties.

▼ The dialog box that appears next is the Properties dialog box for the file that you right-clicked, as indicated in the title bar. To work with the file's attributes, click the General tab.

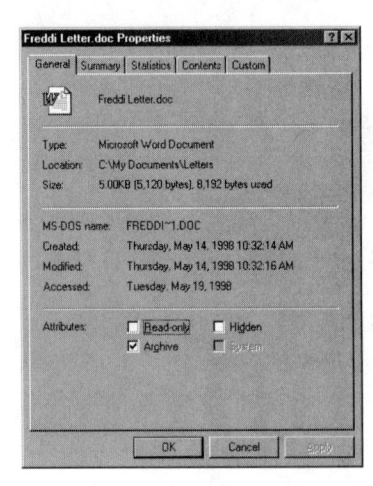

Here in the General tab of the Properties dialog, I can tweak the attributes for the FreddiLetter.doc file.

Attribute Definitions Following is a list of the file attributes and the characteristics of each one.

File Attribute	File Characteristic When Attribute Is Set
Archive	This file has been changed since the last backup (see "Major Backups," coming up in this chapter).
Read-only	This file can be open and read in a program, but cannot be changed within that program.
Hidden	This file will not be visible in My Computer, Windows Explorer, or Find unless the Show All Files option in Folder Options is selected. See the earlier section on the View tab of the Folder Options dialog box.
System	This file is a critical system file. You don't have the option to change this setting.

Of these file attributes, the one most likely to give you a hard time is the Read-only attribute. Whenever you try to change the contents of such a file, any changes you try to save will be rejected. (It's possible to save the modified document under a different name, by choosing File ➔ Save As from the program's menu bar. But you can't save the original file with changes.)

CD-ROM File Attributes Files and folders on CD-ROM are always flagged as Read-only, because the CD is a Read-only medium. There's no way to change a file's attributes when that file is on a CD-ROM. As explained earlier, you can copy any file from a CD-ROM to your hard disk. Only problem is, the file will still be flagged as Read-only even *after* it's copied. If you want to be able to use that file normally, you must turn off its Read-only attribute. You can do so only on the copy that you've already put on your hard disk.

Changing Attributes

Changing the attributes of one or more files is pretty easy:

▼ Use Windows Explorer, My Computer, or Find to browse to the file(s) whose attributes you want to change.

▼ If you want to change the attributes of several files, select those files now.

▼ Right-click the icon of the file you want to change, or right-click any one of the files in the selected group.

▼ Choose Properties from the shortcut menu that appears.

▼ Click the General tab in the Properties dialog box.

▼ To turn an attribute on or off, click its checkbox. Like all other checkbox options, when the checkbox is clear the attribute is turned off; when the checkbox contains a check mark, the attribute is turned on.

When multiple files are selected

If you've selected multiple files and only *some* of those files have an attribute, such as Read-only, then the checkboxes for those items will be light-gray with a dark-gray checkmark. When you change the attribute, *all* selected files are affected. For example, if you clear a gray Read-only checkbox, the checkbox will turn white, and all selected files will have their Read-only attribute turned off.

▼ Click the OK button near the bottom of the dialog box to apply your new settings and close the dialog box.

And that's all there is to that. If you cleared the Read-only attribute from a document file, you can now click (or double-click) its icon to open it up and edit it.

Major Backups

Every hard disk is composed of some moving parts. The disk spins, and the drive head inside the drive moves around to read from and write to that disk. As you undoubtedly know from general life experience with machines, things with moving parts can break. If your hard disk breaks, it's pretty serious: It usually takes everything with it—meaning that you've just lost *all* the files and folders that were stored on that disk.

There's no reason to panic about this. Hard disks don't "just break" very often. In my 15+ years of using dozens of different computers, I've had only one hard disk break down on me. But of course, I did lose everything on that disk the moment it got fried. The answer, rather than to panic, is to **plan ahead** for such a disaster.

Planning Ahead There are two ways to protect yourself from a fatal hard-disk crash. One method is to make frequent **backups** of your entire hard disk. This, unfortunately, is very difficult and time-consuming to do with floppy disks, because today's hard disks can hold as much as *several hundred* floppy disks. Such a job could easily take all day. Obviously not a viable solution.

The workable alternative is to buy special **backup hardware and software**, such as a Zip drive, a Jaz drive, a CD-R drive, or a tape drive. All these gadgets are available at all software stores and generally come with both the hardware and the software required to maintain backups of your hard disk. Each backup device has its own options and characteristics, of course, so I can't really tell you how to use yours. You'll need to rely on the instructions that come with the device to learn how to use it.

Using CDs for Backup A CD-R drive lets you write information to a CD-ROM. And a single CD can hold over 650MB of data, which makes it a good medium for storing large amounts of data. Also, the CD can be read in any computer that has a CD-ROM drive, so those CDs full of data can also be used to transfer copies of files from one computer to another.

Back Up Documents Only If you keep the original copies of all programs you purchase and install on your PC, there really is no need to back up your entire hard disk. As an alternative to investing in special backup hardware, you can use floppy disks to back up only the files you've created yourself. You could do so perhaps at the end of each day, or however often seems reasonable to you. Backing up the files that you've created is just a matter of selecting them and dragging them to floppy disks, as described earlier in this chapter.

If your hard disk does go down at some time in the future, you still have copies of all the files you've worked so hard to create. After you replace the broken hard disk and reload your programs from their original disks or CD-ROMs, you can copy all your personal files from the floppies onto the new hard disk.

"Reload my programs?" you ask. Yes—unfortunately, backing up your documents doesn't help you recover all the applications and other programs that likely were lost when the hard disk went down. But, as we'll discuss in the next chapter, you can use the original disks that you used to install all those programs in the first place, to reinstall them onto your new hard disk. All it costs you is some time.

Guidelines for Backup

As I mentioned just above, deciding whether (and how often) to back up your entire hard disk or just to back up documents as you create and save them is a decision you'll need to make for yourself.

At the very least, you should back up (or copy to floppies) any document in which you've invested a lot of time, as well as any simpler documents that you may just want to refer to later. And do it as often as every day, depending on your situation. Store the copies in a safe place, preferably in another room or other location. That way, you're covered if your hard disk crashes, or your computer gets stolen, or even if the darn room burns down. At least you still have the copies of your most important documents.

Summary

This is a long chapter, but managing files isn't as complicated a task as you might think. The Windows Explorer, My Computer, and Find programs provide not only the means to find the files that you want to manage, but also the tools required to perform the management tasks. Let's take a moment to review the most important points covered in this chapter:

- ▼ The **Folder Options dialog box** (Start ➔ Settings ➔ Folder Options) lets you customize the behavior and appearance of Windows Explorer, My Computer, and Find.

- ▼ When you want to move, copy, delete, or rename a file (or files), you first need to get to those files using Windows Explorer, My Computer, or Find.

- ▼ To **delete** or **rename** a file, right-click its icon and choose the appropriate option from the shortcut menu.

- ▼ To **move** or **copy** files, locate the files first. Then open a destination drive/folder. Select the file(s) to move or copy, and right-drag them from the source to the destination drive/folder. Release the mouse button and choose Copy Here or Move Here from the shortcut menu.

- ▼ To **undo** a recent action, click the Undo button, or press Ctrl+Z. Or choose Edit ➔ Undo from the nearest menu bar. (The Undo command on the menu will reflect the action that's about to be undone.)

- ▼ To **change** a file's attributes, right-click the file's icon. Or, select several files and right-click any one of their icons. Choose Properties from the shortcut menu, open the General tab, and adjust the attributes as needed.

Installing New Programs and Such 8

As you probably know, there are thousands of programs available for Windows PCs. Your computer already has some programs installed on it. Windows 98, for example, is one of those programs. You can find out what other programs are already installed just by clicking the Start button, pointing to Programs, and making selections from the submenus that appear.

In this chapter, however, I'm going to talk about programs that are *not* already on your PC. Specifically, you'll be learning about what you need to do after you purchase a new program, to get it installed and working on your PC.

Installing a New Program

When you buy a new program, it typically comes in a box or other packaging containing some written instructions, with the program itself on a CD-ROM or floppy disks. Before you can use such a program, you need to **install** it on your hard disk.

Among other things, the **installation procedure** copies files from the CD-ROM or floppy disks onto your hard disk, and then sets up a menu so you can start the program from the Start button. You need only install a program once—not each time you want to run that program—unless something goes wrong or you want to alter the original installation.

A General Installation Procedure

Proceed with caution

I can give you a pretty simple procedure that you can use to install just about any program that's delivered to you on floppies or CD-ROM. However, be aware that for each individual program there are *always* exceptions to the general rule, or extra steps to perform, or some additional element to consider. You should always check the installation instructions that came with the program you're installing (generally they're in the printed documentation that comes with the program). A quick glance may alert you to the fact that you need to follow their explicit installation instructions.

There may also be some special installation instructions in the program's **ReadMe file**. To view that file, insert the program's floppy disk or CD-ROM into the appropriate drive. Use Windows Explorer or My Computer to navigate to that drive, and look for a file named ReadMe (or ReadMe.txt or readme.doc, or something like that). If you find such a file, you can just click its icon (or double-click) to read the contents of that file.

Readme.txt

Especially if the ReadMe file is lengthy, you may want to print it out, or just print the instructions. To do this, choose File ➔ Print from the menu bar just above the instructions. To close the instructions, click the Close (X) button near the upper-right corner.

If you don't have any special instructions, or if you just want to get right to installing the program, here's the general procedure that works 99.9% of the time:

Step 1. Close all programs and windows that are currently open, so you're at the Windows 98 desktop.

Step 2. Insert the program's CD-ROM into your CD-ROM drive, or the program's floppy disk (or Disk #1, or whatever) into your floppy drive.

Step 3. If you're installing from a CD-ROM, wait half a minute or so to see if it **autostarts**. (That is, wait to see if a program window appears on the screen automatically, without any help from you.) If a window does pop up and offers you an Install or Setup option, choose that option and then skip the rest of these steps.

If you don't see one of these autostart program windows, proceed to step 4.

Step 4. Click the Windows 98 Start button, and choose Settings → Control Panel.

Step 5. Open the Add/Remove programs icon to bring up the Add/Remove Programs Properties dialog box, and click to open the Install/Uninstall tab (if necessary).

Add/Remove Programs

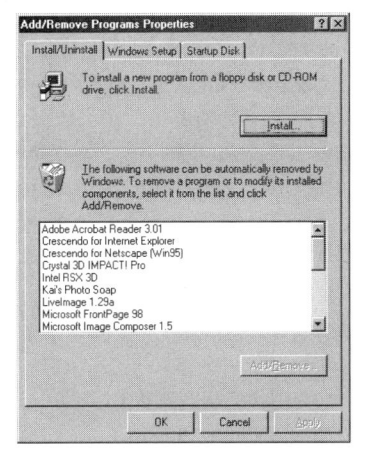

Step 6. Click the Install button.

Step 7. In the next window that appears, click the Next> button. Windows will search for an installation program.

Step 8. If Windows successfully finds the installation program on the inserted floppy or CD-ROM, the command line for starting that program will appear in the next window. Click the Finish button to begin the installation.

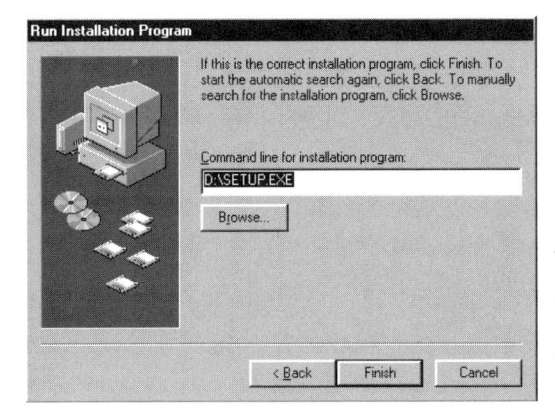

Downloaded Programs: If you've downloaded a new program from the Internet or some other online service, often you can install the program just by opening the icon of the downloaded file. See Chapter 14 for more information.

Add/Remove Programs has found an installation program named SETUP.EXE on the disk in drive D:.

205

Follow Screen Instructions At this point, the installation program for the program you're installing takes over, and what happens next really depends on the program you're installing. Your job is to follow the instructions that appear on the screen, and make choices as appropriate. If you come across a question that you don't know how to answer, your best bet would be to just take the **default** option—that is, whatever option is suggested to you on the screen.

When the installation is complete, you'll see a message telling you so. Some programs may require that you restart your computer after the installation. If you see such an instruction, don't forget to remove any floppy disks and/or CD-ROMs from their drives *before* you restart the computer.

Starting Your New Program Once the installation is complete, you should be able to run the new program right from the Start ➔ Programs menu. You probably won't need to put any disks into drives, because the program will be run from your hard disk from this point on. However, some games and other graphics-intensive programs may require that you to put the CD-ROM into the CD-ROM drive before you start the program. (If you forget to insert the CD, you'll just see a reminder to do that after you try to start the program.)

Finding the Icon The main trick at this point is to *find* the icon for starting the new program. Start by looking around the desktop first, since some programs put startup icons right on the desktop. If you find the new program's icon there, just click (or double-click) it to start the program.

If there's no desktop icon for the new program, look around the menus. First click the Start button and see if an icon for the new program appears right on the Start menu. If so, you can click that icon to start the program. If there is no icon on the Start menu, point to Programs and look through the program groups and icons for whatever icon is needed to start your new program. When you find it, just click it to start the new program.

Once you discover how to get your new program running, you can always use that technique to start the program in the future. Remember, you need not go through the whole installation procedure again in the future, because the program's files have already been copied to your hard disk. You can also create a desktop or Quick Launch shortcut to the new program, using the technques we discussed back in Chapter 7.

Don't forget: If my generic installation instructions don't work for a particular program, you can always look in the program's written instructions or ReadMe file for more information. Similarly, if you can't find a program's startup icon after you've installed the program, the best place to look for that information will be in the program's written documentation or ReadMe file.

Registering a Program

Many programs that you install will ask you to **register** the product. This step is usually optional, but it's a good idea to register. That way, the publisher of the software can send you updates, fixes, or whatever else they have to offer. If you have a modem, you can usually register online by following the instructions that appear on the screen. If you don't have a modem (or don't know how to use it yet), you can usually register by mail. A preaddressed card is usually provided in the software packaging.

Don't Lose the Original Program Stuff

Once you get a program installed and running, you might be quick to forget all about the original disk and instructions. But you'd do well to get all that stuff organized and put away, right now. I recommend that you keep all your program CD-ROMs and disks together in some **safe place**. That way, if you ever accidentally delete a program or if your hard disk crashes, it will be easy to find the original disks and reinstall the program.

Some programs require serial numbers or a CD key to be installed. You most definitely want to carefully save that information! And not at the bottom of your junk drawer, either—I recommend that you make a folder (the paper kind), put every serial number and CD key into that one folder, and file it away in your filing cabinet (the real one). That way, should you be asked for a serial number or CD key when reinstalling the program in the future, you'll know just where to look.

Removing Installed Programs

At some point, you may want to do a little housekeeping on your hard disk and get rid of a program that you don't use anymore. *Be careful when you're doing this!*

You'll remember that we warned you in Chapter 5 about the dangers of deleting entire folders from your hard disk. A similar caution applies here: Removing an installed program from your hard disk is not a simple matter of deleting a file or folder. You should always try to use Windows 98's **Add/Remove Programs** dialog box to remove installed programs, because this technique ensures that the program itself, plus related folders, menu entries, and other components of the program, are all thoroughly removed from your system.

Add/Remove Programs

Here's how to use the Add/Remove Programs dialog box:

▼ First, close all open programs and windows, so you're at the Windows 98 desktop.

▼ Choose Start ➔ Settings ➔ Control Panel.

▼ Open the Add/Remove Programs icon. Of course, the Add/Remove Programs Properties dialog box will look familiar; it's the same one you use to install a new program.

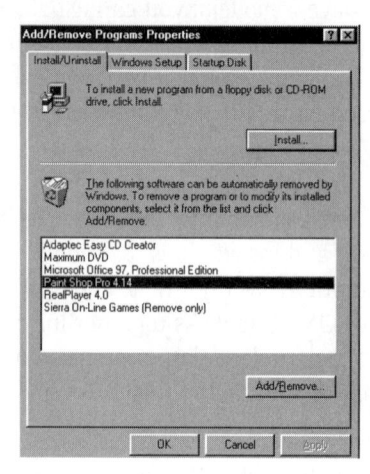

This dialog box lets you remove installed programs, as well as install them.

▼ Look in the list of programs in the middle part of the Install/Uninstall tab, and click the name of the program that you want to remove.

▼ Click the Add/Remove button.

Don't See Your Program? If you don't see the name of the program you want to remove, it may be because there is no "uninstall" routine for that particular program. You'll have to refer to the program's written documentation, ReadMe file, or online help for instructions on removing that program. Or, perhaps the program you're trying to uninstall is a Windows component. These programs must be removed using the Windows Setup tab, as discussed under "Installing Missing Windows Components" later in this chapter.

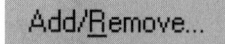

Once again, I must leave you to your own devices at this point, because I cannot know how your uninstall program is going to work from here on out. It all depends on the specific program you're removing. Your job is to read and follow the instructions on the screen until a message indicates that removal of the program is complete. (Or follow the steps in the program's documentation.)

You may need to restart your computer after removing certain programs. If so, you'll see an option on your screen that you can select to "restart the computer now."

Windows 98 comes with a whole bunch of little software **components**, including the WordPad program, some games, the Calculator, and more. (I've also been calling these components **programs**, and sometimes **applets**.) These may or may not have been installed when Windows 98 was first installed on your PC. Most of the components that have, in fact, been installed will be residing in the Accessories program group on the Programs menu.

Installing Missing Windows Components

Let's take a look at the Accessories program group. Click the Start button, point to Programs, and then Accessories. The icons and program groups on the Accessories submenu give you an indication of which applets are already installed.

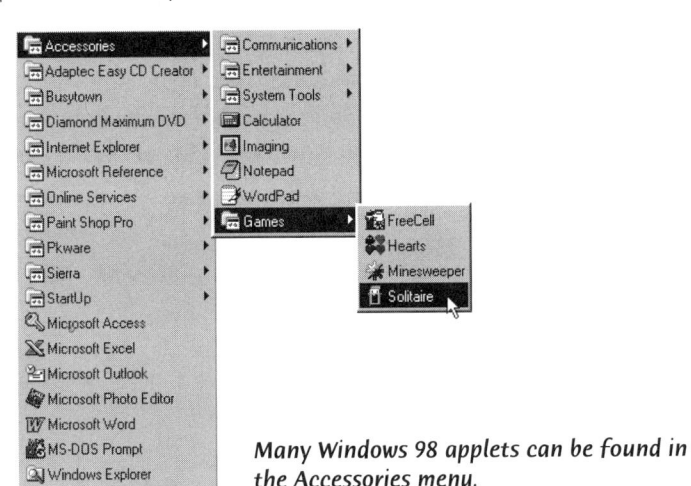

Many Windows 98 applets can be found in the Accessories menu.

Should you discover that a Windows 98 applet (or other component) that you need is missing from your computer, you can easily install that component. Here are the steps:

Steps for Installing

▼ Close all open windows and program to get to a clean Windows 98 desktop.

209

8: INSTALLING NEW PROGRAMS AND SUCH

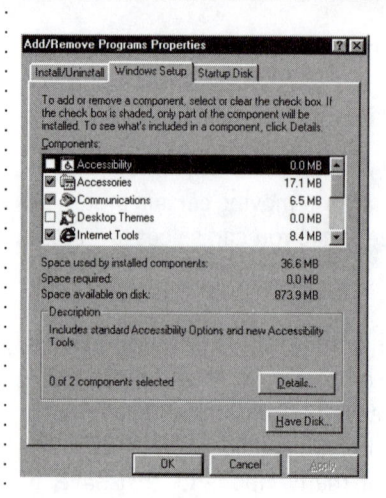

- Gather your original Windows 98 CD-ROM or floppy disks. (If your PC came with Windows 98 already installed, you may be able to skip this step. Just keep following these steps and you'll know soon.)
- Click Start → Settings → Control Panel.
- Open the Add/Remove Programs icon.
- Open the Windows Setup tab.

Browsing the Components

In the Setup tab, notice the checkboxes and component names listed under Components. Most of these are actually *groups* of components. To see if an item is a component of something else, click it. Then look down at the Details button. If the Details button is dimmed, then the highlighted component is an individual component. There are no details to see. If the Details button is available, then the highlighted component is actually a group of components. You can click the Details button to see the items that make up that group.

Since we're interested in Accessories, click that item in the Components list and then click the Details button. You'll see a list of all the applets that make up the Accessories component.

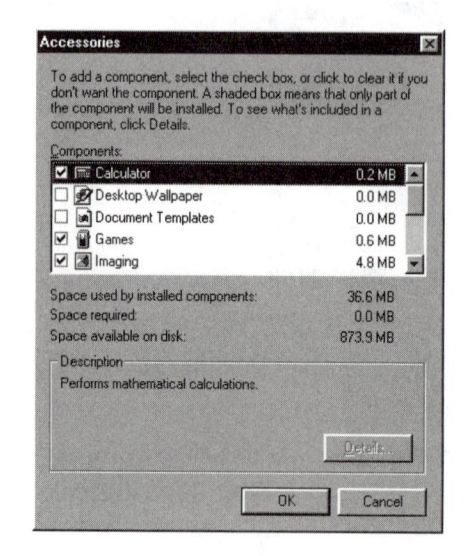

The Accessories component includes lots of applets.

210

Install/Uninstall Checkboxes

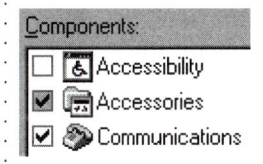

As you browse around through components and groups of components, you'll come across various checkboxes. Here's what the checkbox symbols mean:

- **Empty checkbox**: This component or group of components is not installed on your PC.
- **Checked box, gray background**: Some (but not all) components in this group are already installed.
- **Checked box, white background**: This component or group of components is already installed.

Using these checkboxes, you can enable and disable (install and uninstall) the various Windows components. It's really easy:

- To install a missing component, select (check) that component's checkbox.
- To remove an installed component, clear that component's checkbox.
- To leave the component as is (installed or not installed), leave its checkbox as is.

Once you've selected all the components and installed or removed them as required, click the OK button at the bottom of the dialog box until you see a message on the screen indicating that the files are being copied, or until you receive more instructions on the screen. From here on out, you'll need to follow whatever instructions appear on the screen.

Was Windows preinstalled on your computer?

If your computer came with Windows 98 already installed, you may not need to insert any disks. However, you may have installed Windows 98 yourself, or your PC manufacturer may have installed only certain components of the whole Windows 98 system. In either of these cases, you'll be prompted to insert the Windows 98 CD-ROM or one of the Windows 98 floppy disks. Insert the appropriate disk in the drive as prompted.

When you've completed the installation instructions, the program will be installed and you'll be returned to the Control Panel. Close the Control Panel by clicking its Close (X) button, and go ahead and start your newly installed component in the usual manner. Click Start → Programs and look around for the program's startup icon. When you find it, you can click it to start the accessory.

8: INSTALLING NEW PROGRAMS AND SUCH

Removing a Windows Component

If space on your hard disk starts getting scarce, you can easily recover some space by removing Windows components that you don't use. As I indicated earlier, the steps for removing an installed component are virtually identical to the steps for installing one:

▼ Get to the Windows Setup tab of Add/Remove Programs, and clear the checkboxes of any components you want to remove.

▼ Hit the OK button, and follow any instructions that appear on the screen.

And remember, you can come back and reinstall these components whenever you want.

Installing New Fonts

Installing new fonts is a little different from installing programs. But I suppose that before I tell you how to *install* new fonts, I should tell you what a font *is*, just in case you're not familiar with the term.

A **font**, in this context, is a style of print. To illustrate what I mean, here are examples of five different fonts, including the fun and decorative Wingdings:

I'm Courier Font

I'm Arial Black Font

I'm Times New Roman

I'm Lucida Handwriting

The characters below are Wingdings

TrueType Fonts:
In this book, we're specifically talking about TrueType fonts; that's what the icons' "TT" symbol stands for. TrueType fonts are the ones best suited to work with Windows 98.

You're likely to have an everyday involvement with fonts. For example, when changing the color and appearance of the overall screen on your system, you can choose a font for some kinds of text. (We discussed this under "Screen Colors" back in Chapter 5.) And you can also use fonts in just about any program that allows you to type on the screen. I'll present an example of that under "Using Fonts in Programs" later in this chapter.

Your Windows 98 program came with quite a few fonts built in. Those fonts may be all you ever need. There are, however, thousands of other fonts available for PCs. You can find these at computer stores, and often on the Internet as well.

To see what fonts are currently installed on your computer, you need to go to the **Fonts window**—another item in the Control Panel. If you've purchased or downloaded some new fonts and want to install them on your computer now, you'll need the Fonts window for that, as well. Here's how to get there:

Which Fonts Do You Have?

▼ Click the Windows 98 Start button.

▼ Choose Settings → Control Panel.

▼ Open the Fonts icon.

The Fonts window shows an icon for each installed font. If you want to see how a font looks in print, just double-click its icon. A sample of the font will appear in a smaller window.

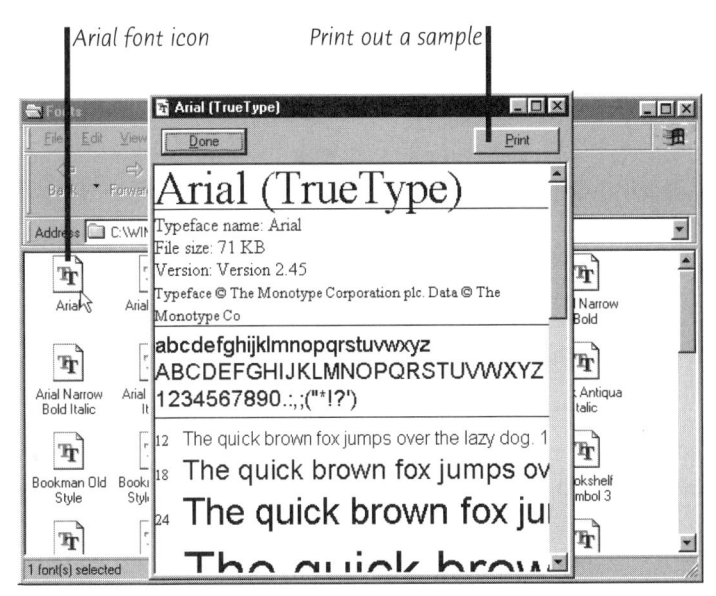

When you double-click the Arial font's icon, you get a look at that font, in different sizes.

You can click the Print button in the font's window to print a sample of the font. Click the Done window when you've finished viewing the font.

To install new fonts, you can try the general steps coming up. These steps will work with *most* TrueType fonts. If you have any problems installing a font, though, you'll need to refer to the written instructions or ReadMe file that came with that font. Some font publishers provide special installation programs for their fonts.

Steps for Installing Fonts

213

The following **general steps** will get you started. Assuming you have one or more TrueType fonts on a floppy disk or CD-ROM that you want to install, here's what you do:

▼ Close all open windows and programs (except the Fonts window, if it's already open).

▼ If the Fonts window isn't open, open it now by clicking Start ➔ Settings ➔ Control Panel, and opening the Fonts icon.

▼ Insert the floppy disk or CD-ROM that contains the font(s) you want to install.

▼ From the Fonts window's menu bar choose File ➔ Install New Font. You'll then see the Add Fonts dialog box.

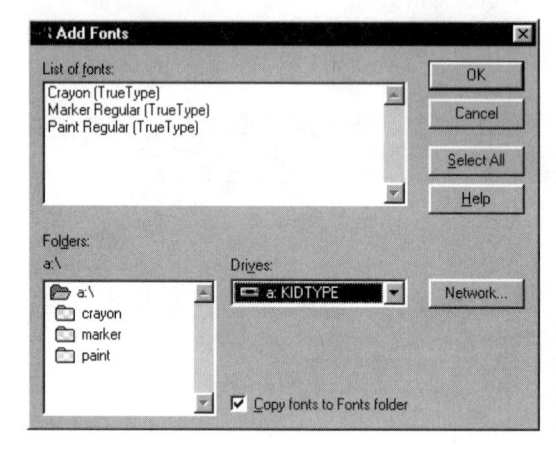

Getting ready to install some fonts from the disk in drive A:.

▼ Under Drives, choose the drive that contains the fonts you want to install. For example, if the fonts are on the floppy disk in drive A:, choose that drive. The names of installable fonts on that disk will then be listed in the scrollable List of Fonts area.

▼ Select the fonts that you want to install. To select one font, click it. Ctrl+click to select additional fonts. Or, click the Select All button to install all the listed fonts.

▼ Make sure the Copy Fonts to Fonts Folder option is selected, as shown here in the margin.

▼ Click OK and wait as the fonts are copied to your hard disk.

Don't see your new font? When copying is complete, you'll be returned to the Fonts window. If you don't see your new fonts listed in that window, you can update that window's contents by pressing the F5 key or by choosing View ➔ Refresh from the Fonts window menu bar.

8: INSTALLING NEW PROGRAMS AND SUCH

Using Fonts in Documents

Just about any program that allows you to create documents will let you use your fonts in those documents. Virtually all programs require the same steps to apply a font: From within the program, you select the text to which you want to apply the font, by dragging the mouse pointer through that text. Then you choose Format ➔ Font from that program's menu bar. Choose your font; set its size, style, and so forth; and click OK—and you're done.

Here's an example, using the WordPad program.

▼ To start WordPad, click Start ➔ Programs ➔ Accessories ➔ WordPad.

▼ When the WordPad program opens, type a word, such as **Welcome**, into the document.

▼ Select that text by dragging the mouse pointer through it.

▼ Choose Format ➔ Font from WordPad's menu bar. The Font dialog box opens up.

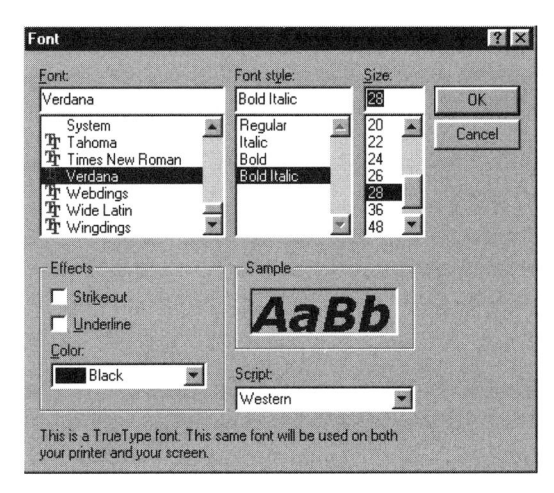

▼ In the dialog box, select the font you want to apply from the scrollable list of fonts.

▼ In addition, you have several options for determining the appearance of the font you are applying: Style (italic or bold, for instance), Size (usually in points), Effects (such as underlining), Color, and Script type. You can set these up to get just the look you want for your text.

▼ Click OK. You'll be returned to your document, where you'll see that the font you chose has been applied to the text you selected.

Arial Regular
Arial Bold
Arial Italic
Bold Italic
~~Strikeout~~
Underlined

215

Installing New Hardware

The procedure for installing new hardware in a PC—whether you're upgrading, enhancing, or repairing your machine—is a huge topic that goes beyond the scope of this book. Suffice it to say that there are many significant factors to take into consideration. Such as, should you get an internal or external device? If it's internal, do you have an available PCI or ISA slot for the device? Do you need SCSI for the device? If it's an external device, do you have an available printer, serial, USB, or other appropriate plug for the device? Is the device plug-and-play? And it gets way more complicated than that.

> **Professional Help**: Often the best alternative is to get the experts in your local computer store or service center to install the new device. Installation is generally simple (when you know what you're doing) and inexpensive. The pros can install the hardware and all appropriate software for you, potentially saving you hours or even days of frustration.

Doing It Yourself

Should you decide to ignore my warning and install the product yourself, make sure you carefully read the manufacturer's instructions on how to install the hardware device. Once the device is physically connected, there's a good chance that Windows can do all the rest of the work necessary to get the device working. This job includes installing the **device drivers** (programs that let Windows "talk to" the new device), perhaps creating some new icons, and updating the various system files that keep track of such things.

What you'll need to do, after physically connecting the device to the PC (or after installing the card inside the PC) is gather any floppy disks or CD-ROMs that came with the hardware device. Also, grab your original Windows 98 CD-ROM or floppies, if you have them. Those disks contain drivers for many hundreds of hardware products. (If Windows 98 came preinstalled on your PC, you may not need to bother with the original Windows 98 CD or floppy disks. Here again, as mentioned earlier, you won't know for sure until after you've started the installation procedure.)

Plug-and-play means less work for you.

When you're ready, start up your PC in the usual manner—with the floppy disk drives and CD-ROM drive empty. If the device you installed is **plug-and-play**, Windows 98 will probably detect it. Plug-and-play essentially means you plug the device in and the computer figures out what to do with it.

If Windows does need any help from you, you'll see instructions on the screen. Follow those instructions to complete the hardware installation.

8: INSTALLING NEW PROGRAMS AND SUCH

If Windows 98 just boots up normally without appearing to have detected your new hardware, here is what you should do next:

- If your new hardware is a modem, click Start ➔ Settings ➔ Control Panel. Open the Modems icon, and follow the instructions in the **Install New Modem Wizard** that appears.
- If your new hardware is a printer, open My Computer, open the Printers icon, and then open the Add Printer icon. Follow the instructions to install a local printer.

For any other devices (or in the event that either of the above instructions fails), try the Add New Hardware Wizard in Control Panel. To get there...

▼ Close all open programs and windows.

▼ Click Start ➔ Settings ➔ Control Panel.

▼ Open the Add New Hardware icon.

▼ When the Add New Hardware Wizard opens, read and follow the instructions that appear in the wizard's progressive windows.

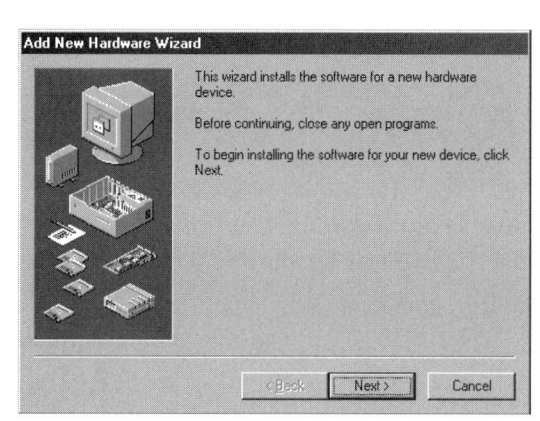

First window in the Add New Hardware Wizard.

I wish you luck with hardware installations. Chances are things will go smoothly and you'll have things working in no time. However, do keep in mind that all hardware devices are different. Beyond what I've just told you, I don't know what the wizard is going to ask. It all depends on the hardware you installed. The only place you'll find instructions for that particular hardware device is *with* that hardware device—if not on paper, then perhaps on a disk that came with the device.

If Windows Doesn't Get It

A **wizard** is simply a series of dialog boxes that ask you questions about a task. Then the wizard does the work for you.

Add New Hardware Wizard

Add New Hardware

Summary

Your PC is a very flexible machine, and can be used to run all kinds of programs, both for work and for play. You can buy new programs at any computer store. Before you can use the program, however, you'll probably need to install it. Installation procedures have been the main focus of this chapter.

- ▼ When you buy a new program, it will usually be delivered to you on a CD-ROM or floppy disk.
- ▼ Before you can use that program, you'll probably need to **install** it on your PC.
- ▼ To install a new program, your best bet is to follow the **installation instructions** that came with that program.
- ▼ You can install most programs just by using a **wizard**. Put the program's floppy disk or CD-ROM into the appropriate drive. Open Control Panel, open Add/Remove Programs, and click the Install button.
- ▼ Always store your program's original disks, and any CD keys or serial numbers in a safe place. They are your **backups** in the event of a disaster!
- ▼ To remove a previously installed program, open Control Panel and open the **Add/Remove Programs icon**. Click on the name of the program you want to remove; then click the Add/Remove button.
- ▼ To install missing Windows components or to get rid of ones you don't need, open Add/Remove Programs and click on the **Windows Setup tab**.
- ▼ To install new Fonts, open the **Fonts icon** in Control Panel, and choose File → Install New Font from its menu bar.
- ▼ To install new hardware, hire someone who knows what they're doing. If you insist on doing it yourself, pay very careful attention to the manufacturer's instructions.

Part Three
Work and Play

Create Your Own Shortcuts 9

As you use your computer more and more, it's likely that you'll start getting tired of navigating through the Start menu every time you want to get to an often-used program. And you might get tired of going through Windows Explorer, My Computer, or Find to get to a folder that you use often. When that starts to happen, you'll definitely want to read this chapter. Here you'll learn how to give yourself shortcuts—that is, one-click access—directly from the Windows 98 Desktop or Quick Launch toolbar, to *anything* that's in your PC.

What Is a Shortcut?

It's really easy to create and delete shortcuts, on an as-needed basis, to give yourself fast access to programs, folders, and documents that you use frequently. However, before you start peppering your PC with shortcut icons, you'll want to be sure that you understand what a shortcut icon really is, and how to recognize one when you see one.

A **shortcut** to a file is not a copy of the file itself—it's just a **pointer** to the actual file. A shortcut icon looks just like the original file's icon, except that it has a little curved arrow in the lower-left corner. Take a look at the following examples of actual icons for a folder, document, and program, and the matching shortcut icons for each of those items.

The "real" icons are on the left, and the shortcuts are on the right.

The most important thing to understand about shortcuts is that you can *always* delete them without hurting the original files or folders that they point to. But when you delete the "real" (nonshortcut) icon for a folder or file, you're actually deleting the entire folder or file. So don't ever do that unless you're absolutely, positively sure you really want to delete that item.

Recycle to the Rescue: As discussed in Chapter 8, if you do delete an item by accident, you can fish it out of the Recycle Bin (using the Restore command), provided you do so before you empty the Recycle Bin.

Creating Desktop Shortcuts

The Windows 98 desktop is a great place to put shortcuts to your favorite programs, folders, and documents, because the desktop is the first thing you see every time you start your computer. And even when the desktop is crowded with lots of open windows, you can still get to it pretty quickly by clicking the Show Desktop button in the Quick Launch toolbar, or by right-clicking the taskbar and choosing Minimize All Windows.

Shortcuts to Menu Items

To create a shortcut to a program that's currently only accessible from your Start menu, first close any open windows so you can see the Windows 98 desktop. Then follow these steps:

▼ Click the Start button.

▼ Follow the usual path to the program for which you want to create a shortcut, by choosing whatever menu options are required to get there. However, when you actually get to your program, leave it highlighted but stop right there—don't click its icon.

▼ Leave the mouse pointer resting on the highlighted menu item, hold down the right mouse button, and drag the little outline that appears out to the Windows 98 desktop. In the following illustration, I've just started right-dragging the icon for the WordPad program out of the Accessories menu.

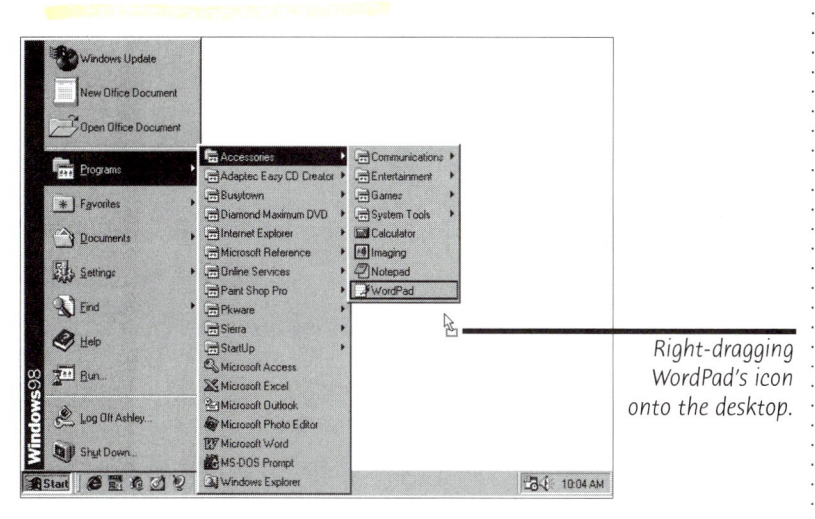

Right-dragging WordPad's icon onto the desktop.

▼ When the mouse pointer gets to the Windows 98 desktop (any part of it), release the mouse button and choose Create Shortcut(s) Here.

▼ You'll see a shortcut icon appear near the mouse pointer. It will have the same name as the original icon, but you can change that if you like. If you want to rename the new shortcut, right-click its icon, choose Rename, and type in a new name.

From now on, you can just click (or double-click, in Classic-style navigation) the shortcut icon on the desktop to open the program. There's no need to go through the menus any more. Should you ever decide to get rid of the new shortcut icon, you can just right-click it and choose Delete from the menu that appears.

9: CREATE YOUR OWN SHORTCUTS

223

9: CREATE YOUR OWN SHORTCUTS

Rearranging shortcut icons

If you don't have your desktop's Auto Arrange setting turned on, and you want to put your new icon into its proper alphabetical position on the screen, right-click a neutral area of the Windows 98 desktop and choose Arrange Icons ➔ By Name. Remember, though, that the icons you create are listed (and alphabetized) *after* the built-in desktop icons, including My Computer, My Documents, and Recycle Bin.

Shortcuts to Files and Folders

You can also create a shortcut from your desktop to any folder or file on your PC. The task is basically the same as what you just did for creating a shortcut item to a menu option. The only difference is that you need to drag the icon out of a browsing program rather than from the menu. Here's how:

▼ Use Windows Explorer, My Computer, or Find to locate the folder or file to which you want to create a shortcut. Don't open that icon, however; just manuever until you can see it.

▼ Right-drag the icon out to the Windows 98 desktop (any part of it).

▼ Release the mouse button and choose Create Shortcut(s) Here. In the following illustration, I've right-dragged the icon for my Little Windows Book folder out of the My Documents folder and onto the desktop.

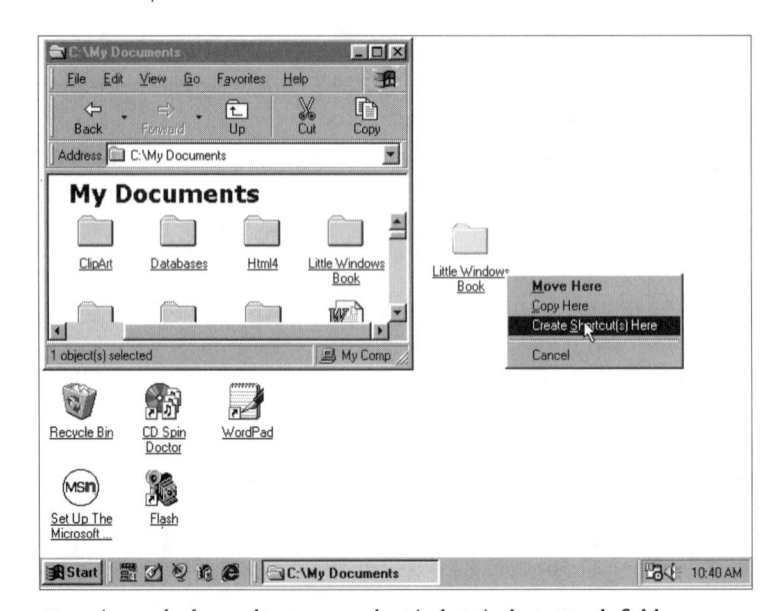

Creating a desktop shortcut to the Little Windows Book folder.

224

▼ You can rename shortcut icons for files and folders just as you can shortcut icons for programs. If you want to rename the shortcut you just created, just right-click it, choose Rename, and type in a new name.

To open the item that your new shortcut points to, just click (or double-click) the shortcut. If you ever decide to get rid of the shortcut, right-click it and choose Delete.

Back in Chapter 3 (under the heading "Taskbar Toolbars") I introduced you to the **Quick Launch toolbar.** That toolbar is a great place to put shortcuts to frequently used programs, folders, and documents. In fact, the advantage to having shortcuts on the Quick Launcher rather than the desktop is that the Quick Launch toolbar never gets covered up by open windows.

Shortcuts on the Quick Launcher

Well, let me restate that. The Quick Launch toolbar never gets covered up—*if* you display it in the taskbar and leave the taskbar set to Always On Top. So, before I show you how to add shortcuts to the Quick Launch toolbar, let's take a moment to make sure it's always going to be visible in your taskbar:

▼ Click the Windows 98 Start button and choose Settings → Taskbar and Start Menu.

Making the Quick Launcher Visible

▼ On the Taskbar Options tab of the Taskbar Properties dialog box, make sure Always On Top is selected. If you want your desktop to behave exactly like mine, set up the other checkboxes on your screen to match those shown here; click OK when you're done.

▼ If you already see the Quick Launch toolbar in your taskbar, you're all set—you can skip the steps that follow.

▼ To make the Quick Launch toolbar visible, right-click a neutral area of the taskbar (between buttons but not on a button).

▼ In the menu that appears, point to Toolbars to display the submenu. If Quick Launch is not selected (checked), click it. If Quick Launch is already selected, just close the menus by clicking somewhere outside them.

225

When you've finished, you should be able to see the taskbar with the Quick Launch toolbar in it. If you want, you can drag (horizontally) the thin vertical bars at the left and right ends of the Quick Launcher to size and position it on the taskbar.

If your Quick Launch toolbar appears floating freely on the desktop, and you want to put it into the taskbar, just drag it from the desktop right into the taskbar.

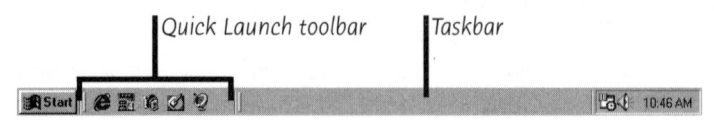

Windows 98 taskbar with the Quick Launch toolbar visible.

Adding the Shortcuts

Adding shortcuts to the Quick Launch toolbar is simple—you just right-drag any icon onto the toolbar, release the mouse button, and choose Create Shortcut(s) Here from the menu that appears. Here are the step-by-step instructions:

▼ Get to the icon for which you want to create a Quick Launcher shortcut. This can be any icon on the desktop, or any icon that's accessible from the Start menu, or any icon that you can locate with Windows Explorer, My Computer, or Find.

▼ Point to (but don't click) the icon that you want to add to the Quick Launcher.

▼ Hold down the secondary (right) mouse button and drag the icon right onto the Quick Launch toolbar. A dark "I-beam" indicator shows you where the icon will be placed.

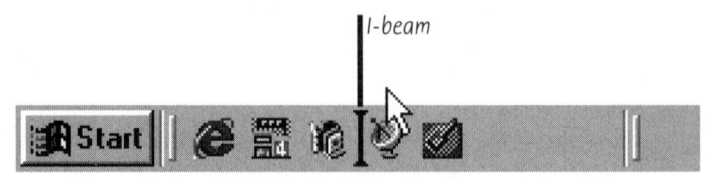

The I-beam in the Quick Launcher shows where a dropped icon will be placed.

Reposition the shortcut if you want

▼ If you want the shortcut to be in a different spot on the toolbar, drag the I-beam left or right until it's in the position you want.

▼ Release the mouse button and choose Create Shortcut(s) Here.

A new button, looking similar to the icon you dragged, is added to the Quick Launch toolbar. Now you have "quick-launch" access to the folder, file, or program that button refers to—one click on the shortcut icon is all it takes.

Each little button in the Quick Launch toolbar has a label that appears in a tooltip when you rest the mouse pointer on that icon. The label also appears under the icon in the toolbar itself, when the Show Text option (in the Quick Launcher's right-click menu) is turned on. You can easily change these labels by following these steps:

Renaming Quick Launch Buttons

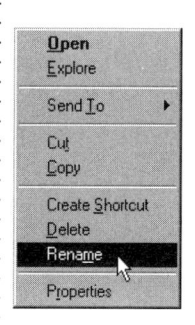

▼ Right-click a neutral area of the Quick Launch toolbar, or on the thin vertical bar at the left of the Quick Launch toolbar (not on a button or icon), and choose Open. This displays the Quick Launch window.

The Quick Launch window lets you rename the toolbar icons.

▼ In the Quick Launch window, right-click the icon that you want to rename, and choose Rename from the shortcut menu.

▼ Type in the new name.

▼ Press Enter or click anywhere outside the icon to save its new name.

▼ You can repeat these steps to rename as many icons as you wish. When you've finished, just close the Quick Launch window by clicking its Close (X) button.

Now when you point to a button in the Quick Launcher, that button's tooltip should display the button's new name. (If it doesn't, right-click the toolbar one more time, and choose Refresh. Then try again.)

Other Quick Launcher Tricks

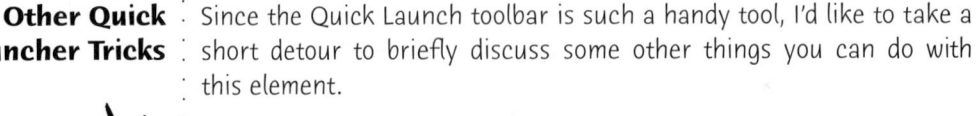

Since the Quick Launch toolbar is such a handy tool, I'd like to take a short detour to briefly discuss some other things you can do with this element.

For starters, don't forget that you can size and position the Quick Launch toolbar by dragging the thin vertical bars at both ends. Double-clicking the vertical bar on the left side automatically sizes the toolbar for an ideal fit.

In addition to controlling the size and position of the toolbar, you can do all of the following to tailor the toolbar to your own needs:

Resize the buttons

- To make the Quick Launcher's buttons large or small, right-click the toolbar (between the buttons but not on a button) or on the thin vertical bar at its left end to get the shortcut menu. Point to View and choose Large or Small from the submenu.

Right-click the Quick Launcher (not on a button, though) to view its shortcut menu.

Rearrange it

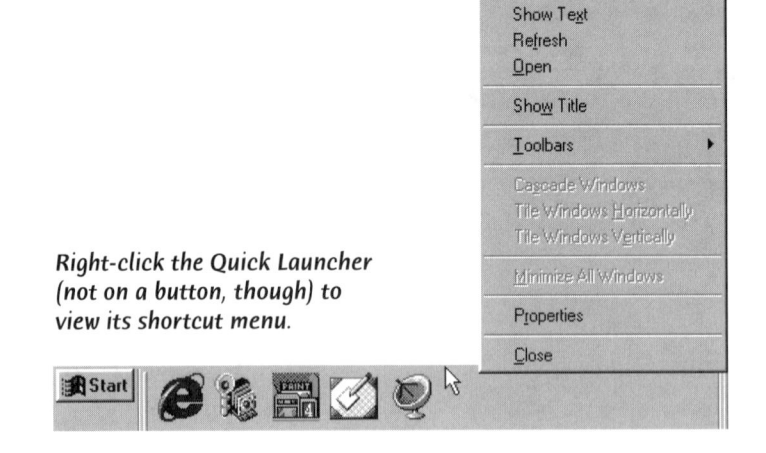

- To rearrange the buttons and shortcuts in the Quick Launcher, just right-drag any button left or right until the I-beam is in the position you want for a button. Then release the mouse button.

Hide/show the tables

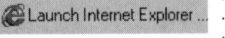

- To hide or show the labels that appear beside icons in the Quick Launch toolbar, right-click the toolbar and choose Show Text. In the example shown here in the margin, you can see the label for the icon that starts the Internet Explorer Web browser.

  Even if you turn off the button labels in the Quick Launcher, you can always see a label just by resting the mouse pointer on that icon and waiting a second or two for its tooltip to appear.

- To hide or show the name of the Quick Launch toolbar, right-click the toolbar and choose Show (or Hide) Title.

- To delete an icon from the Quick Launch toolbar, right-click the icon you want to delete and choose Delete. The icon is moved to the Recycle Bin.

  Oops: If you accidentally delete an icon from the Quick Launcher, you can restore it from the Recycle Bin, as discussed in Chapter 7. The icon's Type will be listed as Shortcut.

- To move or copy a shortcut from the Quick Launcher to the desktop, right-drag the icon to the desktop and then choose Move Here or Copy Here.

- Similarly, you can move or copy an icon from the desktop to the Quick Launcher by right-dragging from the desktop onto the toolbar.

Delete icons

Move/copy shortcuts

Your Start menu is really a collection of shortcuts. Normally, when you install a new program, that program automatically gets added to your Start menu—usually on the Programs submenu or within some program group on the Programs submenu. You can further customize your Start menu, however, adding shortcuts to any file or folder on your PC.

Shortcuts in the Start Menu

The process is virtually identical to creating a shortcut on the desktop or in the Quick Launch toolbar:

Adding a Shortcut to the Start Menu

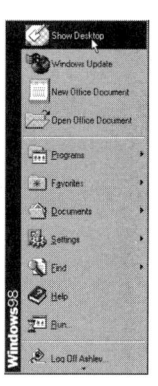

▼ Use Windows Explorer, My Computer, or Find to locate (but not click) the icon to which you want to create a shortcut. Or, pick an icon from the Windows 98 desktop or Quick Launch toolbar. As you can see, just about anything can become a shortcut on your Start menu.

▼ Right-drag the icon onto the Start button, and release the right mouse button to create your shortcut.

Initially, the new shortcut icon will appear at (or near) the top of the Start menu. For example, in this Start menu you see the Show Desktop icon at the top.

That's because I right-dragged the Show Desktop icon out of the Quick Launch toolbar onto the Start button. But you can change the Start menu into an arrangement that works for you. Let's see how.

229

9: CREATE YOUR OWN SHORTCUTS

Rearranging Start Menu Items

If your Start menu seems disorganized, making it hard to find things you need often, you can easily rearrange most items on the menus. (The items that you *can't* rearrange include anything below the "Programs" item.)

The simplest way to move a Start menu item is to do the following:

▼ Click the Start button and navigate through the menus (and submenus) to get to the icon that you want to move.

▼ Rest the mouse pointer on the item you want to move, hold down the primary mouse button, and start dragging the icon to wherever you want it. An I-beam will appear.

▼ When the I-beam gets to where you want to place the icon, release the mouse button. For example, if you want to move something to the Programs menu, drag the icon to Programs until that menu opens up.

Other Start Menu Changes

Working directly with items on the Start menu, as described just above, is one way to get things organized. There's another way, too. If you want to create new program groups, or if you have any trouble getting an icon from "point A" to "point B" by dragging, you can use the alternative method of reorganizing the Start menu—the **Start Menu window**.

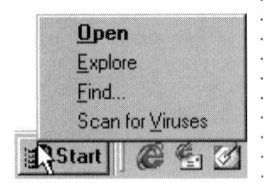

To get started with this method, you need to right-click the Windows 98 Start button and choose Open. This opens the Start Menu window. This window contains the same icons that are in the top part of your Start menu—namely, an icon for the Programs submenu and an icon for each item above it.

For example, here are the Start menu and the Start Menu window on one of my computers.

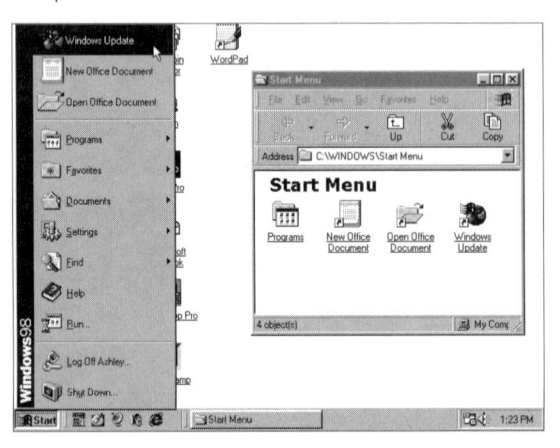

230

Notice that the Start Menu window and the top of the Start menu both contain the same items: Windows Update, New Office Document, Open Office Document, and Programs.

When I open the Programs icon in the Start Menu window, I'll see a bunch of icons for programs and program groups. The title bar for this dialog box reads "Programs," because that's the name of this group of icons. If I then point to the Programs option on the Start menu, I'll see the same set of icons. In the following example, I opened Programs in the Start Menu window and then clicked Start ➔ Programs. You can see that the icons on the Programs menu are identical to the icons in the Programs window.

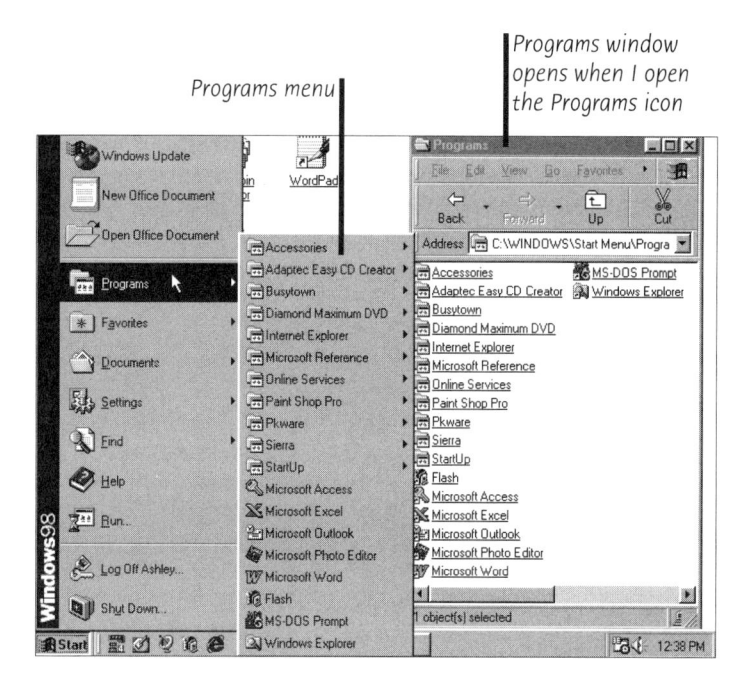

The Start Menu Folder

Icons in the Programs menu are the same as those in the Programs window

It works this way because everything you see in the Start menu is also stored in a **folder named Start Menu**, on your hard disk. Any changes you make to that folder will apply to the Start menu. And any changes you make directly to the Start menu will affect the Start Menu folder. The two are basically one and the same. The Start button is just a handy way to display and choose items that are in the Start Menu folder.

So, as an alternative to moving things around directly on the Start menu, you can move things around inside the Start Menu window.

In case you're wondering, the full path to the Start Menu folder is C:\Windows\Start Menu. Desktop shorcuts are also stored in a regular folder, named C:\Windows\Desktop.

231

Creating a New Program Group

Why should you use the Start Menu window to rearrange the Start menu?

A big advantage to using the Start Menu window is that you can also create your own folders there. These folders, when placed in the Programs menu, actually become **program groups**. I think an example might help illustrate what I mean.

Take another look at the Program menu I last showed you. You'll see that I have several programs from Microsoft Office listed there, including Access, Excel, Outlook, and Photo Editor. Suppose that, rather than keeping all those icons right on the Programs menu, I want them to be in their own little program group, perhaps named Microsoft Office.

Make a New Folder

The first step is to create a new folder, inside the Programs window, named Microsoft Office. To accomplish that:

- Right-click anywhere inside the Programs window (on blank space but not on an icon) and choose New → Folder to create a new folder.

- Rename that folder to whatever name you want to appear in the menu. For example, I might rename mine **Microsoft Office**. The new folder takes on the icon of a program group.

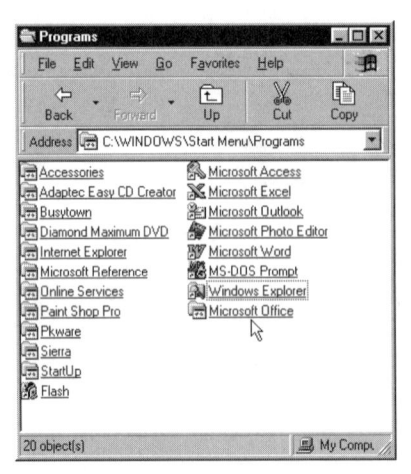

My new folder, named Microsoft Office, near the mouse pointer in my Programs window.

Drag In the Programs

The next step is to gather up all the items you want to have in the new program group.

To move items into the new program group:

- Select all the icons that you want to put into the new folder. In the following example I've selected programs from the Microsoft Office suite.

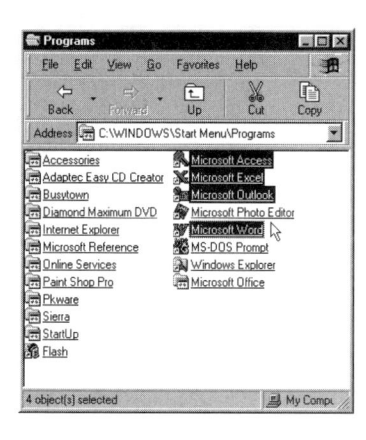

The icons to be moved into Microsoft Office folder are selected.

▼ With those icons selected, right-drag any selected icon until the mouse pointer is resting *right exactly on* that new folder (the one named Microsoft Office in my example).

▼ Release the mouse button and choose Move Here.

The selected icons disappear, because they've been moved into the Microsoft Office folder. (You can easily prove this simply by opening the Microsoft Office folder and looking at its contents.)

With that done, you can now close all open windows to get to the Windows 98 desktop. Next time you open the Start menu on that PC and point to Programs, you'll see your new program group. Opening that group will display whatever icons you dragged into that group. In my example, I'll see a new program group named Microsoft Office. Pointing to that option reveals the icons that I put into that folder.

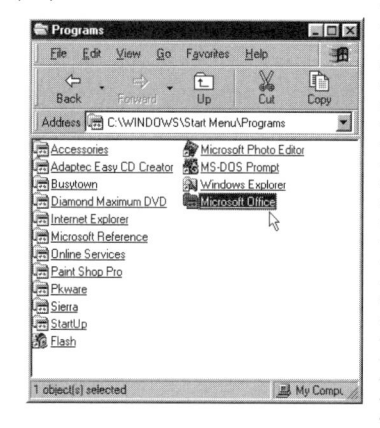

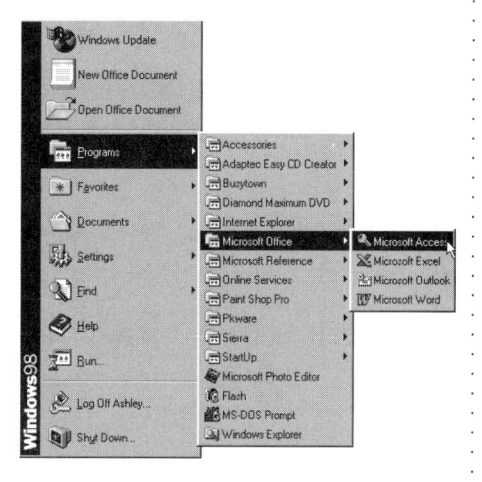

My Programs menu after creating a Microsoft Office program group.

I might point out that after you return to the Programs menu, you might not like where your new program group is placed. But you can fix that, right while you're looking at the Start ➔ Programs menu, simply by dragging the new icon to another position in the menu.

Still More Ways to Create Shortcuts

You'll be able to create any shortcut imaginable using the techniques described so far in this chapter. But Windows 98 offers yet more approaches to creating shortcuts. Choosing one approach or the other is simply a matter of personal preference, or doing whatever seems most convenient at the moment.

Send To ➔ Desktop as Shortcut

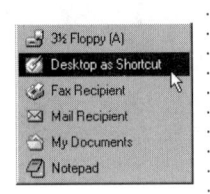

Let's suppose that you're browsing around your hard disk using Windows Explorer, My Computer, or Find. You come across an icon for something you know you're going to use a lot, and for which you'd like to create a shortcut. But suppose the desktop is currently crowded with open windows, and you don't feel like closing all of them at the moment to expose the desktop. Well, that's not a problem—because you don't *have* to right-drag the icon to the desktop to create a shortcut. You can, instead, just right-click that icon and choose Send To ➔ Desktop as Shortcut. Presto—Windows places a little shortcut to that icon right on your desktop.

The Create Shortcut Wizard

Another way to create a new desktop shortcut is to simply right-click the desktop and choose New ➔ Shortcut. This pops up the **Create Shortcut Wizard**. You can use the Browse button there to navigate to the program, folder, or file for which you want the shortcut.

Taskbar Properties Dialog box

As an alternative to working directly on the Start menu, you can use the **Taskbar Properties dialog box** to add and remove Start menu items. Here are the steps:

▼ Click Start ➔ Settings ➔ Taskbar & Start Menu.

▼ Click the Start Menu Programs tab.

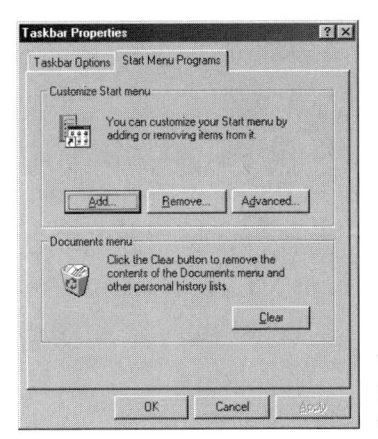

Yet another way to mess around with the Start menu.

▼ In the Start Menu Programs tab, use the Add, Remove, and Advanced buttons to add programs to or remove programs from your Start menu. Here's what to expect:

Add button: Takes you to a Create Shortcut wizard. Here you can create a shortcut by typing a path to the desired file, or by clicking a Browse button and then navigating to the file to which the shortcut will point.

Remove button: Takes you to a Windows Explorer-type view, where you can point to any icon and then click the Remove button to remove that option from the Start menu.

Advanced button: Takes you to a Windows Explorer view of the Start Menu folder. There, you can manipulate the Start menu options in the same way you'd manipulate any other icons in any other window.

> With so many different ways available to create shortcuts, you should be able to set up a shortcut to any file on your PC. To avoid cluttering your desktop or Quick Launch toolbar with too many icons, you might want to create a new set of shortcuts for each project you undertake on your PC. When you've finished with that particular project, you can get rid of its shortcuts as easily as you created them.

Summary

Shortcuts are little icons that provide quick access to frequently used programs, folders, and documents. As you gain experience with your computer, you'll probably want to start creating your own custom shortcuts to the items on your computer that you need to open often. There are several ways to create shortcuts, and a couple of techniques for organizing them:

- ▼ To put a shortcut icon **on the Windows 98 desktop**, locate the icon for which you want to create the shortcut. Then right-drag that icon out to the desktop and choose Create Shortcut(s) Here.

- ▼ Here's another way to put a new shortcut on your Windows 98 desktop. When you find the icon to which you want to create a shortcut, right-click that icon and choose Send To → Desktop as Shortcut.

- ▼ To add a shortcut item **to the Quick Launch toolbar**, just right-drag any icon onto the toolbar, release the mouse button, and choose Create Shortcut(s) Here. To reorganize items in the Quick Launch toolbar, just drag the items right and left.

- ▼ To add a shortcut item **to the Start menu**, drag an icon to the Start button and drop it there. To reorganize items in the Start menu, just drag any item to a new location.

- ▼ You can also organize the Start menu by right-clicking the Start button and choosing Open.

- ▼ Here's yet a third way to customize your Start menu: Click Start → Settings → Taskbar & Start Menu, and then click the Start Menu Programs tab.

Performance, Maintenance, & Troubleshooting

Most machines need a little tune-up and maintenance once in a while, just to keep running smoothly. Your PC is no exception. Fortunately, the task of getting your PC running at its best, and keeping it there, doesn't require any wrenches or messy fluids. You just need to run a few programs. Even with regular maintenance, however, problems can arise. Fortunately, Windows 98 has some built-in troubleshooters to help you deal with those problems. In this chapter we'll look at the various caretaking techniques that you can use to get the most from your PC and keep it running at its full potential. You'll also learn how to troubleshoot many of the problems that routine maintenance cannot prevent or solve.

Converting to FAT 32

Windows 98 can use a relatively new technology called **FAT 32** (the FAT stands for **File Allocation Table**) to manage files stored on a disk. This new technology stores information more compactly and efficiently than the older FAT 16 method used by earlier versions of Windows. The end result is that your programs start faster, and you can actually put more stuff on the hard disk.

Converting your drive to FAT 32 is fairly easy. You need only do it once (in fact, you're only *allowed* to do it once).

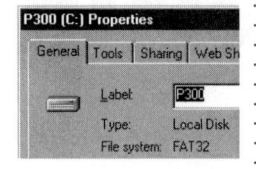

Already Using FAT 32? To see whether or not your hard drive is already using FAT 32, open My Computer, right-click the icon for your hard drive, and choose Properties. The General tab contains an item for the current File System. If yours is already set to FAT 32 like the example shown in the margin, then you can skip the rest of this section. Go on ahead to the section on "Tuning Up Your Hard Disk."

If you do want to convert to FAT32, be forewarned that once you start the process, it runs all by itself—but for several hours! Fortunately, you don't need to be sitting at the PC. So you might want to start the process just before leaving the office or going to a movie or whatever.

Starting the Conversion

When you're ready to give it a whirl, you just need to follow these simple steps:

▼ Save all your work, if necessary, and then close all open programs, windows, documents, and so forth to get to the Windows 98 desktop.

▼ Click the Start button and choose Programs → Accessories → System Tools → Drive Converter (FAT 32).

▼ In the first window of the **Drive Converter (FAT32) Wizard**, click the Next button.

▼ In the next wizard screen, select the drive to convert. Most likely, this will be your main hard drive, C:. Then click the Next button.

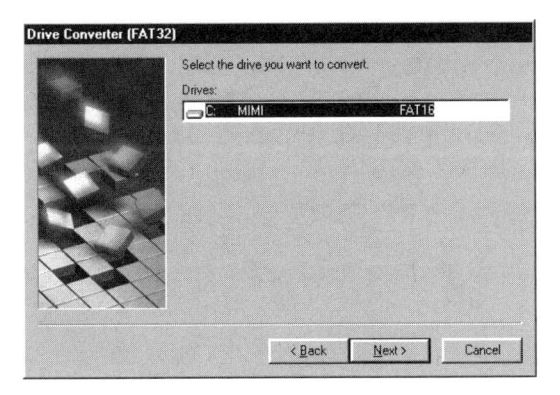

The wizard will start looking for programs that are likely to crash and burn (so to speak) when faced with FAT 32. Exactly what will happen next is difficult to predict. It all depends on what the wizard finds on your PC. You may get a warning about anti-virus programs, like this one:

Wizard Warnings

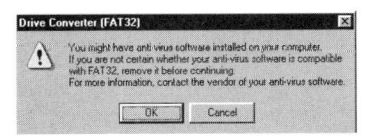

This warning about FAT 32 and anti-virus programs may show up before you start the conversion.

I really can't tell you specifically how to handle this warning because I don't know about your PC. If your PC is at work and you have resident experts, you might want to ask them for help. On a PC at home, if you don't use an anti-virus program often (or don't know an anti-virus program from a cantaloupe), then you probably needn't worry about it. You can click OK to carry on. If you do decide to stop the conversion at this point, clicking Cancel will stop the whole procedure, and the drive is not altered in any way.

▼ Next, you'll probably see this warning:

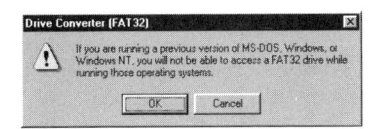

Warning for people who use multiple operating systems on one PC.

In general, this warning occurs if you've configured your PC so that you can boot up in two or more operating systems. Again, I can't make the choice for you of what to do at this point. If, for whatever reason, you are running another operating system, then you may lose

10: PERFORMANCE, MAINTENENCE, AND TROUBLESHOOTING

access to files in the Windows 98 partition when you boot up in the alternative system. So if that's gonna be a problem, you can click the Cancel button to stop the conversion right now.

> **Booting to DOS**: Actually, the ability to boot up into DOS is built right into Windows 98; it's available on the Shut Down menu (Start ➜ Shut Down). Booting to DOS, however, does *not* count as a separate operating system—at least, not in a context that's relevant here.

On the other hand, if you are like 99% of the rest of us and have only one operating system (Windows 98) on your PC, then this is not an issue. You can just click the OK button to move on.

Incompatible Programs

▼ Which brings you to the next wizard window, listing any other potentially incompatible programs. Yours may look like the following example, in which no programs are listed, and then you're home free. Click the Next button and ignore the next paragraph.

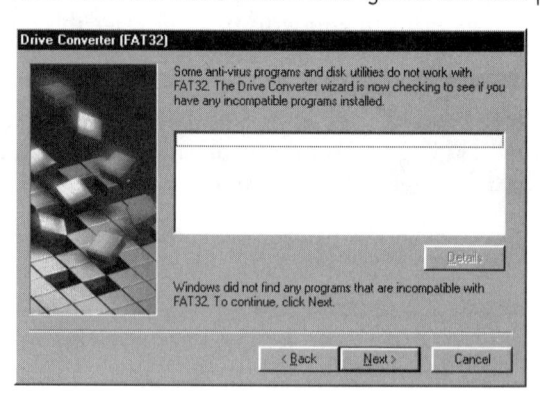

No FAT 32-incompatible programs found; this system is ready to convert.

If you do have incompatible programs, it's decision time.

Should you see a list of potentially incompatible programs, however, then I'm afraid you'll have to decide for yourself whether to forge ahead and lose the use of those programs, or to cancel the whole conversion. (Again, if you're at work, consult a resident expert before proceeding.) To with the conversion, click the Next button. Or, if you want to bail out now, click the Cancel button.

Backing Up

▼ Proceeding with the conversion, the next wizard screen asks if you want to back up your hard drive first. If you have a device for backing up your drive and you know how to use it, it's likely that you've already backed up your hard disk. Otherwise, you can back it up right now. This is a safety precaution, just in case something goes really wrong during or after the conversion.

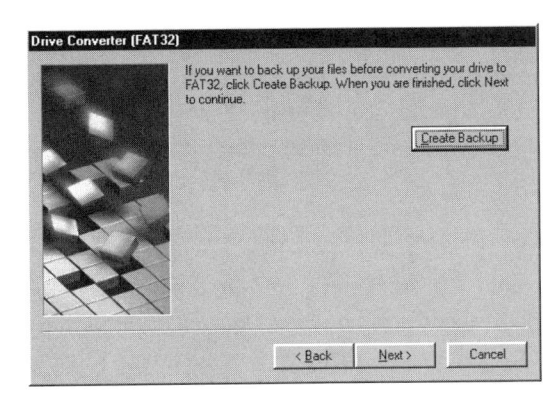

You get an opportunity to back up your entire hard drive before proceeding.

It's Best to Back Up. If you don't have any means of backing up your entire hard disk, you can go ahead with the conversion and take your chances. But remember, in the unlikely event that the conversion fails, you could lose everything on your hard disk. So once again, the decision is your own.

▼ If you do want to proceed, click the Next button to get to the last of the wizard's options

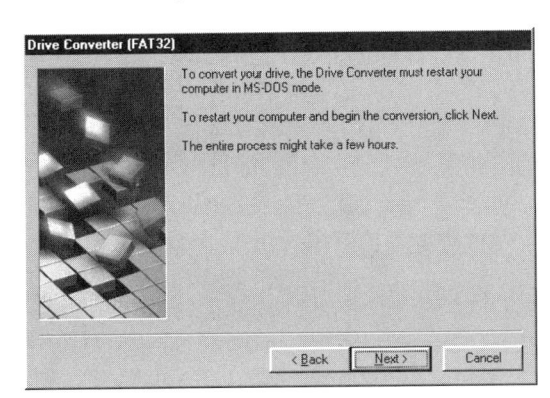

Last chance to change your mind before converting to FAT 32.

Right now would be a really good time to check your PC and make sure there is no floppy disk in drive A:. For that matter, you might as well remove all floppy disks and CD-ROMs. If you have any doubts, this is your last chance to change your mind—that Cancel button is still available to you.

▼ But if it's all systems go, click the Next button. You won't need to answer any more questions. You can just leave the PC running now, and go to lunch, bed, or wherever. When the conversion is complete, the wizard will pop up a window telling you so, and that window will just sit there and wait until you show up.

Completing the Conversion

When you do get there, just click the Finish button to carry on. You won't notice any change when you get to the Windows 98 desktop. But after you perform the tune-ups described in the sections that follow, you might notice that large programs start up more quickly than they used to.

Tuning Up Your Hard Disk

On any PC, the hard disk is one component that's likely to become a bottleneck, preventing your PC from operating at top speed. When a hard disk isn't working at peak performance, you may notice that it takes quite a long time to open programs and documents. (That is, there's a long delay between your mouse click and the actual appearance of the requested file on the screen.) Three factors contribute to the hard disk's slowing down:

- **Too many files**: When you have a lot of unnecessary old temporary files on your hard disk, you're not only wasting space but may also be making the hard disk work harder by having to look through more files.

- **Bad sectors**: It's possible for a hard disk to develop bad sectors (sort of like little rough spots on the disk) that can no longer store data. Too many bad sectors can also slow the performance of your PC.

- **Fragmentation**: A fragmented file is one that is "spread out" over the hard disk rather than being in one place. Reading such a file causes the drive head to work harder and longer. **Defragmenting** your hard disk helps prevent that kind of slowdown.

System Tools

Windows comes with several easy-to-use programs that you can run to take care of these disk housekeeping chores and get your hard disk running at its full potential again. The names of these helper programs are listed in the following table, along with information on how long it might take each program to complete its job once you start it. All three programs are available as **system tools** (click the Start button and point to Programs → Accessories → System Tools). To run any of those programs, just select its name from the System Tools menu and follow the instructions that appear on the screen.

10: PERFORMANCE, MAINTENENCE, AND TROUBLESHOOTING

Program	Purpose	Run Duration
Disk Cleanup	Delete unnecessary files	A few seconds
ScanDisk	Check and repair bad sectors	A few minutes
Disk Defragmenter	Fix fragmented files	An hour or more

> Before you spend a lot of time waiting for some of these programs to do their job, let me give you some perspective on what to expect. If your PC is the digital equivalent of a 1976 Ford Pinto, doing a tune-up on that PC won't turn it into a Ferrari. Rather, the tune-up will make that PC run like a 1976 Ford Pinto with a tune-up. So please don't expect miracles!

Which One First?

Should you decide to run each of the system maintenance programs manually, you should run Disk Cleanup first, followed by ScanDisk, and then Disk Defragmenter.

But before you get started, there's an alternative to running each program manually and waiting for each job to finish: You can have your Windows system do these maintenance tasks for you, automatically, while you're away from the computer. This makes more sense because it doesn't waste your time. Plus, it's pretty easy to schedule these tasks to take place in your absence. So what the heck—let's look at it from that perspective.

Automating Maintenance Tasks

The best way to maintain your hard disk's efficiency is to simply choose a time—perhaps once a week—when you can leave the PC on all night. And then schedule the maintenance tasks to take place during that night.

> To schedule periodic maintenance in this manner, you must first make sure your PC's calendar and clock are accurate. If you don't remember how to do that, see "Setting Date/Time" in Chapter 5.

When you're sure your clock and calendar are correct, follow these steps to schedule your maintenance tasks:

▼ Click the Windows 98 Start button and choose Programs ➔ Accessories ➔ System Tools ➔ Maintenance Wizard.

If asked what you want to do next, choose the option for "Change my maintenance settings or schedule" and click OK. Then you'll come to the first **Maintenance Wizard** screen.

243

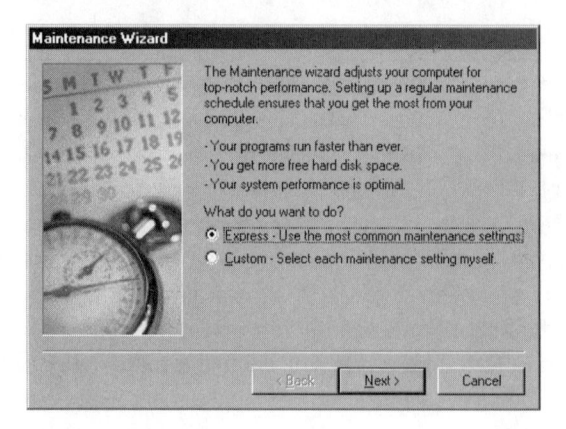

10: PERFORMANCE, MAINTENENCE, AND TROUBLESHOOTING

▼ Choose the Express option, and click the Next button to move to the second wizard screen.

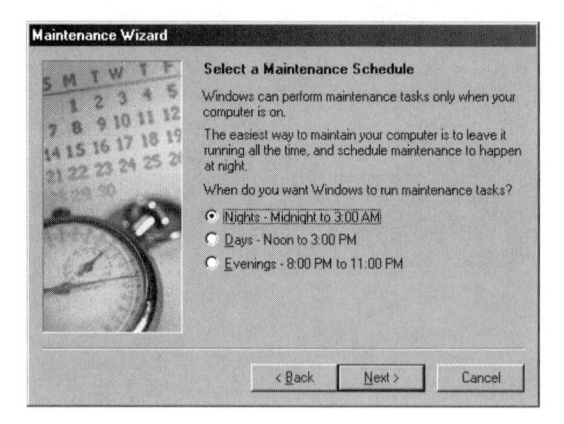

What Time of Day?

▼ This screen offers three different **time-period options** for your regular maintenance. Each option performs the maintenance weekly (though you can change that if you wish, which I'll discuss shortly). So you just need to choose the time when you're least likely to be using your computer. For example, you can see that I've chosen "Nights - Midnight to 3:00 AM."

▼ When you've made your selection, click the Next button. You'll come to the third and final wizard screen.

244

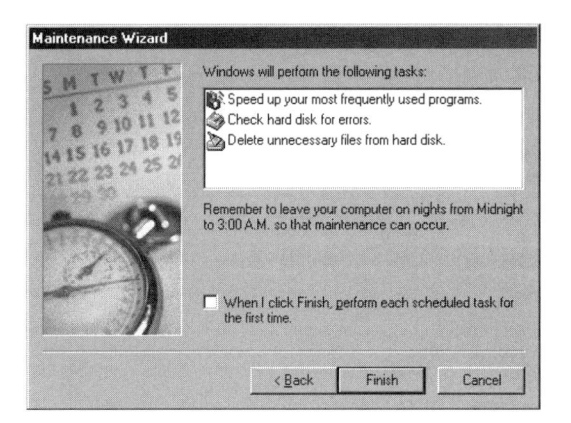

Don't forget to leave your computer on when the scheduled maintainence will happen.

▼ The last wizard screen contains a list telling you which tasks are scheduled, and a message about when you'll need to leave your computer on to perform those tasks. It also offers a checkbox option that lets you run the scheduled tasks immediately. Since we're not going to do that right now, leave this checkbox empty and click the Finish button.

You're done, and your scheduled maintenace will get done at the time you've designated. In this example, the three tasks that the wizard scheduled will take place only once a week, on Sunday.

You may find you've picked the wrong day or time of day for your computer maintenance (maybe it's not easy for you to leave your computer on all night every Sunday after all). If so, you can make changes and refinements to the schedule without going through the wizard. To do so, you need to open the **Scheduled Tasks window**. Use either of the following techniques, whichever is most convenient at the moment:

- Click the Start button and choose Programs → Accessories → System Tools → Scheduled Tasks.
- Or, double-click the tiny Task Scheduler icon in the Indicators section of the Windows 98 taskbar.

Changing the Schedule

10: PERFORMANCE, MAINTENENCE, AND TROUBLESHOOTING

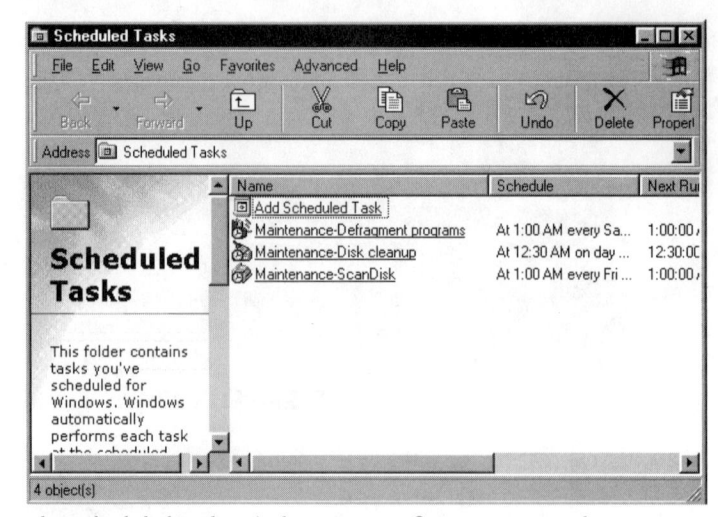

The Scheduled Tasks window on one of my PCs, opened up so I can alter the maintenance schedule.

Rescheduling a Task You can easily reschedule any item in the Tasks list just by clicking it (or double-clicking it in Classic-style navigation). A dialog box appears, showing the name of the program and various options for when and if the program is run. For example, you can click the Schedule tab of the dialog box to get to the details of that item's schedule.

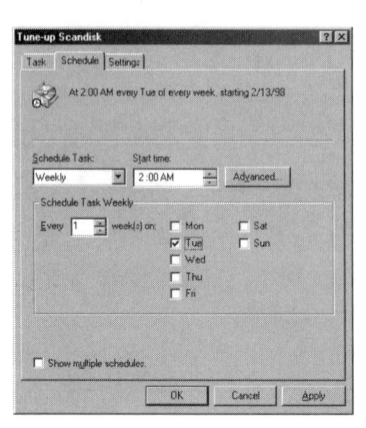

Here's the Schedule tab for the ScanDisk maintenance task.

To reschedule this task, make selections from the options shown. In the screen just above, I've rescheduled ScanDisk to run every Tuesday morning at 2:00 A.M. I could do the same for the other scheduled tasks. Then I would need to remember to leave my computer running overnight on Monday night, so all the work gets done in the wee hours of Tuesday morning.

You may want to widen the first two columns of the dialog box, so you can read them more easily. Just drag the border on the right-hand side of the Name and/or Schedule column headings to the left or right, until you get to the desired width. In the window just below, you can see that I've rescheduled Disk Cleanup, ScanDisk, and Defragment to run at various times early on Tuesday mornings. The widened columns make it easier to see the program names and start times.

Making the Scheduled Tasks window easier to read

> **Stay in Order**: If you elect to reschedule the times for running the tune-up programs, try to maintain the same sequential order for the programs. Have Disk Cleanup run first, followed by ScanDisk, and Disk Defragmenter last, as in the example shown in this section.

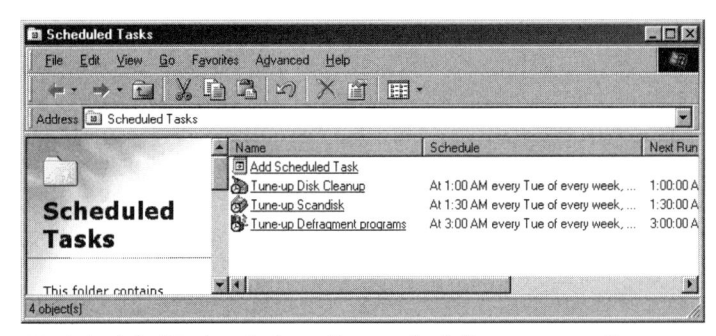

My Scheduled Tasks window after rescheduling tune-ups for Tuesday mornings.

It's easy to add tune-up tasks of your own to the list of Scheduled Tasks. Just click the Add Scheduled Task option in the Scheduled Tasks dialog box, and let the wizard guide you through the process. If for whatever reason you need to schedule programs to run at a very specific time, and only under certain conditions, there are more options to choose from. You'll find that they're all fairly self-explanatory. To check them out, click any task listed in your Task Scheduler. Then, on the Schedule tab, click the Advanced button to make changes and refinements to the task's scheduling and execution.

Adding Other Maintenance Tasks

To adjust *how* the program is run at the scheduled time, click the Settings tab. For more information on any option, remember that you can click the question-mark button near the upper-right corner of the dialog box. Then click the option about which you're seeking help. As always, you can also get detailed help from the Windows help system. Press F1, click the Index tab, and type **sch** to jump down to the information on scheduled tasks.

Troubleshooting

When problems arise and you just can't seem to get something working correctly, the built-in Windows 98 **Troubleshooters** can be your saving grace. These take you step-by-step through the process of tracking down and correcting many common problems that people face with their PCs. The Troubleshooters are actually built into the Windows help system.

To start the Troubleshooters:

- ▼ Save any work in progress and close all open windows and programs.
- ▼ Click the Start button and choose Help. If necessary, click the Contents tab to open it up.
- ▼ Open the Troubleshooting book.
- ▼ In the list of new book icons that appears, choose Windows 98 Troubleshooters. Here's the Windows 98 Help window showing the Troubleshooters list:

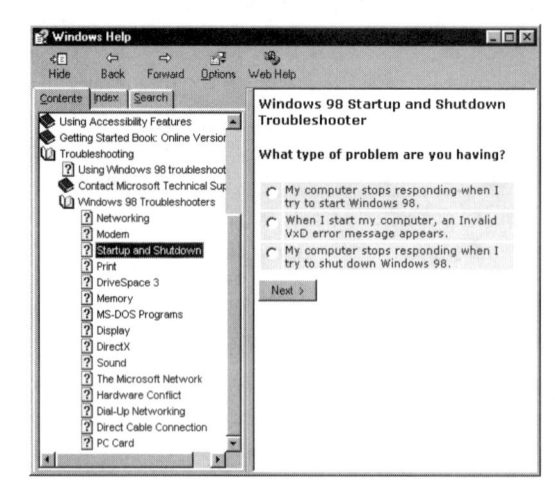

The Windows 98 Troubleshooters can solve lots of problems.

- ▼ From the list of Troubleshooters topics, click whichever topic best describes the area of your problem.
- ▼ In the pane on the right, choose an item that best describes your problem or question, and click the Next button.

From here on out, it's up to you to read and respond to questions as they appear on the screen. I can't help you out much here because each problem is likely to have its own particular solution. But as a rule, you'll find the Troubleshooters quite easy to use, and successful at solving many little difficulties.

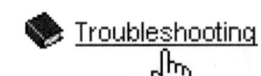

Those of you who already have access to the Internet and know a little about using a Web browser, such as Microsoft Internet Explorer or Netscape Navigator, may want to check in at the **Windows 98 Update Web site** from time to time, just to see what's new. If you don't have Internet access or don't know how to use it yet, or if you have any problems following the steps below, there's no harm in skipping the rest of this chapter for the moment. Stick a post-it on this page and come back after you've read Part IV of the book.

Experienced Internet users who are ready to find out how Windows Update works can follow these steps to get to the Windows Update site:

▼ Click the Start button.
▼ Choose Windows Update from the top of the Start menu.

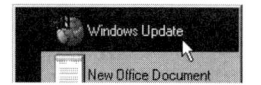

Your Web browser will start, and you'll be taken to the Microsoft Windows Update site at **http://update.microsoft.com**

This page changes from time to time, and so do its authors. Here's an example of how it looked today when I browsed to it:

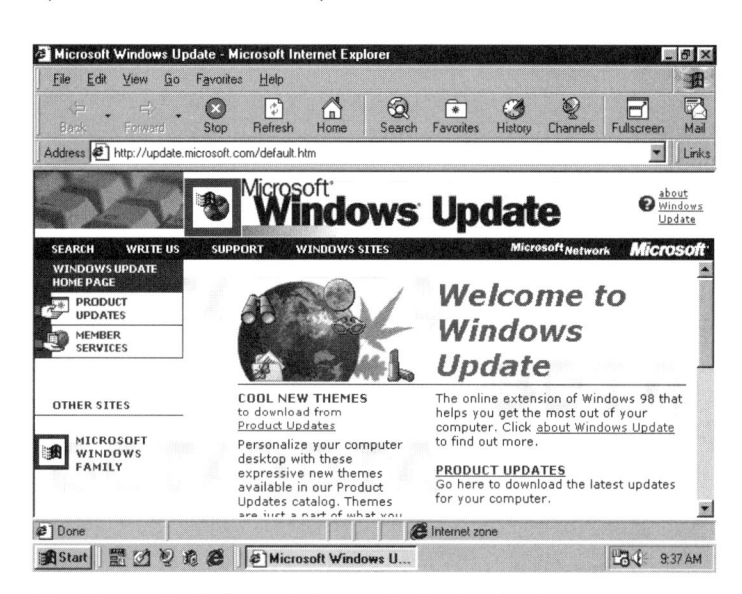

The Microsoft Windows Update Web site in July 1998.

Once again, you're on your own. Feel free to explore and see what's new. You certainly can't do any harm just by browsing around, and you're likely to find at least a few items of interest.

Keeping Windows Up-to-Date

Windows Update Site

Other Places to Nose Around

Windows 98 can dish up highly detailed technical information about your PC. For the most part, average users like you and me don't really need to see that much technical information. Engineers, technicians, and repair people are the ones who use that information to help them do more "heavy-duty" troubleshooting and repair. Nevertheless, you may be interested.

My goal for this book certainly isn't to overwhelm you with all kinds of behind-the-scenes technical information that isn't relevant to everyday use of Windows. But if you're curious about what's inside your PC, or if someone has asked you for detailed information on a component in your PC, you may need to know where to get the answer.

Looking Under the Hood

You can probably find out what you need to know just by exploring your system's technical innards. There are two ways to do so, and choosing one or the other is largely a matter of personal preference. You can use either the Microsoft System Information dialog box, or the System Properties dialog box.

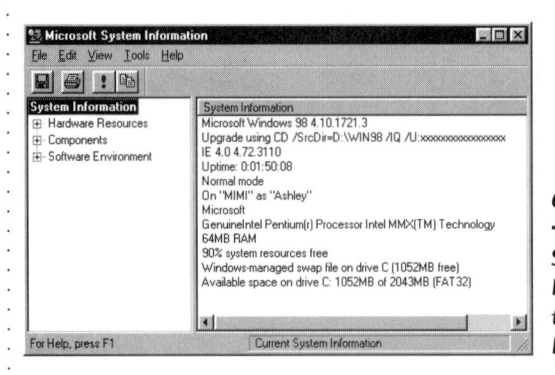

Click Start → Programs → Accessories → System Tools → System Information to get to the Microsoft System Information dialog box.

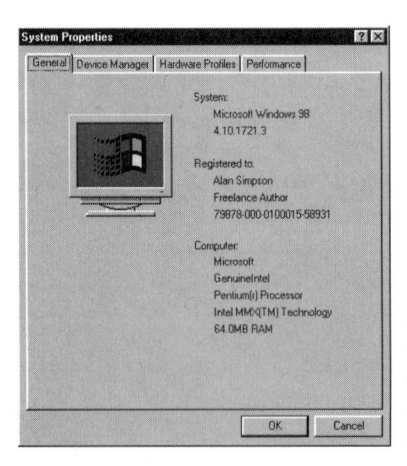

Click Start → Settings → Control Panel and open the System icon to get to the System Properties dialog box.

These two programs are just two different ways to explore and in some cases change some of the deep-down nitty-gritty settings inside your PC. Many of you won't be concerned with much more than just looking around at the brand names and capabilities of various components, such as your display card, CD-ROM drive, and so forth.

You can also print information from both of these programs. In Microsoft System Information, just choose File ➔ Print from the menu bar. In the System Properties dialog box, click the Device Manager tab and then click the Print button.

In fact, it's an excellent idea to print up all the system information that you can, from one program or the other, and put that printed document someplace where you can easily find it in the future. If your machine ever breaks down and you need to take it to a repair shop or describe a problem over the phone, you'll have this printed information available for the repair or support person's reference. It's a good bet that at least some of the information will be helpful in getting your repair done more quickly and inexpensively.

Printing a Hardware Record

Summary

In this chapter we've looked at tools and techniques for keeping your PC running at its full potential. The information presented here will help you to focus on what you're most likely to need to know, without having to turn yourself into some kind of full-time PC repair technician.

- ▼ Most options for tuning and maintaining your PC are on the **System Tools menu** (click the Start button and choose Programs → Accessories → System Tools).

- ▼ The new **FAT 32** capability in Windows 98 can help your hard disk store information more efficiently and your programs start more quickly.

- ▼ To convert your C: drive to FAT 32, click Start → Programs → Accessories → System Tools → Drive Converter (FAT 32), and then follow the instructions that appear on the screen.

- ▼ To get your hard disk running at its best, run the **Disk Cleanup**, **ScanDisk**, and **Disk Defragmenter** programs (in that order) from the System Tools menu. To keep your hard disk running at top speed, use the Task Scheduler to do run these tasks weekly, while you're away from the computer.

- ▼ To open the **Task Scheduler**, click Start → Programs → Accessories → System Tools → Scheduled Tasks. Or double-click the Task Scheduler indicator in the taskbar.

- ▼ To troubleshoot common problems, click Start → Help. On the Contents tab, open the Troubleshooting book and then open the **Windows 98 Troubleshooters** book.

- ▼ If you have Internet access, you can run **Windows Update** from the Start menu to check for recent updates and enhancements for Windows 98.

Windows 98 Entertainment

In this chapter we'll look at some of the new Entertainment features that come with Windows 98. Please be aware, however, that the features described in this chapter only work if your PC has the appropriate hardware built in. For example, you can't play audio CDs unless your PC has a CD-ROM drive and sound capabilities. You can't watch TV on your PC unless it has a TV adapter, or a built-in multifunction display card (such as ATI's All-In-Wonder card).

If some of the features in this chapter are of interest to you but your PC is missing the required hardware, check with your local dealer or repair shop to see what it will cost to equip your machine with what's needed.

Music, TV, and More

In addition to the media control features of Windows 98, you should be aware that many multimedia hardware devices come with programs of their own. Also, PC manufacturers often provide their own multimedia control programs to support the multimedia capabilities of that particular PC.

Whether you use the manufacturer's programs or the Windows 98 programs discussed in this chapter is purely a matter of personal preference. The Windows 98 programs are somewhat generic, in that they're designed to work with a wide variety of devices. You may find that the program that came with your PC or multimedia hardware actually provides more options!

Playing Audio CDs

On PCs that have a CD-ROM drive, you can use that drive as an audio CD player. In other words, you can stick a regular audio CD—the kind you normally use on your sound system or CD player—into the computer's CD-ROM drive and listen to the CD. You can listen through the computer's speakers or a pair of headphones.

> **Set Speaker Volume First.** If you're going to play CDs on your computer, you need to learn to control the volume of your speakers or headphones. For instructions, or if you need a refresher, see "Controlling Sound" in Chapter 5.

Windows CD Player

When you're ready to play an audio CD in your PC, follow these steps:

The icon shows that there's an audio CD in drive D:.

- ▼ Put the audio CD into your CD-ROM drive, label side up.
- ▼ Wait 30 seconds or so to see if the CD starts playing automatically.
- ▼ If the CD doesn't start playing automatically, open My Computer. Right-click the icon for your CD-ROM drive and choose Play from the shortcut menu.

Typically, you'll hear the CD playing, and a button for the **CD Player applet** appears down in the taskbar. When you click that taskbar button, the CD Player applet will open. You can work the player in much the same way you'd work a normal CD player. In this case, of course, you'll need to work the buttons using the mouse rather than pushing in buttons on an electronic control panel.

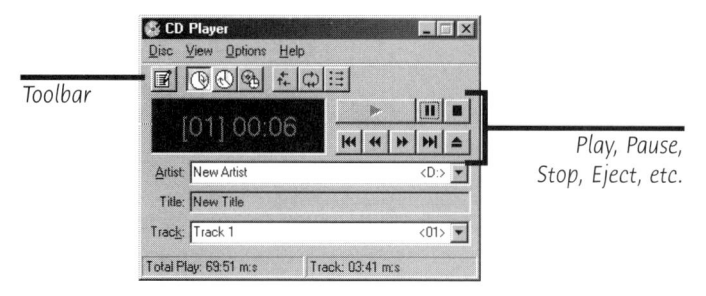

Toolbar

Play, Pause, Stop, Eject, etc.

The Windows 98 Audio CD Player applet.

You can also start CD Player by clicking the Start button and choosing Programs → Accessories → Entertainment → CD Player.

Using the Entertainment Menu

> If CD Player isn't available on the Entertainment menu, that means it isn't installed. You can install it following the steps described under "Installing Missing Windows Components" in Chapter 8. Entertainment components are listed under Multimedia in the Components list.

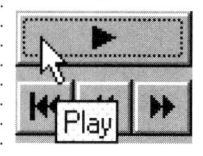

Most of the buttons and indicators of CD Player will undoubtedly look quite familiar to you. If you're not sure which button is which, just point to the button to view its tooltip. The main play buttons are virtually identical to the buttons on a regular CD player. You can play an entire CD, or just listen to particular tracks (songs). The buttons all have tooltips, as listed below:

CD Player's Buttons

Button	Function
Play	Starts playing the CD (dimmed while CD is playing)
Pause	Pause/resume play at current position
Stop	Stop playing the CD
Previous Track	Go back one track
Skip Backwards	Move back within current track
Skip Forwards	Move forward within current track
Next Track	Move to next track
Eject	Stop playing the CD and eject it from the CD-ROM drive

CD Player's Options

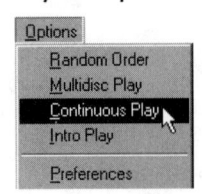

The CD Player's menus and toolbar buttons provide additional options and commands. You can turn the toolbar and other parts of the CD Player on and off using options on the View menu. You can also use the following features from the toolbar and Options menu:

Feature	Function
Random Order	Plays tracks in random order
Multidisc Play	Allows you to play more than one CD, if your CD-ROM drive is capable of holding multiple CDs
Continuous Play	When the last song on the CD is finished, starts over again at the first song for continuous music
Intro Play	Plays only the first few seconds of each track

All in all, it's pretty simple. Just like a car stereo, really. You won't need any more help from me to enjoy your CD player. If you want it, CD Player has its own built-in online help. So if you have any questions, you'll probably find the answers just by clicking on Help in the menu bar and then browsing around in the help topics.

The optional Windows 98 Plus! program comes with a **Deluxe CD Player** that's a bit fancier than the one built into Windows 98. In fact, if you have an Internet connection, the Deluxe CD Player will identify your audio CD, then download a list of song titles and play times from the Internet. So instead of seeing Track 1, Track 2, and so forth in the Tracks list, you see the actual name and play time of each song. Very cool!

WebTV for Windows

WebTV for Windows is a new technology that promises to make television of the future a whole new experience for consumers.

Get the hardware first

To use WebTV, your computer must have a Windows 98-compatible TV tuner. As mentioned at the outset of this chapter, if you don't have a TV adapter (or other entertainment component) in your PC, you can have one installed at any computer store that does upgrades and repairs. Check with your dealer for pricing. Make sure they understand that you want a card that's compatible with Windows 98.

Once your PC is equipped with a TV tuner, you can use the Windows 98 WebTV program to watch normal television programs right on your Windows 98 desktop. You can display WebTV in full-screen mode or in a window, even while using other programs. You'll also be able to watch the new and emerging **enhanced TV programs** that blend traditional television with the interactive nature of the PC. In addition, you'll be able to get updated program listings—sort of an electronic version of *TV Guide*—through your PC.

There are basically three components to WebTV for Windows:

WebTV Components

WebTV Component	Description
TV Configuration	TV Config (as it's typically called) is a wizard, of sorts, that helps you set up your TV tuner card to work properly with Windows 98 and WebTV for Windows.
Program Guide	Sort of an electronic *TV Guide*, the Program Guide lets you see what's on TV today. Can be updated automatically each night, while you sleep.
TV Viewer	This is the actual TV screen on your monitor, complete with its own channel-changer. You can watch TV full screen, or in a window.

To use WebTV for Windows, follow these steps:

Starting WebTV

▼ Click the Launch Web TV for Windows button in the Quick Launch toolbar. **Or,** click the Windows 98 Start button and point to Programs → Accessories → Entertainment.

▼ Choose WebTV for Windows.

> If your PC has a TV tuner card but WebTV for Windows is not available on the Entertainment menu, you need to install WebTV. Do this through the Windows Setup tab of Add/Remove Programs, as discussed under "Installing Missing Windows Components" in Chapter 8.

Exactly what happens next depends on whether or not you've used WebTV before.

▼ If the WebTV Configuration "wizard" starts up, see the upcoming section "WebTV Configuration."

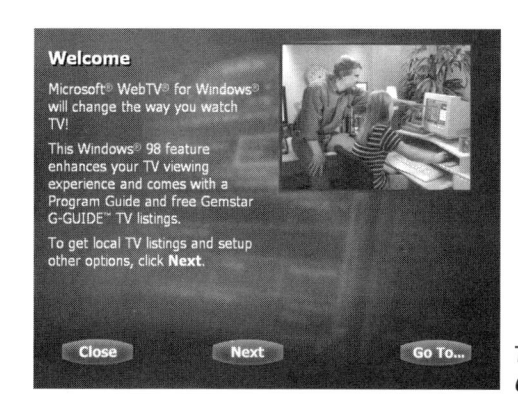

The WebTV for Windows Configuration wizard.

▼ If the WebTV Program Guide appears, see the later section "WebTV Program Guide."

The WebTV for Windows Program Guide.

▼ If the TV Viewer appears, either full-screen or in a window, go to the section "WebTV Viewer."

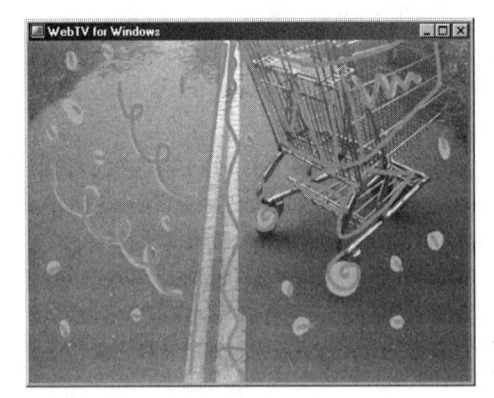

The Windows 98 TV Viewer.

WebTV Configuration

The WebTV Configuration program usually appears the very first time you start WebTV for Windows. The Configuration program is like a wizard, in that it asks questions, presents options, and waits for you to make a selection. You just need to keep following instructions and responding to questions as they appear on screen.

If you are in the Program Guide or TV Viewer and need to get to the configuration program, do one or the other of the following:

- From the TV Viewer, press F10 to reveal the TV banner (you'll get a look at this in a moment). Then click the Guide button to get to the Program Guide.

- From the Program Guide, use the scroll bars to get to the channel named TV Configuration. (It may be Channel 96, Channel 1, or some other number.) Then click the Watch button.

No matter where you start, your goal is to get to the first page of TV Config, which was illustrated a little earlier in this chapter. Configuring your TV is easy—just follow the written (and spoken) instructions as they progress. You'll be given options to scan for active channels, get current program lisings, and so forth. The wizard is smart, and self-explanatory, so you should have no problem just following along until you get to the Configuration Complete page. Click the Finish button, and you'll be taken to the Program Guide, discussed next.

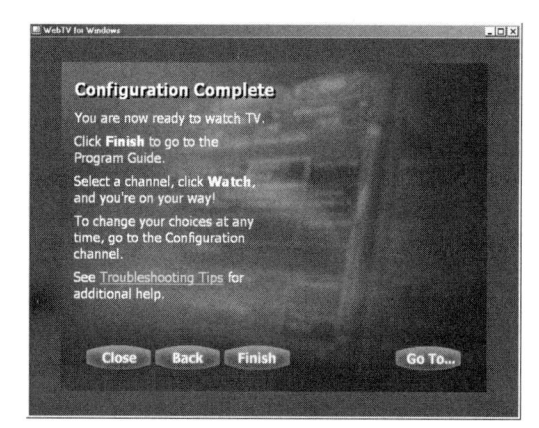

When you reach the last page of the WebTV Configuration wizard, you can move on to the Program Guide.

WebTV Program Guide

The Program Guide portion of WebTV for Windows is your "electronic TV Guide." The information presented in the guide is downloaded to your PC when you go through the TV Config wizard. The Program Guide needs to be updated daily, but you can schedule that task to take place while you're away from your computer. (You probably discovered this while going through the screens of the TV Config wizard.)

Nothing in your listing?

If no programming information is available in your Program Guide, you need to download current listings. Go to TV Config, as discussed in the preceding section. There, you click the Go To button and choose Get TV Listings. This takes you straight to the TV listing sections, where you can update your Program Guide.

11: WINDOWS 98 ENTERTAINMENT

Navigating the Program Guide

Using the Program Guide is easy. Listed down the left side of the Guide are all the available channels. Shows scheduled for a channel are in blocks going horizontally off to the right. Normally, shows that are playing right now have green backgrounds and are usually listed right next to the channel numbers. You can just click any channel, or on a green-colored current show, to view that show and information about it in the small TV screen and information panel in the right-hand frame of the Program Guide.

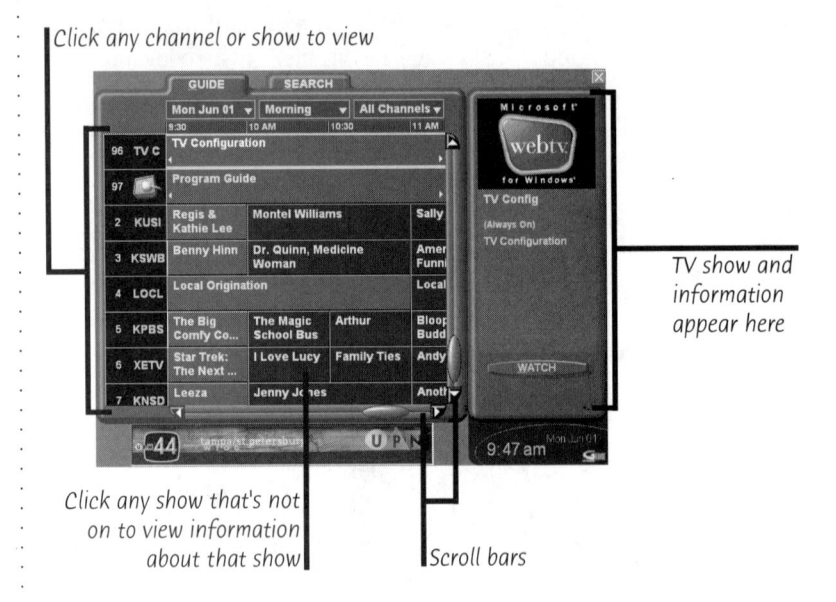

Click any channel or show to view

TV show and information appear here

Click any show that's not on to view information about that show

Scroll bars

Basic tools for using the WebTV's Program Guide.

Scroll bars

You can use the scroll bars to move horizontally and vertically to view the entire schedule. To get more information on a show that isn't airing at the moment, scroll to it and just click the name of the show. Information about that show appears over in the right-hand side of the Program Guide.

If while scrolling around the Program Guide you lose track of shows that are currently on, just click the current time indicator near the lower-right corner. The schedule will shift so that currently airing shows are re-aligned next to the channel numbers.

Time indicator

In addition to the scroll bars, three buttons near the top of the Program Guide give you alternative methods for managing information in the Program Guide. For instance, in the preceding image of the Program Guide, you can see program information for Monday June 1. The second button tells you you're seeing Morning shows, and the third button tells you that All Channels are included in this view of the Guide. To choose other dates, times, and channels for your display of the Guide, you can click on those buttons. You'll be given a drop-down list of options, as shown here in the margin. Just click whatever option you want.

Date, time, and channel buttons

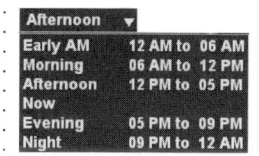

The **Search tab** at the top of the Program Guide lets you look around for programs that might interest you. When you click the Search tab, your view of the Program Guide changes.

Searching for Programs

As shown in the following illustration, you can define the Program Guide display by clicking any category in the left-hand column—for example, Movies. The Program Guide will then display only programs that fit that category.

Search a predefined category

Pick a category, or . . .

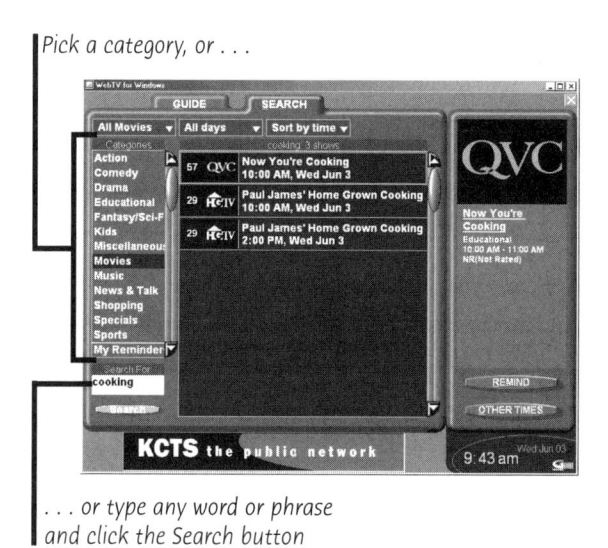

. . . or type any word or phrase and click the Search button

You can also search for shows in a category or on a subject of your own choosing. Just type any word or phrase into the small "Search For" text box, then click the Search button. For example, in the screen shown just above, I searched for shows on **cooking**. Now the Program Guide lists only three shows. As you can see, all three have something to do with cooking.

Specify your own search criteria

11: WINDOWS 98 ENTERTAINMENT

Coolest Feature! One of the coolest things about the Program Guide, which makes it vastly superior to any printed schedule, is that you can see all the times when a particular show will air. For example, suppose you come across a TV show in which you're interested, but it's not being broadcast on a day or time that is convenient for you. The Program Guide will show you other times when the program will be on, if repeat showings are scheduled. Click the Other Times button to see when that same show might be airing again.

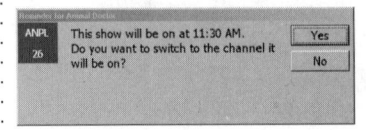

When you find a convenient show and time, you can click the Remind button to set up a little reminder. A few minutes before the show starts, a little reminder like the example here will pop up on your Windows 98 desktop, reminding you to watch the show. Just click the Yes button to open the TV Viewer and switch to the appropriate channel.

Viewing the Banner The Program Guide and the TV Viewer (discussed shortly) both share the **TV banner**. The banner is usually invisible and out of your way. When you need it, there are two simple techniques to bring it out of hiding:

- Press F10.
- **Or**, if you're viewing the Program Guide at full screen, just move the mouse pointer to the top of the screen and hold it there for a couple of seconds.

Let's take a look at the various items in the TV banner, illustrated here:

The buttons near the upper-right corner play the same role as equivalent buttons in other windows. Use them to Maximize, Restore, or Close the Program Guide or TV Viewer window in which the banner is being used.

Moving over to the left side of the banner, you can use the small spin buttons near the upper-left corner to change channels. You can also type a specific channel number in the box next to the buttons and press Enter to go to that channel. Or, use the Page Up and Page Down keys on your keyboard to flip through channels.

262

Clicking the Guide button takes you to the Program Guide (if you're not already there).

The Settings button lets you choose channels to view/hide. You could, for example, hide (exclude) channels in which you're not at all interested. Or hide channels from the kids.

And the Help button, of course, provides help on using WebTV.

The Add button in the TV banner lets you add the channel you're watching to your collection of favorite channels. Each channel you make a favorite will get its own button in the TV banner. You can quickly switch to any favorite channel simply by clicking its button.

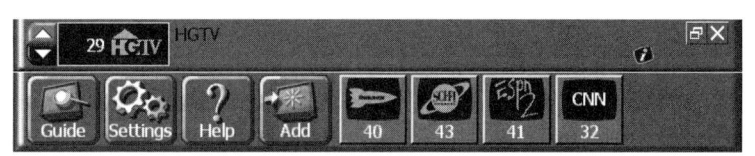

Favorite channels

Use the Add button to make a collection of favorite channels, which are then represented with their own buttons in the banner.

To remove a button from your list of favorites, first click the button that you want to get rid of. The Add button will change to a Remove button. And you can click that Remove button to delete the current channel button.

You can leave the Program Guide at any time using any one of the following methods:

Leaving Program Guide

- To leave the Program Guide and go to the TV Viewer, click the Watch button in the right-hand frame. (This button is available only in the Guide and not in the Search window.)
- To leave the Program Guide and go to TV Config, scroll or otherwise navigate to the TV Config channel and double-click it.
- To leave the Program Guide and close WebTV, click the Close button near the upper-right corner of the TV banner.

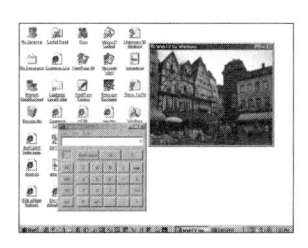

The TV Viewer is essentially a TV screen on your computer monitor. You can watch TV in full-screen mode, or in a window, as shown here. When the viewer is in a window and not full screen, you can size and position the window just as you can any other.

TV Viewer

263

11: WINDOWS 98 ENTERTAINMENT

Here are the basic TV viewing operations:

- If TV Viewer is full screen and you want to shrink it, press the F10 key or move the mouse pointer to the top of the screen. When the TV banner appears, click its Restore button.
- When the TV Viewer isn't in full-screen mode, you can drag any edge or corner of its window to size it.
- To move the TV Viewer window, just drag it by its title bar.
- Whenever you need to view the TV banner, press F10 or right-click the TV Viewer screen.
- To expand the TV Viewer to full screen, click the Maximize button near the upper-right corner of the TV Viewer window.

Interactive TV — Near the top-right of the TV banner, you might notice a small button with an *i* on it. This button allows **interactive TV shows** to work properly. Currently, interactive TV is still a thing of the future; however, you may be located in an area that's experimenting with the technology and have the opportunity to participate.

You can enable your WebTV setup to do this, by making sure the Interactive TV capability is turned on. Click the *i* button, and you'll see the Interactive TV indicator shown here in the margin. This indicator is a toggle; you can turn it on and off by clicking it. To leave the Interactive TV option at its current setting, click somewhere outside the button.

Need More Help? — You should be able to master WebTV for Windows just by clicking around and experimenting with it. If you need additional help at any time, you can just open up the TV banner and click the Help button. The Help window that appears explains all aspects of WebTV and provides a Troubleshooting section in case you have problems.

Using WaveTop

WaveTop is another optional TV-related component of Windows 98. Unlike WebTV for Windows, which is essentially standard TV displayed on a computer screen, WaveTop is a **nationwide data-broadcast medium** that delivers other media content, such as news, magazines, software, and even Internet Web pages, to your Windows 98 desktop. If your PC is equipped with a TV tuner, if you live in the USA, and if you can receive PBS broadcasts over-the-air or through cable, you'll be able to get information and Internet content free—without slow, costly telephone connections and Internet accounts.

264

11: WINDOWS 98 ENTERTAINMENT

If the WaveTop component has been installed on your PC, you've probably already seen it offer its services, via the window shown here, several times.

The WaveTop component waiting to be initialized.

If WaveTop isn't installed yet (or you're not sure if it is or not), you can follow these steps to install it:

Installing WaveTop

▼ Save any work in progress, and close all open windows and programs.
▼ Grab your original Windows 98 CD or floppy disks. (You may be able to skip this step if Windows 98 came preinstalled on your PC.)
▼ Click the Start button and point to Settings ➔ Control Panel.
▼ Open the Add/Remove Programs icon, and click the Windows Setup tab.
▼ Scroll down to and click the WebTV For Windows option at the bottom of the list.
▼ Click the Details button.
▼ If the WaveTop Data Broadcasting option is *not* checked, as shown in the following illustration, click its checkbox.

In this example, WaveTop Data Broadcasting is not yet enabled.

Note: *If you find that WaveTop is already checked, that component is already installed. You can just click the Cancel buttons at the bottom of the dialog boxes to back out without uninstalling WaveTop.*

265

11: WINDOWS 98 ENTERTAINMENT

- ▼ Choose OK to close Details, and choose OK to close Add/Remove programs.
- ▼ Follow the instructions that appear on the screen to install WaveTop.
- ▼ After you install WaveTop, you'll be asked to restart your PC. Go ahead and do so.

Running WaveTop

After you restart your PC and come back to the desktop, the WaveTop window illustrated earlier will appear. To get going with WaveTop, click the Yes button and follow the instructions on screen. You'll be going online, so I can't tell you exactly what to expect. It will depend on what WaveTop finds in your broadcast area. But the basic skills you've learned up to this point should be all you need to complete the initialization process.

Once WaveTop is installed, you can use it at any time by clicking the Start button and choosing Programs ➔ Accessories ➔ WaveTop.

WaveTop Help and Information

For help solving any problems you encounter, you can contact WavePhore—the company that brings you WaveTop. Reach them by phone at (800) 868-2152.

If you already have Internet access, you can also learn more about WaveTop by visiting WavePhore's web site at **http://www.wavetop.net**

Dismissing WaveTop's Window

WaveTop may not be available in your area yet, and you may want to get rid of the WaveTop dialog box that pops up periodically. To do so, you'll have to uninstall that component.

Just go back to Windows Setup (Start ➔ Settings ➔ Control Panel ➔ Add/Remove Programs). When you get to the WaveTop Data Broadcasting component, clear its checkbox to disable it, and click the OK buttons to remove the entire component.

Summary

Windows 98's new Entertainment features really allow you to enjoy music, TV, and perhaps some features of the Internet on your PC. Of course, the extent to which you can use those features depends on the hardware capabilities of your PC, as well as what's being broadcast in your area.

- To play an **audio CD** in your PC, you probably just need to insert the CD into your PC's CD-ROM drive.
- If your PC has a TV tuner built into it, you can watch TV using the **WebTV for Windows** component.
- To start WebTV for Windows, click Start → Programs → Accessories → Entertainment → WebTV for Windows. Or, click the Launch WebTV for Windows button in the Quick Launch toolbar.
- While in WebTV for Windows, you can press F10 to view the **TV banner**, which offers several access options.
- The **Program Guide** component of WebTV for Windows lists current television offerings, such as a printed TV listing.
- **WaveTop** is yet another TV-related technology that allows you to get Internet access through broadcast media, such as your local PBS station. Once WaveTop is installed, you can access it by clicking Start → Programs → Accessories → WaveTop.

Part Four
Cruising the Internet

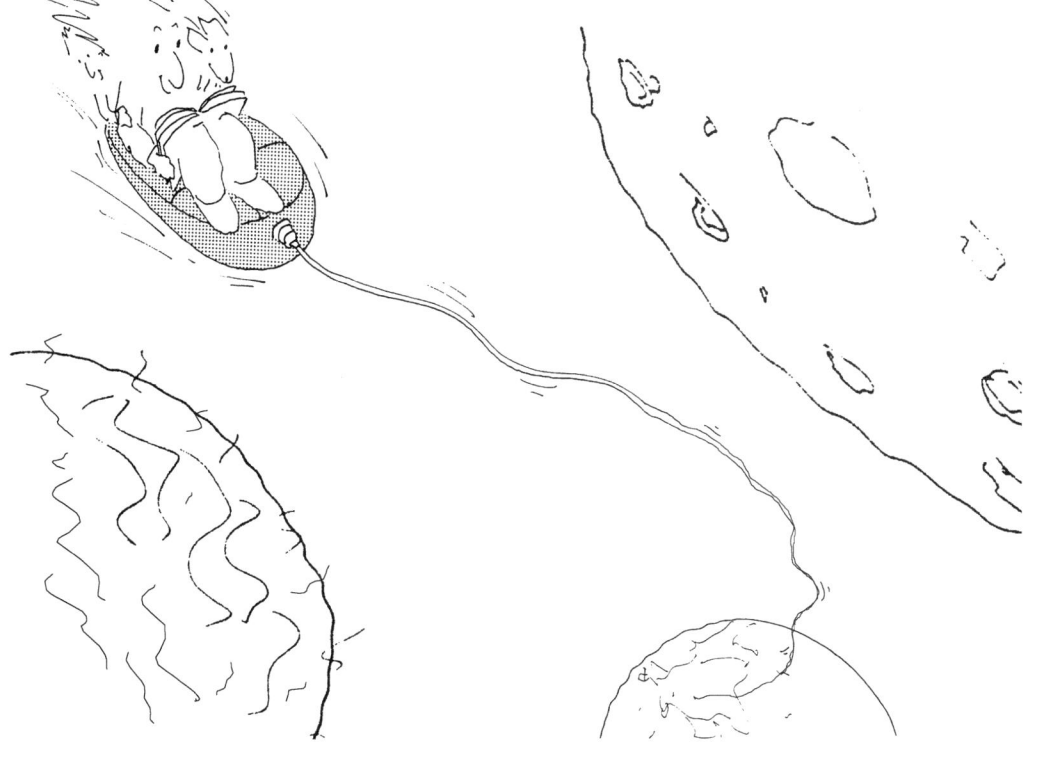

Connecting to the Internet 12

Unless you've been stranded on some *really* deserted island somewhere for a few years, you've no doubt heard of the Internet. You probably have at least some idea of what the Internet offers—such as e-mail and the World Wide Web—and you may already have some experience using it. What you may not know, however, is how to get your own PC connected to the Internet. If that's the case, you've come to the right place. This chapter is all about connecting your own desktop PC and/or laptop computer to the Internet.

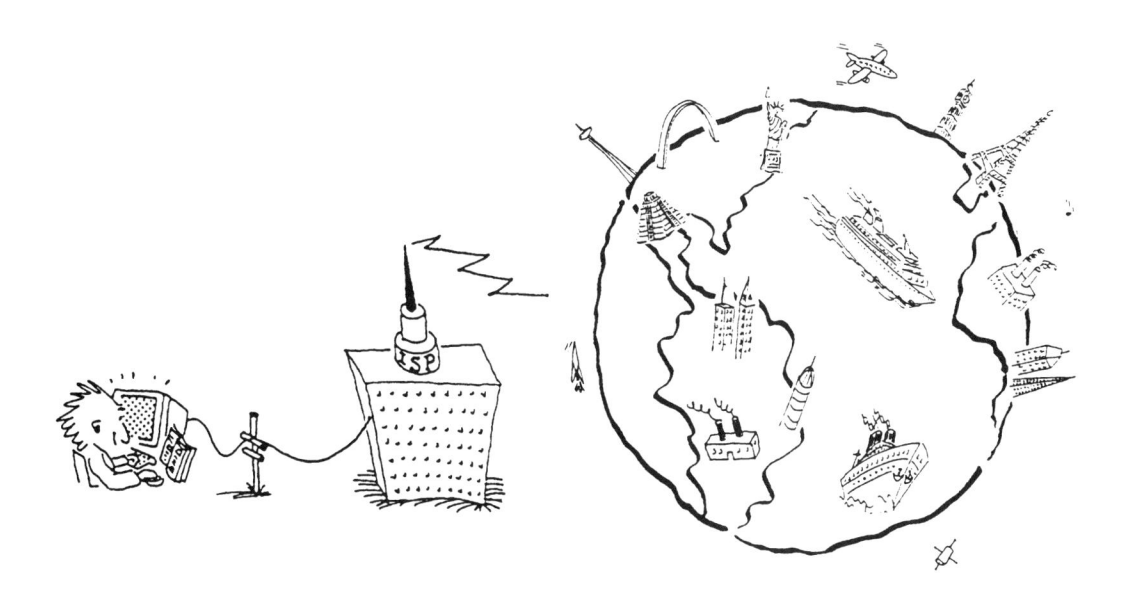

12: CONNECTING TO THE INTERNET

Getting Connected

In a nutshell, you need two things to get your PC connected to the Internet:

- An account with an **Internet Service Provider (ISP)** or other online service that provides access to the Internet.
- A **modem** to connect your PC to the phone lines or to the cable-TV cable.

Let's take a moment to discuss the various options available to you, to help you make a good decision.

Choosing an ISP

An **Internet Service Provider** is any service that can give you access to the Internet. Shopping for an ISP is largely a matter of getting the most bang for your buck. Here are some factors to consider when choosing an ISP:

- Many cable-TV companies now offer Internet access. (The same is true of some satellite-dish TV systems). If you have cable or satellite TV, I suggest you contact your provider for availability and pricing of their Internet connection services.
- If you already have an account with America Online, CompuServe, Microsoft Network (MSN), or Prodigy, you don't need anything else. You can access the Internet through all of those services.
- If you already have a modem, you can go online to shop for an ISP. See "Using the Internet Connection Wizard" later in this chapter for more information.

Many of the ISPs suggested by the Internet Connection Wizard will offer free trial periods, which you can begin to use right away.

- You can also check your local Yellow Pages, the newspaper, many mainstream magazines, or the various computer magazines to find out about Internet Service Providers in your area.
- And finally, if you know people who have Internet connections, ask them about their service. Word-of-mouth recommendations are often the best kind!

Concentrate on the basics

When choosing an ISP, you may be faced with literally dozens of services to choose from. If you feel overwhelmed by all these options, remember that as a beginner, you only need a basic **dial-up account** that gives you an e-mail setup and access to the World Wide Web. An account like that usually costs somewhere in the range of $10 to $40 dollars a month. Should you become a whiz at surfing and need to add more options to your Internet connection, you can always upgrade your account.

It's likely that you already have a modem in your PC, but if not, you'll need to get one.

Installing a Modem

Choosing a Modem: If you choose an Internet Service Provider before choosing a modem, your ISP can probably recommend a good modem to complement their service. Or, to connect through a cable TV or satellite service, you may need to buy a specific **cable modem** from that service.

If you want to purchase and install a modem before choosing an ISP, be sure to get a modem that's compatible with Windows 98 (or Windows 95). Also, you'd do well to choose the fastest modem you can get. The size and complexity of files that produce Web pages for your viewing are steadily increasing, and you'll probably grow impatient if you have to wait for a slower modem to download the Internet content you try to access. As this book goes to press, the 56K modems are the fastest modems for standard telephone lines. You can buy such modems and have them installed at your local computer store.

Go for speed and compatibility

Once you purchase a modem, you'll need to get it hooked up.

Hooking Up the Modem

Internal Modems: If you purchased an internal modem and it's already installed inside your PC, hooking it up is generally pretty easy. You just need to make sure to shut down Windows and your PC, and connect the Line jack on the modem to a standard telephone wall jack. Then connect the Phone jack on the modem to your telephone instrument. Then turn on the PC.

External Modems: If you buy an external modem and want to install it yourself, follow the modem manufacturer's instructions. Make sure the modem is properly connected to your PC and phone line, and also plugged into the wall and turned on before you turn your computer back on.

There may be other steps to getting your internal or external modem hooked up, depending on the particulars of the modem you've purchased. But if you just follow the installation instructions that came with your modem, you should have no problems.

12: CONNECTING TO THE INTERNET

The Internet Connection Wizard

The **Internet Connection Wizard** makes it pretty easy to connect your PC to an ISP. As described in the preceeding section, you'll want to have your modem installed, hooked up, and in working order before you use the wizard—because the wizard needs to use the modem.

Connect to the Internet

To start the Internet Connection Wizard, just open the Connect to the Internet icon on your Windows 98 desktop. Or, if you don't see that icon:

- ▼ Click the Start button, and choose Programs → Internet Explorer → Internet Connection Wizard.

- ▼ If you see a message indicating that Windows wants to install a new modem, then Windows is not yet aware of your modem. Assuming your modem is installed, plugged in, turned on, and hooked up, you should be able to just follow the instructions in the wizard screens to make Windows aware of the modem now.

What Do You Want to Do?

If your modem is all ready to go when you start up the wizard, you'll come to the first page of the Internet Connection Wizard. Here you'll need to choose among three connection options; select the one that best describes your situation.

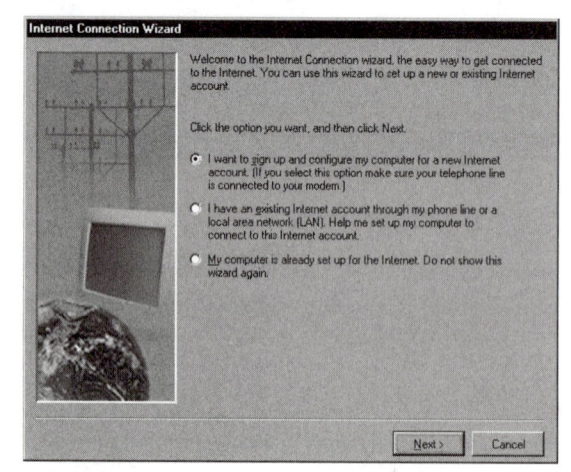

First page of the Internet Connection Wizard.

For example:

- If you have no access to the Internet and have never opened an account with an ISP, and you want to choose an ISP now, choose the first option.

- If you already have an account with an ISP, or you want to connect to the Internet via America Online, CompuServe, MSN, or Prodigy, choose the second option.

- Choose the third option only if you can already use the Internet from this computer and don't want to change anything about your current connection.

Click the Next button after making your choice.

The next page to appear depends on what you chose in the first wizard page. Here again, you're on your own. Follow the instructions on the screen, and respond to prompts as they appear, until the wizard tells you you're done.

Signing Up with an ISP

> You need to set up an Internet account only once. Once you've established an account, you can access the Internet at any time without going through all the steps described in this section.

Although I can't specifically describe the kinds of choices you'll be making in this segment of the connection process, I can take you through an example of signing up with a provider for the first time. I'll use AT&T WorldNet as the sample ISP.

An example: AT&T WorldNet

Let's say I've already started the Internet Connection Wizard and selected the first option from the wizard's first page. After clicking the Next button, I see this message:

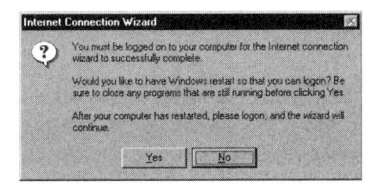

Logging On

I need to log on to my own PC before setting up a new Internet account.

When I choose Yes, the computer whirs and buzzes for a while as it prepares to accept a **logon name**.

> If you're following along in a similar manner on your own PC, you might notice a new icon named **Network Neighborhood** appearing on your desktop. That icon is needed for networking —and when you're connected to the Internet, your PC is, indeed, part of a large network.

After choosing Yes, my computer restarts. If you try this and your computer doesn't restart automatically within a few minutes after answering Yes to the logon inquiry, you can probably follow these steps to log on manually:

275

- Click the Start button, and choose Log Off from the Start menu.
- Choose Yes when asked if you're sure.
- When you get to the Enter Windows Password dialog box, type in your first name (or whatever you want to use as a logon user name). You can leave the Password box empty. Then click the OK button.

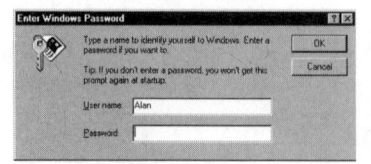

I'll use Alan as my logon user name.

You should be taken back to the Windows 98 desktop, and the Internet Connection Wizard should restart automatically. If this doesn't happen, go ahead and restart it manually. That is, click Start→ Programs → Internet Explorer → Connection Wizard.

Getting back to my example, where everything did restart by itself, I again choose the first option from the first Wizard page and click the Next button.

Picking the ISP

Since I've now logged on, I'll next see a page that dials up Microsoft's **Internet Referral Service**. Once that connection is made (and it might take a couple of minutes or more), a list of ISPs in my area appears on the screen, looking something like the example shown here.

In my current example, I have only one ISP available—AT&T WorldNet. Your list is likely to be longer than that. It will depend on the ISPs available in your area.

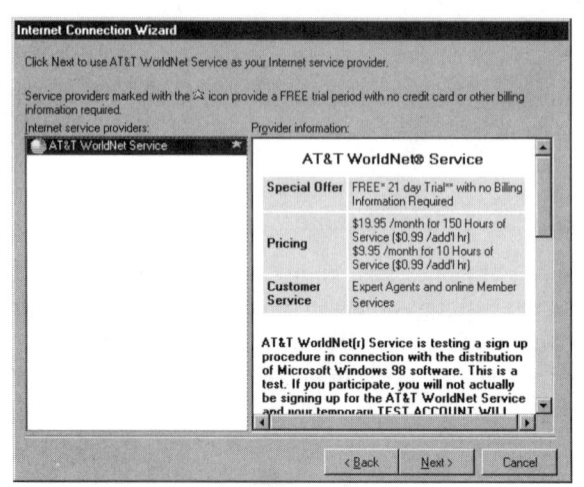

The wizard lists ISPs in your area, with provider information about each one.

Since this is only an example, I'll go ahead and choose AT&T WorldNet as my ISP by clicking that name in the list and then clicking the Next button.

The next page of the wizard asks that I identify myself. Here I just fill in the blanks and click the Next button.

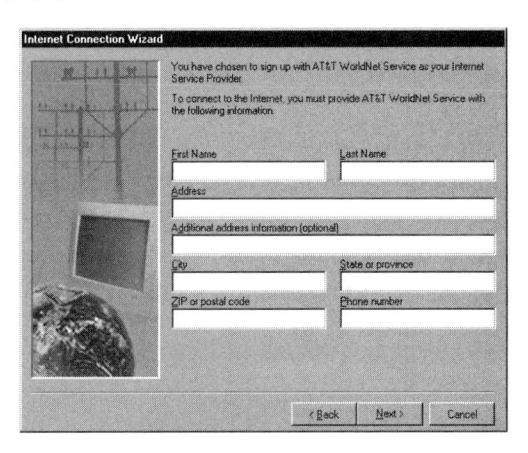

ID and Credit Card Info

Clicking the Next button takes me to the Internet Service Provider I chose, (AT&T WorldNet). Once connected, AT&T asks me for credit card information. Once I've filled in the blanks, I can click the Next button to move to the next wizard page.

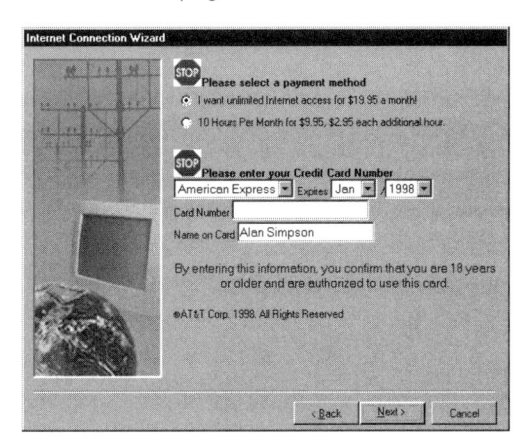

The next page gives me a list of phone numbers that I can use to dial in to the Internet.

Dial-in Access Number

If you follow along as in my example, and you're given several dial-in options, you might want to grab your local telephone directory (the white pages), and look up your own dialing prefix in the front of the

12: CONNECTING TO THE INTERNET

book. (For example, I would look up 756 because those are the first three numbers of my phone number after the area code.) The white pages will show you a list of phone number prefixes that you can dial for free. Ideally, to avoid toll charges while you're online, the dial-up phone number you choose should have one of these toll-free prefixes.

You'll also want to choose a number that supports your modem's speed. For example, if you have a 56K modem, choose a phone number that supports at least 56K speeds (or faster).

E-mail Address

Let's return to my example once again. After choosing a phone number, I can click the Next button. The next page lets me write part of my own Internet e-mail address. For example, in the following illustration I've opted to make my e-mail address Alan@alpha.cistest.att.net.

Alan's E-mail: *I'm just creating a hypothetical account here. My real e-mail address, should you decide to write me, is alan@coolnerds.com. Don't try to sending mail to the address shown in the example.*

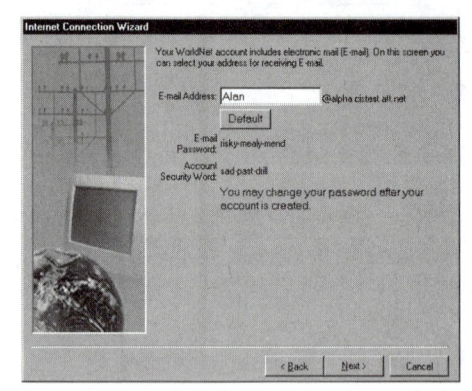

AT&T WorldNet lets me make up part of my own e-mail address.

Agreement and Confirmation

The next wizard page is a sort of contract that I can read and accept, agreeing that AT&T will act as my service provider. Choosing "I accept the agreement" and clicking the Next button takes me to the final page of the wizard. On this page, my e-mail address, password, and account security password are displayed.

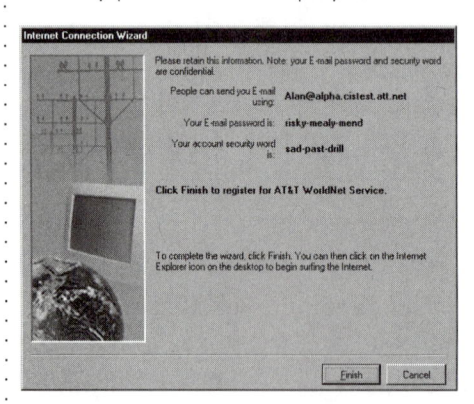

When you get information about your new Internet account, write it down!

278

It is important to write this information down, because you never know when you'll need it again. Use the exact same upper- and lowercase letters!

For example, I might jot down the following on a piece of paper, and then file that paper away in a safe place where I can find it later, if needed.

> **Internet Account**: AT&T WorldNet Service
> **My E-Mail Address**: Alan@alpha.cistest.att.net
> **My E-Mail Password**: risky-mealy-mend
> **My account security word**: sad-past-drill

At this point, I am done. I can click the Finish button and respond to any prompts that appear on the screen. The next step is to test to see if my new account works.

Most of the ISPs listed in the Internet Connection Wizard provide immediate access to the Internet. So in my example, after clicking the Finish button and returning to the Windows 98 desktop, I should be able to hop right on the Internet. Doing so is simply a matter of starting Microsoft Internet Explorer and answering a few prompts as they appear. Here are the example steps I (or you) would follow at this point:

Testing the Connection

▼ Open Microsoft Internet Explorer, either by clicking its icon on the Windows 98 desktop or on the Quick Launch toolbar, or by clicking the Start button and choosing Programs → Internet Explorer → Internet Explorer. A dialog box similar to this one appears:

Internet Explorer

My PC is about to connect to AT&T WorldNet Service.

12: CONNECTING TO THE INTERNET

- ▼ If I plan to have only one ISP (like 99% of the other people in the world), I would check the Connect Automatically checkbox. That way, whenever I start up Microsoft Internet Explorer in the future, it will automatically make the connection for me. I won't need to go through the Dial-up Connection dialog box any more.
- ▼ To actually get online, click the Connect button.

You're In! It might take a minute or more for the connection to be made. When properly connected, the dialog box disappears, and Internet Explorer displays a **home page** from the Internet's World Wide Web. If you connect with a modem, you'll probably also see a little connection icon in the Indicators section of the taskbar. The indicator tells you that your modem is active and that you are currently online.

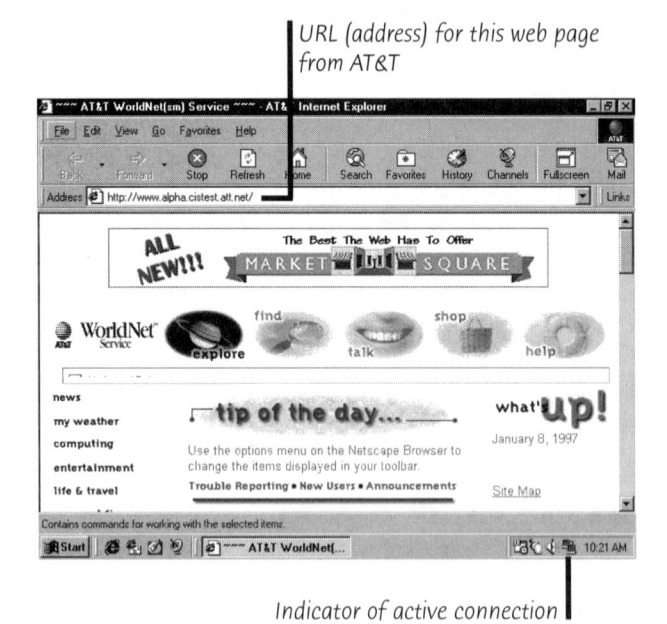

URL (address) for this web page from AT&T

Indicator of active connection

Success! I am connected to AT&T's home page on the World Wide Web.

Alan's Web site When you make a connection on your own PC, you may want to try visiting another Web site on the Internet. You can try mine for starters. To visit my site, you have to enter my Web site URL (address) in the Address bar. Replace whatever address is currently shown there (in our example, it's http://www.alpha.cistest.all.net/) with the URL of the Web site you want to visit (http://www.coolnerds.com for my Web site).

280

Then press the Enter key and wait a minute or so. If you're properly connected, you'll end up at the Coolnerds home page. (I may change that page, though, before you visit. So don't be surprised if it doesn't look exactly like the page shown here.)

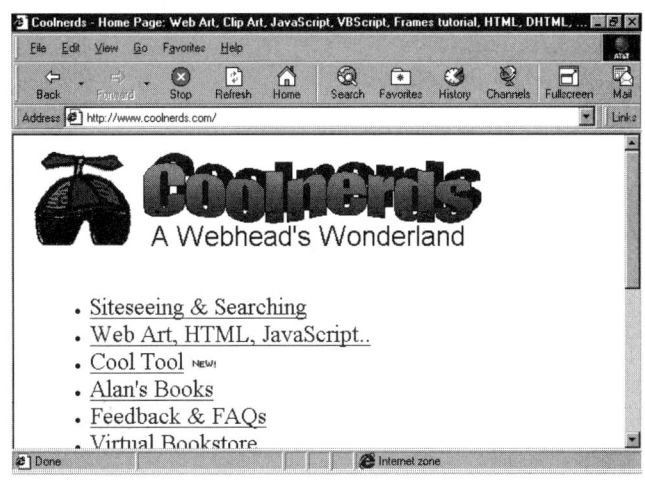

Now visiting Alan's Web site at http://www.coolnerds.com.

If you need a refresher on typing and changing text, see the sections titled "Text Boxes" and "Changing Text" in Chapter 4.

I'll talk more about Microsoft Internet Explorer and the World Wide Web in Chapter 14. For now, you've just learned about creating and testing an Internet connection.

Note: By the way, once you've set up an Internet account, the Connect to the Internet shortcut disappears from the Windows 98 desktop. But you can always restart the Connection Wizard by going through the Programs menu, if need be.

About Dial-Up Networking

Before we leave this chapter, I'd like to point out some facts about a program called **Dial-Up Networking,** which you'll probably be using to connect to the Internet.

When you set up an account with an ISP via the Internet Connection Wizard, the wizard sets up what's called a **Dial-Up Networking connectoid** that gives your modem the information it needs to make the connection. If you'd like to take a peek at that element or perhaps change something about your Internet account, you can do so through the Dial-Up Networking window. Here's how:

Dial-Up Networking

- ▼ Open My Computer.
- ▼ Open the Dial Up Networking icon. This opens the following window:

The Dial-Up Networking window on one of my PCs.

The Dial-Up Networking window includes an icon named Make New Connection, plus one icon for each dial-up account you create. If you've followed the instructions in this chapter and used the Internet Connection Wizard to set up your account, you may never again need to mess with that Make New Connection icon—because the wizard sets up the connection for you. For instance, the AT&T WorldNet Service icon was created automatically when I used the wizard earlier in this chapter.

- ▼ To see what information the connectoid contains about your account, right-click the icon for your dial-up connection and choose Properties.

  It's unlikely that you'll ever need to alter your dial-up connection's settings at this point. But if you do ever have to change some setting, such as the telephone number to which you dial in, then this would be the place to do it: the connectoid's Properties dialog box.

Manual Dial-In

You can also use the Dial-Up Networking window to make a connection to your ISP. Whether or not you actually ever have to do this depends on how you set things up later, as I'll discuss in the next two chapters. But just in case you ever do need to dial in "manually," here's what you do:

- ▼ Open the Dial-Up Networking window and click (or double-click) on the connectoid you want to activate.
- ▼ In the Connect To dialog box that appears, click the Connect button, and the connection will start. You'll see some activity on the screen

in dialog boxes. You'll know you're online when the little modem indicator appears in the Indicators section of the taskbar.

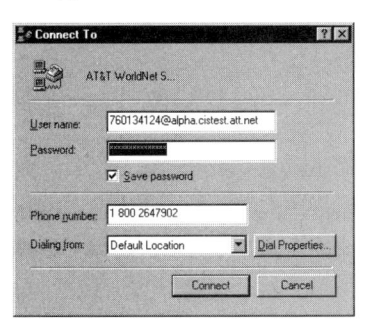

Connecting to the Internet through Dial-Up Networking connectoid.

In certain situations, you'll want to pay close attention to when you are and are not connected to the Internet. Perhaps your ISP account includes provisions that limit you to a certain number of hours per month, or that charge you per hour of access. Or maybe you can't seem to find a toll-free connection to the Internet

Whether these situations apply to you or not, *you should always disconnect if you're not actually using the Internet*. Chances are, you'll be given the opportunity to disconnect, automatically, whenever you close some Internet-related program. Or you'll be reminded to after a particular interval of inactivity.

There's a simple way to disconnect no matter what's showing on the screen at the moment:

▼ Right-click the connection indicator in the taskbar.

▼ Choose Disconnect from the shortcut menu that appears.

When the little connection indicator disappears from the taskbar, that's your way of knowing that you are no longer online.

Disconnecting from the Internet

Summary

To access the Internet, you need some kind of an account with an Internet Service Provider (ISP), and a modem to connect to your ISP. In this chapter we've discussed several options for pursuing an account. Let's review the main points:

- ▼ To use the Internet, you must set up an account with an **ISP**.
- ▼ If you have cable TV or a satellite dish, you might want to contact that service provider first, to see if they offer Internet service.
- ▼ If you're a member of America Online, CompuServe, MSN, Prodigy, or some other **commercial online service**, you may be able to access the Internet through that service. In that case, there's no need to set up an additional account for Internet connection.
- ▼ In lieu of going through a cable company or commercial online service, you can set up an instant Internet account, on-the-fly, using the **Internet Connection Wizard**.
- ▼ To use the Internet Connection Wizard, you first need have a modem installed on your computer and hooked up to a phone line or cable-TV cable.
- ▼ The two main factors to consider when choosing a modem are **speed** (today, 56K is the fastest possible speed) and **compatibility** with either Windows 98 or 95.
- ▼ When you've completed the Internet Connection Wizard, you should be able to immediately get onto the **World Wide Web** (one service of the Internet), just by opening your Microsoft Internet Explorer or other browser.
- ▼ Whenever you're connected to your ISP, a little **modem indicator** appears in the taskbar.
- ▼ Always **remember to disconnect** from your service when not using the Internet. To do so, right-click the connection indicator in the taskbar and choose Disconnect from the shortcut menu.

Doing Internet E-mail 13

As you may know, **e-mail** is all about sending letters (messages) to other people over the Internet, as opposed to going through the Postal Service. E-mail has two big advantages over "snail mail" (paper mail): One, no matter where you send the letter, it gets there in a matter of seconds; and two, it doesn't cost anything to send the message. E-mail also helps prevent those awful telephone-tag scenarios where, for hours or days or even weeks at a time, two people leave endless messages to each other and never have a meaningful conversation.

Everyone is doing e-mail these days. In fact, e-mail is the busiest service that the Internet provides.

13: DOING INTERNET E-MAIL

What You Need for E-mail

E-mail is short for "electronic mail"

To use Internet e-mail on your own PC, you need to have a few things installed and configured, including

- A program for doing e-mail (also called an **e-mail client**)
- An e-mail account with your Internet Service Provider (or with just about any online service, really, since most of them today offer e-mail as part of the package)
- An e-mail address (to which people send your e-mail)
- A password for reading your e-mail

The first item, a program for doing e-mail, is easy—you already have an e-mail program called **Microsoft Outlook Express**, which comes with Windows 98. The other three items really depend on your Internet access account. You must have some kind of online access, as we discussed in Chapter 12. Assuming that you *do* have Internet access, then there are three possible scenarios for you to follow:

You Used the Internet Connection Wizard

If you used the Internet Connection Wizard to set up your Internet account, then you're probably ready to do e-mail already. Go to this chapter's section titled "Introducing Outlook Express."

You Hired an ISP

If you set up an Internet account without using the Internet Connection Wizard, your ISP will have provided information about your e-mail account. You'll need to skip to the section "Setting Up a New E-mail Account" later in this chapter.

You're Online but Don't Have E-mail

If you have Internet access but no e-mail, you can add free e-mail to your service using services such as these:

- **Hotmail** (http://www.hotmail.com)
- **Yahoo** (http://www.yahoo.com)
- **Women's Wire** (http://www.women.com).

In the event you're going to use the e-mail program provided by an online service, you should skip this chapter for now, go to Chapter 14, and learn to use your Web browser. Then point your browser to the address of whatever mail service you want to use, and follow the instructions presented at that site to set up your new e-mail account.

Regardless of which type of service you choose, you can use your Microsoft Outlook Express program to read and write e-mail. Let's see how it works.

286

Microsoft Outlook Express is an easy-to-use e-mail program that comes with Windows 98. (If Outlook Express isn't installed on your PC, see "Installing Missing Windows Components" in Chapter 5.)

To start Outlook Express, do any of the following:

- Click the Outlook Express icon on your desktop.
- **Or,** click the Launch Outlook Express button on the Quick Launch toolbar.
- **Or,** click the Start button and choose Programs → Internet Explorer → Outlook Express.

Where Do You Want to Store E-mail? The very first time you open Outlook Express, you'll see a dialog box asking where you want to store e-mail messages—although that will happen only if you haven't already told the program where to store messages. If you do see a dialog box asking for this storage location, I suggest that you just choose the suggested folder and move to the next dialog box.

Going Straight to E-mail. Another dialog box you might see when you you open Outlook Express the first time is the one shown here, giving you the option to connect right now. (It *won't* appear if you or someone else has already instructed Outlook Express to go online automatically.)

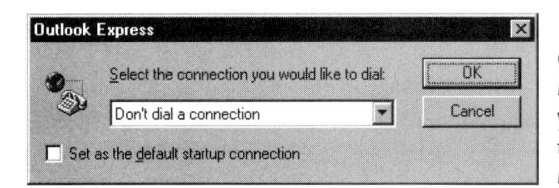

Outlook Express giving you an option to go online right now.

If you already have an e-mail account, you can select that account from the drop-down list, check the "Set as the default startup connection" option, and then click OK. Doing so will make Outlook Express connect to your **e-mail server** automatically at startup. If you don't already have an e-mail account (or if you just don't want to connect right now), choose "Don't dial a connection" from the drop-down list, and click OK.

The **e-mail server** is a computer that's connected to the Internet seven days a week, 24 hours a day. Any e-mail that's sent to you is initially just stored on that server. When you tell Outlook Express that you want to read your e-mail, it uses your modem to copy all e-mail messages from the e-mail server to your PC, so you can read them.

Introducing Outlook Express

About E-mail Servers

Logging On

If you do opt to connect to your e-mail server now, you'll see a Connect To dialog box like this one:

```
┌─ Connect to AT&T WorldNet Service ──────────── [X] ┐
│    📞    Enter a user name and password with access to the │
│          remote network domain.                             │
│  ┌─ Logon ─────────────────────────────────────┐            │
│  │ User Name:  760134124@alpha.cistest.att.net │            │
│  │ Password:   ******************              │            │
│  │ Phone:      <Default>                       │            │
│  │             ☑ Save Password                 │            │
│  └─────────────────────────────────────────────┘            │
│            [  OK  ]  [ Cancel ]  [ Edit Connection... ]    │
└─────────────────────────────────────────────────────────────┘
```

- ▼ To make the connection, fill in your User Name and Password (if they aren't already supplied for you). You establish both of these elements when you sign up with your ISP, and you should have them written down somewhere by now.

    Remember the sample account with AT&T WorldNet described in Chapter 12? In that example I was given the e-mail password **risky-mealy-mend**, and that's what I would type in as the password here.

    > If you don't want to have to type in your password each time you access your e-mail, you can enable (check) the Save Password option.

- ▼ Fill in the phone number you dial to go online. You can leave it set at <Default>, which will tell Outlook Express to use the number you normally use for connecting to the Internet.

- ▼ Click OK when you're done, to make the connection to your e-mail service.

If you don't want to connect at this moment, no big deal. Just click the Cancel button to go into Outlook Express without making a connection first.

When the Outlook Express program is open, it will look something like this:

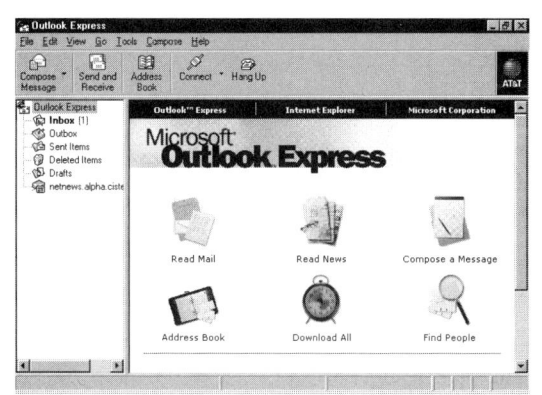

Outlook Express opening window.

If your Outlook Express opening window looks radically different, you might want to adjust your view to match or be similar to mine. Here's how:

View Options

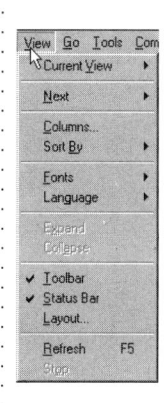

- In the left-hand column of the window, click the Inbox folder.
- Choose View from the Outlook Express menu bar.
- Make sure both Toolbar and Status Bar are enabled (checked).
- In the View menu, choose the Layout option.
- In the Layout Properties dialog box, select options to match mine, as shown just below. Then click OK to save your settings and close the dialog box.

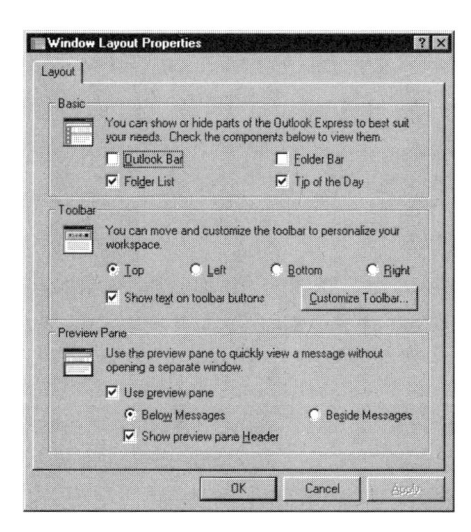

One way to set up your Outlook Express view layout.

When you've finished, you should be able to see folders listed down the left pane. As in Windows Explorer, you can click any folder to see what's in there. For the moment, you're only concerned with two folders:

Inbox   This is where messages that have been sent to you are stored. Unread messages are listed in boldface.

Outbox This is where messages you've written, but have not yet sent, are stored. Sort of like the outbox on your real desktop.

Composing an E-mail Message

To get started writing an e-mail, just do any of the following to get the New Message window:

- Click the Compose Message button in the Outlook Express toolbar.
- **Or,** choose Compose → New Message from the Outlook Express menu bar.
- **Or,** just press Ctrl+N (the shortcut key for New Message).

The New Message window, where you compose new e-mail messages.

Recipients: The first step is to fill in the e-mail address of the recipient. For example, to send a message to me, you'd fill out the To: box with my e-mail address, alan@coolnerds.com.

> **Address Book**: After you build up a collection of e-mail addresses, you'll be able to e-mail recipients right from your Address Book. More on this topic later in the chapter.

Multiple Recipients: You can send copies of your message to other recipients, as well. Put that person's e-mail address in the Cc: box. You can also send "blind" copies (in which recipients can't see who else got the message), by typing those recipients' addresses into the Bcc: box. All three boxes—To:, Cc:, and Bcc:—can contain multiple e-mail addresses, provided you separate the addresses with semicolons (;). For example, addressing an e-mail to **alan@coolnerds.com; someone@ somewhere.com** would send the same message to both those addresses.

Subject: In the Subject line, type a brief description of what the message is about. That line will appear in the recipient's inbox when they're checking their e-mail.

Message Content: When you're ready to type the actual message, just click in the large message composition area and type your message. You can use all the standard text-editing techniques described under "Changing Text" back in Chapter 4 to make changes and corrections as you type. If you type up and send the exact same e-mail message shown just above, addressed to me, I'll actually get it in my e-mail inbox.

Sending an E-mail Message

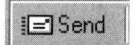

After you've composed and addressed your e-mail message, sending it to its recipient is easy. Just do any of the following while you're still in the New Message window:

- Click the Send button near the left end of the New Message window's toolbar.
- **Or,** choose File ➔ Send Message from the message window's menu bar.
- **Or,** press Alt+S (the shortcut key for Send Message).

One of two things will happen next. If Outlook Express is set up to send mail immediately, the message will be sent on its way to the recipients. Otherwise, you'll probably see a message box like this:

Using the Outbox

As the box says, your e-mail message will be put into your **Outbox** but will not actually be mailed yet.

> Later in this chapter you'll find out how you can designate whether or not you want to use the Outbox, under "Personalizing Outlook Express."

13: DOING INTERNET E-MAIL

To actually transmit all messages that are in your Outbox, do either of the following:

- Click the Send and Receive button in the Outlook Express toolbar. Messages in your Outbox will be sent out, and new incoming messages will be downloaded from your e-mail server to your PC.
- **Or**, choose Tools → Send, which sends your current outgoing mail but doesn't check for new e-mail that came in to you.

If you're not already connected to your ISP when you tell Outlook Express to send out your mail, you may see a dialog box giving you the option to connect. Fill in your e-mail password, then click OK, and another dialog box will appear to keep you informed of how the message transmission is going. After all messages in your Outbox have been sent, the progress dialog box disappears.

The number next to the Outbox folder tells you how many messages are waiting to be sent.

If you close Outlook Express before you send out messages that are in your Outbox, you'll automatically be given an option to send those messages before Outlook Express closes.

Checking Your E-mail

When someone sends an e-mail message to you, that message finds its way to your ISP, and then to your e-mail server. In order to read your e-mail messages, you need to connect to your ISP and retrieve your messages. Here's how:

▼ Open Outlook Express as described earlier in this chapter.

▼ If given the option to connect to your ISP, go ahead and do so.

▼ When you get into the Outlook Express window, do any of the following:

- Click the Send and Receive button in the toolbar.
- **Or**, choose Tools → Download all from the Outlook Express menu bar.
- **Or**, press Ctrl+Shift+M (the shortcut key for downloading incoming mail).

As Outlook Express downloads messages from your e-mail server to your PC, you'll see a message box telling you how the download is progressing. When all your e-mail messages have been retrieved, that message box disappears and you're returned to the Outlook Express window.

To see your new messages, open (click) the **Inbox** folder. New messages that you've never read before are shown in boldface. If a lot of messages are waiting for you in your Inbox, a scroll bar will appear to help you move up and down through the entire list of messages. To read a message, just click it. The message content appears in the lower pane, as shown here:

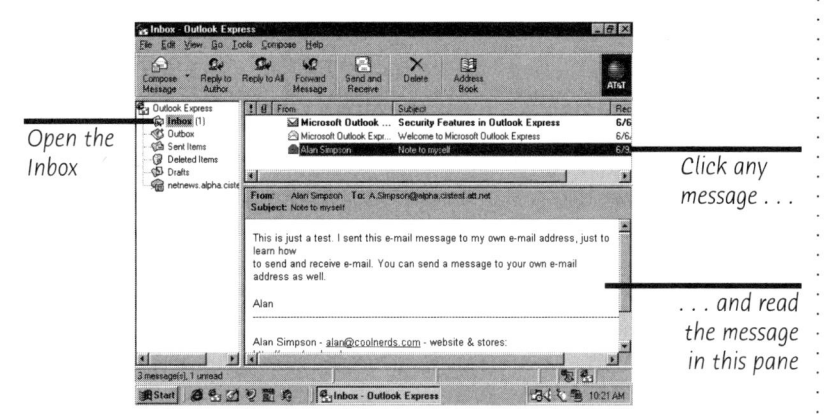

Open the Inbox

Click any message . . .

. . . and read the message in this pane

If the message is too large to fit inside the viewing pane, you can scroll around in that pane. Just click anywhere in the viewing pane, and then:

- Use the scroll bar to the right of the message to scroll up and down.
- If your mouse has a wheel, you can spin the wheel to scroll up and down.
- You can also scroll using the arrow keys, Page Up, and Page Down.

Just use whichever method is the most comfortable or convenient for you at the moment.

After reading a message, you can send an immediate **reply** if you like. Just do any of the following:

To reply to the original author only:

- Click the Reply to Author button in the Outlook Express toolbar.
- **Or,** choose Compose ➔ Reply to Author from the menu bar.
- **Or,** press Ctrl+R (the shortcut key for Reply).

Reading Your E-mail

The number next to the Inbox folder tells you how many unread messages are in your Inbox.

Replying to a Message

293

To reply to everyone, including people who received cc's and bcc's:

- Click the Reply to All button.
- **Or,** choose Compose ➜ Reply to All from the menu bar.
- **Or,** press Ctrl+Shift+R (the shortcut key for Reply to All).

The Reply Window

The Reply window is much like the message composition window, except that the recipient's address and the Subject line are already filled in for you. (You can change the Subject line if you wish.)

The message you're replying to appears in the message pane, under the heading "Original Message." Leave that there, so the recipient can see the message you're responding to. Type your new message—the reply—near the top of the window. For instance, in the following example I typed the response **Got your e-mail. Seems to be working just fine.**

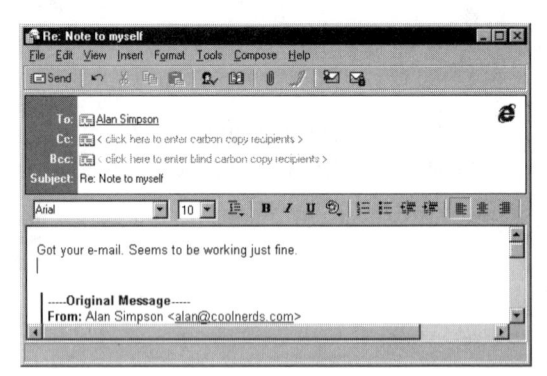

Replying to a message.

To send the completed reply, just click the Send button in the Reply window's toolbar. Or choose File ➜ Send Message from the nearest menu bar. The reply message will be put in your Outbox (or sent, if Outlook Express is set up to send immediately).

Forwarding a Message

If you get a message that you want to pass on to or share with someone else, you can **forward** the message. By now you're familiar with the three choices Outlook Express gives you: Click the Forward Message button in the toolbar, or choose Compose ➜ Forward from the menu bar, or press Ctrl+F (the shortcut key for Forward).

You'll see a window similar to the Reply window, but with "Fw:" in the title bar. To send this forwarded message on its way, type in the e-mail address of the new recipient. Then click the Send button near the upper-left corner of that window. It's as simple as that.

You don't want your Inbox getting piled up with too many messages—and it can happen before you know it. So after you've finished reading a message, you can delete it. You have the option to place it in a **Deleted Items folder** from which you can later recover it if necessary (similar to the Windows Recycle Bin). Or you can delete the message permanently.

Deleting a Message

Just to play it safe, I suggest you use the Deleted Items folder. (You can see this folder in the tree in the left-hand frame of the main Outlook Express window.)

Deleted Items Folder

▼ In the messages list, click the message you want to delete (that is, place in the Deleted Items folder).

▼ Click the Delete button in the toolbar, or press the Delete (Del) key on your keyboard.

The message disappears from your Inbox folder and is moved into the Deleted Items folder. This folder is similar to the Windows Recycle Bin. Deleted messages stay in the Deleted Items folder until you're absolutely sure you want to delete them. So if you delete a message by accident and need to get it back, you can just open (click) the Deleted Items folder. Then click the message you want to recover.

To permanently delete a message so that it's no longer even in your Deleted Items folder, just delete the item from that folder.

Permanently Deleting Messages

▼ To permanently delete a single message from the Deleted Items folder, right-click the message you want to delete and choose Delete from the shortcut menu. **Or** click the item within the folder and click the Delete button in the toolbar, **or** press the Delete (Del) key on your keyboard.

▼ Then use any of the usual methods to delete the selected messages: The Delete button in the toolbar, or the Delete (Del) key, or the Delete option on the message's shortcut (right-click) menu.

Optionally, you can delete everything from the Deleted Items folder all at once. Choose Edit → Select All from the Outlook Express menu bar.

When you want to send someone a file from your PC, the simplest way to do so is to compose an e-mail message and then add the file to the message as an **attachment**. The attached file can be literally any file on your hard disk, or on any disk drive on your computer at the moment.

E-mail Attachments

295

13: DOING INTERNET E-MAIL

Sending an Attachment

Here are the steps to follow to send somebody a file from your PC:

▼ Open Outlook Express, and click the Compose button to create a new message.

▼ Fill in the To: and Subject: lines. Type your message, if you have one, in the message area. You might want to include a brief mention that there's a file attached.

▼ Click the Insert File button (the paper clip icon) in the toolbar, or choose Insert → File Attachment from the menu bar.

▼ In the Insert Attachment dialog box that appears, open the Look In drop-down list and select the folder that contains the file you want to send.

> You can choose to display only files of a certain type in each directory. To do this, select something other than All Files (*.*) from the Files of Type drop-down list near the bottom of the dialog box.

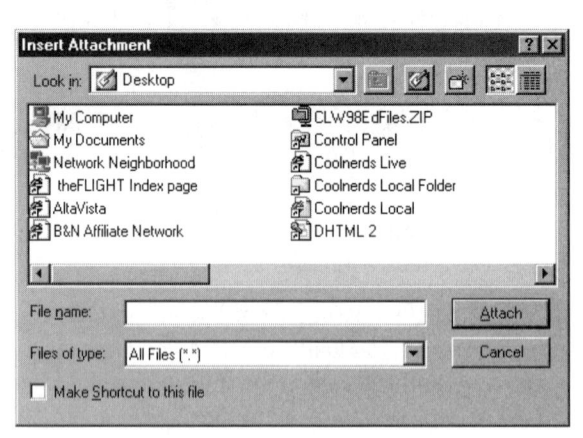

The Insert Attachment dialog box.

▼ When you find the file you want to attach to your e-mail message, click its name and then click the Attach button. (If you need to attach multiple files to the message, just click the Internet File button again and select the additional files.)

Each file you attach will appear as an icon at the bottom of the e-mail message. For example, I've attached a file named myphoto.bmp to the following e-mail message:

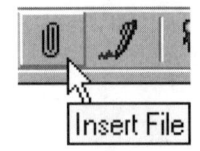

296

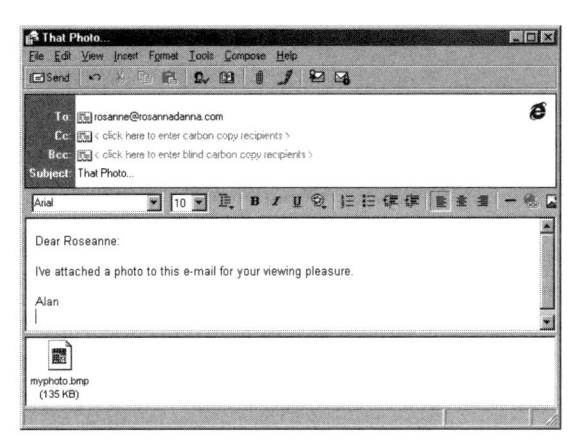

The file myphoto.bmp is attached to this e-mail message.

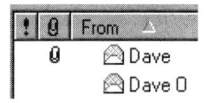

When somebody sends you an attachment along with an e-mail message, that message's entry in the Inbox will include a little paper clip icon, as shown here next to the message from Dave. When you read Dave's message, the gray bar over that message will also contain a paper clip icon that turns into a button when you point to it. Clicking on the paper clip reveals a list of all the files that are attached to the current message:

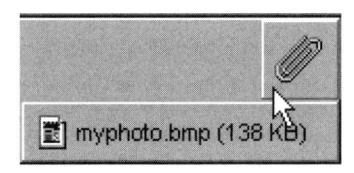

Reading an Attachment

You can just click any of the listed filenames to open that attachment.

Opening an attachment is similar to clicking a document icon in Windows. If Windows can find the appropriate program for opening whatever type of document is in the attachment, that program will be launched and will display the contents of the attachment. While in that program you can choose File → Print to print the attachment. You can also choose File → Save to save the attachment as a normal document in any folder on your hard drive.

Sometimes Windows doesn't recognize the filename extension (the dot followed by one or more letters at the end of the name) of an attached file. Or you may have set up Outlook Express to always ask before opening this type of file. In these cases, Windows will ask you what you want to do with the attachment. Here's the message you see:

Filename Extensions on Attachments

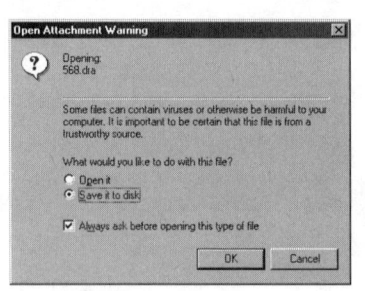

The Open Attachment Warning box lets you decide whether you want to save an attachment, or to first open and examine it.

The all-purpose "virus warning" statement

Don't be alarmed by the tone of this message—it implies that there may be some grave danger here, but that's rarely the case. The purpose of the message is perhaps less to warn you than it is to protect Microsoft from getting sued every time some poor soul opens a virus-infected attachment. What it's really trying to tell you is not to accept candy from strangers. If the attachment is something you're expecting or is from someone you know, there's little chance that the file will contain any sort of virus or prank. So just be aware of your options; to be absolutely safe, open the file and examine it online rather than saving it to disk right away.

The Associated Application

What happens next depends on the choices you make, and what Windows can determine about the attached file. For example, if you choose to open the attachment, Windows will look at the document's filename extension. If that extension is associated with a particular program on your computer, then that program will open and display the attachment. For example, if the attachment is a file named tagalong.doc, Windows will open the attachment in WordPad or Microsoft Word (if you have that program installed).

Windows may need your advice on what program to use.

Otherwise, if Windows can't figure out which program it needs to open the file, you'll see a message on the screen telling you so. Your best bet would be just to save (rather than open) that attachment. Then perhaps send a message to whomever sent you the attachment, and ask them what program you should use to open it. Or, you can just wing it and try using a few different programs on your PC to open the file.

Be careful, however, not to save the file *after* opening it, because you could change and even damage the file's contents. If you're going to experiment with opening the file in a few programs, it's a good idea to first make a copy of the attachment after you've saved it to disk. Then monkey around with the copy so you can't hurt the original.

Finally, notice that "Always ask before opening this type of file" checkbox at the bottom of the Open Attachment Warning box. If you select (check) that box, Outlook Express will *always* present this warning box when you view an attachment that has the current filename extension. If you disable this "Always ask" option and Windows knows what program to use to open this type of file, then you won't see this dialog box any more. The attachment will just open in whatever program is associated with that filename extension.

Always ask?

Should you decide to save rather than open an attached file, you'll come to the Save Attachment As dialog box.

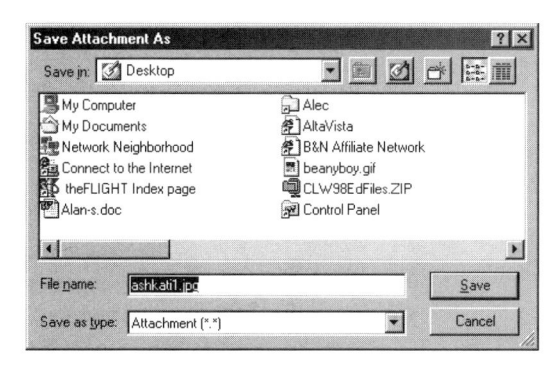

Saving an Attachment

Before you click that Save button, think about *where* you want to save this file, so you'll be able to find it easily later. Then set the Save In drop-down list to the appropriate folder.

Think first

> **Saving to the Desktop**: You may want to just save the file to the desktop where it will be easy to spot. To choose the Windows 98 Desktop as the destination, open the drop-down list and choose Desktop (the first option on the list).

The File Name box will contain a suggested filename, which you may keep or change as you wish. Should you decide to change the filename, change only the first part of the name, not the extension. Remember, the filename extension tells Windows which program to use to open the file, and you don't want to change that information right here and now.

When you're ready to save, just click the Save button. Not much seems to happen; however, you can rest assured that the attachment you saved is now on your hard disk, in whatever folder you put it in, with whatever filename you gave to it. You can now treat it as any other file on your hard disk. So, for example, if you saved the file attachment to the Windows 98 desktop, the next time you return to the desktop you'll see an icon for that file. You can click (or double-click) the icon to open it, or right-click for a shortcut menu. You can also move or copy the icon using any of the standard techniques discussed back in Chapter 7.

About Zip Files People often send **zip files** as attachments with e-mail messages. A zip file consists of one or more "regular" files (either documents or programs) that have been compressed (zipped) into a single, smaller file to speed up delivery over the Internet.

To create zip files, and to open zip files sent to you by other people, you'll need an appropriate program. I can confidently recommend WinZip, which I've used for years. Once you have access to the World Wide Web, you can download a shareware evaluation copy of WinZip and try it out free for a while. Just point your Web browser to **http://www/winzip.com** and look around for downloading instructions.

If you don't have access to the Web, you can contact the publishers for ordering information:

Nico Mak Computing, Inc.
P.O. Box 540
Mansfield, CT 06268-0540   USA
E-mail: help@winzip.com

Personalizing Outlook Express Like most programs (including Windows), Outlook Express offers many options that let you configure things the way you want. After you gain some experience with Outlook Express, you might want to look around and experiment with some of these options. They're pretty self-explanatory, so I'll keep it short here and just tell you how to get into the appropriate dialog boxes.

Assuming you're in Outlook Express, here's what you do:

- To change the setup of your view in Outlook Express, select options from the View menu.
- To personalize other features of Outlook Express, choose Tools → Options from Outlook Express's menu bar.
- If you just want to adjust the size of panes inside the Outlook Express window, move the pointer to the border that separates any two panes. When the pointer turns into the two-headed arrow, you can drag the border to expand or shrink the pane.

Windows 98 also comes with a handy **Address Book,** which you can use to record people's e-mail addresses. In fact, you can use the Address Book to track all kinds of information about people.

Using Your Address Book

The easiest way to use the Address Book for e-mail is to have Outlook Express automatically keep track of names and addresses for you. Here's how:

▼ If you're not already in the Outlook Express program, start it now as discussed earlier in this chapter.

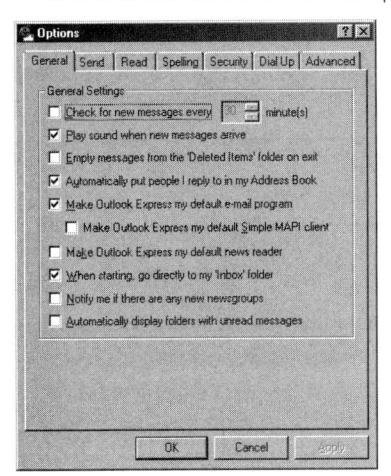

▼ Choose Tools → Options from the Outlook Express menu bar.

▼ If the General tab isn't visible in the Options dialog box, click that tab now.

▼ Select (check) the option to "Automatically put people I reply to in my Address Book."

▼ Click OK to save your selection and close the dialog box.

You won't notice any difference in how Outlook Express looks or behaves. But from now on, any time you reply to an e-mail message you've received, Outlook Express will put the reply recipient's name and e-mail address into your Address Book (assuming it's not already there, of course). Those addresses are likely to come in handy sometime in the future.

The automatic technique you activated in the preceding section is just one way to record names and addresses in your Address Book. You can also type in information whenever you please. There are lots of ways to do it, too:

Adding Names

- If you're in Outlook Express, click Address Book in the toolbar, or choose Tools → Address Book from the menu bar, or press the shortcut key Ctrl+Shift+B.

- **Or,** if you're composing or replying to a message, choose Tools → Address Book from the message window's menu bar, or press Ctrl+Shift+B.

- **Or,** if you're at the Windows 98 Desktop, click the Start button and choose Programs → Internet Explorer → Address Book.

When the Address Book window appears, click the New Contact button in the toolbar. You'll come to a dialog box that looks something like the one just below, except all the fields (text boxes) will be empty. Your task now is to type in as much (or as little) about the person as you care to. Type in a first and last name, as I've done for **Howie Doone** in the example.

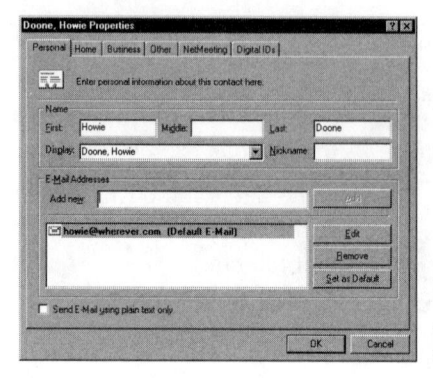

The Properties dialog box for Howie Doone's entry in the Address Book.

Take advantage of Address Book's alphabetical arrangement

In the Display box, you can type in the person's name exactly as you want it displayed in the Address Book. Since the names of contacts are always shown in alphabetical order, you might be wise to display all names with last name first. For example, I've typed in **Doone, Howie** into my Display text box to make sure this contact is alphabetized under the letter D.

Properties Dialog Box

Your Properties dialog box for a particular person should contain at least as much information as the one shown here for Howie. As stated earlier, however, there are many more options for keeping track of your friends, business contacts, and everyone else you know. For example, notice the Nickname text box.

Let's take a look at some other features in the Address Book's Properties dialog box.

Multiple Addresses for a Contact: Occasionally you may want to maintain more than one e-mail address for a contact (a special address while traveling, for instance, or on another server). You can enter another address for the person in the Add New text box and then click the Add button to add that address to the list.

I personally don't know anyone who asks me to e-mail them at different addresses except when they have separate addresses for business and other types of e-mail. Following are some additional options, however, should you need them.

Other Contact Info: If you want to record more information about this contact, just click any of the other tabs. For example, the Home tab lets you record a home address and phone number. The Business tab lets you record business information such as company, job title, business address, phone number, fax, Web site, and so forth.

When you've finished typing in all the information you want to keep for this contact, click the OK button. The Properties dialog box closes, and the new contact is added to the list of existing contacts. For example, here's my Address Book after adding the record for Howie Doone. (The other names were already in there.)

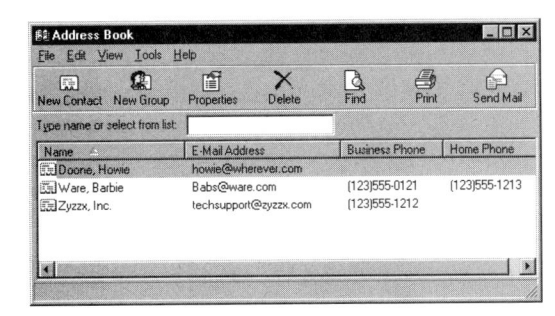

Howie Doone, among others, in my Address Book.

You can add, remove, change, print, and view the records in your Address Book at any time. Just open the Address Book using any of the methods described under "Adding Names" earlier in this chapter. In the list of names, click any name to select it, as shown for Barbie Ware in the example just below. Then click the Properties button to open that record.

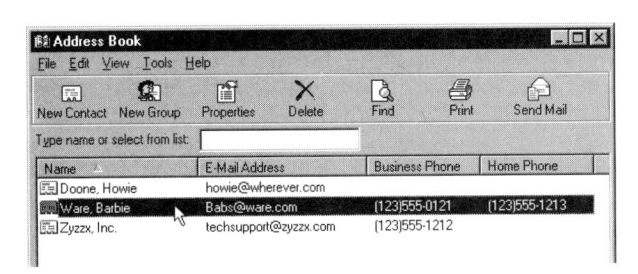

Managing Addresses

Once an Address Book record is displayed, you can view more detail on this person and change any of it as needed. To remove this item from the Address Book, click the Delete button.

> You can also just right-click any line in the Address Book to get the shortcut menu. Choose Properties to change that person's info, or Delete to remove that entry.

Addressing E-mail to Contacts

When sending an e-mail message, you can easily look up the addresses you need in your Address Book. Just open Outlook Express in the usual manner and click the Compose button to write a message. In the New Message window, click the little index card next to the To:, Cc:, or Bcc: field:

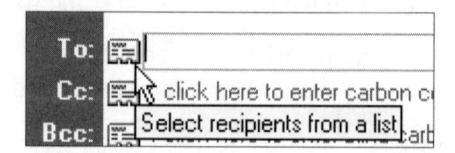

Or you can click the Select Recipients button in the toolbar. Next you'll see the Select Recipients dialog box:

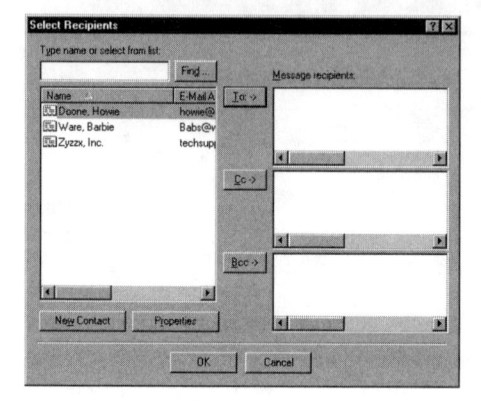

Finding a Recipient

If your list of contacts in the Select Recipients dialog box is long, a fast way to get to the name you want is to start typing the first few letters of the recipient's name in the top text box, and then click the Find button. When the name you're looking for is highlighted, click the To:➔, Cc:➔, or Bcc➔ button to move that name to one of the lists of recipients on the right. You can designate as many recipients as you wish in this manner.

After selecting your recipients, just click the OK button. The recipients' actual names (not their e-mail addresses) will appear in the address portion of your message. But when you send the message, Windows will automatically use the correct e-mail address for each person.

Printing Your Address Book

You can also print information from your Address Book. The technique is the same as it is in most programs. When you're in the Address Book, just click the Print button in its toolbar, or choose File ➔ Print from its menu bar. In the Print dialog box, specify the options you want for this print job.

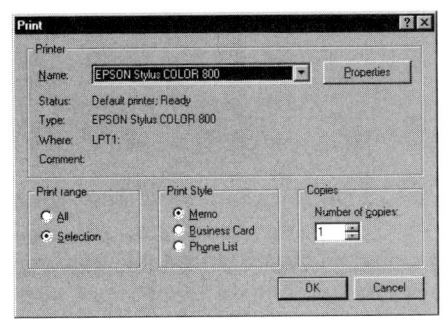

The Print dialog box for the Outlook Express Address Book.

Print Range: You can print all the names and addresses in the Address Book, or just the one that's selected (highlighted) in the Address Book right now.

> You can also use the Ctrl+click method to select multiple addresses to print, and then choose File → Print to print just those selected addresses.

Print Style: Choose Memo, Business Card, or Phone List. Try printing a few names using each style, so you can see exactly what each one looks like.

Copies: Type in or "dial up" the number of copies to print, and then click the OK button.

If you used the Internet Connection Wizard to create your Internet account, your e-mail account is probably all set up and ready to go. In that case, you don't have to bother with the tasks described here. Otherwise, however, you'll need to set up your account manually. To do that, get the following information from your ISP or other e-mail account provider:

- Your e-mail address, to be used by other people who send e-mail to you.
- Your User Name for logging on to your mail server (this is probably the same as your User Name for connecting to the Internet).
- The password for downloading messages from your mail server.
- The type of server used for incoming mail (this will be either **POP3** or **IMAP**).
- The name of your incoming mail server.
- The name of your outgoing mail server (also called an **SMTP server**).

Manual Setup of E-mail Accounts

13: DOING INTERNET E-MAIL

The following table shows some examples of these pieces of information, to give you a sense of the formats you'll encounter. You can use the third column in the table to jot down your own e-mail account information, if you like. Remember, all this information will come from your Internet Service Provider or e-mail service.

Information	Example	Write Yours Here
E-mail address	alan@wherever.com	
User name (or POP account name)	Alan	
E-mail password	risky-mealy-mend	
Incoming mail server type	POP3	
Outgoing mail server	pop3.wherever.com	
Incoming mail server	smtp.wherever.com	

Creating Your Account

When you have the required information, follow these steps to get started setting up an Outlook Express account for sending and receiving e-mail:

▼ Start Outlook Express. (Open the Outlook Express desktop icon, or click its Quick Launch toolbar button, or click Start → Programs → Internet Explorer → Outlook Express.)

▼ If prompted to connect to the Internet, you can skip that for now. You don't need to be online to set up an e-mail account on your PC.

▼ Choose Tools → Accounts from the Outlook Express menu bar.

▼ In the Internet Accounts dialog box, click the Mail tab.

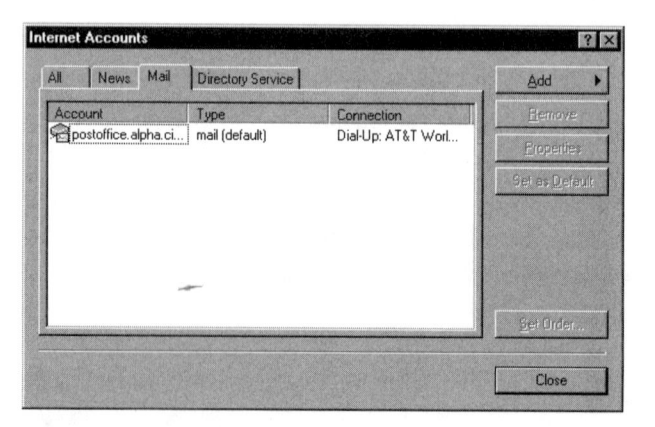

If you (or the Internet Connection Wizard) have already set up an e-mail account, that account will be listed in the Mail tab. You can click that account name and choose Properties to see information about your account. For right now, though, you're looking to add a new account. So click the Add button and choose Mail from the menu that appears. You'll be taken to a different version of the Internet Connection Wizard that just helps you set up your e-mail account.

On the first wizard page, type your name as you want it to appear in your outgoing messages. In the example, I've just typed my everyday first and last name. Click the Next button to move to the next page.

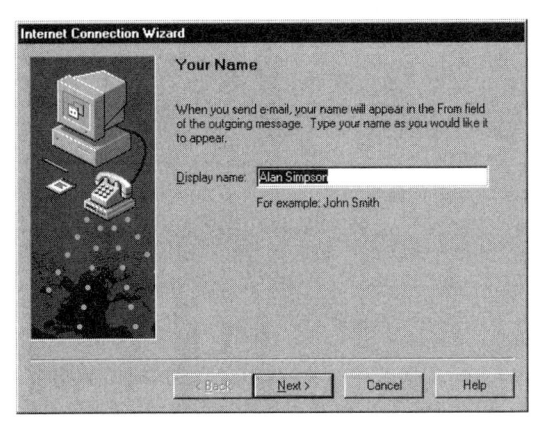

Using Connection Wizard

Internet Connection Wizard for setting up an e-mail account.

The second page of the wizard prompts you for your e-mail address. This must be the exact e-mail address, as provided by your ISP or e-mail provider, that people will use to send your messages. Go ahead and type it in—carefully! You don't want to make any mistakes here. Click the Next button when you're ready to move on.

E-mail address

In the third wizard window, specify the type of server to be used for incoming mail (POP3 or IMAP). Then in the two lower text boxes, *carefully* type the exact names of your incoming and outgoing mail servers. Make sure you type these *exactly* as indicated by your Internet or e-mail service provider, and it's best to use the same upper/lowercase letters that your service provider has used. Click the Next button to proceed.

E-mail server names

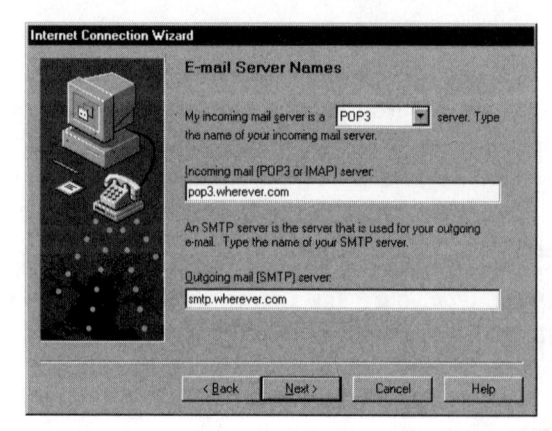

Wizard page asking for e-mail server information.

Continue filling out the remaining pages in the wizard, which will be self-explanatory. In one page you'll be asked how you want to log on to the Internet in order to send and receive mail. Make sure you type your POP account name (or User Name), and your e-mail password exactly as provided by your ISP. For instance, my entries (as shown in the table of examples in the preceding section) would be **Alan** as the POP account name, and **risky-mealy-mend** as the password. Remember: Use the same uppercase and lowercase letters that your ISP used.

After completing this wizard page and clicking the Next button, you'll be asked to provide a "friendly name" for his account. Enter any text that you think will help you identify this particular account in the future.

Dial-up connection for e-mail

The wizard will also ask how you want to connect to your e-mail server. Unless your ISP has told you otherwise, you'll probably want to chose the first option, Connect Using My Phone Line. That's the option you select when you're connected to the Internet via a modem.

When you get to the Dial-Up Connection page, choose the option to use an existing dial-up connection, and click the name of the connectoid you want to use. (This will be your Dial-Up Networking connectoid for getting on the Internet.) Then click the Next button.

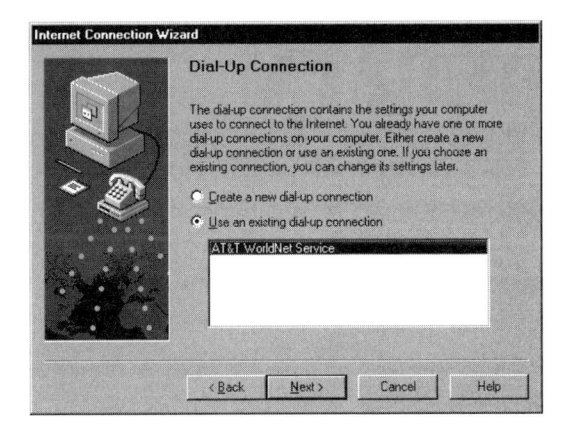

Finally, you'll come to the last page of the wizard, which is just a "Congratulations!" screen. Click the Finish button, and you'll return to the Internet Accounts dialog box. From there, you can just click the Close button to save your new account and return to Outlook Express. If you want to try your new account, go back to the section in this chapter titled "Introducing Outlook Express."

More on Outlook Express and Address Book

If you really want to get deep into Outlook Express, check out its online help system. Very informative! From the Outlook Express menu bar choose Help → Contents and Index. Or you can press the F1 key if Outlook Express is currently the active window. The Outlook Express Help window looks like any other Windows-style help accessory. Click the Contents tab (if it's not already selected). Then just start reading the help pages starting with the first one, "Introducing Outlook Express."

The Address Book offers some other options that you may find handy. For example, the New Group button in the Address Book's toolbar makes helps you set up a mailing list that you can use to send messages to an entire group of recipients. You can explore these options on your own if you wish—once you've learned the e-mail basics as discussed in this chapter, you won't have any problem using these other features. And, of course, the Address Book also has plenty of online help should you need further assistance.

Summary

What you've accomplished in this chapter should make you something of a whiz at Internet e-mail. Getting an e-mail account established and working the service correctly on your computer are the biggest challenges. But once you get your e-mail account working, the rest is pretty easy. Here's a quick review of the main topics covered in this chapter:

- ▼ To do **Internet e-mail**, you need access to the Internet, an e-mail account, an e-mail address, and an e-mail program.

- ▼ You can use **Outlook Express**, which comes with Windows 98, as your e-mail program.

- ▼ To type up a new e-mail message in Outlook Express, click its **Compose Message** button.

- ▼ To send a completed e-mail, click the **Send button** just above the message you wrote.

- ▼ If sent messages go to your **Outbox** rather than straight to your mail server, you have to choose Tools → Send from the menu bar or click the Send and Receive button in the toolbar to send the messages from your Outbox to the recipients.

- ▼ You can use the **Insert Attachment** button to attach virtually any file from your PC to an e-mail message.

- ▼ **To read** your e-mail, open Outlook Express and click the Send and Receive button. If necessary, you'll be prompted to connect to your ISP first.

- ▼ New messages will appears in Outlook Express's **Inbox** folder. Unread messages are listed in boldface text. To read a message, click it. The lower pane of the message window will display the message contents.

- ▼ To reply to the sender, click the **Reply to Author** button and type up your new message.

- ▼ You can use the Windows **Address Book** to keep track of names and addresses, including e-mail addresses.

Browsing the World Wide Web

14

This chapter is all about using the Internet's World Wide Web and the Internet Explorer browser. The World Wide Web is perhaps the most famous and certainly one of the most popular uses of the Internet. **The Web**, as it is usually called, is a collection of documents, or **Web pages**—millions of them in fact—spread throughout the world on millions of computers. You can find Web pages dealing with every topic imaginable. It's a great place to find information on any topic that interests you, and also a good way to network with other people who share similar interests.

14: BROWSING THE WORLD WIDE WEB

Introducing Internet Explorer

To browse the World Wide Web you need access to the Internet (as discussed in Chapter 12), and a particular type of program called a **Web browser**. There are many Web browser programs for you to choose among, and you may already be familiar with names such as Netscape Navigator and Microsoft Internet Explorer. You can certainly use whatever Web browser you like. In this book our browser discussion is limited to Microsoft Internet Explorer, version 4, because it comes with Windows 98 and you have it readily available.

Starting Internet Explorer

You can start up Internet Explorer using any of the following methods:

- Click (or double-click) the Internet Explorer icon on your desktop.
- **Or,** click the Launch Internet Explorer button on the Quick Launch toolbar.
- **Or,** click the Start button and choose Programs ➔ Internet Explorer ➔ Internet Explorer.

Internet Explorer can, and will, start itself when appropriate. For example, let's say you're reading an e-mail message that contains a blue, underlined item that looks something like the following. The blue (usually) and underlined attributes, by the way, tell you this is a link to another site on the Internet (more on links later in the chapter).

http://www.coolnerds.com

URLs

When you click this link, Windows 98 recognizes the **http://www.** as the first letters of a Web site's **URL**, or address. So Windows will automatically start up your Web browser (Internet Explorer in this case) and take you right to that address.

> URL stands for Uniform Resource Locator. The acronym URL is usually pronounced by saying the letters, "U R L," or sometimes by saying the word "earl."

You may have to log on. Exactly what happens next depends on several factors. If you're not already online, and your PC has no way of going online automatically, then you'll probably see the Dial-up Conection dialog box, inviting you to log on now. You'll need to fill in your Internet user name and password, and click the Connect button.

Internet Explorer wants to log on to the Internet.

If for some reason you're reading this chapter before getting set up with an Internet Service Provider and an Internet account, and you don't yet have a user name and password, stop here and go back to Chapter 12. You won't be able to access the Web until you're connected.

Once you are online, your Web browser will display a **home page**. This is your default home page, or the page at whatever URL you clicked on. Your **default home page** is the page first displayed when you open your Web browser. I can't show you exactly what that will look like, because it depends on the Web page that is designated as your home page and what that page looks like when you visit it. But here's an illustration of the Internet Explorer program itself. The large white area in that figure is where the Web pages you visit will be displayed.

You Start Out at a Homepage

You'll find more information about home pages and URLs in a section coming up shortly, along with information about how to designate a particular Web site as your default home page. You can choose a site you use often, and start out there automatically every day.

View Options

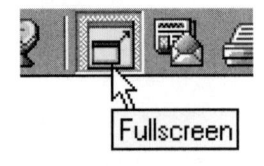

Like most programs, Internet Explorer has a View menu that enables you to control how you view the contents of the Web. Let's discuss some of these options, to help you find a view that works well for you.

For starters, if you click the Fullscreen button in Internet Explorer's toolbar, or choose View ➔ Full Screen from the menu bar, the screen changes radically and focuses on the Web site display. As shown in the following example, you get a special toolbar and the page display, and the rest of the Interent Explorer window goes away. To return to the normal view, click the Fullscreen button again.

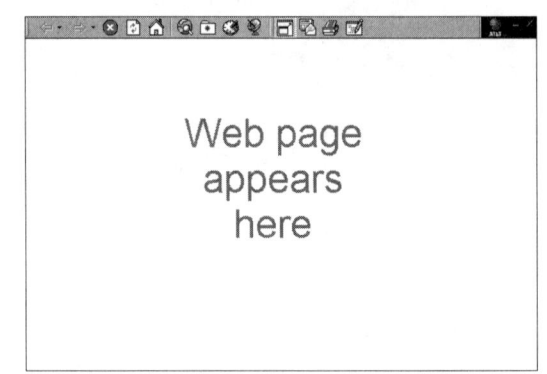

Internet Explorer in Full Screen view.

You can also use the View menu to choose which toolbars you do and don't want to see. You might wish to start out with the same settings I use, with the Standard buttons, Address bar, status bar, and text labels all visible as shown on the View menu illustrated just below. Of course, you should feel free to experiment, if you'd like.

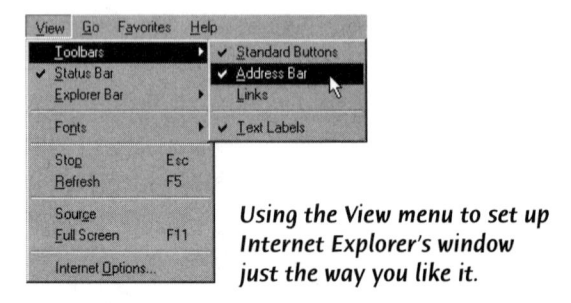

Using the View menu to set up Internet Explorer's window just the way you like it.

Now, it's time to take a closer look at those home pages and their URLs. And then I'll show you how to point your Web browser to any page on the Web.

Home Pages and URLs

Just as every house has its own unique address and phone number, every page on the Web has its own URL. All URLs for pages on the Web start with *http://www*. The *http* stands for **HyperText Transfer Protocol**, which is the name of a particular technology that the Web uses. The *www* part, of course, stands for World Wide Web.

Domains

After the site name part of the URL (*coolnerds*, in my site's URL) comes a dot and a few letters (usually three), such as *.com* or *.edu*. Those few letters represent the organizational **domain** of a particular site. The following table lists some common domain designators and the organizational units they represent.

Organization Designator	Type of Web Site
.com	Commercial (private or corporate)
.gov	U.S. government
.mil	Military
.edu	Educational institution
.net	An entire network of computers, as opposed to one computer

Now that you know a little about their structure, take a look at the following list of some real URLs.

Place or Organization	URL
The White House	http://www.whitehouse.gov
Harvard University	http://www.harvard.edu
United States Army	http://www.army.mil
AT&T Network	http://www.att.net
Microsoft	http://www.microsoft.com
Peachpit Press	http://www.peachpit.com

I'm sure you've seen many other examples, because so many enterprises and organizations maintain Web sites these days—television shows, corporations, retail enterprises of every imaginable type, dating services, game forums, financial and legal entities, social and health resources, news agencies and publications, job banks, football teams ... I could go on forever.

Your Default Home Page

If you want to designate a particular Web page as your default home page, follow these steps:

- ▼ Point your Web browser to the page you want to use as your default home page.
- ▼ When the page is in full view, choose View → Internet Options.
- ▼ Open the General tab, click the Use Current button, and click OK.

From now on, whenever you first start Internet Explorer, you'll begin at this home page.

Browsing the Web

To get to a specific site on the World Wide Web:

- ▼ Just type its URL into the Address bar of the Web browser, and then press the Tab or Enter key. In Internet Explorer:
  - If the Address bar isn't visible, you'll need to choose View → Toolbars → Address Bar from Internet Explorer's menu bar.
  - If the menu bar itself isn't visible, click the Fullscreen button to get back to the Internet Explorer program window.

For example, to visit Microsoft's Web site you'd type in the URL **http://www.microsoft.com** as shown here:

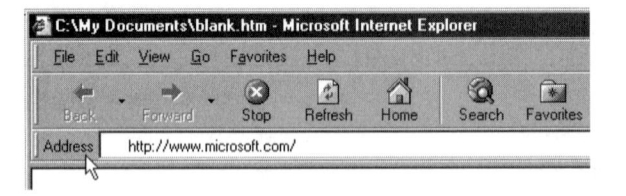

- ▼ Press the Enter or Tab key, and wait a bit for the page from Microsoft to appear in your browser window. (Exactly how long this takes will depend mainly on the speed of your modem.)

URL Typing Tips

Since URLs are often very much alike, you don't always necessarily have to retype every URL from scratch. Way back in Chapter 2, you learned how to highlight and type over a filename; you can use that same technique here to edit the URL that's currently in the Address bar. For example, if you're currently at http://www.microsoft.com, and you want to go to http://www.coolnerds.com, you can just select (highlight) the part of the existing URL that needs to be changed:

Then type the new part—just the word **coolnerds** in this example. The newly typed text replaces the selected text:

> Address http://www.coolnerds.com/

So now you just have to press Tab or Enter to go to the coolnerds Web site. (Again, you might have a minute's wait, depending on the speed of your modem/Internet connection.)

Typing lengthy URLs into the Address bar can become tedious. In addition to the highlight-and-retype technique described just above, following are some other tricks you can use to reduce the amount of typing involved in entering the addresses of the sites you want to visit.

Other URL Quickies

You really don't ever need to type the **http://** part. As long as you type the **www.** part, Internet Explorer will "know" to add the **http://** to the front of the URL.

Skip the http://

To completely erase the URL that's currently in the Address box, just click anywhere on that URL. This automaticaly selects the entire URL. Then you can press the Delete key to remove the whole URL, or just start typing in a new URL to replace the selected URL.

Overtyping

Internet Explorer remembers many of the URLs you type, and uses that information to "auto-complete" the URL you're typing. For example, let's say you recently visited http://www.coolnerds.com. You decide to revisit that site. You start typing **www.cool...** into the Address box. Suddenly, Internet Explorer takes over and completes the typing for you. Of course, the browser won't always guess right; if it correctly completes the URL that you in fact want to visit, you can just press Tab or Enter to use that URL. But when you see that Internet Explorer's assumption is wrong, you can just keep typing the URL you intended in the first place. The auto-complete feature won't prevent you from typing the URL correctly.

Auto-completion of the URL you start typing

You can also select a URL from the list of recently visited sites that Internet Explorer maintains for you in the Address box's drop-down list. Just click the arrow button at the far right of the Address bar to view the list. If you see the URL that you want to visit, click it to place it in the Address bar.

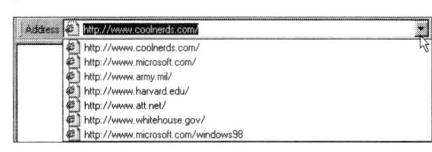

List of recently visited URLs

> Address http://www.coolnerds.com/
>   http://www.coolnerds.com/
>   http://www.microsoft.com/
>   http://www.army.mil/
>   http://www.harvard.edu/
>   http://www.alt.net/
>   http://www.whitehouse.gov/
>   http://www.microsoft.com/windows98

The History Explorer Bar

The Address bar drop-down list is just one place where Internet Explorer keeps track of recently visited URLs. A more complete list is available in the **History Explorer bar**. To open that bar, click the History button in Internet Explorer's toolbar, or choose View → Explorer Bar → History from the menu bar. The History list opens on the left side of the screen:

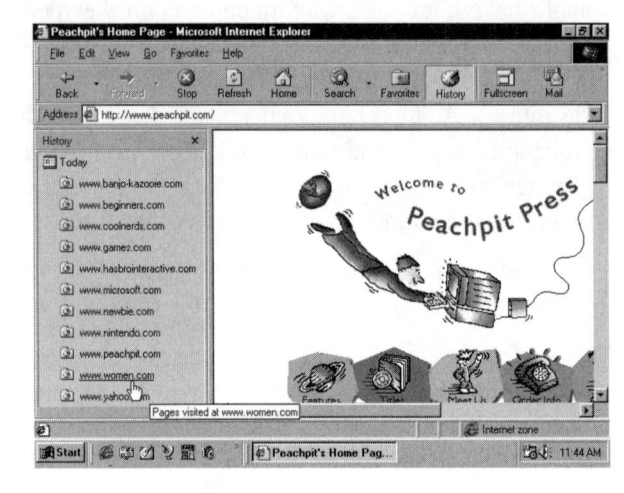

> **The Explorer Bars**: Internet Explorer has several Explorer bars, which can come out of hiding at the left edge of the screen. As you'll learn, there are Explorer bars for displaying a history of sites visited, your list of Favorites, a list of search engines for finding stuff on the Web, and Channels. To call up an Explorer bar, click the Search, Favorites, History, or Channels button in the toolbar. Or you can choose one from the View → Explorer Bar submenu. To close an Explorer bar, click the Close (X) button at the top.

Internet Explorer's History list in the Explorer bar.

To revisit a site from the History list, first click the folder icon that represents the site you want to visit. A list of pages within that site appears below the folder icon. To visit one of those pages, just click the URL. To close the History list, click again on the History button in the toolbar, or click the X at the top-right of the History list.

Surfing in a Nutshell

So let's review: The bottom line on Web browsing is simply that you need to

- ▼ Start up Internet Explorer and get online.
- ▼ To visit a specific Web site, just type its URL into the Address box, press the Enter or Tab key, and wait.

    Optionally, to revisit a site you've been to recently, find and click that site's URL in the Address bar drop-down list, or in the History Explorer Bar.

Then, once you've entered a URL and pressed Tab or Enter, you'll be taken to the Web site. Unless the URL you entered specifies otherwise, you'll probably be taken to the home page of that site. That page will likely have links to other pages in the site. You can use those links as another means of exploring the World Wide Web, as discussed next.

Using Links and Buttons

Many Web pages offer **links** that you can click to get to other Web pages. Text links are usually blue and underlined, although they can be whatever color the author of the Web page wants them to be. Many (but not all) graphics images are also **clickable** links. The best way to know if something on a Web page is a clickable link is simply to point to it. If the mouse pointer turns into a little hand, the thing under the mouse pointer is clickable. So you can click it to see where it takes you.

Toolbar Buttons

Internet Explorer's toolbar contains several buttons for navigating around Web sites:

The **Back** and **Forward** buttons take you ahead and/or backward among the pages you're visiting. When you click the Back button, you'll return to whatever page preceded the one you're viewing now, whether that page was in the same Web site or a different one. After you press the Back button, the Forward button beomes available, and you can click it to return to whatever page you just retreated from.

If you've specified a page you want to visit, and it seems to be taking *forever* for the page to appear on the screen, you can cancel your visit by clicking the **Stop** button.

The **Refresh** button rereads the currently displayed page of the Web server, to ensure you're getting the most up-to-date version of that page.

The **Home** button takes you to your default home page—the page that comes up every time you start Internet Explorer. That page might be your ISP's home page, or Microsoft's home page, or a page you've specifically designated as your home page.

Suffice it to say, once you're actually on the Web and viewing a Web site, you have dozens of different ways to get around and find things.

Searching the Web

The Web is a collection of millions of pages covering every topic imaginable—and sometimes the sheer depth and breadth of all that stuff can be overwhelming. In an effort to make all this information more accessible to everyone, special Web sites called **search engines** continually build indexes of pages on the World Wide Web. These search engines can be accessed at any time to help you determine what's out there and find exactly the pieces of information you need.

14: BROWSING THE WORLD WIDE WEB

You can use any search engine to look up any word or phrase. (Although you'll discover that some searchers are better than others at finding particular types of information.) Probably the easiest way to get to search engines is through the **Search Explorer bar**. To open that bar:

- Click the Search button in Internet Explorer's menu bar.
- **Or,** choose View → Explorer Bar → Search.

The Search bar opens up at the left side of the Internet Explorer window.

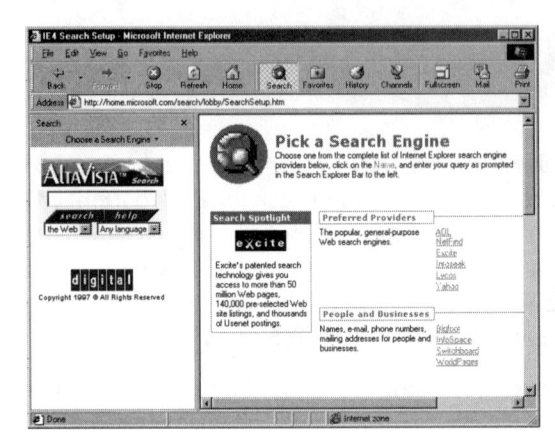

The Search Explorer bar in the left frame of the Internet Explorer window.

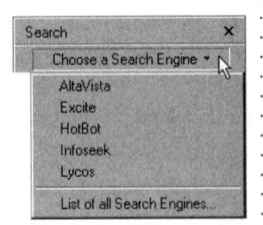

Near the top of the Search Explorer bar, you'll see a button titled Choose a Search Engine. Clicking that button reveals a list of popular search engines, as shown here in the margin. To search the Web, first choose any search engine. They all provide a broad search of the Web, so don't worry about picking the "right" or "wrong" one. (If you want my advice, though, I suggest you start with AltaVista.)

Performing a Search

To actually perform the search, you need to type some word or phrase into the text box provided in the Search Explorer bar. Then click the Search button (in other search engines, this button may say something like "Find" or "Go Get It"). The Search Explorer bar will then list Web sites and/or documents pertaining to the word or phrase you searched for.

Each engine displays this information in a slightly different format, but as a rule the Explorer bar will show you a list of blue underlined hyperlinks to the related Web pages. When you click one of those links, the actual page shows up over in the right frame, and the Explorer bar stays open next to it. Typically there's an indication of how many matches

320

were found, and a list of links to the first 10 or 15 pages. To go to a page, just click its link. When your search turns up lots of pages, buttons such as Next and Previous will appear to help you move among the pages and examine the ones you think will helpful.

Let's look at an example of a search using AltaVista. In the figure coming up, I'm searching AltaVista for the phrase *beanie babies*. After clicking the Search button, I discover that there are some 400,000 pages (documents) on the Web having to do with Beanie Babies. The first 10 of those pages are listed beneath the counter, and I can click any of those links to go its page. Optionally, to see other related Web sites, I can click the Next button down near the bottom of the list to view the next group of 10 sites located in my search.

AltaVista Search Example

Search Explorer bar's results of searching AltaVista for "beanie babies."

When you're finished using the Search Explorer bar, you can easily put it back into hiding. Just click the Search button in the toolbar again, or click the Close button (X) near the top of the Explorer bar.

In my own Web site I have a multiple-engine search page, Coolnerds MegaSearch, that you might find a little easier to use than the Search Explorer bar. To get there, point your Web browser to **http://www/coolnerds.com** and look for the Sitseeing & Searching option. Beneath that, click on the Coolnerds MegaSearch link. (Optionally, you can just point your Web browser to **http://www.coolnerds.com/sitesee/search.htm**.)

Coolnerds MegaSearch
Alan's Web site

Just type your search word or phrase into the Step 1 text box in the left-hand frame. (In the illustration just below, I've entered **UFO**

Abduction.) Then choose a search engine from the list in Step 2, and click the Do the Search button. After a brief delay, the right-hand frame will display the results of your search. As always, you can click any link in the search results to go to that page or site.

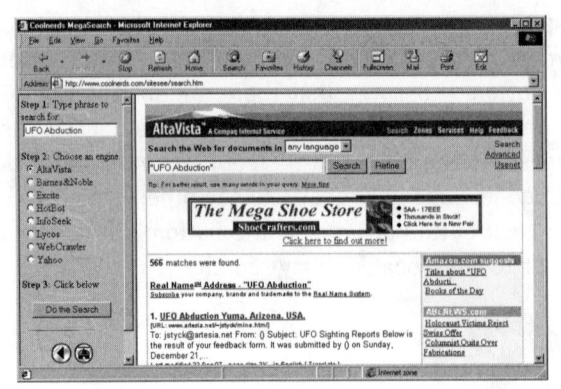

Coolnerds MegaSearch for "UFO abduction."

Note: The Barnes&Noble option in Coolnerds MegaSearch isn't a search engine. Rather, it links you to Barnes and Noble's online database, where you can search for books on the topic you're interested in.

If you want to search with a different engine, just click the one you want, over in the left-hand frame. Then click Do the Search again.

Popular Search Engines

The Search Explorer bar and Coolnerds MegaSearch are just utilities to give you quick access to the most popular search engines. Many of those search engines offer other tools, such as special characters and operators, that you can use to refine your searches and find exactly the information you need. To see everything a particular search engine has to offer, you should point your Web browser directly to that site and then use it.

Designing searches is a skill you'll want to develop. The more you practice, the better you'll get at finding exactly what you want, quickly.

Here's a handy list of search engine URLs.

Search Engine	URL
AltaVista	http://www.altavista.digital.com
Excite	http://www.excite.com
HotBot	http://www.hotbot.com
InfoSeek	http://www.infoseek.com
Lycos	http://www.lycos.com
WebCrawler	http://www.webcrawler.com
Yahoo	http://www.yahoo.com

Keeping Track of Favorite Sites

As you browse around and explore the Web, you'll find sites that you'd like to revisit later, either occasionally or regularly. Rather than having to remember all those sites and their URLs, Internet Explorer helps you maintain a list of your favorite sites.

The job is simple. When you are at a site that you think you'd like to have on your list of **Favorites**, choose Favorites ➔ Add to Favorites from Internet Explorer's menu bar. You'll come to this dialog box:

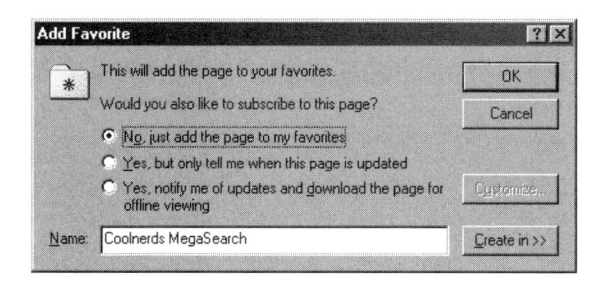

*Two options in the Add Favorites dialog box allow you to set up a **subscription** to a Web site, which is a bit more sophisticated than a Favorites link. Subscriptions are discussed in Chapter 15.*

Choose the first option (No, Just Add . . .), and then click the OK button. That's all there is to it. Anytime you want to revisit this site in the future, you can just click Favorites in the menu bar. The Web sites you've placed in your Favorites list will be displayed on the Favorites pull-down menu, ready for your selection.

You can also open up and select from your list of favorites in the **Favorites Explorer bar**. Just click the Favorites button in the toolbar or choose View ➔ Explorer Bar ➔ Favorites. Your list of favorites will appear in the explorer bar on the left. To close the Favorites Explorer bar, just click the X button at the top of the bar, or click the Favorites button in the toolbar again.

Downloading Files from the Web

One of the primary reasons for browsing the Web is to locate information that you need. Often you will want to have a copy of an article, document, graphic, or some other item of interest that you've come across. Or you may have found a shareware program that you want to try for free, or a new version of one of your software applications may have become available.

Many sites let you do this; they offer the option to **download** files—or almost anything, really—to your PC. To *download* a file means to copy it from a server on the Internet to your own computer. If a particular Web site does offer files for downloading, you'll see some kind of link on the page that you can click to start the download.

Print Those Instructions! Typically the site's sponsor or author will have provided instructions explaining how to use the file after you've downloaded it. If you do come across a page with those instructions, you'd do well to print it. Just click the Print button in the Internet Explorer toolbar to start printing right away. Optionally, you can choose File ➔ Print or press Ctrl+P to get to the Print dialog box. From there, you can specify printing options, and then click the OK button to start printing.

It's Best to Save First When the download actually begins, you'll come to the File Download dialog box. Unless the Web site's download instructions specifically tell you otherwise, *you should choose the option to "Save this program to disk" rather than to run the program from the site.*

"Always ask" option It's also a good idea to leave the "Always ask . . ." checkbox checked, to make sure you always get to make this save-or-run choice. Then click the OK button.

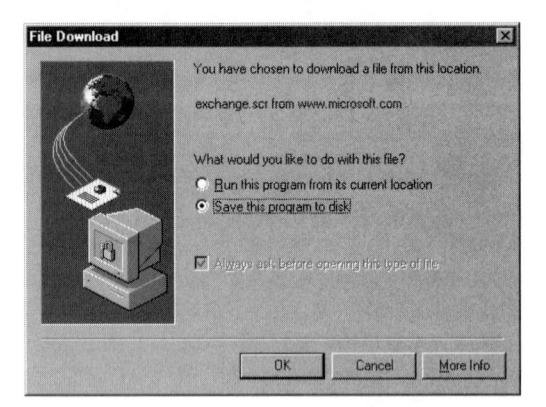

Note the Path & Filename! The Save As dialog box, shown just below, appears next. This is where most people make their big mistake. They don't pay attention to the folder where the file is being downloaded, and under what filename. So after the download is complete, they can't find the file they just downloaded!

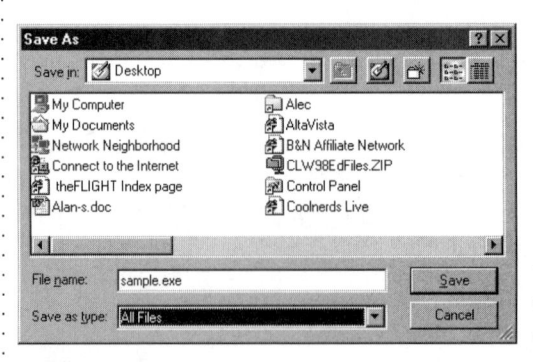

This file will be saved to the Windows 98 desktop as file sample.exe.

You'll want to be sure and pay attention to what you do at this point. For starters, you should make a conscious choice of the folder that will receive the downloaded file. One way to make sure you won't lose the file is just to put it right on your desktop. To do that, choose Desktop from the top of the Save In drop-down list, as I've done in the preceding example. Pay attention to the File Name box as well. That tells you the name of the file that you're about to download.

Choose the destination folder carefully!

When you're ready to go, click the Save button. A progress meter will appear, telling you how the download is going. When the download is complete, you'll see a message to that effect.

After downloading a file, you can continue browsing the Web, or you can close Internet Explorer and focus on the file you just downloaded. Unless your download instructions say otherwise, you can open your new file by clicking (or double-clicking) its icon, as usual.

If you'd like to get an idea of what kinds of things you can download from the Web, I suggest you visit some of the sites that specialize in downloads. Here's a list of some places you may want to visit.

Cool Download Sites

Download Site	URL
Five-Star Shareware	http://www.5star-shareware.com
Happy Puppy	http://www.happypuppy.com
Microsoft Download	http://www.microsoft.com/msdownload
PC Magazine	http://www.zdnet.com/pcmag/pctech/download/index.html
SimTel	http://oak.oakland.edu/simtel.net
Software USA	http://www.softusa.com
Tucows	http://www.tucows.com
Windex	http://windex.daci.net
WinFiles	http://www.winfiles.com
Wugnet	http://www.wugnet.com

Protecting the Kids

If you're setting up Internet browsing in a household, school, or anyplace else where kids and teens will be accessing the Web, it's important to keep in mind that the Internet is a *very* public place with virtually no censorship. And there are lots of Web sites that you definitely don't want youngsters to stumble across, much less log on to.

For help in this area, there are some programs that you can use to prevent access to inappropriate material. To learn more about any of the products included in the following list, just visit its Web site using the URL shown.

Product/Resource	URL
CyberSitter	http://www.solidoak.com
Net Nanny	http://www.netnanny.com
Surf Watch	http://www.surfwatch.com

Summary

The World Wide Web is one of the Internet's most popular services. All kinds of organizations, businesses, and individuals have sites on the Web that you can visit. To use the Web you need some kind of connection to the Internet, and a Web browser program. **Microsoft Internet Explorer**, which comes with Windows 98, is just such a browser.

- ▼ To get on the Web, just open your Web browser, Internet Explorer. If prompted, go ahead and log on to your Internet account.
- ▼ To go to a specific Web site, just type the site's **URL** into Internet Explorer's Address bar, and press Enter or the Tab key.
- ▼ Many Web pages contain **links** to other pages, which you can just click to go to another page. Textual links are usually blue and underlined, letting you know they're clickable. Some graphic images —in some cases even a portion of an image—are also clickable.
- ▼ Whenever the mouse pointer is on something that can be clicked, the pointer turns to a little hand with the index finger raised.
- ▼ **Search engines** are special Web sites that help you to look up information on the Web. You can get quick access to many search engines just by clicking the Search button in Internet Explorer's toolbar, or by choosing View → Explorer Bar → Search.
- ▼ To **download** a file means to copy it from some computer on the Internet (or any other computer, for that matter) to your own computer.
- ▼ There are several products on the market that parents and schools can use to **block out material** that isn't appropriate for children.

Subscriptions, Channels, & Active Desktop

If you've made it through the book to this point, you now know your way around the Windows 98 operating system. And you've worked through the fundamental setup and usage of Internet Explorer 4 to browse the World Wide Web. In this final chapter, I'm going to show you some unique ways provided by Windows 98 and Explorer, together, for accessing information on the Web.

You can **subscribe** to Web sites, and you can also subscribe to special Web sites called **channels**. Your Windows 98 desktop can also host **active desktop items**. These are miniprograms that live right on your desktop and can stay hooked into the Internet full time. Desktop items can feed you up-to-the-minute news, stock quotes, weather reports, and other information—live, right from the Web, as you do your day-to-day work with your PC.

Before we get started, bear in mind that the features described in this chapter will work only if your Internet connection is up and running, as discussed in Chapter 12. And you'll also want to be familiar with the basics of Web browsing, as discussed in Chapter 14.

15: SUBSCRIPTIONS, CHANNELS, & ACTIVE DESKTOP

Subscriptions Probably the biggest complaint that most people have about the Word Wide Web is that it's too slow. After pointing your Web browser to a site, it may take a minute or more for the page to actually appear. That long wait time isn't really caused by the Web, per se. It's caused by the relatively slow dial-up connections that most of us use to access the Internet from our PCs.

High-speed, dedicated connections are much faster. But these lines can cost hundreds or even thousands of dollars each month, which puts them out of reach for most of us normal folk. Cable-TV modems are much faster than dial-up modems. But not everyone has access to cable Internet or can afford the added expense of the cable company's fees.

Subscriptions are sort of a "no-cost" solution to slow Internet connections.

Subscribing to a Site Here's the idea: When you add a new Web site to your Favorites list in Internet Explorer, you can also **subscribe** to the site. Then you can schedule a time, preferably when you're sleeping or whatever, to have your PC go out and visit all your favorite Web sites. When that time arrives, your PC connects to the Internet and visits all the sites you've subscribed to. If it finds that something has changed at that site since your last visit, it marks the site's icon in the Favorites list with a little red gleam (see the example in the margin).

After your PC has finished checking all your subscribed Web sites, it disconnects itself from the Internet. When you next check your favorite Web sites, in the morning or when you get home from work or whenever, the red gleams tell you which sites have changed since your last visit. You can just click any one of those icons to go to the Web site and see what's new. You save time by not visiting sites that have not changed since your last visit.

Subscribe and Download: It's also possible to subscribe to a Web site in such a way that when your PC finds the site has changed since your last visit, everything from that site is actually downloaded right onto your hard disk. With this arrangement, when you click any icon with a red gleam, you *instantly* see the entire Web site. You don't have to wait for any lengthy download because that's already been taken care of, while you were away from your computer.

Browsing Offline Having Internet Explorer download material to your PC (at night or in the very early morning, or at another selected time) offers another advantage: It allows you to **browse offline**. You can examine all the

Web pages that have changed since your last visit, without even being connected to the Internet. For example, if you set up this sort of arrangement on a laptop, you could review all the new Web content anywhere—say, on the way to work (though preferably not if you're driving or riding your bike to get there!).

Unlike subscriptions in the magazine world, the kind of subscriptions I'm talking about here—set up via the Favorites menu in Internet Explorer—don't come with any extra fees attached. The way these subscriptions work is pretty simple and is handled entirely by your own computer, not the Internet. Each time you visit a Web page, Internet Explorer puts a copy of that page on your hard disk, in a special folder called the **Internet cache** (pronounced "cash"). Along with that page is stored the page's **timestamp**, which is the date and time the file was put on your hard disk.

A Little Technical Stuff

When your PC goes out and prowls your subscribed Web sites, the timestamp of a page that's in your Internet cache is compared to the timestamp of the page that's currently on the Web. If the page on the Web site is newer than the one in your Internet cache, then that site's Favorites icon earns the red gleam. If you told Internet Explorer that you also want to download new content, that new content will be downloaded to your Internet cache for your offline browsing.

> **Not All Subscriptions Are Free**: I don't want to imply that *everything* on the Internet is free. There are private newsletters and such that do charge you for subscribing. But that type of subscription is different from the subscriptions you set up through Internet Explorer's Favorites menu.

And speaking of charges, any connect-time charges that normally apply while you are browsing the Web will apply equally to the connect time used for updating subscriptions. Whoever is doing the billing at your ISP doesn't know, or care, whether a human or a machine placed the call ;-)

Connect-time charges

To subscribe to a Web site, you first need to get to that site. It must be on the screen, with its URL in the Address bar. Use Internet Explorer 4 and the techniques we discussed in Chapter 14 to do that, or you may already be up and browsing and come across a site you'd like to subscribe to.

How to Subscribe

Here are the steps to do a quick-and-easy subscription to a Web site currently on your screen:

▼ From Internet Explorer's menu bar, choose Favorites ➔ Add to Favorites. You'll see the Add Favorite dialog box.

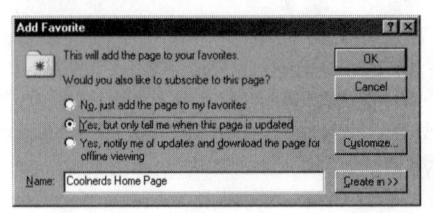

Adding a Web site to your list of Favorites.

▼ If you want Internet Explorer to mark changes to this site with a red gleam, but *not* download everything from the site, choose the second option.

▼ If you want Internet Explorer to mark changes to this site with a red gleam *and* download everything from the site, as well, choose the third option.

▼ Click the OK button.

That's all there is to it—the subscribing part anyway. You can use these same simple steps to subscribe to any Web page, anytime. And, of course, you can subscribe to as many or as few Web sites as you wish.

Managing Your Subscriptions

Subscribing to Web sites is easy. But there are other aspects of subscriptions that need to be attended to. Such as how often you want your PC to go out and scour the Web for you. And at what time of the day this should happen.

Getting Ready

It's pretty easy to set the schedule, but there are a couple of important things to take into consideration first:

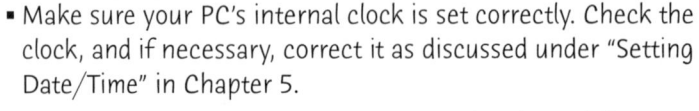

- Make sure your PC's internal clock is set correctly. Check the clock, and if necessary, correct it as discussed under "Setting Date/Time" in Chapter 5.

- If you've scheduled any other tasks to take place while you're away from your computer, such as backup and disk cleanup, make sure you know when those tasks are scheduled to run. That way, you can schedule subscriptions for a time when the PC isn't busy with those other scheduled tasks. See "Automating Maintenance Tasks" in Chapter 10 if you need a reminder on how all that works.

Let's start by taking a look at the Subscriptions window in which you'll work on managing your subscriptions.

▼ Open Internet Explorer.

▼ Choose Favorites ➔ Manage Subscriptions from Internet Explorer's menu bar.

Here is the special My Computer window that you'll see next, showing you a list of Web sites to which you've subscribed:

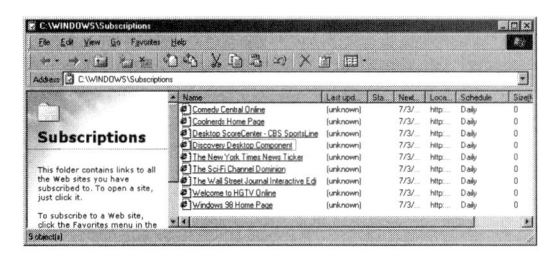

The Subscriptions Window

Special My Computer window for managing Web subscriptions.

What you're actually viewing here is a folder named C:\WINDOWS\Subscriptions, which is a special folder where all subscription information is stored. You're viewing the folder through My Computer.

> Because you're in a My Computer window, you can choose various view characteristics from the View menu. In the Subscriptions window, I'm viewing the folder in Details view and have narrowed the columns by dragging the vertical bars in the column headings. This makes the Subscriptions window easier to work with.

Take a look at the Schedule column. Notice all of the items in my Subscriptions list sport a dog-eared page icon with the distinctive Explorer "e" icon—those items are all subscriptions. (If you have added sites to your Channel bar, those items will be listed, too, with their own characteristic icons. We'll get to the Channels topic later in this chapter.) Notice that all the subscriptions are scheduled to be updated Daily. But you can change that to whatever schedule you want, as we'll discuss next.

To determine when and how often your PC goes online and checks your subscribed Web sites, you need to create a schedule. Or you can tailor an existing schedule to fit your own requirements. You can do that right here in the My Computer view of your Subscriptions folder.

Make Your Schedules

333

Here are the steps to get to the dialog box that allows you to create and tweak schedules:

- ▼ Right-click any subscription item in the Subscription window. (Remember, a subscribed item is any page icon that has the little "e"-on-a-page icon and is scheduled for updates.)
- ▼ Choose Properties from the shortcut menu.
- ▼ When the Properties dialog box appears, click the Schedule tab.

Just below is an illustration of the Properties dialog for a sample site on the Daily schedule. Other schedules, accessible from the drop-down list, include Weekly and Monthly. Your first decision is whether you want to use one of the existing schedules, perhaps tweaked a bit to your own liking. Or do you want to create an entirely new schedule?

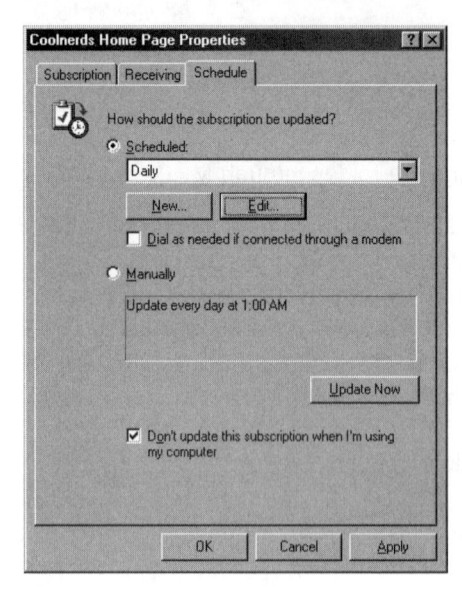

This subscription gets updated every day at 1:00 A.M.

Predefined Schedules   Before you decide about scheduling, let me tell you what the three predefined schedules allow you to do.

Daily   Choose this option if you want to check subscriptions daily, or just on weekdays, or several times a day, or more than once a week.

Monthly   Choose this option if you want to check subscriptions only once per month or less frequently, such as every two months.

Weekly   Choose this option if you want to check subscriptions once a week, or on several different days of the week (such as Monday, Wednesday, and Friday), or less often than once a week but more often than once a month.

The simplest thing to do, in most cases, is to choose which one of the existing schedules best describes the kind of schedule you want, and then tweak that schedule.

It's important to understand that all the subscribed sites designated for Daily updates will be affected by any change you make to the Daily schedule. Likewise, any subscription that you put on a Weekly or Monthly schedule will be updated according to whatever you have defined for those schedules. You do not have to tweak each subscription's start time individually. By the same token, be sure to consider any subscriptions that are exceptions to a schedule before you set that schedule up.

When you change a schedule, you change the update timing for all subscriptions on that schedule.

For example, let's say you want your PC to update your subscriptions at 4:30 A.M. on weekdays. In the Schedule tab of the Properties dialog box, choose Daily from the drop-down list. Then click the Edit button to tweak this schedule named Daily.

Modifying the Daily Schedule

The next dialog box to appear is the Custom Schedule dialog box, in which you get to define just what "Daily" means on your PC. In the following example, I've defined Daily to mean weekdays at 4:30 A.M. You can choose whatever options you'd like in this dialog box, to set a schedule that works for you. I chose 4:30 A.M. because it gives my other scheduled computer maintenance tasks, which start at 1:00 A.M., plenty of time to finish. Also, this early-morning timing gives all the Web site publishers most of the night to get their new content for the day posted. (An earlier update time, such as 11:00 P.M., would miss all the new pages that were put on the Web later that night.)

Pick a time of day that is convenient for your life as well as suitable for the site.

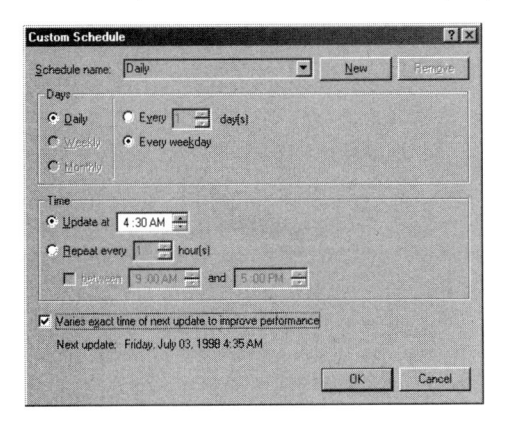

The Custom Schedule dialog box also offers an option that "varies exact time of next update to improve performance" (see the checkbox near the bottom of the dialog). Enabling that option gives Windows some extra leeway in deciding exactly when the update takes place. Windows will use the extra leeway to figure out an ideal time, based on network traffic and other factors, for updating your subscriptions.

335

> `Update every weekday at 4:30 AM`

When you've finished modifying the current Daily schedule for this subscription, click OK to save your changes and return to the Schedule tab. The schedule described within that dialog box now matches the schedule you've just defined.

Before we move on, let's look at one more example of editing an existing schedule.

Modifying the Weekly Schedule

Suppose you prefer to schedule your updates to happen every Monday, Wednesday, and Friday at 6:00 A.M. Choose the Weekly schedule from the drop-down list, and then click the Edit button. In the Custom Schedule dialog box, set your schedule as shown here:

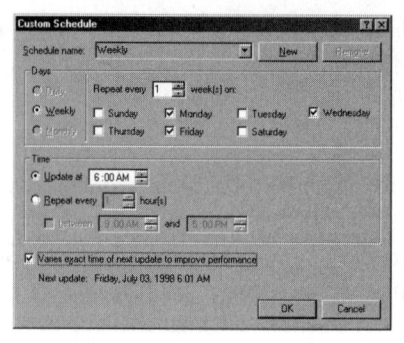

In this schedule, Weekly is defined to mean every Monday, Wednesday, and Friday at 6:00 A.M.

Clicking the OK button will save the change, and when you return to the Schedule tab, the description of your weekly schedule will reflect your three-times-weekly schedule.

> Don't forget to leave the computer running on nights that you've scheduled updates! If the computer isn't on when the scheduled time arrives, your PC can't go out and update your subscriptions.

Modifying the Monthly Schedule

There's not much to modifying the Monthly schedule. You can choose which day of the month you want the subscriptions to be updated. You can also skip months—for example, have the subscription updated on the 15th of every other month. And, as with the other schedules, you can choose what time of day you want the subscription update to start.

Scheduling a Subscription

Not all subscriptions have to be on the same schedule. For instance, you might want to have your news-related sites updated daily. Other sites, which you know don't change that often, can be put on other schedules. To designate a particular schedule for a particular subscription, follow these steps:

- In the My Computer view of your Subscriptions folder, right-click the subscription you want to reschedule.
- Choose Properties from the shortcut menu.
- Click the Schedule tab.
- Choose a schedule from the Scheduled drop-down list.
- Click the OK button to save the change and close the dialog box.

The subscription you changed will display its new update schedule in the Details view of the Subscriptions folder. In the following example, I've scheduled some subscriptions to be updated daily, and others weekly.

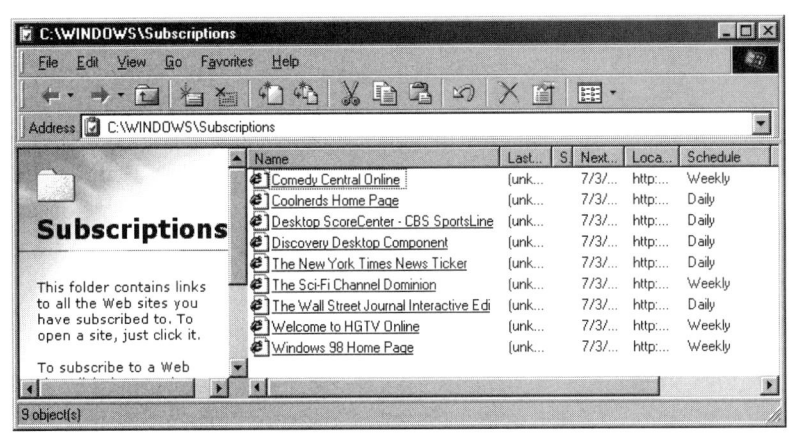

You can designate a particular schedule for every subscription.

Changing Individual Subscriptions

The Properties dialog box for a subscription offers other options in addition to scheduling. To review and manage the options being applied to a particular subscribed item:

- Right-click the subscription you want to work with, and choose Properties from the shortcut menu.
- Select the options you want to apply to the subscription, as explained in the following paragraphs.
- Click the OK button after making your selections to save your changes and close the Properties dialog box.

15: SUBSCRIPTIONS, CHANNELS, & ACTIVE DESKTOP

Update Options
Some options for updating Web content are located on the Receiving tab of the Properties dialog box.

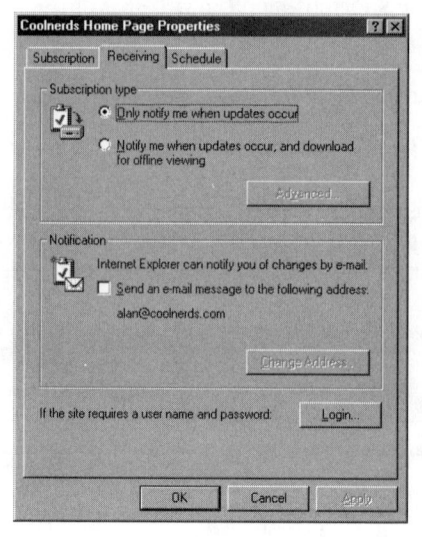

The Receiving tab lets you arrange how you are to be notified of new content.

Update Notifications
Under Subscription Type, you designate whether or not new content is automatically downloaded to your PC for offline browsing (discussed earlier in this chapter). Remember that regardless of which of those options you choose, the icons for sites that have changed since your last visit will be marked with a gleam.

E-mail Notifications: The checkbox under Notification lets you go a step beyond the red gleam as your notification of a change to the Web site. If you enable this option, Internet Explorer will send an e-mail message to your address telling you when a site has changed. Click the Change Address button and specify the e-mail address to which you want these notifications sent. In the future, whenever Internet Explorer discovers new content on a subscribed web site, it will write up and send an e-mail message telling you of the change. The site's icon will still earn the red gleam, as well.

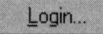

Arranging for Login During Updates:
If the site you're scheduling requires you to log in, you'll need to arrange this login for the updating operation. In the Receiving tab, click the Login button, and then type in the User Name and Password that you use to log in to that site.

338

Arranging for Manual Update of a Subscription:
You may not want a subscription to be updated automatically and would rather do it yourself. In that case, you can select the Manually option on the Schedule tab, and the site will only be updated when you tell the PC to update the subscription.

If you want to update this subscription only, right now, regardless of any schedules, click the Update Now button.

> **Avoiding Update Cross-Traffic:** To make sure that subscription updates don't kick in while you're trying to use the computer, go to the Schedule tab and enable the option for Don't Update This Subscription When I'm Using My Computer.

If you access the Internet through a dial-up modem connection, you need to make sure your computer will dial on cue. Click the Schedule tab, and select the checkbox for Dial as Needed If Connected Through a Modem.

Arranging for Dial-up

When you have set up some subscriptions to be updated manually (with the Manually option in the Schedule tab, as described earlier), or if you ever want to update all your subscriptions on the spot without regard to the schedule, you can follow these steps:

Manual Updates

▼ If you haven't already done so, start Internet Explorer.
▼ Choose Favorites ➔ Update All Subscriptions from Internet Explorer's menu bar.

A progress indicator will keep you posted on how the updates are going. When they're finished, the dialog box will disappear by itself.

You can check your subscriptions at any time to see which Web sites have changed since the last update. Start Internet Explorer, if necessary, and choose Favorites ➔ Manage Subscriptions. When you get to the Subscriptions folder, you might want to switch to Large Icons view (choose View ➔ Large Icons from the Subscription window's menu bar). With the icons enlarged, it's really easy to see which icons have a red gleam, as shown in this next example. To visit any Web site that has changed, just click its icon.

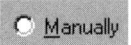

Checking Your Subscriptions

339

15: SUBSCRIPTIONS, CHANNELS, & ACTIVE DESKTOP

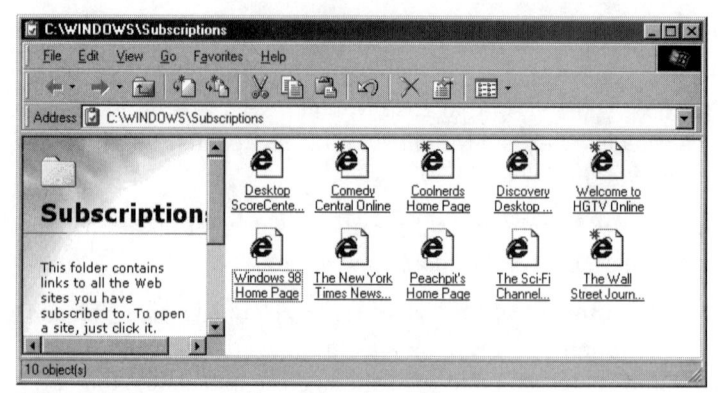

The Subscriptions window with enlarged icons, so it's easy to see which sites are marked with a red gleam.

Subscribed sites will also show up in your Favorites list. (Click the Favorites button in Internet Explorer's toolbar or choose View ➔ Explorer Bar ➔ Favorites from the menu bar.) Subscribed Web sites that have changed since your last visit are marked with the same red gleam that you see in the Subscriptions window. To visit any site, just click its name in the Favorites list.

To Unsubscribe

If you want to remove a subscription from your list, open the Subscription tab and click the Unsubscribe button.

How to Browse Offline

As mentioned earlier in this chapter, you have the option to automatically download new material from subscribed sites for **offline browsing**. If you choose that option, you'll want to make sure Internet Explorer is working offline while you're browsing around. Otherwise, Internet Explorer will attempt to go online and view the page live. To put Internet Explorer into offline mode:

- ▼ Choose File ➔ Work Offline from Internet Explorer's menu bar.

    Now when you click a favorite site that has changed, Internet Explorer will "know" to read the new material out of the Internet cache on your hard disk, rather than attempt to go online.

- ▼ When you've finished working offline and want to go back to normal online browsing, just choose File ➔ Work Offline again to clear the option.

Channels

Some (though certainly not all) Web sites support the Windows 98 **Channel bar**. A **channel** is pretty much the same thing as a subscription, in that you can schedule updates to sites that are designated as channels. A channel is different from a subscription, however, in the following ways:

- The Channel bar gives you one-click access to any of its channels.
- Although you can subscribe to *any* Web site, only Web sites that sport this "Add Active Channel" button can be added to your Channel bar.
- When you designate a site as a channel, you can allow the publisher of the Web site to determine an ideal update schedule for you.

If you don't see the Channel bar on your own Windows 98 desktop, don't worry abut it. I'll show you the bar, and how to display it, in the section coming up.

When you open a channel, it is displayed in Internet Explorer's full-screen view, usually with the **Channels Explorer bar** open on the left. (The Channels Explorer bar and the Channels bar are two different elements, although they contain many of the same items.) Here's what the Disney channel, and the accompanying Channels Explorer bar, look like on screen:

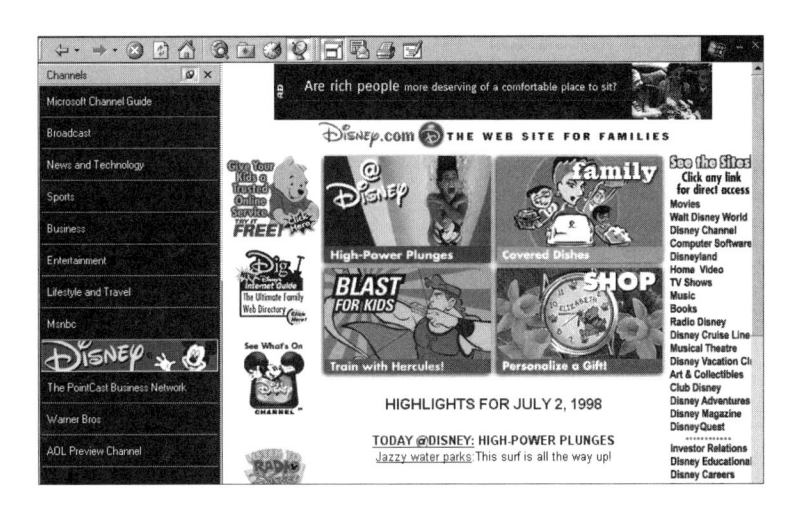

To play around with channels, the first thing you'll probably want to do is to put the Channel bar on your desktop. If you don't already see the Channel bar, follow these steps to bring it up:

- Right-click a neutral area of the Windows 98 desktop and choose Properties from the shortcut menu.

Accessing the Channel Bar

- Click the Web tab in the Display Properties dialog box.
- Make sure the following two items are both selected (checked):

  ☑ View my Active Desktop as a web page
  ☑ Internet Explorer Channel Bar

- Click the OK button to save your selections and return to the desktop.

When it appears on your desktop, the Channel bar should look something like the following example—though yours might contain different buttons). The labels within the pictures show what the various parts of the Channel bar are for. Note that the gray title bar and frame appear *only* while the mouse pointer is actually touching the Channel bar. When you move the mouse pointer away from the Channel bar, that gray frame will disappear.

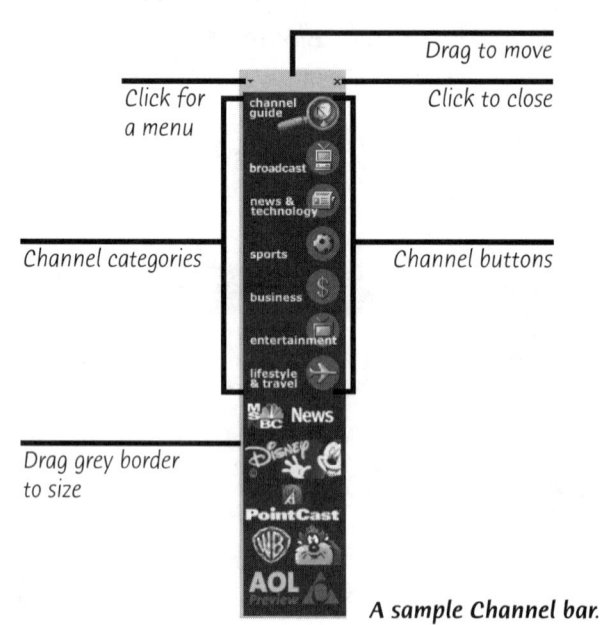

A sample Channel bar.

Channels Explorer Bar

You can also view channels in the Channels Explorer bar. To do so:

- Click any button in the Channel bar.
- **Or**, click the View Channels button in the Quick Launch toolbar.

- **Or,** if you're in Internet Explorer, click the Channels button in the toolbar, or choose View ➔ Explorer Bar ➔ Channels from the menu bar.

You can display the Channels Explorer bar in both the regular and full-screen (as in the next example) views. Remember, you can switch between the regular and full-screen views just by clicking the Fullscreen button in Internet Explorer's toolbar.

When you work in full-screen view, you'll find that the Channels Explorer bar will slide out of your way from time to time, as you explore channels. To bring the bar out of hiding, just move the mouse pointer to the far-left edge of your screen. If you don't want the Explorer bar to slide out of view at all, click the little push-pin icon at the top of the explorer bar.

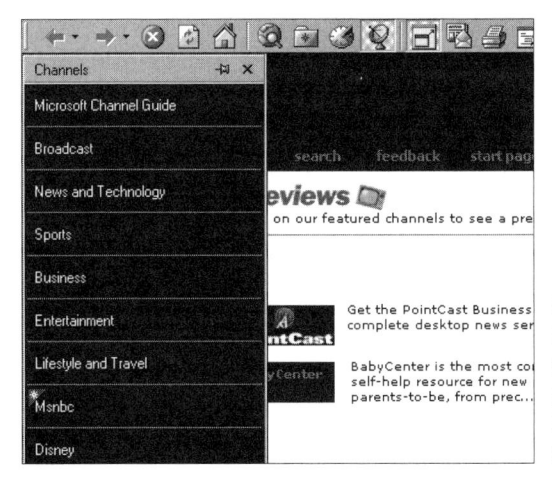

The Channels Explorer bar at the left side of a full-screen Internet Explorer view.

As I mentioned, you can't add just any old Web site to your Channel bar. Only Web sites that bear the Add Active Channel logo can be added to the Channel bar. But you don't have to wait until you just happen to stumble across such a site to add it to your Channel bar. Instead, you can visit the suggested sample channels that are already in your Channel bar. Choose which ones you want to subscribe to, and which ones you don't, using the following steps.

▼ Open Internet Explorer if it isn't open already.

▼ Display the Channels Explorer bar.

▼ Click a category that interests you, such as News & Technology.

Subscribing to Channels

Step 1: Open a category

15: SUBSCRIPTIONS, CHANNELS, & ACTIVE DESKTOP

The category expands to show individual channels available within the category, along with their icons. For example, in the upcoming example, I've opened the News & Technology category. The icons and names beneath that category name (including Snap! Online, *The New York Times*, and so on) represent channels in that category. The main frame to the right of the Channels Explorer bar also provides quick links to the News & Technology channels.

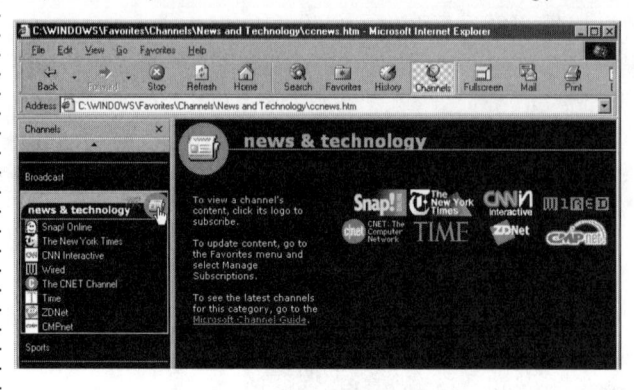

The News & Technology category of channels.

Step 2: Visit the channel

▼ Click any Channel icon, either in the Channels explorer bar or in the main page, to visit the channel.

Exactly what appears next depends on the channel, of course, but chances are you'll be given the opportunity to browse around and take a look at the site.

▼ Find the Add Active Channel button somewhere in that site.

Step 3: Choose a subscription setup

▼ You actually have three choices of what to do with each channel you visit:

- If you don't want to subscribe to the site, but you'd like to have a button for the channel in your Channel bar anyway, do nothing. Just move on to the next site in the list, or to your next task.

- If you don't want to subscribe, and you also want to remove the channel from your Channel bar, right-click the channel's icon in the Explorer bar and choose Delete from the shortcut menu.

- If you do want to subscribe to the channel, click the Add Active Channel button within the site.

Step 4: Choose an update arrangement

▼ When you do add a channel to your Channel bar, you'll be given some options for how you want those Channels updated automatically. These options are similar to the ones for regular subscriptions:

344

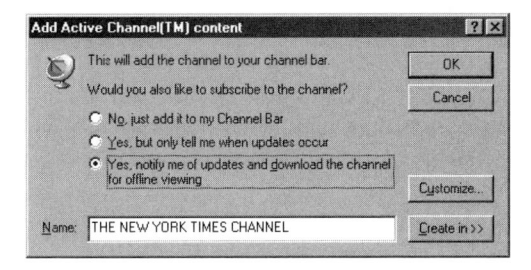

- **No, just add it to my Channel bar**: When you choose this option, your PC will never check this Web site for updates. A button for the channel does, however, remain in your Channel bar.
- **Yes, but only tell me when updates occur**: In this case, your PC will look for channels that have changed since your last visit and mark them with a red gleam in the Channel bar and Channels Explorer bar.
- **Yes, notify me of updates and download the channel for offline viewing**: This option works the same as the second option and, in addition, new content is downloaded to your PC for faster viewing and/or offline browsing.

You can browse around in this manner and subscribe to as many (or as few) channels as you wish. Any sites on which you click the Add Active Channel button will add a button to your Channel bar.

Organizing the Channel bar

As you add and remove Channel bar buttons, you may want to reorganize those buttons from time to time. The job is a pretty easy one. Just get to the Channels Explorer bar in Internet Explorer. Then:

- To open a Channel category, click that group.
- To move an icon out of a group and into its own position on the Channel bar, just drag the icon from the group and drop it somewhere on the Channel bar, outside of any group.
- To move an icon into a group, just drag the icon to the group's button and drop it there.
- To delete a Channel icon, right-click it and choose Delete.

Once you get the hang of it, you shouldn't have any trouble organizing and arranging items in the Channels explorer bar. Any change you make there will also be reflected in the Channel bar that appears on the desktop.

Scheduling Channel Updates

Unlike subscriptions, most channels come with a predefined updating schedule. The publisher of the Web site decides what would be a good time to check for updates. That information is automatically applied to the channel—although, like everything else on the PC, you're not stuck with the publisher's suggested schedule. You can schedule channel updates however you wish. Use the Subscriptions window, just as you would for regular subscriptions. The steps to get started are as follows:

▼ Open Internet Explorer (if it's not already open). If Internet Explorer is in full-screen view, click the Fullscreen button so you can view the menu bar.

▼ Choose Favorites → Manage Subscriptions.

Channel Icons

In the Subscriptions folder, channels generally sport their own unique icon (different from the little Explorer "e" icon). For instance, notice the icon next to THE NEW YORK TIMES CHANNEL in the upcoming illustration. All the rest of the items in this Subscriptions window are subscriptions.

Also, look at the Schedule column for THE NEW YORK TIMES CHANNEL. It reads "Publisher's recommended schedule" (though the last word isn't visible in the illustration).

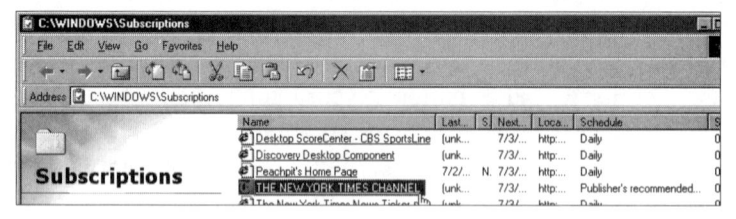

Channels have special icons in the Subscriptions window.

Channel Updates

To change a channel's update schedule, right-click its icon in the Channels Explorer bar, and choose Properties from the shortcut menu. The Properties dialog box for a channel offers options nearly identical to those for regular subscriptions. Here's the Subscription tab, for example:

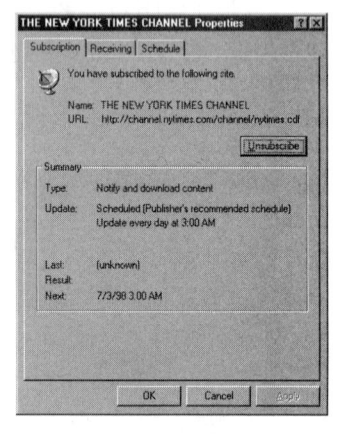

As with regular subscriptions, you can do the following:

- To unsubscribe the channel, click the Unsubscribe button on the Subscription tab.
- To choose how you're notified of changes to the channel, and whether or not you want new content downloaded to your PC, choose the appropriate options from the Receiving tab.
- To change the dates and times when the updates will occur, choose the appropriate options from the Schedule tab.

After making your selections, click the OK button to save your changes and close the dialog box.

Channel Surfing

Once you have your channels all squared away and have scheduled them for automatic updates, channel surfing becomes easy. Any channels that have changed since your last visit will be marked by a red gleam in your Channel bar. You can just click that red gleam Channel bar to go straight to the Web site and see what's new. Of course, if you opted to download new content, you can also browse offline, using the same techniques described under "How to Browse Offline" earlier in this chapter.

Active Desktop Items

Windows 98 supports a new type of program called an **active desktop item**. These items are different from other programs in that they can be hooked into the Internet ("live"). While connected, they get a steady stream of data from the Internet. This allows you to get up-to-the-minute news, stock prices, weather conditions, sports scores, and more, right on your desktop as you're using your PC.

Some active desktop items aren't plugged into the Internet full time, but they can still provide one-click access to favorite Web sites. For example, the Channel bar you learned about in the preceding section is actually an active desktop item. The Channel bar is, in fact, the only desktop item that comes with Windows 98. And you can find a whole lot more active desktop items on the World Wide Web.

The Active Desktop Layer

The active desktop is actually a **layer of content** on your screen. It resides between your desktop icons and your Windows 98 desktop. For example, suppose I apply a pinstripe-style wallpaper to my Windows 98 desktop, just to make it more visible (as shown in the following illustration). Let's say I also have the active desktop turned on and showing the Channel bar. If I were to drag the Channel bar over to the desktop

15: SUBSCRIPTIONS, CHANNELS, & ACTIVE DESKTOP

> **Wallpaper**: If you'd like to wallpaper your own Windows 98 desktop, see "Your Own Wallpaper" in Chapter 5.

icons, you could see that the Channel bar is on top of the wallpaper but beneath the icons, as on the left of this example:

Desktop icons (top layer)

Windows 98 desktop (bottom layer)

Active desktop item (middle layer)

When View As Web Page is turned off, active desktop layer is inactive and invisible

When visible, active desktop items like the Channel bar are sandwiched between the Windows 98 desktop and your desktop icons.

Active Desktop On/Off

Turning the active desktop on and off is as simple as can be. Here are the steps:

▼ Right click the Windows 98 desktop.

▼ Point to Active Desktop.

▼ If the View As Web Page option is checked, then your active desktop is turned on and functioning. If that option is not checked, then your active desktop is turned off and invisible.

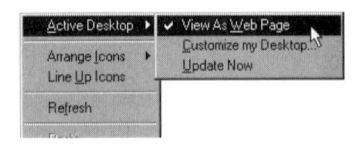

▼ To switch from on to off or vice versa, just click the View As Web Page option.

The one thing you *don't* want to do is get mixed up about the Windows 98 desktop folder vs. the active desktop. To control the appearance and behavior of the folder, you use the techniques we discussed in Chapter 7. To turn the active desktop on or off, you want to start right from the desktop.

Finding Active Desktop Items

I mentioned earlier that, in addition to the Channel bar, there are many more active desktop items available on the Internet. In fact, lots of the big companies give them away for free. It's cheap advertising—puts their logo right on your desktop! Or, to use corporate Web-speak,

348

15: SUBSCRIPTIONS, CHANNELS, & ACTIVE DESKTOP

I should say "…outs their logo on your active desktop layer." But you get the idea.

Anyway, to go hunting for these active desktop freebies, you need to go to the Microsoft Active Channel Guide. Follow these steps:

▼ If you're not already in Internet Explorer, go ahead and open it now.

▼ Open the Channels explorer bar if necessary. (Just in case you forget how to do this—click the Channels button in Internet Explorer's toolbar or choose View ➔ Explorer Bar ➔ Channels.)

▼ Click the Microsoft Active Channel Guide button in the toolbar. Wait for the Web page to load.

> You can close the Channels Explorer bar now to make more room for the Web pages you'll be viewing. Just click the Close (X) button at the top of the Explorer bar, or click the Channels button in the toolbar.

From this point on, you'll be somewhat on your own, because you're going to visit a Microsoft Web page now. Although I can't predict exactly what that page will look like on the day you visit, I can walk you through the process as it played out for me.

Clicking on the Microsoft Active Channel Guide button in my example took me to the Windows Media Showcase Web page shown here. If you look at the column titled Cool Media, the third item down is "active desktop items." Clicking that option would take you to yet another page.

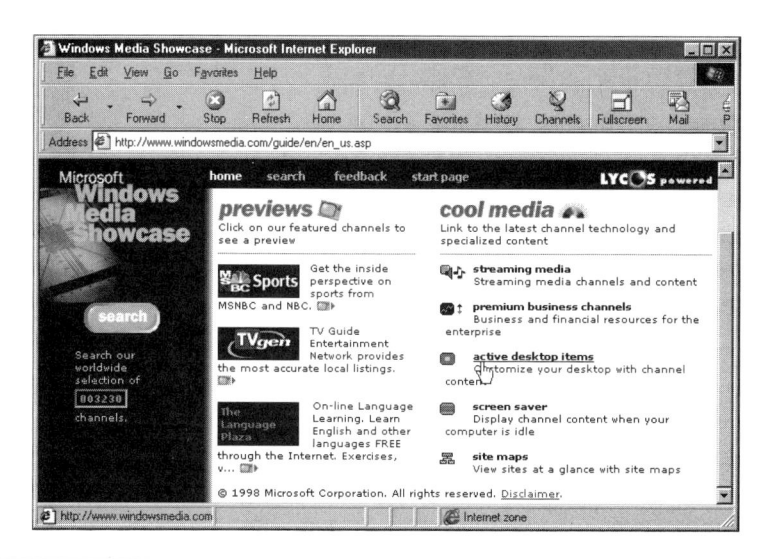

Look for an option that'll help you find active desktop items.

349

The next page lets me search for different kinds of active desktop items. I wanted to see them all, so I chose All and clicked the Search button. Several pages of active desktop items appear in the left-hand column. To learn more about a particular active desktop item, I can click its logo. The page numbers tell me I can view additional pages of logos. I can either click one of the page numbers, or click the Next Page button at the bottom of the logos list.

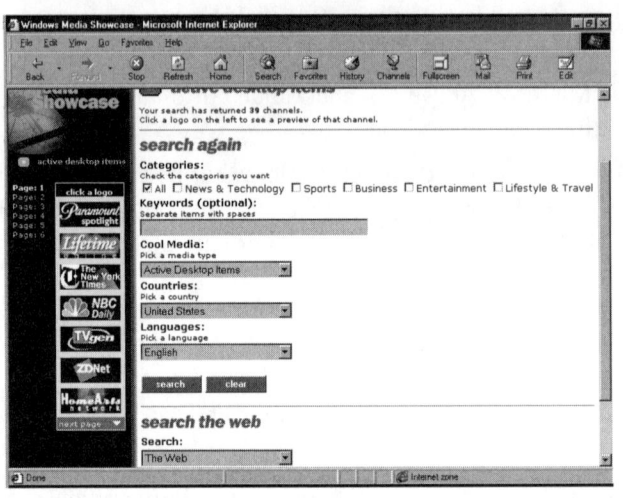

I can click one of the logos in the left-hand frame to see information about that company's active desktop items.

Adding an Item

Clicking one of the logos in the Microsoft Web page takes me to the active desktop item represented by that logo. When you're doing this search for yourself, the option to add active desktop components will most likely be yellow and look something like the example here in the margin. Just click it to try the item.

Can't find any active desktop items?

If a particular Web page doesn't offer any active desktop items, you might have to go looking around the publisher's Web site. Look for a Visit Active Channel button, and click it. Once you're on the site, you can search there for information on downloading active desktop items.

Download Warnings: If the download begins right away, you may be warned about viruses or other dangers. But I doubt any of the active desktop items you download through the Microsoft Active Channel Guide will ever cause you any grief.

15: SUBSCRIPTIONS, CHANNELS, & ACTIVE DESKTOP

The next dialog box to greet you will probably be the one just below, whose job is mainly just to ask for confirmation. Since you've learned all about subscription schedules in the earlier part of this chapter, you might want to schedule the updates for this item right now. It's a convenient time.

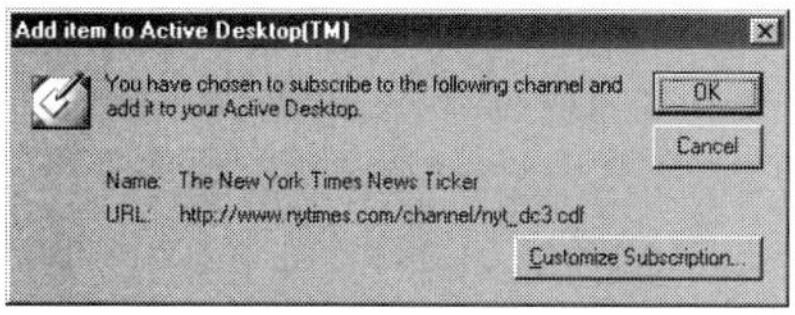

Schedule Updates, Too

Confirm your chosen active desktop item and, optionally, schedule updates for that item.

Just click the Customize Subscription button to jump to a little one-page Subscription Wizard. There you can choose a schedule in the drop-down list (Daily or Weekly). Then click the wizard's Finish button to get back to where you left off.

Click the OK button to begin the download of your active desktop item. You shouldn't have to do anything except wait. A progress meter will keep you posted on the download's progress. If any instructions do appear on the screen, be sure to follow them. When the download is done, the active desktop item should be right on your desktop. It may be covered by open windows, but you can just minimize all your open program windows to get to the new item on your screen.

> **Reminder**: In case you've forgotten how to minimize all the open windows on your desktop, here are two choices for you: Either click the Show Desktop icon in the Quick Launch toolbar, or right-click a neutral spot on the taskbar and choose Minimize All Windows.

The following example of my screen shows that I've added several active desktop items to my screen.

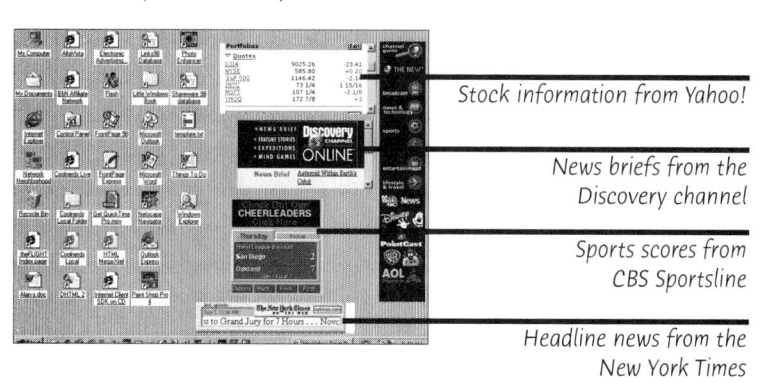

Stock information from Yahoo!

News briefs from the Discovery channel

Sports scores from CBS Sportsline

Headline news from the New York Times

351

Managing Active Desktop Items

When you do get an active desktop item on your desktop, don't think that it's stuck in place. You can size and drag active desktop items in the same way you move and size windows. The main difference is that the active desktop item doesn't have the normal title bar and borders. In fact, no borders at all are visible until you point to the desktop item (as is the case with the Channel bar). When the mouse pointer is resting on the desktop item, you'll be able to see the gray frame around the item. Once visible, these borders act much like the title bar and borders on a normal window.

Point to an active desktop item to view the gray frame.

Once you see the gray frame, you can do any of the following:

- To move the item, drag it by the wide gray frame across the top of the item.
- To size the item, drag any gray border.
- To close the item, click the Close (X) button.
- To see what other options are available for this active desktop item, click the little down-pointing triangle at the left edge of the top gray bar.

Some desktop items will also have hot spots that, when clicked, open a Web site or perform some other function. You can find such hot spots by pointing to different-colored or otherwise emphasized words or graphics in the desktop item. If the mouse pointer changes to a pointing hand, that means you're pointing to something clickable.

Hiding the Regular Icons

Sometime active desktop items are covered or obscured by the regular desktop icons. You can get better access by hiding all the desktop icons, leaving only the active desktop items visible. To do so:

▼ Right-click the Windows 98 desktop and choose Properties, or open the Control Panel and click the Display icon. Either way, you'll end up at the Display Properties dialog box.

▼ Click the Effects tab in the Display Properties dialog box.

▼ Chech the option to Hide Icons When the Desktop Is Viewed as a Web Page.

☑ Hide icons when the desktop is viewed as a Web page

▼ Click the OK button to close the dialog box.

Now you'll have plenty of room to arrange your active desktop items. When you want to bring your desktop icons back out of hiding, just repeat the steps above and turn off the Hide Icons When the Desktop Is Viewed as a Web Page option in the Effects tab.

You can also hide the active desktop items and leave the desktop icons in view. To do this, just turn off the active desktop. Right-click the Windows 98 desktop and point to Active Desktop on the shortcut menu. The View as Web Page option can then be toggled off (or on) to hide (or redisplay) the active desktop items.

Hiding Active Desktop Items

You can pick and choose which active desktop items you want to display at any given time.

Customizing Active Desktop

> As illustrated earlier, in "The Channel Bar" section, make sure the option for View My Active Desktop As a Web Page is selected; otherwise, active desktop items won't appear on the screen.

Here are the steps to customize active desktop items:

▼ Right-click the Windows 98 desktop and choose Active Desktop → Customize My Desktop. You'll be taken to the Web tab of the Display Properties dialog box, where you'll see a list of active desktop items installed on your system. Here's an example:

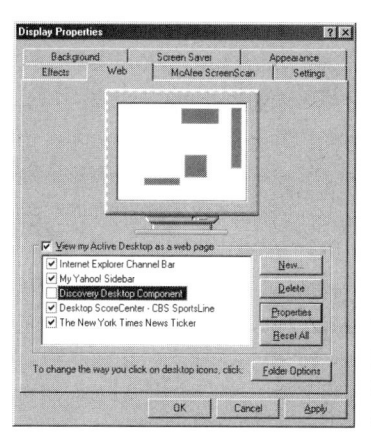

The Web tab in Display Properties lets you manage active desktop items.

These same steps will also let you remove any active desktop items that you don't want on your system anymore.

15: SUBSCRIPTIONS, CHANNELS, & ACTIVE DESKTOP

▼ Make your selections from the options presented.

- To **hide an active desktop icon** so it's not visible on the desktop, clear its checkbox. To redisplay the item, check it again.
- To **delete an active desktop item from your system**, click to highlight the item you want to delete, and click the Delete button.
- To **check and/or change an item's update schedule**, click to highlight the item and then click the Properties button.
- To **remove all active desktop items** (except the Channel bar), click the Reset All button.

▼ When you've finished making your selections, click the OK button.

Updates to Active Desktop Items

Any active desktop items that you add to your system will be listed along with your Web subscriptions in the Subscriptions window. That means you can schedule updates for active desktop items from within Microsoft Internet Explorer, just as you can for subscriptions and channels.

When scheduling the frequency of updates to your active desktop items, don't forget that your Internet connect-time or toll charges, if any, still apply.

Choose Favorites → Manage Subscriptions from Internet Explorer's menu bar to get to the Subscriptions window as discussed earlier in this chapter.

Manually Updating Items

You can update your active desktop items at any time—you don't need to wait for the scheduled time to arrive. This is especially handy with active desktop items that display news and other information that you want to be up-to-the-minute. When you want to know what's going on right now, just update your active desktop items. Here's how:

▼ To update all active desktop items, right-click the Windows 98 desktop, and from the shortcut menu choose Active Desktop → Update Now.

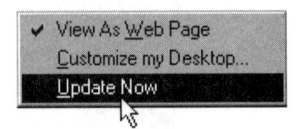

354

Some active desktop items have a built-in Update button that you can click to update that one item's information. You can also update an individual item right from the desktop. Here are the steps:

Use the built-in update button if there is one.

▼ Right-click the Windows 98 desktop and, from the shortcut menu, choose Active Desktop → Customize My Desktop. Next up is the Web tab of the Display Properties dialog box.

▼ In the list of active desktop items, click the one you want to update and then click the Properties button.

▼ In the item's Properties dialog box, open the Schedule tab and click the Update Now button. Then click OK.

▼ Back in the Web tab, click OK again to close the Display Properties dialog box.

Summary

Windows 98 comes with several features designed to make your activities on the Internet's World Wide Web faster, easier, and more productive. The three features we discussed in this chapter include subscribing to Web sites, accessing Web site channels, and taking advantage of active desktop items.

- ▼ A **subscription** to a Web site is a means of having your PC visit the site from time to time, and notify you when the site has changed. When you open Internet Explorer's Favorites menu or the Explorer bar, subscribed Web sites that have changed since your last visit will be marked with a red gleam.

- ▼ To **schedule** the frequency and timing of your PC's checks for updates on the Internet, open Internet Explorer and choose Favorites ➔ Manage Subscriptions.

- ▼ **Channels** are Web sites that support special features available only in Microsoft Internet Explorer 4. Some channels are readily available from your Channel bar.

- ▼ To view the **Channel bar**, right-click the your Windows 98 desktop and choose Active Desktop ➔ Customize My Desktop. Make sure these two options are checked: View My Active Deskop As A Web Page, and Internet Explorer Channel Bar.

- ▼ To see channels that are currently available on the Internet, click the **Channel Guide** button at the top of the Channel bar. Or if you're already in Internet Explorer, you can click the Channels button to open the Channels Explorer bar. Then click the button titled Microsoft Active Channel Guide.

- ▼ The **active desktop** is a layer of content sandwiched between your Windows 98 desktop and your desktop icons.

- ▼ To show or hide the active desktop, right-click the Windows 98 desktop and choose Active Desktop ➔ View As Web Page.

- ▼ You can place active desktop items on the desktop if you wish. Many sites will offer a simple button or link to download and use an active desktop item. Optionally, you can just go to Microsoft's Active Channel Guide, and search for information on active desktop items.

Installing Windows 98

If your computer came with Windows 98 already installed on it, you can ignore this entire appendix. If you're upgrading from Windows 95 or Windows 3.11, this appendix will provide all the information you need to perform the update.

A: INSTALLING WINDOWS 98

What You Need Windows 98 doesn't require a brand-new computer or even particularly new technology. If your system meets the following minumum requirements, you can install Windows 98.

- At least a 486DX/66 MHz or higher processor.
- At least 16MB of memory (though more memory will definitely speed up your PC's performance).
- About 195MB of free hard-disk space, but may range between 120MB to 295MB, depending on your system configuration and the options you choose to install.
- A CD-ROM drive or DVD-ROM drive. (If you only have 3.5" high-density floppy disks, you can purchase Windows 98 in that format for an additional charge).
- VGA or higher-resolution monitor.
- Microsoft mouse or compatible pointing device.

Of course, those are the minimum requirements. If your PC has more horsepower than that, Windows 98 will take advantage of it. For example, Windows 98 fully supports modern Pentium II and Pentium MMX microprocessors.

Windows 3.11 users You can upgrade from either Windows 95 or Windows 3.11.

Performing the Installation The installation process for Windows 98 is fairly automatic. You just need to get the process started and then follow the instructions that appear on the screen.

Be forewarned—the procedure can take up to an hour. So plan your time accordingly.

CD-ROM Installation If you are installing Windows 98 from a CD-ROM drive, follow these steps:

▼ **Step 1**: Insert the Windows 98 CD-ROM into your PC's CD-ROM drive.

▼ **Step 2**: Wait a minute or so to see if the following message appears. If it does, it means your PC can autostart the Windows 98 CD-ROM. Click the Yes button and skip steps 3 and 4.

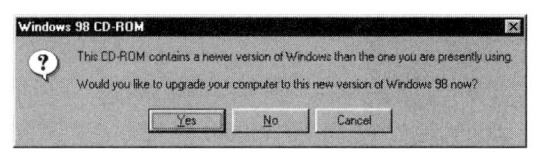

You may see this message if your PC will run the CD automatically.

▼ **Step 3**: If you don't receive the message shown just above, click the Windows 95 Start button and choose Run.

Or, if you're upgrading from Windows 3.11, choose File → Run from Program Manager's menu bar.

Windows 3.11

▼ **Step 4**: In the Run dialog box, type **D:\setup.exe**, where **D:** is the drive letter of your CD-ROM drive. (If your CD-ROM drive is not drive D:, then you'll need to type in the correct letter.) Then press Enter.

▼ You should now see a Windows 98 Setup dialog box like the one shown here. Just click the Continue button, and then follow the instructions that appear on the screen.

Ready to install Windows 98.

If you're installing Windows 98 from floppy disks, follow these steps instead:

Floppy-Disk Installation

▼ **Step 1**: Put the Windows 98 Setup disk (Disk #1) in drive A: of your PC.

▼ **Step 2**: Click the Windows 95 Start button and choose Run.

Or, if you're upgrading from Windows 3.11, choose File → Run from Program Manager's menu bar.

Windows 3.11

▼ **Step 3**: Type **a:\setup.exe** and press Enter.

A: INSTALLING WINDOWS 98

Restart the PC

▼ **Step 4**: Follow the instructions that appear on the screen.

Don't be alarmed if your PC needs to be restarted several times. It might take a few tries for Window 98 to get all your installed hardware working correctly.

Once Windows 98 does start up and seems to be sitting idly, ready to go, you can then move to Chapter 1 of this book and start learning how to put Windows 98 to work for you.

Keyboard Shortcuts   B

Windows 98 is designed with mouse users in mind. And in most cases, the mouse is indeed the easiest way to get things done. However, there are many keyboard shortcuts that you can use in place of the mouse, when your hands happen to be on the keyboard, or just because you prefer another method of doing things. This Appendix describes the following categories of shortcuts:

- General Windows shortcuts
- Windows Natural Keyboard shortcuts
- Shortcuts for use in dialog boxes
- Shortcuts in My Computer
- Shortcuts in Windows Explorer
- Shortcuts available in Windows-compatible programs
- Shortcuts used with drag-and-drop operations
- Accessibility features for users with special needs

B: KEYBOARD SHORTCUTS

General Shortcuts

The keyboard shortcuts listed in the following table generally work throughout Windows 98 and your Windows programs.

Operation	Shortcut Keys
Bypass CD-ROM autoplay	Hold down Shift while inserting the CD-ROM
Cancel a dialog box	Esc
Cancel drag-and-drop	Esc
Capture screen to Clipboard	Print Scrn
Capture active window to Clipboard	Alt+Print Scrn
Choose command or option	Alt+underlined letter
Close a program/window	Alt+F4
Command prompt boot-up	Press F8 when "Starting Windows 98" message appears
Copy	Ctrl+C
Cut	Ctrl+X
Delete	Delete or Del
Delete, with no Recycle Bin copy	Shift+Del
Find files or folders	F3
Help	F1
Paste	Ctrl+V
Properties	Alt+Enter
Refresh	F5
Rename	F2
Shortcut menu	Shift+F10
Shut down	Alt+F4 after all windows closed
Start menu	Ctrl+Esc, or Windows key
Step-by-step startup	Shift+F8 at startup beep
Switch to another program	Alt+Tab
System menu	Alt+- (hyphen)
Undo	Ctrl+Z

Windows Natural Keyboard

If you have a Microsoft Natural Keyboard, or you're using a similar program with an extra Windows key and Application key, you can use these shortcuts.

Operation	Shortcut Keys
Cycle through taskbar buttons	Windows+Tab
Find files and folders	Windows+F
Help	Windows+F1
Minimize/restore all windows	Windows+D
Run	Windows+R
Shortcut menu	Application key
System properties	Windows+Break
Undo minimize all windows	Shift+Windows+M
Windows Explorer	Windows+E

Dialog Boxes

These keys are for getting around in dialog boxes and making selections.

Operation	Shortcut Keys
Cancel without saving	Esc
Checkbox on/off	Spacebar
Choose option	Alt+underlined letter
Click the default (dark-rimmed) button	Enter
Click the selected button	Spacebar
Cursor to end of line (move)	End
Cursor to start of line (move)	Home
Drop-down list (open)	Alt+down arrow
Next option	Tab
Parent folder (go to)	Backspace
Previous option (go to)	Shift+Tab
Scroll	Up arrow, down arrow, Page Up, Page Down
Slider left/right (move)	Left arrow, right arrow
Spin box up/down (select higher/lower values)	Up arrow, down arrow
Tab (next)	Ctrl+Tab
Tab (previous)	Ctrl+Shift+Tab

B: KEYBOARD SHORTCUTS

My Computer and Windows Explorer

Your My Computer and Windows Explorer programs support these special shortcut keys. (Windows Explorer gives you a few additional ones, too, described in the next table.)

Operation	Shortcut Keys
Back	Alt+left arrow
Close	Alt+F4
Close active and parent windows	Hold Shift while clicking Close (X) button
Copy selected items	Ctrl+C
Cut selected items	Ctrl+X
Delete, with no Recycle Bin copy	Shift+Delete
Find Files and Folders	F3
Forward (move cursor)	Alt+right arrow
Paste	Ctrl+V
Properties	Shift+Enter
Refresh	F5
Rename	F2
Select all	Ctrl+A
Up to parent folder (move)	Backspace

Windows Explorer

In addition to the shortcut keys listed in the preceding table, Windows Explorer supports the following shortcut keys. These keys work in the left-hand frame of Windows Explorer, which displays folders in hierarchical fashion.

Operation	Shortcut Key(s)
Collapse expanded folder	Left arrow
Parent folder (go to)	Left arrow
Expand folder	Right arrow
Collapse selected folder	Num Lock +- (hyphen)
Select first subfolder	Right arrow
Expand all folders below current folder	Num Lock +* (asterisk)
Switch between left/right panes	F6

Program Shortcuts

Most program that are specifically designed for Windows 98 (or Windows 95) will support the following shortcut keys.

Operation	Shortcut Keys
Cancel	Esc
Close document	Ctrl+F4
Close program	Alt+F4
Copy	Ctrl+C
Cut	Ctrl+X
Delete	Delete or Del
End of document (go to)	Ctrl+End
End of line (go to)	End
Find	Ctrl+F
Help	F1
Menu	F10
New document (open)	Ctrl+N
Open (existing) document	Ctrl+O
Paste	Ctrl+V
Print	Ctrl+P
Pull down a menu	Alt+underlined letter
Replace	Ctrl+H
Save	Ctrl+S
Select all	Ctrl+A
Select item from open menu	Underlined letter
Start of line (go to)	Home
Top of document (go to)	Ctrl+Home
Undo	Ctrl+Z
What's this?	Shift+F1

Drag-and-Drop These keys let you control drag-and-drop operations.

Operation	Shortcut Keys
Cancel the drag-and-drop operation	Esc
Copy the file(s) being dragged	Ctrl+drag
Create shortcut(s) to the dragged item(s)	Ctrl+Shift+drag
Move the file(s) being dragged	Alt+drag

Accessibility Features Windows 98 provides accessibility features to give people with various physical and sensory handicaps alternative ways of interacting with the PC. The accessibility features can be installed via Add/Remove Programs, as discussed under "Installing Missing Windows Components" in Chapter 8. Here are the keyboard shortcuts associated with those accessibility features.

Operation	Shortcut Keys
Filter keys on/off	Hold down right-hand Shift key for 8 seconds
High Contrast on/off	Left Alt+Left Shift+Print Scrn
Mouse keys on/off	Left Alt+Left Shift+Num Lock
Sticky keys on/off	Press Shift 5 times
Toggle keys on/off	Hold down Num Lock for 5 seconds

Glossary

Numbers/Symbols

+ (plus sign)
When used in the context of *key+key*, indicates a combination keystroke in which you hold down the first *key* then tap the second *key*.

A

active desktop
A layer of content between your Windows 98 desktop and its icons, used to display the Channel bar and other Internet-related items.

active desktop item
A small program that can display, right on your desktop, up-to-date news and other current information from the Internet.

active window
The only window that can accept keyboard input. The active window is always on top of all other open windows, and has a brighter-colored title bar. Clicking any open window instantly makes it the active window.

Alt
A key on the keyboard; short for Alternate. A combination keystroke that includes the Alt key (Alt+*key*) means "hold down the Alt key, tap the second *key*, then release the Alt key."

AOL
Short for America Online, a popular service for PC users.

app
Short for application program, a program you run on your PC to do work.

applet
A small application program such as Notepad or Calculator, which comes with Windows 98.

application
Another name for a program—software you purchase to perform work on your PC.

attachment
A file that's stuck onto an e-mail message and transferred along with that message. Microsoft Outlook Express lets you add attachments to your messages, as well as use attachments others have sent to you.

audio CD
The type of CD that you normally play in a stereo.

B

bandwidth
The amount of information that can come across a wire at one time. The higher the bandwidth, the quicker the access.

baud
The speed at which information is sent through a modem. The higher the baud, the faster the information transfer.

bitmap
A type of graphic image that's composed of tiny dots.

browse
To look around your computer using a program like My Computer or Windows Explorer, or to look around the World Wide Web using Microsoft Internet Explorer or another browser.

byte
The amount of storage required to store a single character, such as the letter A.

C

cache
Pronounced *cash*, a place used to store information temporarily, to help speed up operations.

case-sensitive
A situation where upper/lowercase letters are treated as unequal. For example, if your password is Sesame and that password is case-sensitive, typing SESAME or sesame or sEsAmE won't do. You have to type Sesame.

CD-ROM
Acronym for Compact Disk Read-Only Memory. Looks like a regular music CD, but stores computer software rather than music.

channel
A special Web site that takes full advantage of Microsoft Internet Explorer and can be accessed from the Channel bar on the active desktop.

character
Any single letter or punctuation mark, such as the letter A or an exclamation point (!).

Classic view
A way of interacting with a computer that resembles older versions of Windows, in which you have to double-click an icon to open it.

click
To rest the mouse pointer on some item, then press and release the primary mouse button.

client
A computer that's attached to a larger network. When you use the Internet, your PC is an Internet client.

Clipboard
An invisible storage area in the computer used to hold information for a brief time, usually for the purpose of moving or copying that information from one place to another.

close
To remove from the desktop, typically by clicking the Close (X) button in the upper-right corner of the program or object.

combination keystroke
Something you do at the keyboard that requires pressing two or more keys. Usually expressed as *key+key*, you hold down the first *key*, tap the second *key*, then release the first *key*. Also called key-combination.

command
Another name for an option on a menu.

connectoid
A small file containing information that tells Dial-Up Networking how to connect to a particular service. Icons for connectoids appear in Dial-Up Networking, which is accessible from within My Computer.

control
Any little text box, button, checkbox, or other item on the screen that you can control or in some way act upon to make a selection.

Control Panel
A special window in Windows 98 that contains icons for making personal settings. To open Control Panel, click the Start button and choose Settings → Control Panel.

CPU
Acronym for Central Processing Unit, the microchip inside your computer that does the work.

Ctrl
A key on the keyboard; short for Control. To type a Ctrl+*key* combination keystroke, hold down the Ctrl key, tap the second *key*, and release the Ctrl key.

Ctrl+click
To hold down the Ctrl key while clicking the primary mouse button.

Ctrl+drag
To hold down the Ctrl key while dragging an item with the primary mouse button held down.

cursor
The blinking line on the screen that indicates where the next character you type will appear.

D

default
A setting that's been preselected for you, in case you don't know which setting would be best or most typical.

desktop
Short for Windows 98 desktop; the main part of the screen when Windows 98 is running. Acts as your "home base"—you can start programs from the desktop, and when you exit a program you're taken back to the desktop.

desktop icon
An icon on the Windows 98 desktop representing a program or other item that can be started from the desktop. *See also* icon.

dialog box
A special window that contains a set of items from which you can make selections.

directory
A place on a disk where files are stored; actually called a "folder" in Windows 98.

disk drive
A gadget in your computer that can spin a disk around and store and retrieve information. Each disk drive has a one-letter name. Your main hard disk, for example, is drive C:.

document
An item you create on your computer, such as a piece of correspondence, a report, or a picture, using a program that runs on your computer. For example, you use a word processing program to create written documents.

DOS
Acronym for Disk Operating System; the first operating system for PCs. Remnants of it remain in Windows 98 to allow DOS programs to run on the PC.

double-click
To rest the mouse pointer on an item and then press and release the primary mouse button twice, in rapid succession.

download
To copy something from the Internet or some other network to your own PC.

drag
To hold down the primary mouse button while moving the mouse.

drag-and-drop
A method used to move and copy files and other information. So called because you point to an item, hold down the primary mouse button while dragging the item, then release the mouse button to drop the item in a new location.

drive
Short for disk drive.

drop-down list
A text box-style control that has a small down-pointing arrow button at the right side. When you click that button, a list of items appears, from which you can make a selection.

DVD
Acronym for Digital Versatile Disk (or Digital Video Disk, depending on whom you ask). Similar to a CD-ROM but capable of storing much more information—enough to show a full-length feature movie.

E

e-mail
Electronic mail that's delivered from one computer to another, without any paper involved.

e-mail address
A place to which you send electronic mail, typically expressed in the format **someone@ somewhere.com**.

edit
To change something, such as a document you've created. You must open an item (in a program) before you can edit it.

Esc
Short for the Escape key, which you can press to get you out of unfamiliar territory, and often to back out of something when you change your mind. Typically labeled Esc, Escape, or Cancel on the keyboard.

event
Anything that happens on the screen that the computer can detect. Opening an icon is such an event, as is closing a window.

Explorer bar
A pane that appears at the left side of Internet Explorer's window when you choose an option from the View → Explorer Bar menus, or click an equivalent button in Internet Explorer's toolbar. Explorer bars include Search, Favorites, History, and Channels.

extension
The three-letter (or perhaps longer) addition at the end of a filename, after a period character. Tells Windows what kind of information is inside the file. For example, a .doc file typically contains a document that can be edited with WordPad or Microsoft Word.

F

FAQ
Frequently Asked Question.

FAT/FAT32
The technology Windows uses to store information on a disk. FAT32 is new to Windows 98 and offers some advantages over the original FAT (or FAT16).

file
A single unit of storage on a computer disk, perhaps similar to a file in a filing cabinet. A letter you type and save, for instance, is stored in a file.

file attributes
Characteristics of a file that can be changed. To see a file's attributes, right-click the file's icon and choose Properties.

filename
The name assigned to a particular file. Appears below or next to the file's icon.

filename extension
The dot and (usually) three-letter extension that's added to the end of a file name to associate the file with a program. For example, when you open a file that has the extension .doc, it will automatically be displayed in Microsoft Word or WordPad.

fixed disk
Another name for a computer's internal hard disk.

floppy or floppy disk
A small, thin disk encased in a hard plastic shell, with a sliding door that opens when the disk is placed in the PC's floppy disk drive.

folder
A place on a disk where files are stored. Generally used to categorize and organize files to make it easier to find them later.

font
A style of lettering or print.

function keys
The keys labeled F1, F2, and so forth on the keyboard.

ftp
Acronym for File Transfer Protocol, a set of standards used for uploading and downloading Internet files.

G

G, GB, gig
Abbreviation for gigabyte.

gigabyte
Roughly a billion bytes.

graphics
Pictures, as opposed to written text, that can be created, stored, and displayed on a computer.

GUI
Acronym for Graphical User Interface, the type of interface employed between you and Windows, through which you get things done by clicking on pictures (icons) and such, rather than by typing complex computer instructions.

H

hard disk
The disk that's inside your computer, permanently, and doesn't come out. Your hard disk is typically drive C:.

hardware
The physical parts of a computer such as the system unit and its electronic components, and peripheral equipment such as the mouse, keyboard, printer, and monitor.

Help key
Usually the function key labeled F1, which you can press to display helpful information on the screen.

home page
The first page you come to when you visit a Web site.

hyperlink
A chunk of text or picture that, when clicked, takes you to some other page on the Internet.

I

I-beam
A character on the screen that looks like the letter I, used to indicate where a dropped item will appear, or where the cursor will jump to if you click.

icon
A small, labeled picture on your screen. Clicking (or double-clicking) an icon generally opens whatever is represented by that icon into a window.

indicators
Tiny icons in the taskbar or lower-right corner of a program window; they tell you which features are in use at the moment. You can usually click or right-click an indicator for information and options.

install
To set something up for use on your PC. Installing a program generally involves running a setup.exe file that is stored on the program's floppy disk or CD-ROM.

Internet
An enormous network of interconnected computers spanning the entire globe.

Internet Explorer
A browser program that comes with Windows 98; allows you to browse the World Wide Web and some other Internet services.

ISP
Acronym for Internet Service Provider, a company that can give you an account through which you can access the Internet.

J-K

K or KB
Short for kilobyte.

keyboard
The part of a PC that looks like a typewriter.

kilobyte
Roughly 1,000 bytes.

L

LAN
Acronym for Local Area Network, a collection of connected computers, usually within a single office or building.

M

M, MB, meg
Abbreviation for megabyte.

maximize
To expand a window so that it fills the entire screen.

megabyte
Roughly one million bytes.

megahertz
The speed at which a microprocessor runs; abbreviated mHz.

memory
Generally refers to random access memory (RAM), rendered by microchips in the computer, that stores whatever you're working on at the moment.

menu
A list of options from which you can make a selection simply by clicking on whatever item you want.

menu bar
The strip of menu names just under a program's title bar; typically contains menus named File, Edit, Help, and so forth, that drop down when you click their names.

message box
A small, informative message that appears on the screen to tell you of something.

mHz
An abbreviation for megahertz.

MIDI
Acronym for Musical Instrument Digital Interface, which is music composed and stored on a computer. Often used as background music in games and Web sites.

minimize
To shrink a window to its smallest size (a taskbar button) without actually closing the window.

MMX
Acronym for Multimedia Extensions, a feature of modern Pentium and Pentium II processors that provides better graphics and sound. Windows 98 fully supports MMX PCs.

modem
A device that connects your PC to a telephone line, so you can send e-mail and access the Internet and other online services.

monitor
The part of a PC that looks like a TV.

mouse
A small device with buttons that you roll around on your desk or keyboard table, to move the mouse pointer on the screen.

mouse pointer
The little arrow (or other symbol) that moves on the screen in the same direction that you move the mouse.

Multiple Display Support
The ability to connect two or more monitors to a single PC, and use those monitors as one large Windows 98 desktop.

N

network
Two or more interconnected computers.

newbie
A person who is new to PCs, or new to the Internet.

Num Lock
A toggle key on the keyboard (typically labeled Num Lock) that determines whether the keys on the numeric keypad function as number keys, or as keys for cursor movement.

O

offline
Not currently connected to the Internet or some other network.

open
To bring a file or other item to the screen (and into RAM) so you can see and work with it.

operating system
A required piece of software that determines how you interact with your PC. Windows 98 is an operating system.

OS
Abbreviation for operating system.

P-Q

parent
The items that are one level "up" in a hierarchy. For example, in the path C:\My Documents\Photos, the folder named My Documents is the parent to the folder named Photos.

path
The location of a file on a disk expressed as the disk drive followed by one or more folder names. For example, the path C:\My Documents\MyLetter.doc tells the PC that the file named MyLetter.doc is stored in a folder named My Documents on hard disk drive C.

Pentium
A brand of microprocessor created by Intel Corporation. Most modern PCs are sold with Pentium processors inside.

pixels
See resolution.

plug-and-play
A standard that simplifies the process of adding new devices to your PC.

point
To move the mouse pointer so that it is resting on some item. In typography, a unit of measurement for the height of each letter in a font, where one point equals roughly 1/72 of a inch.

pointer
Short for "mouse pointer," the little arrow (or other symbol) that moves on the screen in the same direction that you move the mouse.

pointing device
A generic term for mouse, trackball, or other device that allows you to move the mouse pointer around on a computer screen.

primary mouse button
The main button used for clicking and dragging; usually the button on the left side of the mouse.

program
Software that you generally buy and install on your PC (as opposed to a document, which is generally something you create yourself).

Quick Launch toolbar
A toolbar that can be placed in the Windows 98 taskbar; provides easy access to favorite programs.

R

R/O
Abbreviation for read-only.

RAM
Acronym for Random Access Memory; the speedy memory inside your computer that stores only the items you are working on at the moment.

read-only
A type of file or disk that can be opened and viewed, but not changed. See also file attributes.

Recycle Bin
A special folder that stores files that have been deleted from your hard disk.

registered file type
A file that has a filename extension that associates the file with some program, such that when you open the file, the appropriate program for viewing and editing that file also opens.

removable media
Disks that can be removed from their drives and stored outside the computer, such as floppy disks and CD-ROMs.

resolution
A measurement of how many *pixels* (tiny dots) are visible on the screen at once; also called the *screen area*. Common resolution settings include 640x480 and 800x600.

restore
To bring a window down from full-screen size to window-size. To do this, click the Restore button near the upper-right corner of the window.

right-click
To rest the mouse pointer on some item then press and release the secondary mouse button (typically the button on the right-hand side of the mouse).

right-drag
To right-drag an item, hold down the secondary mouse button rather than the primary mouse button, while moving the mouse.

root directory
The topmost folder on a disk, indicated by a backslash character (\ ). For example, C:\ refers to the root folder of hard disk drive C.

S

save
To copy a document on the screen and in RAM to a permanent file on a disk, so you can retrieve it again later.

screen
The part of a PC monitor on which you view and work with data in your computer.

scroll bar
A gray (usually) bar that appears along the horizontal or vertical edge of a window, to indicate that there's more content than what's currently visible. Allows you to scroll through that content.

search engine
A place on the Internet that provides the capability of searching for Web pages about a certain subject, like "Great Dane" or "CBS news" or "turtle dove romance." For instance, there's a search engine at http://www.hotbot.com.

secondary mouse button
Typically the mouse button on the right-hand side of the mouse.

select
To choose something either by clicking it or dragging the mouse pointer through it.

server
A computer that's connected to the Internet (or some other network) seven days a week, 24 hours a day, that provides services to clients (people who use the network).

shareware
Software that you can try before you buy.

Shift
The key on the keyboard that you hold down to type an uppercase letter. Also used in combination keystrokes such as Shift+F1.

Shift+click
To hold down the Shift key on the keyboard while clicking the primary mouse button.

Shift+drag
To hold down the Shift key on the keyboard while dragging an item using the primary mouse button.

shortcut
An alternative, and perhaps easier way of doing something. A *shortcut icon* is an icon on the desktop or in a menu that provides easy access to a file "deeper down" in the folder structure. A *shortcut key* is a keyboard alternative to an action such as a menu command.

shortcut menu
A menu of options that appears when you right-click on the desktop, an icon, or other element of the Windows interface or Windows-compatible program.

snail mail
A slang term for traditional paper mail, used by e-mail aficionados.

software
"Invisible" instructions recorded on a disk that tell the computer how to behave. All applications and programs are software.

standby
A state in which the computer consumes little or no energy, but can be turned on simply by moving the mouse or tapping any key.

Start button
The button labeled Start, usually at the left end of the Windows 98 taskbar; used to start fundamental Windows 98 operations and other programs.

Start menu
The menu that appears when you click on the Start button, or press Ctrl+Esc. On a Microsoft Natural Keyboard you can also press the Windows key to bring up the Start menu.

status bar
The gray (usually) bar along the bottom of an open program's window; contains various information about the running program.

string
The computer term for "a chunk of text" as opposed to a number. For example, 123.45 is a number, but "Hello" is a string.

subfolder
A folder that is contained within some other folder. The containing folder is called the *parent folder*.

subscribe
A way of adding a Web site to your list of favorites in Internet Explorer, so that you'll be notified whenever that Web site changes.

System menu
A menu that provides options allowing you to move and size a window using the keyboard. Pressing Alt+Spacebar usually opens a program's System menu. Pressing Alt+- (hyphen) opens a document's System menu.

T

taskbar
The gray (usually) strip typically positioned along the very bottom of your Windows 98 desktop; contains the Start button, various indicators, and other information about running programs and open files.

title bar
The colored strip across the very top of a window that displays the name of the program or document displayed within that window; at the far-right end of the title bar are the Minimize/Restore, Maximize, and Close buttons.

toggle
An option that has only two settings, on or off, like a light bulb. Choosing a toggle option automatically changes it from its current setting to the opposite setting.

tooltip
A tiny informative message that appears when you point to a button or some other item on the screen.

U-V

upload
To copy a file from your PC to some other computer in a network.

URL
Acronym for Uniform Resource Locator, which is the "home address" of a page or other resource on the Web. For example, the URL for my Web site is http://www.coolnerds.com.

USB
Stands for Universal Serial Bus; a type of plug on the back of newer PCs that allows you to install and use a new device simply by plugging it into the PC.

virus
A destructive program specifically designed to play a joke or do some harm; is spread from computer to computer through uploads and downloads, or via shared floppy disks.

W

wallpaper
A pattern or picture that you can place on the Windows 98 desktop.

wave file
A file with a .wav extension that contains sound stored in Microsoft "wave" format. Often used to store small sound effects.

Web
Short for World Wide Web.

Web browser
A program specifically designed for accessing the World Wide Web. Microsoft Internet Explorer, which comes with Windows 98, is just such a program; Netscape Navigator is another popular browser.

Web content
Text and/or graphics that appear along the left side of a folder when the folder is viewed as a Web page.

Web view
A new method of interacting with your PC that resembles the way in which you interact with the World Wide Web. In Web view, you just have to click an item once to open it, rather than double-clicking it as in old (Classic style) Windows.

window
A framed box on the screen that displays one program or one document. Every program you start appears in its own window.

wizard
A series of step-by-step instructions and options that appear on the screen to help you complete a job.

World Wide Web
One of the most popular Internet services, providing millions of pages of text and graphics, all easily accessible through URLs and hyperlinks between pages.

WWW
Abbreviation for World Wide Web.

X-Y-Z

zip file
A file that has been compressed to a smaller size for faster transfer over a network. Must be unzipped before use.

Index

Numbers and Symbols

386 microprocessor, 7
486 microprocessor, 7
*** (asterisks), in password text box, 10
\ (backslash) character, use of in directory names, 146
/ (forward slash) character, 146
? (Help) button, in dialog boxes, 80-81, 94

A

Accessories submenu, Programs menu, 31
 using Install/Uninstall checkboxes, 211
 installing missing applets from, 209-211
active desktop
 adding an item to, 350
 customizing, 353-354
 downloading items from channels, 350
 finding active items, 348-350
 hiding the active desktop items, 353
 hiding the regular desktop icons, 352
 items, 347
 layer of content, 347-348
 managing items, 352
 manually updating items, 354-355
 scheduling updates, 351
 turning on or off, 348
 updates to items, 354
active window, identifying, 61
Add Favorites dialog box, 323
Add New Hardware Wizard, installing new hardware with, 217
Add/Remove Programs Properties dialog box
 Install/Uninstall tab in, 205
 installing programs with, 203-206
 opening, 205
 uninstalling programs, 207-209

Address Book, Windows 98 Outlook Express
 adding names to, 301-302
 addressing e-mail to contacts, 304
 finding a recipient in Select Recipients dialog box, 304
 getting additional information about, 309
 printing, 304-305
 Properties dialog box, 302-303
Address toolbar, in taskbar, 68
Advanced Power Settings tab, Power Management Properties dialog box, 125
Alt (Alternate) key, 15
Alt+Esc, bringing window to top when several are open, 60
Alt+F4, closing windows with, 19
Alt+Print Screen, printing currently open window with, 44
Alt+Spacebar, opening System menu with, 63
Alt+Tab, bringing a window to the forefront with, 61
Alt+V, opening View menu with, 33
Appearance tab, Display Properties dialog box, 79
 changeable desktop items list, 108
 changing appearance items, 109-110
 changing screen colors in, 107
applets. *See* **software/software applications; programs**
applications/application programs. *See* **programs; software/software applications**
Apply button, 79
archiving files and folders, 188
Arrange Icons submenu, arranging desktop icons from, 53
arrow keys, 16, 17
asterisks (***), in password text box, 10
audio CDs, playing on your computer, 131-132, 254-256
Auto Arrange option, 53-54
 turning off, 54

B

Background tab, Display Properties dialog box, 79
backslash (\) character, use of in directory names, 146
Backspace key
 deleting characters in documents with, 36
 deleting characters in text boxes with, 85
backups, system
 copying files and folders for, 188
 guidelines for, 201
 importance of, 199
 media for, 200
 of documents only, 200
 using CDs for, 200
blinking cursor, 36
boot/booting up, 10
browsing the Web, offline, 340
byte, 6

C

Calculator program
 closing, 33
 keyboard shortcut for opening Edit menu in, 33
 Scientific view, 32
 starting, 30
 using, 31-32
Cancel button in dialog boxes, 79
cascading windows, 64
CD Player, Windows
 buttons for, 255
 options, 256
 playing audio CDs with, 254-255
CD-ROM disks, 8
 copying and moving files from, 189
 file attributes/properties, 198
CD-ROM drive, 144
Central Processing Units (CPUs), Intel, 7

377

Change Icon button, Effects tab in Display Properties dialog box, 110
Change Password dialog box, setting a screen-saver password in, 105
channels
  changing the update schedule, 346-347
  choosing update notification option, 347
  scheduling updates, 346
  special icons for, 346
  subscribing to, 343-345
  surfing, 347
  unsubscribing, 347
  versus subscriptions, 341
Channels bar, accessing, 341-342, 345
Channels Explorer bar, 341
  organizing the buttons on, 345
  viewing channels in, 342-343
checkboxes
  checking and clearing, 24
  in dialog boxes, 81
  in Accessories components list, 211
Classic-style navigation
  choosing in Folder Options dialog box, 21
  setting Windows 98 to work in, 20
Classic view, 22
clicking, mouse button, 13
Clipboard, 194
  moving and copying with, 193
  steps for using, 194
clock, showing in taskbar, 66
Close (X) button, 56, 57
  closing programs and windows with, 19, 24, 33
closing windows, 19
Collate checkbox, Print dialog box, 43
Color Depth, choosing for display, 113
combination keystrokes, 16
combo boxes. See drop-down lists
commands, accessing via menus, 32
Compose Message button, in Outlook Express, 290
compressed files, opening, 300
connect-time charges, by ISPs, 331
Contents tab, Windows 98 Help window, 91

Control Panel
  accessing, 100-101
  adjusting date and time, 101-102
copying and moving files and folders
  canceling action before completed, 189
  copying versus moving, 188
  reasons to copy, 188
  reasons to move, 188
  using disks and other removable media for, 190-192
  using Invert Selection command for highlighting text, 192
  using multiple floppy disks for, 192
Coolnerds MegaSearch site, 321-322
CPUs, 7
Create Shortcut(s) Here
  creating shortcuts to files and folders with, 224-225
  creating shortcuts to Start Menu items with, 223
Create Shortcut Wizard, 234
Ctrl (Control) key, 15
Ctrl+ (down arrow), jumping to bottom of list in list box with, 83
Ctrl+ (up arrow), jumping to top of list in list box with, 83
Ctrl+P key combination, 42
Ctrl+Z, undoing recent actions with, 89, 195
cursor
  blinking, 36
  moving with arrow keys, 16
Cursor Blink Rate option, Keyboard Properties dialog box, 118
Custom Settings dialog box
  mouse clicking settings, 176-177
  opening, 174
  setting for Web content, 175-176

D

Date/Time Properties dialog box
  adjusting PC's internal clock in, 101
  checking date and time before automating maintenance tasks, 243
  choosing Time Zone in, 102
  displaying current time in taskbar, 102
default dialog-box button, 79
default home page, Web browser, 313
  designating, 316
Del (Delete) key, 15
  deleting characters in documents with, 36

  deleting characters in text boxes with, 85
Deleted Items folder, Outlook Express, 295
deleting files and folders, 184-185
desktop, Windows 98. See Windows 98 desktop
desktop icons, 11, 12
  arranging, 53-54, 113
  changing, 110
  moving, 52-53
  moving to Quick Launcher toolbar, 229
  opening and closing, 49-51
  rearranging in Start submenus, 54
  using, 48-49
desktop shortcuts, 222
  creating, 56, 222
  creating with Send To Desktop as Shortcut command, 234
  rearranging icons for, 224
  to files and folders, 224-225
  to menu items, 223
desktop themes, 114
  applying, 116
  changing, 116
  choosing in Desktop Themes dialog box, 115
  deleting, 117
  previewing theme settings, 115
  removing, 116-117
  rotating monthly, 115
Desktop toolbar, in taskbar, 68
destination drive and folder, 189
Details view, Windows Explorer, 153-154
Dial-Up Networking
  checking Dial-Up Networking connectoid settings, 281-282
  manually dialing your ISP, 282-283
dialog box
  buttons, 79
  checkboxes in, 81
  controls, 78
  entering information into, 10
  Help (?) button in, 80-81
  option (radio) buttons in, 81
  slider controls, 82
  using keyboard to navigate in, 87
dimmed (disabled) controls, 80
  System menu, 63
disabled/enabled options, 63
Discover Windows 98 option, 23
Disk Cleanup tool, 243
Disk Defragmenter tool, 243
disk drives, 144-145

FILES

Display Properties dialog box
   adjusting screen display settings in, 78
   buttons in, 79
   changeable desktop items list in, 109–110
   changing screen colors in, 107
   changing appearance items in, 109–110
   changing icons in, 110
   changing visual effects in, 111
   choosing desktop wallpaper in, 103
   opening, 103
   tabs in, 79
   with Background tab on top, 103
.doc filename extension, 37
documents
   closing, 38, 41
   creating, 34–36, 196–197
   inserting new text into, 36
   opening a saved, 160
   opening from the Documents Menu, 40–41
   opening from within a program, 39
   printing, 36–37
   printing multiple copies of, 36
   reopening, 39
   saving, 37–38
Documents Menu, opening documents from, 40–41
domains, World Wide Web, 315
double-clicking, mouse button, 13
   resetting to single click, 20
   setting speed of, 119
downloading files from the World Wide Web, 323–325
   cool download sites, 325
   printing instructions after downloading, 324
   saving the downloaded programs to disk, 324–325
dragging
   windows from one monitor to another, 59
   with mouse pointer, 13
Drive Converter (FAT32) Wizard
   backing up system before conversion, 240–241
   completing the conversion, 241–242
   starting the conversion to FAT32 in, 238–239
   warning messages, 239–241
drop-down lists, accessing, 82

E

Effects tab, Display Properties dialog box, 79
   changing icons in, 110
   changing visual effects in, 111
e-mail (electronic mail)
   accounts, setting up with Internet Connection Wizard, 307–309
   addressing in Outlook Express, 290
   attachments, 295–300
   checking for, 292
   choosing an address, 278
   components needed for, 286
   composing in Outlook Express, 290–291
   deleting messages, 295
   free services, 286
   forwarding a message, 294
   getting free from sources other than ISP, 286
   manual setup of accounts, 305–306
   permanently deleting messages, 295
   reading in Outlook Express, 292
   replying to a message, 293–294
   sending from Outlook Express, 291
   sending to multiple recipients, 290–291
   using the Outbox in Outlook Express, 291–292
e-mail attachments
   all-purpose virus warning screen, 298
   associated application for, 298
   filename extensions on, 297
   reading, 297–299
   saving, 299–300
   sending, 296–297
e-mail client, 286
e-mail server
   logging on to, 288
   setting automatic connection to in Outlook Express, 287
End key, numeric keypad, 17
Enter or Return key, 15, 35
   using in WordPad, 35
Entertainment features
   playing audio CDs with Windows CD Player, 254–256
   WaveTop, 264–265
   WebTV, 256–264
Esc (Escape) key, 15

Exit command, closing documents with, 38, 41
Explorer. *See* **Windows Explorer**
Explorer bars, 318
extensions, filename, 37, 158

F

F1 key, getting context-sensitive help with, 94
faded/grayed-out options, System menu, 63
FAT32
   checking system for, 238
   converting to, 238–242
Favorite sites
   keeping track of, 323
   subscribing to, 323
Favorites Explorer bar, 323
file attributes/properties
   CD-ROM, 198
   changing, 199
   definitions, 198
   showing in Details view, 197
   viewing in Properties dialog box, 197
File command, printing WordPad documents from
File menu, closing documents from, 38
file types, choosing for saving documents, 159
filename extensions, 37, 158
filenames
   changing, 183–184
   choosing for saving your work, 158
   forbidden characters in, 158
   maximum length of, 37
files, 145
   attributes, 197–198
   CD-ROM file attributes, 198
   changing name of, 183–184
   choosing a filename, 158
   choosing a path for saving, 157
   copying and moving to removable media, 190–194
   copying within folders, 193
   creating shortcuts to, 224–225
   deleting, 184–185
   finding with the Find program, 180–181
   finding with My Computer, 179
   finding with Windows Explorer, 180
   highlighting in list with Invert Selection command, 192
   identifying shortcut versus real, 165

379

moving and copying, 188–194
navigating to a folder in Save As dialog box, 157
renaming, 183–184
saving, 159
saving to the desktop, 158
searching for in Find dialog box, 164–170
selecting all icons from Edit menu, 183
selecting with the keyboard, 183
selection techniques, 181–183
settings for in Folder Options dialog box, 177–178
using care not to overwrite when saving, 160

Find dialog box
identifying real files versus shortcut files, 165
finding files and folders with, 164–170, 180–181
Include Subfolders checkbox in, 165
searching for by filename, 165
searching for document content, 166
searching by date, 167–168
searching by file type or size, 169–170
sorting found files in, 169

fixed disk drives. *See hard disk drives*

floppy disks, 8
copying/moving files and folders to, 191–192
importance of labeling, 192

floppy disk drive, 144
checking before starting Windows 98, 10

Folder Options dialog box, 174
custom settings in, 174–175
opening, 174
setting navigation style in, 20, 21
setting visual effects in, 111
View option settings in, 177–179
visual settings in, 178–179

folders, 145–146
changing name of, 183–184
copying and moving to removable media, 190–194
copying files and folders within, 193
creating new, 195–196
creating shortcuts to, 224–225
deleting, 184–185
hierarchical arrangement of, 145
moving and copying, 188–194
parents, children, and siblings, 151
renaming, 183–184

selecting all icons from Edit menu, 183
selecting with the keyboard, 183
settings for in Folder Options dialog box, 177–178

fonts
checking for installed, 213
installing new, 212–214
TrueType, 212
using in documents,

forward slash (/) character, 146
function keys, 15

G

General tab in Folder Options dialog box, setting navigation style in, 21
gigabytes, 6
glossary, 367–375
grayed-out/faded options, 63
Guided Tour, on Windows 98 CD-ROM, 22–24

H

hand pointer, 22
Hands-on review, first three lessons, 24
hard disk drive, 5, 144
automating maintenance tasks for, 243–247
changing the label on, 146
files and folders on, 145–147
housekeeping tasks, 173–201
size versus system speed, 6
slowing down of, 242
system tools for maximizing performance of, 242–243
tuning up, 242–247

hardware
device drivers for, 216
installing new, 216–217
installing plug-and-play, 216
printing a record of, 251
using wizards to install, 217

Help, getting instant, 90–96
Help (?) button, in dialog boxes, 80–81, 94
Help keyboard shortcut key, 94
Help window, Windows 98, 90
bringing to forefront when hidden, 94
closing, 94
Contents tab in, 91
Index tab in, 91–92
navigating in, 93–94

resizing, 93
Search tab in, 92–93
toolbar options, 93

hidden files, settings for in Folder Options dialog box, 178
highlighting (selecting) and replacing text, 86–87, 181–183
History Explorer bar, Microsoft Internet Explorer, 318
Home key, numeric keypad, 17
home page in Web browser, 313
horizontal tiling of windows, 64
hot text, 21
housekeeping tasks (hard drive), 173–201
http (HyperText Transfer Protocol), in URLs, 315

I

icons
arranging on desktop, 53–54, 113, 194
hiding when Desktop is viewed as Web page, 178
moving, 52–53
opening and closing, 49–51
rearranging in a Start submenu, 55
using, 48–49

Index tab, Windows 98 Help window, 91–92
indicators, Windows 98 desktop, 11, 13
insert mode, versus overwrite mode, 85
inserting, new text into documents, 36
Install/Uninstall tab, in Add/Remove Programs Properties dialog box, 205
installing
hardware, 217
missing Windows components, 209–211
new programs, 203–206
software, 9
Windows 98, 357–360

Intel microprocessors, 7
Internet
connecting to, 271–281
disconnecting from, 284

Internet cache folder, 331
Internet Connection Wizard
agreement and confirmation, 278
choosing an e-mail address, 278

getting dial-in access numbers, 277-278
giving ID and credit card information, 277
recording setup information and storing in a safe place, 279
setting up connection to ISP with, 274-275
testing the connection, 279-281
Internet e-mail. *See* **e-mail**
Internet Explorer. *See* **Microsoft Internet Explorer**
Internet Referral Service, Microsoft
picking an ISP from, 276
Internet Service Provider (ISP)
choosing, 272-273, 276
logging on, 275
testing connection, 279-280

J-K

keyboard, 5
accessing menus from, 33
special keys on, 15
using in lieu of dialog box buttons, 79-80
using to navigate in dialog boxes, 87
Keyboard Properties dialog box
changing typematic delay and rate with, 117-118
opening, 117
keyboard shortcuts, 361-366
accessibility features, 366
accessing View menu, 33
bringing windows to top when several are open, 60-61
closing windows, 19
drag-and-drop operations, 366
general, 362
getting around in dialog boxes and making selections, 363
Help, 94
jumping to top or bottom of list boxes, 83
opening Edit pull-down menu in Calculator program, 33
opening the System menu, 63
printing currently open window, 44
printing documents, 42
saving documents, 89
selecting pull-down menu items, 33
supported by My Computer and Windows Explorer, 364
supported by Windows 95 or 98 programs, 365

supported in left-hand frame of Windows Explorer, 364
Undo command, 89, 195
using arrow keys with, 33
Windows Natural Keyboard, 363
keystroke combinations, 16, 33
kilobytes, 6

L

label on hard drive, changing, 146
Large Icons view, Windows Explorer, 152, 153
lassoing files and folders, 182
techniques for, 183
Layout Properties dialog box in Outlook Express 289-290
links on Web pages, 319
Links toolbar, in Taskbar, 68
list boxes, selecting multiple items in, 83
List view, Windows Explorer, 153
logon name, for accessing your ISP, 275

M

Maintenance Wizard
automating maintenance tasks with, 243-247
changing schedules in Scheduled Tasks window, 245-246
rescheduling a task, 246
scheduling time of day in, 243-244
time-period options in, 244
Master Volume Control, 129
controlling your computer volume with, 130-134
for headphones used with computers, 131
making accessible from the desktop, 130
Maximize button, 56, 57
megabytes, 6
megahertz, 7
memory. *See also* **RAM (Random Access Memory)**
versus hard disk drive, 5
menu bar, 56, 57
selecting options in, 32
with an associated toolbar, 88
menus
operating with the keyboard, 33
operating with the mouse, 32
using in programs, 32-33, 88-89
microprocessor, 7

Microsoft Internet Explorer
accessing search engines through Search Explorer bar, 320
Explorer bars, 318
exploring the Web, 280-281
keeping track of favorite sites, 323
searching the Web with, 319-322
starting, 312
testing your new ISP connection, 279-280
toolbar buttons for navigating around Web sites, 319
View options in, 314
Microsoft Internet Referral Service, picking an ISP from, 276
Microsoft Outlook Express. *See* **Outlook Express**
Microsoft Paint, using to print screen dumps, 44
Microsoft System Information dialog box, 250
Minimize button, 56, 57
MMX (multimedia extensions) technology, 7
modem
choosing, 273
hooking up external, 273
hooking up internal, 273
installing with Install New Modem Wizard, 217
setting up with Internet Connection Wizard, 274-275
monitor, 4. *See also* **multiple display support; screen**
dragging windows from one to another, 59
power management of, 125
mouse, 5
anatomy of, 13
click settings in Custom dialog box, 176-177
customizing, 118
left-handed use, 14, 119
operating menus with, 32
scrolling with, 14
secondary (right) button, 13
setting double-click speed for, 119
terminology, 14
three-button, 14
Mouse icon in Control Panel, 118
mouse pointer, Windows 98 desktop, 11, 12
activating trails in Mouse Properties dialog box, 121
installing additional from Windows 98 CD-ROM, 121

Mouse Properties dialog box

moving around the desktop, 14
resizing windows with, 59

Mouse Properties dialog box
activating pointer trails in, 121
changing mouse pointer in, 120
customizing mouse behavior in, 118
Motion tab in, 121–122
saving new settings as a theme, 121
setting double-click speed in, 119
setting pointer speed in, 121
settings for left-handed use, 119
turning on mouse wheel checkbox, 122–123

moving and copying files and folders
canceling action before completed, 189
moving versus copying, 188
reasons to copy, 188
reasons to move, 188
using disks and other removable media, 190–192

Multimedia Sound Schemes and Sample Sounds component, 135

multiple display support, 137–138
arranging multiple monitors, 139–140
guidelines, 140–141
two monitors, one desktop, 138

My Computer, 18
changing file attributes/properties in, 199
creating new documents in, 196–197
creating new folders in, 195–196
exploring your PC with, 143–147
finding files with, 179
icon, 18
levels/hierarchy in, 155
practicing opening and closing documents in, 18–19
versus Windows Explorer, 154
view options in, 156

N

name on hard drive, changing, 146
navigation style, setting, 20
New Message window, Outlook Express
composing e-mail messages in, 290–291
nonremovable disk drives. *See* **hard disk drives**
Num Lock key, numeric keypad, 17
numbers, typing, 16, 17
numeric keypad, 16, 17

O

offline Web browsing, 340
OK dialog box button, 79
opening saved documents
from a File menu, 161
from Explorer or My Computer, 160
from the Documents menu, 160
from the Open dialog box, 161–162
Open dialog box, 161
opening documents from, 161–162
operating system, 9. *See also* **software/software applications; Windows 98**
option (radio) buttons, in dialog boxes, 81
OS. *See* **operating system**
Outlook Express
adding names to Address Book, 301–302
addressing e-mail messages, 290
addressing e-mail to contacts, 304
as e-mail client, 286
checking e-mail, 292
choosing e-mail storage location, 287
composing e-mail messages in, 290–291
Deleted Items folder, 295
deleting an e-mail message, 295
e-mail attachments in, 295–300
finding a recipient address in Select Recipients dialog box, 304
forwarding a message, 294
permanently deleting messages, 295
personalizing, 300
printing the Address Book, 304–305
Properties dialog box, 302–303
reading e-mail, 292
replying to an e-mail message, 293–294
sending e-mail messages, 291
sending messages to multiple recipients, 290–291
setting automatic connection to e-mail server, 287
setting view options in Layout Properties dialog box, 289–290
starting, 287
using the Outbox, 291–292
view options, 289–290
overwrite mode, versus insert mode, 85

P

Paint program, 44
Password Properties dialog box
adding a password in, 127
changing a password in, 128
passwords
changing, 128
entering in dialog box, 10, 127
importance of remembering, 127
protecting your privacy with, 126–127
removing, 128
setting for screen saver, 105
using, 128
using on a network, 128
paths, parts of, 150–151
PC (personal computer)
basics, 4–7
exploring, 143–171
performance enhancing techniques, 238–242
personalizing, 99–142
PC hardware devices, 4
Pentium II microprocessor, 7
Pentium microprocessor, 7
PgDn (Page Down) key, numeric keypad, 17
PgUp (Page Up) key, numeric keypad, 17
pixels, 112
Power Management Properties dialog box
Advanced settings tab, 125
choosing a power scheme, 124–125
EPA guidelines, 123
managing your computer's power in, 123
opening, 124
Prompt for password before leaving Standby mode, 125
showing power meter on taskbar, 125
primary (left) mouse button, 13
Print dialog box, 36, 42
Print Range option in, 43, 305
Print dialog box for Outlook Express Address Book, using, 304–305
Print pull-down menu, opening Print dialog box from, 36
Print Range option, Print dialog box, 43
Print Screen (Prnt Scrn) key, taking a screen snapshot with, 44

printers
  selecting from multiple, 43
  sheet-fed versus tractor-fed, 41-42
printing
  documents, 36-37
  paper for, 41-42
  screen dumps, 44
  when doing other tasks, 44
processor, 7
program files, cautions about, 152
program groups
  starting and running programs from submenu, 30-33
  creating new, 232
  moving items into, 232-233
Program Guide, WebTV, 259
  exiting to TV Viewer, 263
  navigating, 260-261
  searching for programs in, 261-261
  viewing the TV banner, 262-263
programs. *See also* **software/software applications**
  finding the icon for newly installed, 206
  general installation procedure for, 204-206
  installing after downloading from Internet, 205
  installing new, 203-206
  registering, 207
  removing installed, 207-209
  starting and running, 30-33, 206
  storing original program stuff after loading, 207
  understanding, 29
Programs menu. *See also* **Accessories submenu**
  dragging icons around on, 56
  Master Volume Control in, 129
  starting a program from, 30
Programs submenu
  starting and running programs from, 30-33
  rearranging icons in, 54-55
Programs window, making new folders in, 232
properties. *See* **file attributes/properties**
Properties button, Print dialog box, 43
Properties dialog box
  changing file attributes in, 199
  viewing file attributes in, 197-198

Properties dialog box, Windows 98 Address Book
  adding multiple addresses for a contact, 302
  adding other contact information, 303
  managing addresses, 303
pull-down menus, 88
  using, 88-89

Q

Quick Launch toolbar, 68
  adding shortcuts to, 226-227
  deleting icons from, 229
  hiding/showing labels, 228
  hiding/showing name of toolbar, 229
  making visible, 225-226
  moving or copying shortcuts, 229
  rearranging, 228
  renaming buttons on, 227
  repositioning shortcut before releasing mouse button, 226
  resizing buttons on, 228

R

radio buttons, in dialog boxes, 81
RAM (Random Access Memory), 5
  effect on system speed, 6
ReadMe file, 204
Recycle Bin, 185
  emptying, 186-188
  restoring/undeleting files from, 187
  using, 186
Regional Settings Properties dialog box
  changing individual items in, 137
  selecting your country in, 136
removable media, 144
  copying and moving files and folders to, 190-194
removing
  installed programs, 207-209
  Windows components, 212
renaming files and folders, 183-184
resizing windows, 57
resolution. *See* **screen resolution**
restarting your computer, 10-11, 25
Restore button, 58
Return or Enter key, 15, 35
right-clicking, 13
right-dragging, 13
root folder/root directory, 146
  other folders under, 147

S

Save As dialog box, 157
  saving WordPad documents with, 37, 156-157
  saving work before shutting down your PC, 25
Save Attachment As dialog box, 299
saving your work, 5, 156-160
  choosing a filename, 158
  choosing a path, 157
  navigating to a folder, 157
  steps to save a file, 159
  to the desktop, 158
  using care not to overwrite files, 160
ScanDisk tool, 243
Scheduled Tasks window
  adding additional maintenance tasks to, 247
  changing the maintenance schedule in, 245
  rescheduling a ScanDisk maintenance task in, 246
  making the window easier to read, 247
screen, 4. *See also* **monitor; multiple display support**
  changing color scheme of, 107
Screen Area
  options, 113
  setting in Display properties dialog box, 112
screen dumps, printing, 44
screen fonts, smoothing edges of, 178
screen resolution, setting in Settings tab, 112
Screen Saver tab, Display Properties dialog box, 79
  adjusting screen saver settings in, 104
  previewing the screen saver, 106
  setting the wait time for the screen saver in, 104
  turning password protection off, 106
scroll arrows, 71, 72
scroll bars, 71
  scrolling through documents with, 72
search engines
  accessing from Search Explorer bar, 320
  list of popular, 322
  searching the Web with, 319-322
Search tab, Windows 98 Help window, 92-93

383

SEARCH EXPLORER BAR

Search Explorer bar, Microsoft Internet Explorer
accessing Coolnerds MegaSearch page, 321-322
accessing search engines through, 320
AltaVista search example, 321
performing a Web search with, 320-321

searching for files, in Find dialog box
identifying real files versus shortcut files, 165
finding files and folders with, 164-170
Include Subfolders checkbox, 165
searching by content, 166-167
searching by date, 167-169
searching by filename, 165
starting a new search, 170
techniques for narrowing the search, 166-167

secondary (right) mouse button, 13
Select Recipients dialog box, finding an address in, 304
selecting and replacing text, 86-87, 181-183
selection (highlighting) techniques
for files and folders, 181
steps for, 182

Send To Desktop as Shortcut command, 234
Settings submenu in Folder Options dialog box, setting navigation style in, 20
Settings tab, Display Properties dialog box, 79
choosing the Screen Area in, 112

sheet-fed printers, versus tractor-fed, 41-42
Shift keys, 15
shortcut files, versus real files, 165
shortcut menus, displaying, 51-52
shortcuts. *See* **desktop shortcuts; keyboard shortcuts**
Show Desktop button, hiding and showing open windows with, 62-63
Show this screen next time Windows 98 starts option, 24
Shut Down command in Start menu, 25
shutting down your PC, 24-25
sizing windows, 58
sizing pad, resizing and/or reshaping windows with, 56, 57
sleep mode, for PCs, using instead of turning off computer, 26

slider controls, in dialog boxes, 82
Small Icons view, Windows Explorer, 152, 153
snapshots of computer screen, printing, 44
software/software applications
basics of, 8-9
bundled versus new, 8
general installation procedure for, 204-206
installing new, 9, 203-206
starting and running, 30-33
understanding, 29

sorting, in Find dialog box, 169
sound
controlling, 129
priority of settings, 129

sound effects, changing, 134-136
sound events, changing, 135-136
Sound Properties dialog box
adding additional sound schemes, 135
changing sound effects in, 134-136
choosing sound schemes, 135

sound scheme, 135
saving new, 136

source drive and folder, 189
speakers, volume controls for, 129
spin buttons, in text boxes, 84
Standby mode
forcing, 126
Prompt for password when computer goes off Standby option, 125
using instead of turning off computer, 26

Start button, 11, 12
Start Menu, 12, 88
adding a shortcut to, 229
creating a new program group in, 232-234
rearranging items in, 230
shortcuts in, 229-231

Start Menu folder, 231
Start Menu items
adding and removing, 234-235
creating desktop shortcuts for, 223
rearranging, 230

Start Menu window, making changes in, 230-231
status bar, 56, 57
subfolders, 145
subscribing to Web sites, 329
the quick and easy way, 331-332

subscriptions to Web sites, managing, 332-340

arranging for dial-up, 339
arranging for login during updates, 338
arranging for manual updates, 339
avoiding update cross-traffic, 339
changing individual subscriptions, 337
checking your subscriptions for updates, 339-340
e-mail notification of updates, 338
getting ready for, 332
making your schedule, 333-334
manual updates, 339
modifying the schedule, 335-336
scheduling, 336-337
unsubscribing, 340
update notification, 338
using predefined schedules, 334-335
the Subscriptions window, 333

surfing the Web, 311-327
in a nutshell, 318
using links and buttons, 319

system backups
copying files and folders for, 188
guidelines for, 201
importance of, 199
media for, 200
of documents only, 200
using CDs for, 200

system files, protecting by hiding, 178
System Information dialog box, Microsoft, 250
exploring your system with, 250-251

System menu, using to move, close, and size windows with keyboard 56, 57
System Properties dialog box, 250
exploring your system with, 250-251

system speed, effect of hard disk size and RAM on, 6, 7
system unit, 4

T

Tab key, 15
navigating in dialog boxes with, 10

taskbar, 11, 12
hiding and/or displaying toolbars in, 68-69
managing toolbars in, 69-70
options, 66
Options tab in shortcut menu, 65
positioning and/or resizing, 67
setting visibility settings, 65

Show Desktop button on, 62-63
toolbars, 68
Taskbar Options tab, settings in, 66
Taskbar Properties dialog box, 65, 66
  adding and removing Start menu items with, 234-234
  making Quick Launch toolbar visible with, 225-226
terabytes, 6
text boxes
  changing text in, 84
  controls for, 84
  editing techniques, 85
  entering information into, 10, 83, 84
tiling windows, 64
title bar, 18
  maximizing windows with, 57
timestamp, for Web pages in Internet cache folder, 331
toggles, for menu options, 89
toolbars, 56
  button equivalents for menu options, 89
  changing the appearance of, 70-72
  managing, 69-70
  using, 88-89
tools
  Disk Cleanup, 243
  Disk Defragmenter, 243
tooltips, 51
  identifying buttons and icons with, 95
tractor-fed printers, versus sheet-fed, 41-42
triple keypress, 16
troubleshooting, 248
Troubleshooters, 248
TV banner, 262-263
TV tuner hardware, needed to use WebTV, 256
TV Viewer, basic operation of, 263-264
typematic delay, 117
typematic rate, 117

U

Undo button, 89, 195
Undo command, Edit menu, 195
uninstalling programs, 207-209
updating Windows 98, 249
URLs (Uniform Resource Locators), 312, 315
  list of recently visited, 317-318
  typing tips, 316-317

user name, entering in dialog box, 10
utilities
  Disk Cleanup, 243
  Disk Defragmenter, 243

V

vertical tiling of windows, 64
view, classic, 22
View menu, opening from keyboard, 33
View options, Microsoft Internet Explorer, 314
View tab, Folder Options dialog box
  settings for files and folders, 177-178
  settings for hidden files, 178
  visual settings, 178-179
view, web, 21-22
virus warning screen, e-mail, 298
visual effects
  description list, 111
  setting in Display Properties dialog box, 111
visual settings, Folder Options dialog box, 178-179
Volume Control dialog box
  controls in, 132-133
  saving the settings, 134
  selecting volume controls in, 133-134
volume controls
  Master Volume Control, 129-134
  priority of settings, 129
  speakers, 129

W

WaveTop
  help and information, 266
  installing/uninstalling, 265-266
  running, 266
  using, 264-265
Web browser, 312
Web content settings, Custom Settings dialog box, 175-176
Web pages, 311
Web-style navigation
  choosing in Folder Options dialog box, 21
  setting Windows 98 to work in, 20
Web tab, of Display Properties dialog box, 79
  choosing Active Desktop features in, 112

WebTV for Windows, 256-257
  components of, 257
  configuration, 258-259
  interactive TV, 264
  Program Guide. *See* **Program Guide**
  starting, 257-258
  TV Viewer, 263-264
  viewing the TV banner, 262-263
WebTV for Windows Configuration wizard, 257-259
Web view, 22
  using, 21-22
Welcome to Windows 98 program
  opening, 23
  reinforcing what you learned, 72-73
  turning off, 24
Wheel tab, Mouse Properties dialog box
  activating mouse wheel with, 122
  options available, 123
window border, 56, 57
windows
  anatomy of typical, 56
  arranging multiple, 64
  bringing to the top when several are open, 60-61
  cascading or tiling, 64
  changing size and shape of, 57, 58
  closing, 19
  disabled/enabled options in, 63
  dragging from one monitor to another, 59
  hiding and showing open, 62-63
  moving and sizing with the keyboard, 63
  moving with mouse, 59
Windows 98
  Address Book, 301-305
  components list, 210
  Entertainment features, 253-267
  Help window, 90-96
  installing from CD-ROM, 358-359
  installing from floppy disks, 359-360
  installing missing components, 209-211
  minimum memory and hard disk requirements, 6
  operating system, 9
  removing a component, 212
  Start menu, 12
  starting, 10-11
Windows 98 desktop, 11-13
  changing the color of, 109
  choosing wallpaper for, 103

385

WINDOWS 98 PLUS!

hiding and showing open windows, 62–63
hosting active desktop items, 329
saving a file to, 158
saving your custom color scheme, 110

Windows 98 Plus!, Deluxe CD Player in, 256

Windows 98 Troubleshooters, starting and using, 248

Windows 98 Update Web site, keeping Windows up-to-date with, 249

Windows CD Player
buttons for, 255
options, 256
playing audio CDs with, 254–255

Windows Explorer
changing file attributes/properties in, 199
closing, 154
creating a shortcut for, 148
creating new documents in, 196–197
creating new folders in, 195–196
exploring your PC with, 147–154
finding files with, 180
starting, 147–148
view options, 152–154
window as guide to hard disk, 148–149
working with, 149–150

WinZip program, publisher information and Web site address, 300

World Wide Web (The Web)
addresses (URLs), 315
browsing, 311–327
browsing offline, 330–331, 340
domains, 315
getting to a specific site on, 316
home page, 313
Internet cache folder for downloaded pages, 331
keeping inappropriate sites from children, 326
subscribe and download feature, 330
subscribing to channels, 329
subscribing to Web sites, 329, 330
URL typing tips, 316–317

WordPad program
creating a document in, 34–36
opening screen on Windows 98 desktop, 34
saving documents in, 37
starting, 34

X-Z

zip files, program for creating and opening, 300